TWIN SPICA

2

Kou Yaginuma

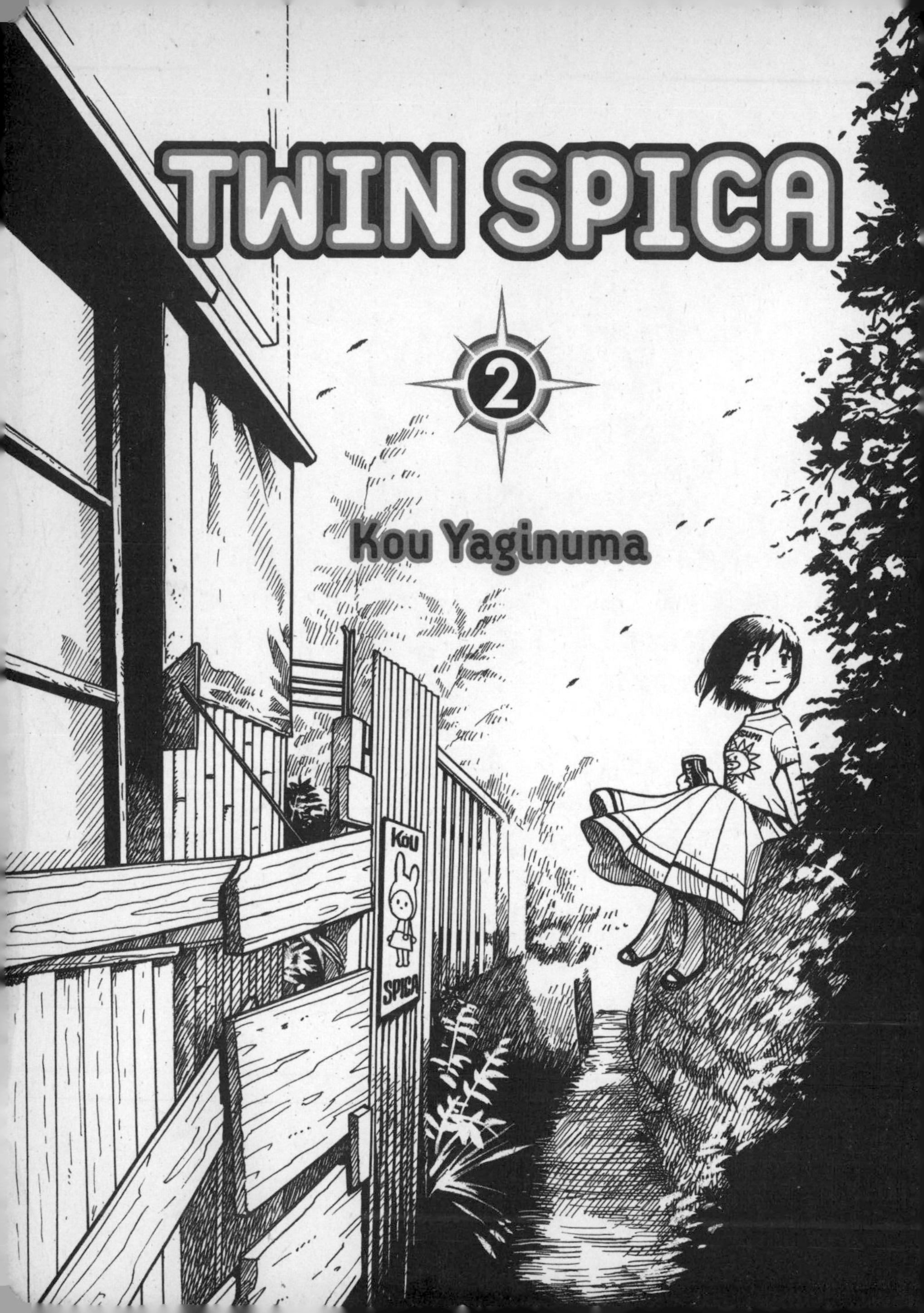
KOU
SPICA

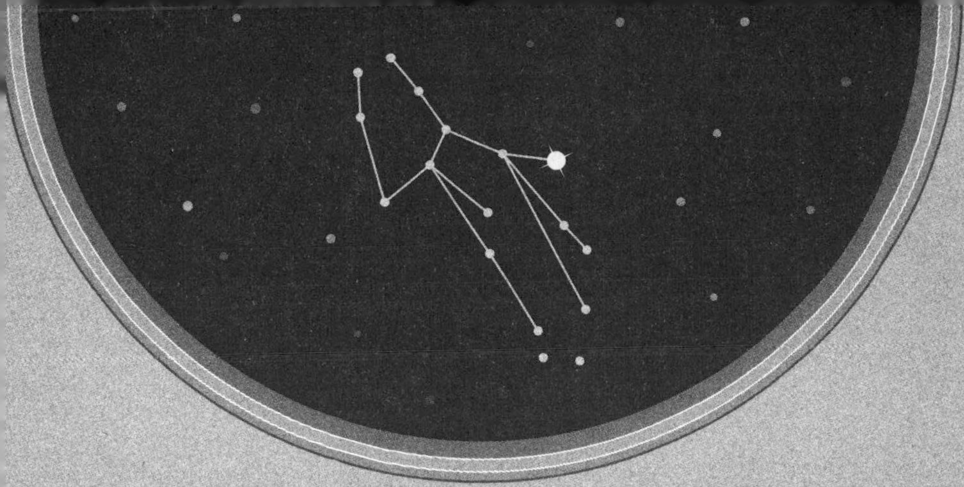

CONTENTS

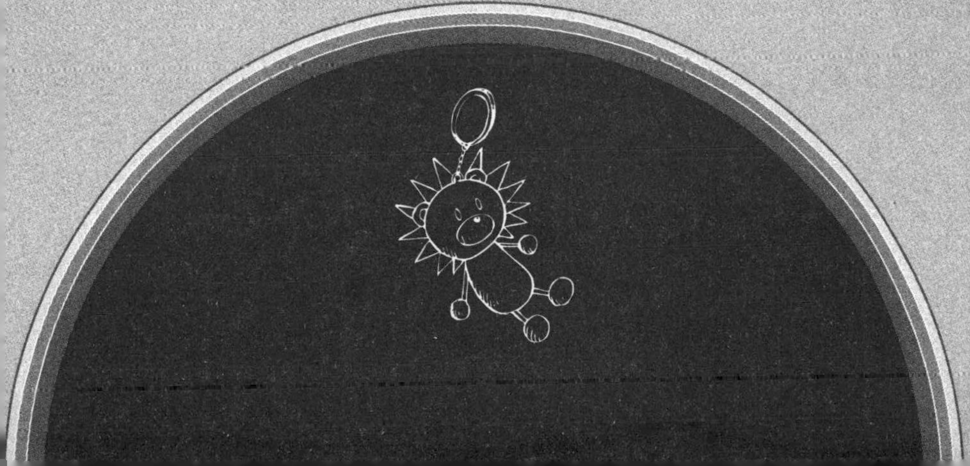

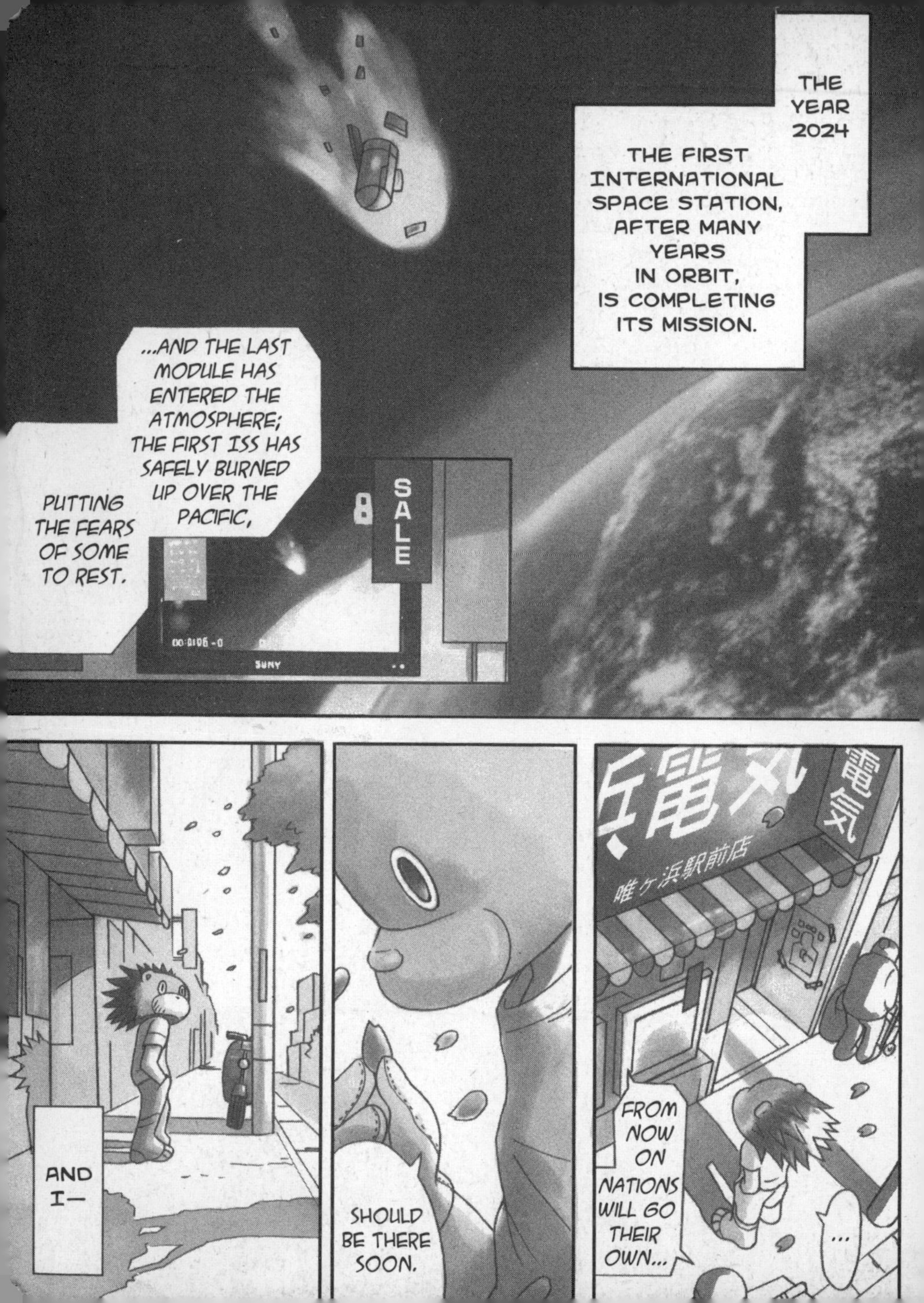
THE YEAR 2024
THE FIRST INTERNATIONAL SPACE STATION, AFTER MANY YEARS IN ORBIT, IS COMPLETING ITS MISSION.
...AND THE LAST MODULE HAS ENTERED THE ATMOSPHERE; THE FIRST ISS HAS SAFELY BURNED UP OVER THE PACIFIC,
SALE
PUTTING THE FEARS OF SOME TO REST.
SUNY
電気
唯ケ浜駅前店
FROM NOW ON NATIONS WILL GO THEIR OWN...
...
SHOULD BE THERE SOON.
AND I—

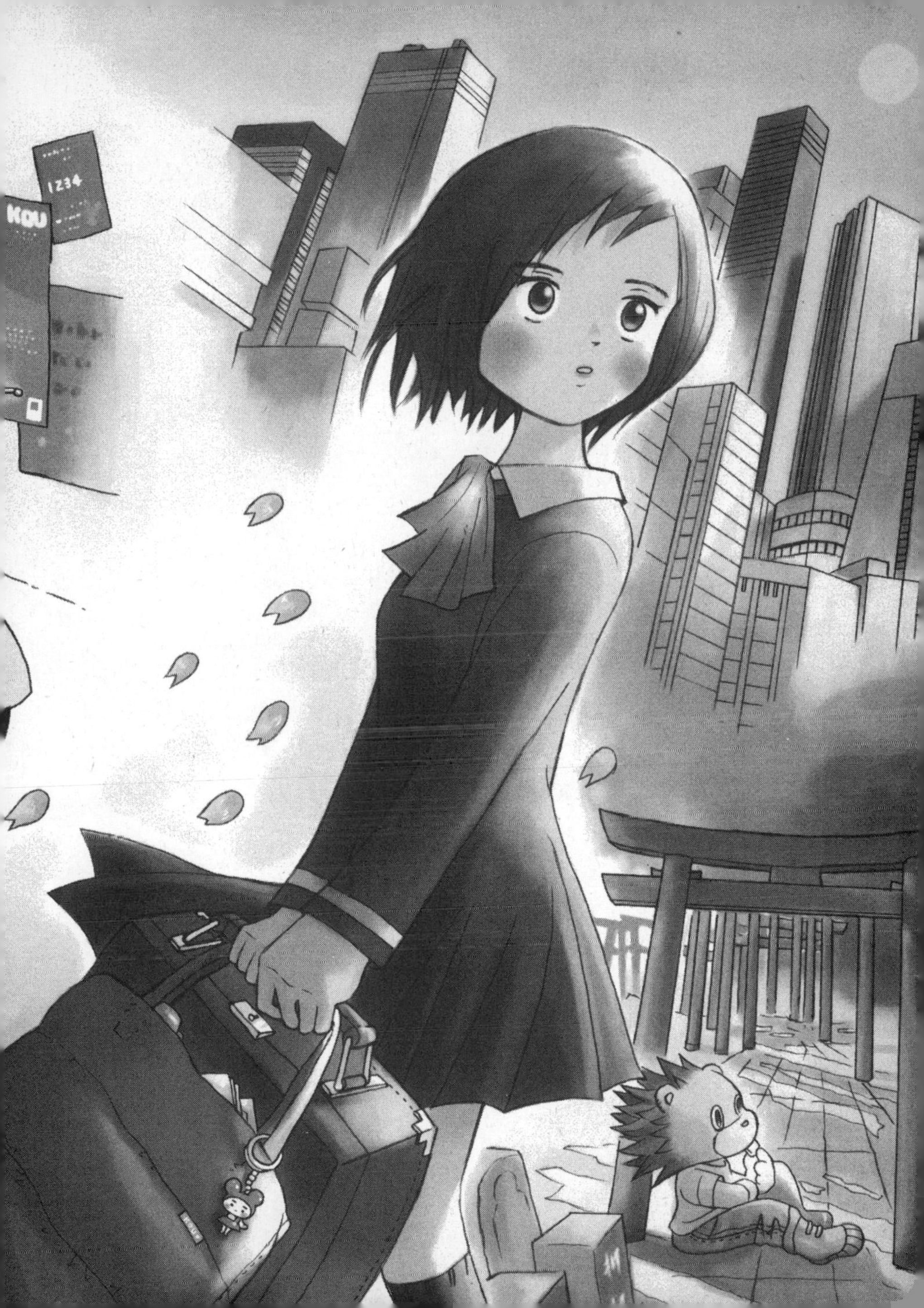
1234
KOU

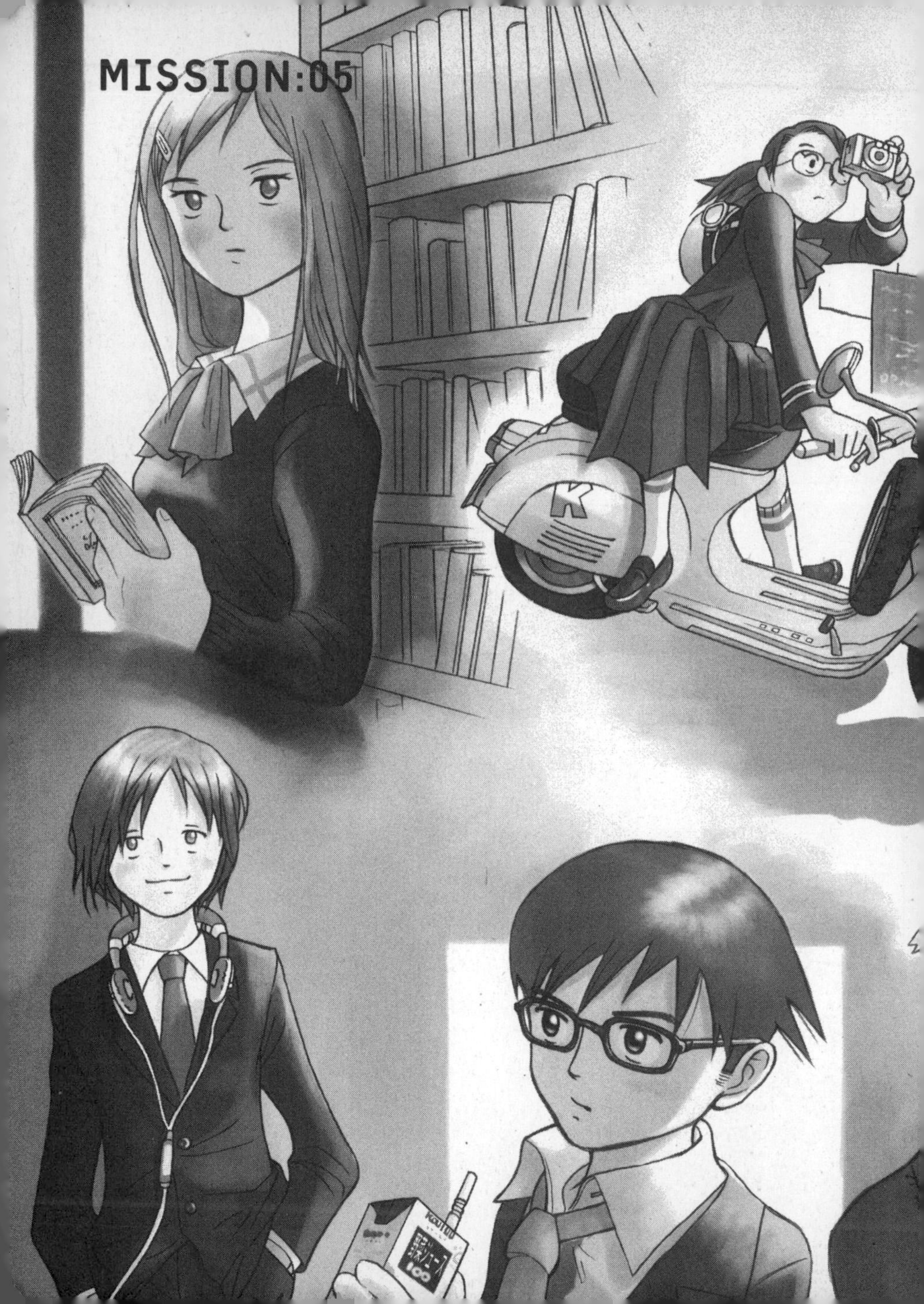
MISSION:05

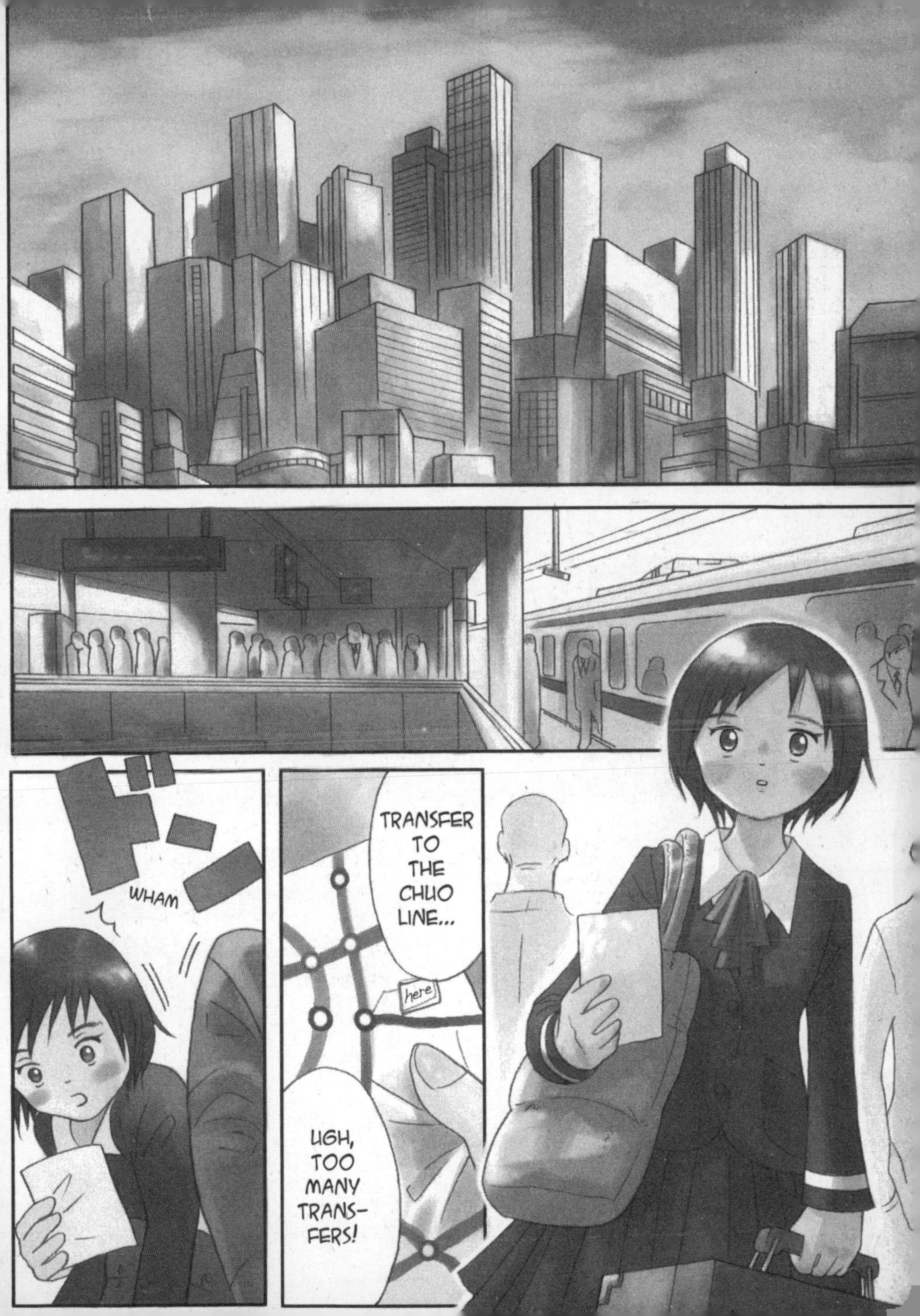
TRANSFER TO THE CHUO LINE...
here
UGH, TOO MANY TRANS-FERS!
WHAM

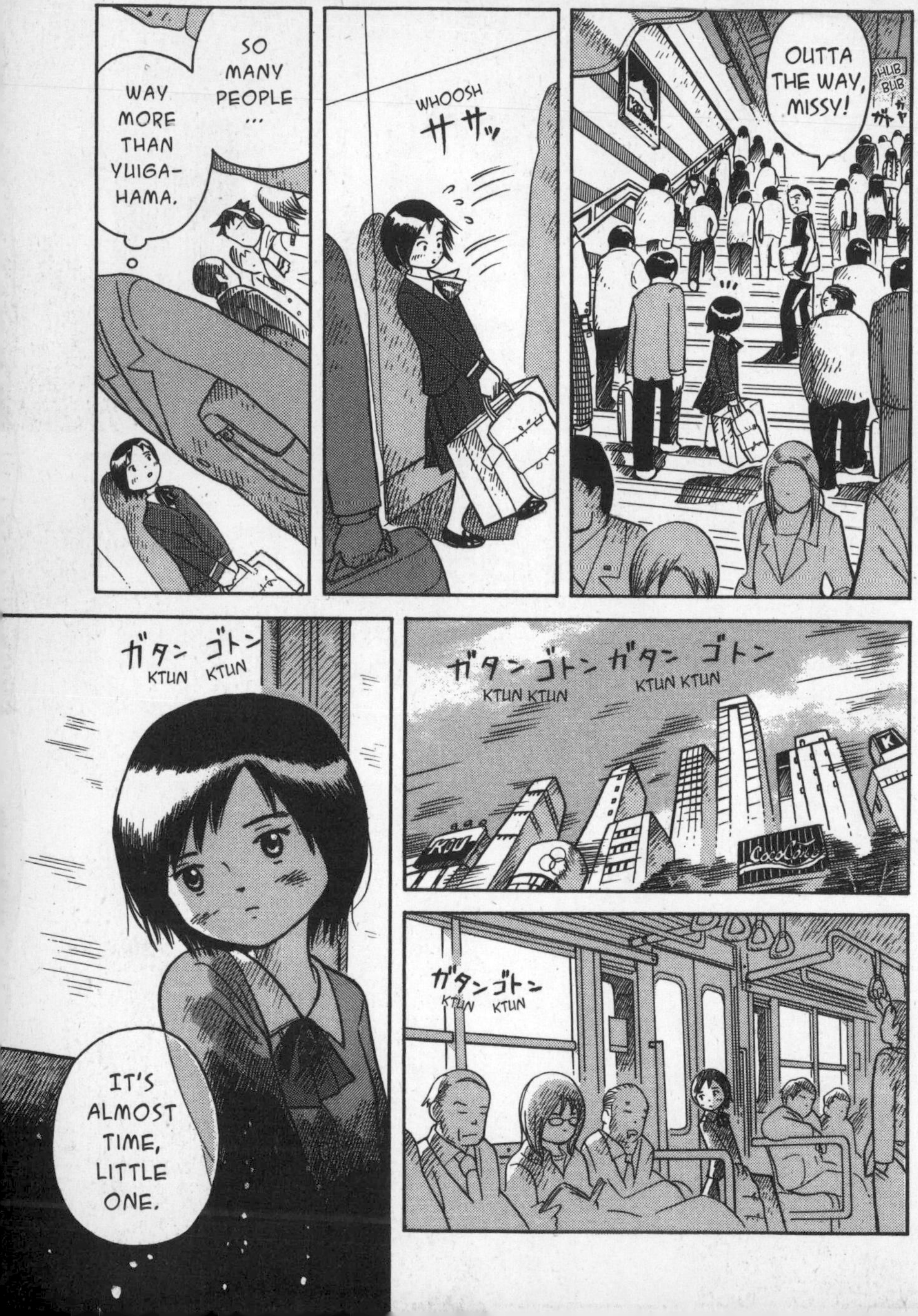
OUTTA THE WAY, MISSY!
HUB BUB
ガヤガヤ
WHOOSH
ササッ
SO MANY PEOPLE ...
WAY MORE THAN YUIGA-HAMA.
ガタンゴトンガタン ゴトン
KTUN KTUN
KTUN KTUN
ガタンゴトン
KTUN KTUN
ガタン ゴトン
KTUN KTUN
IT'S ALMOST TIME, LITTLE ONE.

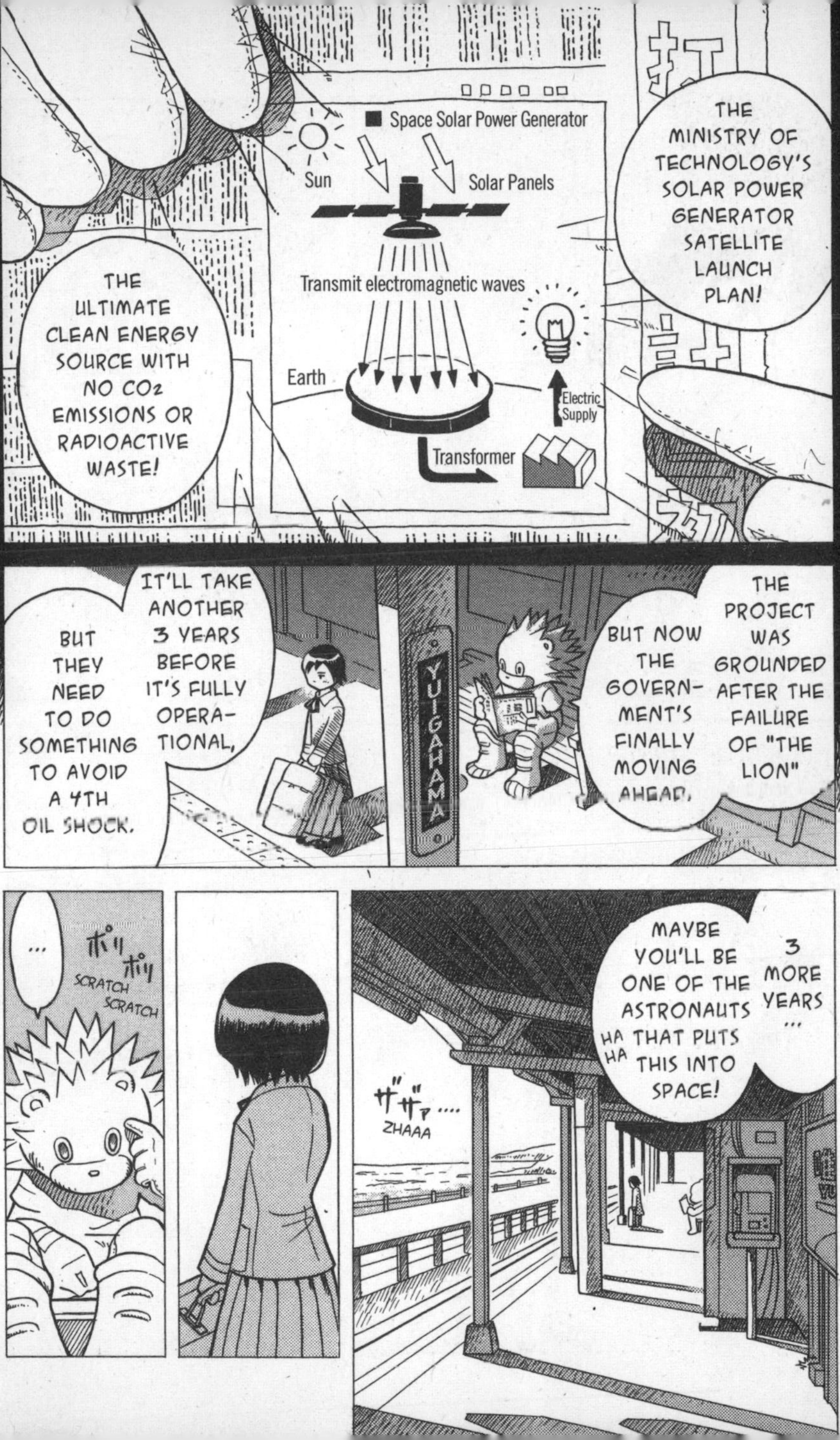
THE MINISTRY OF TECHNOLOGY'S SOLAR POWER GENERATOR SATELLITE LAUNCH PLAN!
■ Space Solar Power Generator
Sun
Solar Panels
Transmit electromagnetic waves
Earth
Electric Supply
Transformer
THE ULTIMATE CLEAN ENERGY SOURCE WITH NO CO_2 EMISSIONS OR RADIOACTIVE WASTE!
THE PROJECT WAS GROUNDED AFTER THE FAILURE OF "THE LION"
BUT NOW THE GOVERNMENT'S FINALLY MOVING AHEAD.
YUIGAHAMA
IT'LL TAKE ANOTHER 3 YEARS BEFORE IT'S FULLY OPERATIONAL,
BUT THEY NEED TO DO SOMETHING TO AVOID A 4TH OIL SHOCK.
3 MORE YEARS...
MAYBE YOU'LL BE ONE OF THE ASTRONAUTS THAT PUTS THIS INTO SPACE!
HA HA
ザザァ....
ZHAAA
...
ポリポリ
SCRATCH SCRATCH

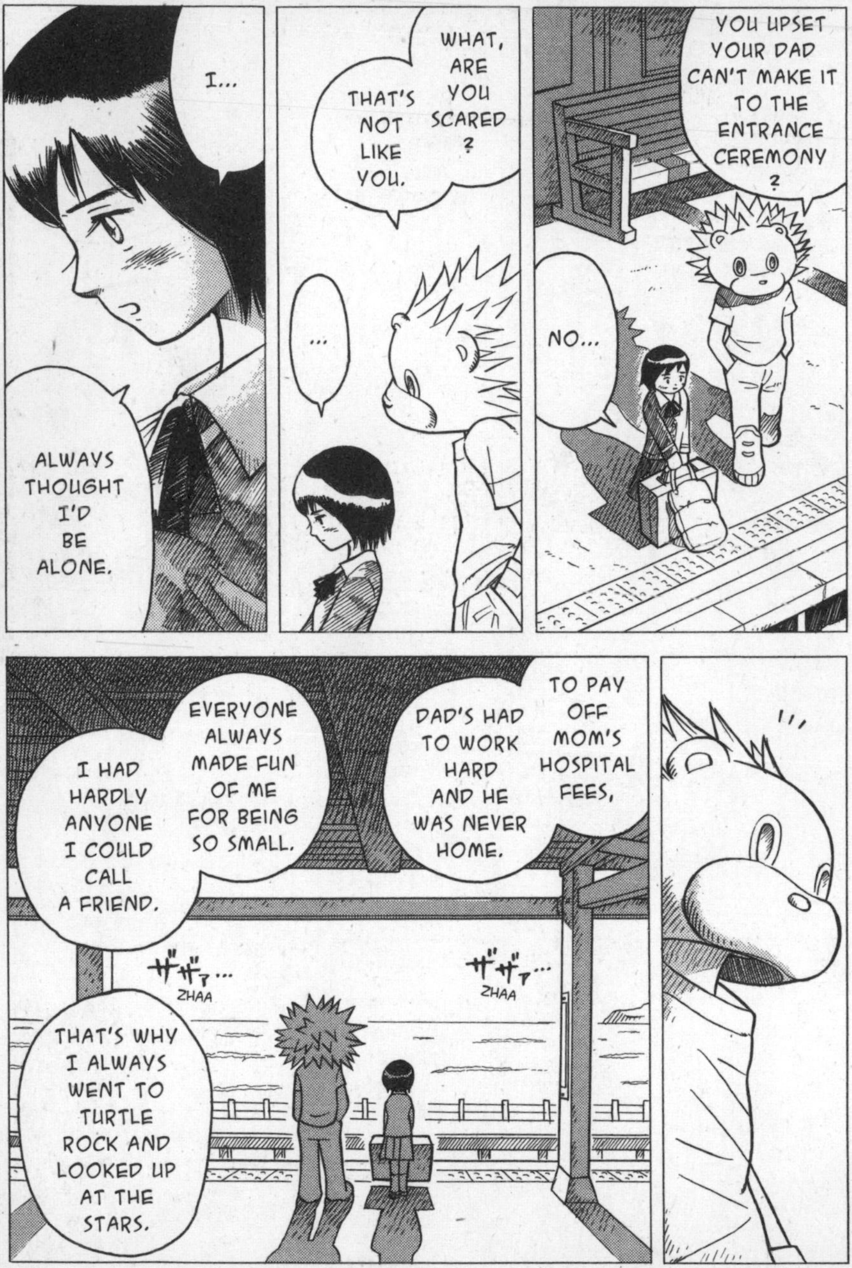

YOU UPSET YOUR DAD CAN'T MAKE IT TO THE ENTRANCE CEREMONY?
NO...
WHAT, ARE YOU SCARED?
THAT'S NOT LIKE YOU.
...
I...
ALWAYS THOUGHT I'D BE ALONE.
TO PAY OFF MOM'S HOSPITAL FEES,
DAD'S HAD TO WORK HARD AND HE WAS NEVER HOME.
EVERYONE ALWAYS MADE FUN OF ME FOR BEING SO SMALL.
I HAD HARDLY ANYONE I COULD CALL A FRIEND.
ザザァ… ZHAA
ザザァ… ZHAA
THAT'S WHY I ALWAYS WENT TO TURTLE ROCK AND LOOKED UP AT THE STARS.

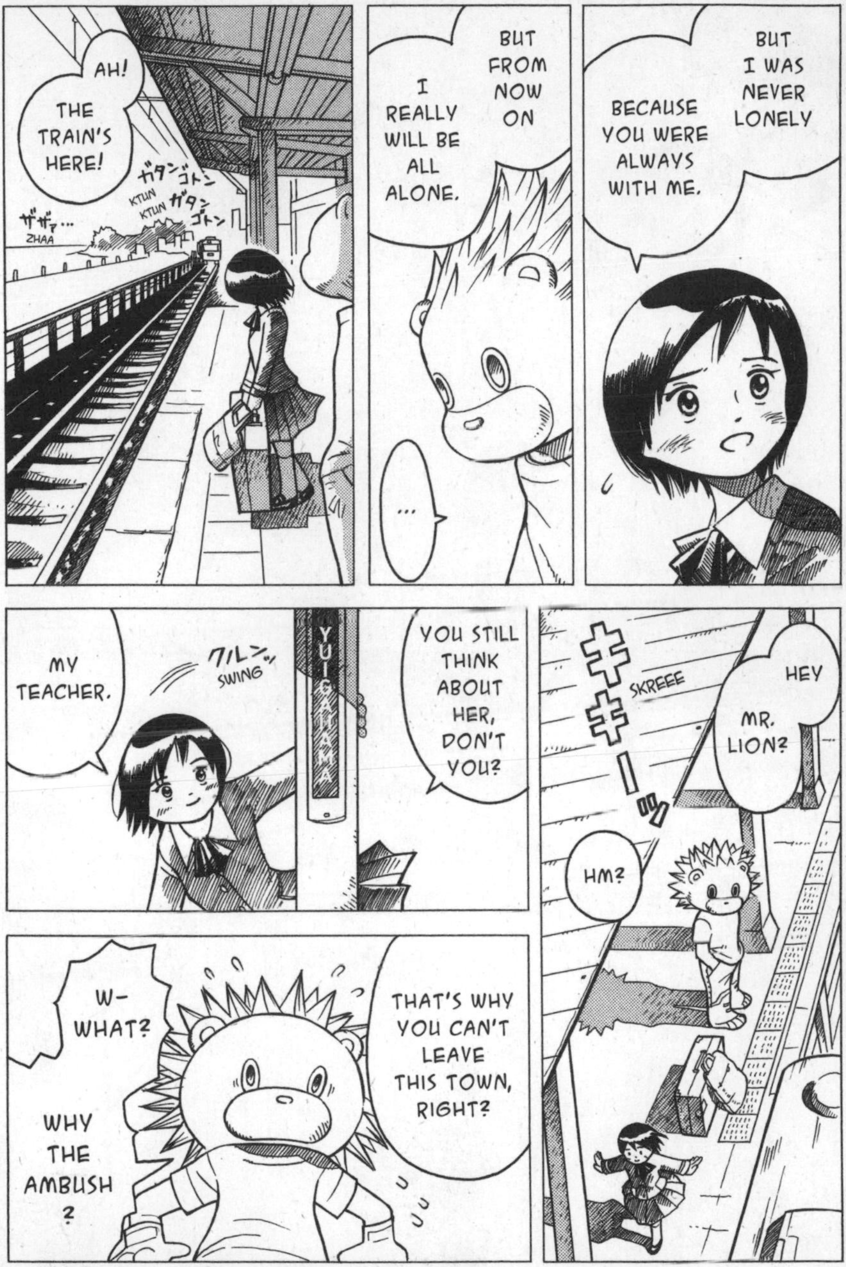
BUT I WAS NEVER LONELY
BECAUSE YOU WERE ALWAYS WITH ME.
BUT FROM NOW ON
I REALLY WILL BE ALL ALONE.
...
AH!
THE TRAIN'S HERE!
ガタン ゴトン KTUN
ガタン ゴトン KTUN
ザザァ... ZHAA
HEY
MR. LION?
キキーッ SKREEE
HM?
YOU STILL THINK ABOUT HER, DON'T YOU?
YUIGAHAMA
クルンッ SWING
MY TEACHER.
THAT'S WHY YOU CAN'T LEAVE THIS TOWN, RIGHT?
W-WHAT?
WHY THE AMBUSH?

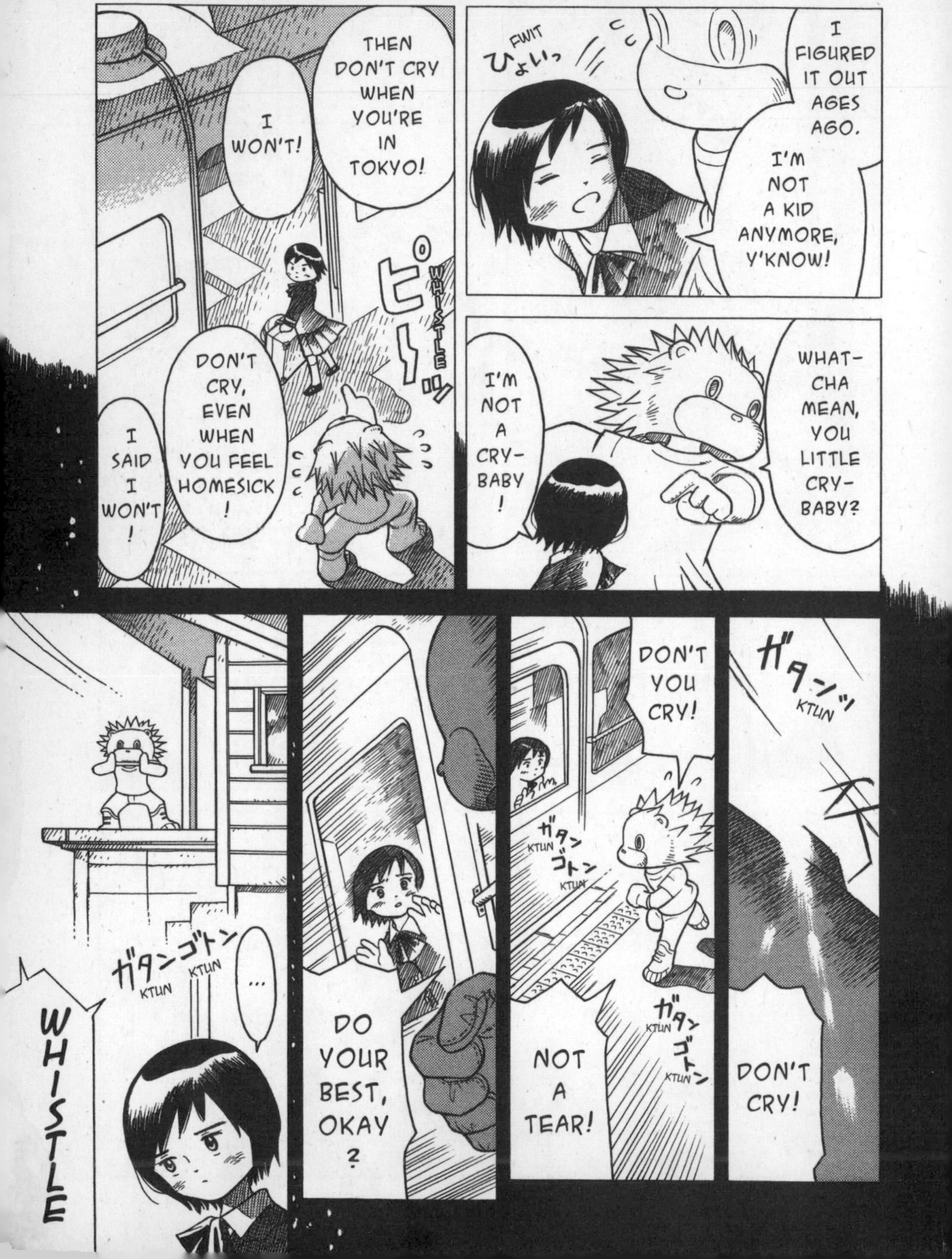
I FIGURED IT OUT AGES AGO.
I'M NOT A KID ANYMORE, Y'KNOW!
ひょいっ FWIT
WHATCHA MEAN, YOU LITTLE CRY-BABY?
I'M NOT A CRY-BABY!
THEN DON'T CRY WHEN YOU'RE IN TOKYO!
I WON'T!
ピーッ WHISTLE
DON'T CRY, EVEN WHEN YOU FEEL HOMESICK!
I SAID I WON'T!
ガタンッ KTUN
DON'T CRY!
DON'T YOU CRY!
ガタン KTUN ゴトン KTUN
ガタン KTUN ゴトン KTUN
NOT A TEAR!
DO YOUR BEST, OKAY?
ガタンゴトン KTUN KTUN
...
WHISTLE

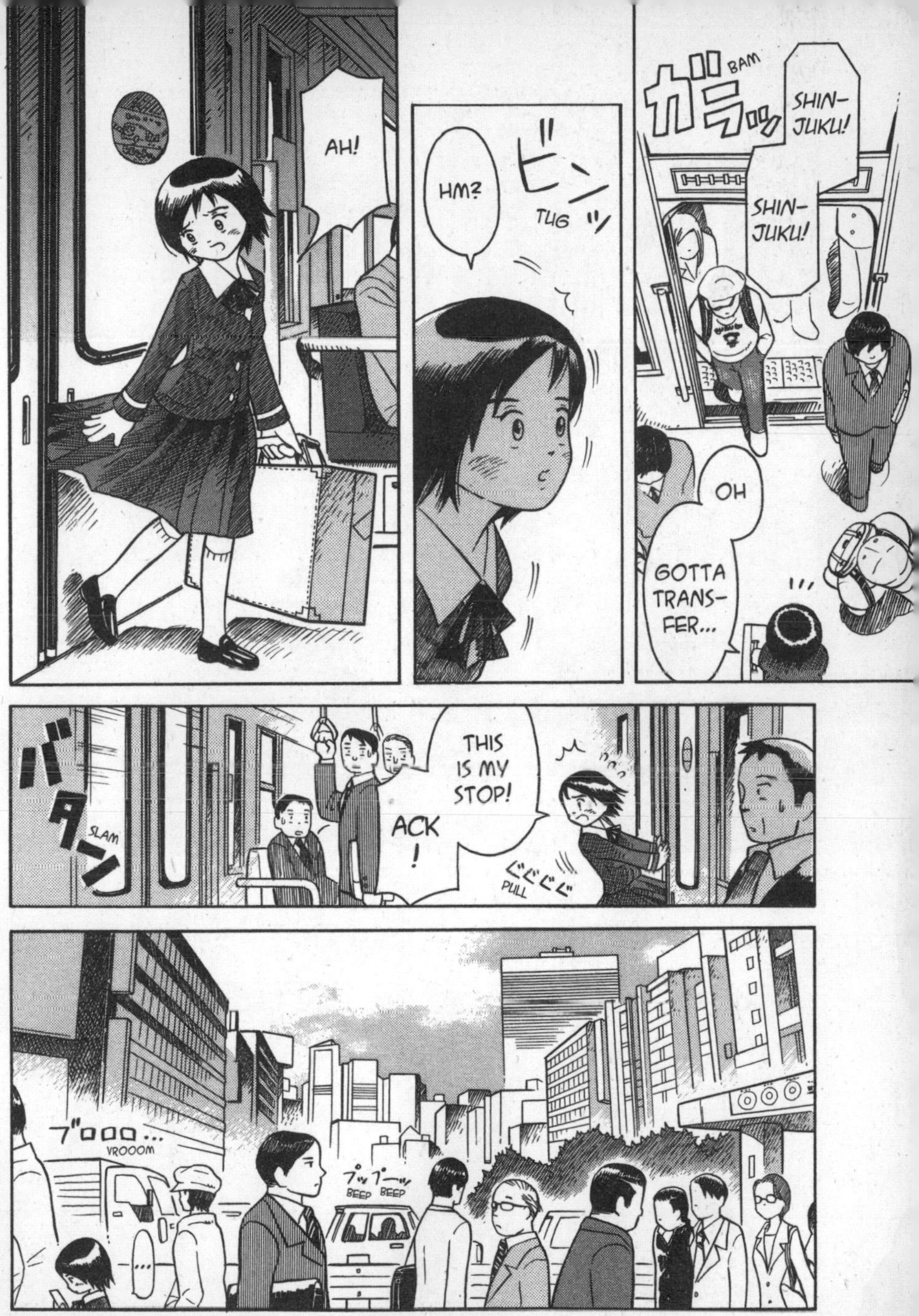
BAM
SHIN-JUKU!
SHIN-JUKU!
OH
GOTTA TRANSFER...
HM?
TUG
AH!
THIS IS MY STOP!
PULL
ACK!
SLAM
BEEP BEEP
VROOOM
...

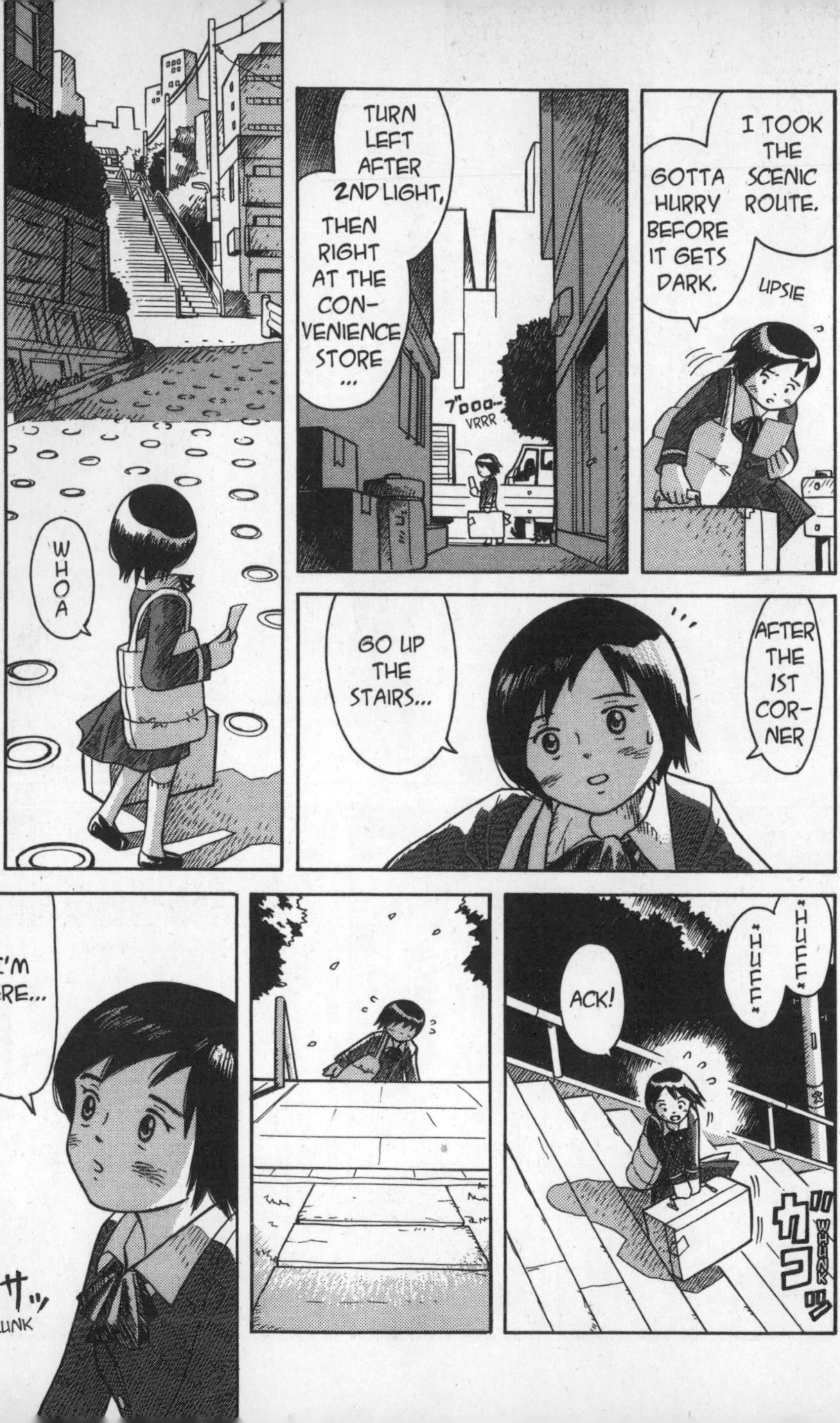
I TOOK THE SCENIC ROUTE.
GOTTA HURRY BEFORE IT GETS DARK.
UPSIE
TURN LEFT AFTER 2ND LIGHT,
THEN RIGHT AT THE CONVENIENCE STORE ...
ブロロロ…
VRRR
AFTER THE 1ST CORNER
GO UP THE STAIRS...
WHOA
HUFF *HUFF*
ACK!
ガコッ
WHUNK
I'M HERE...
ドサッ
KLUNK

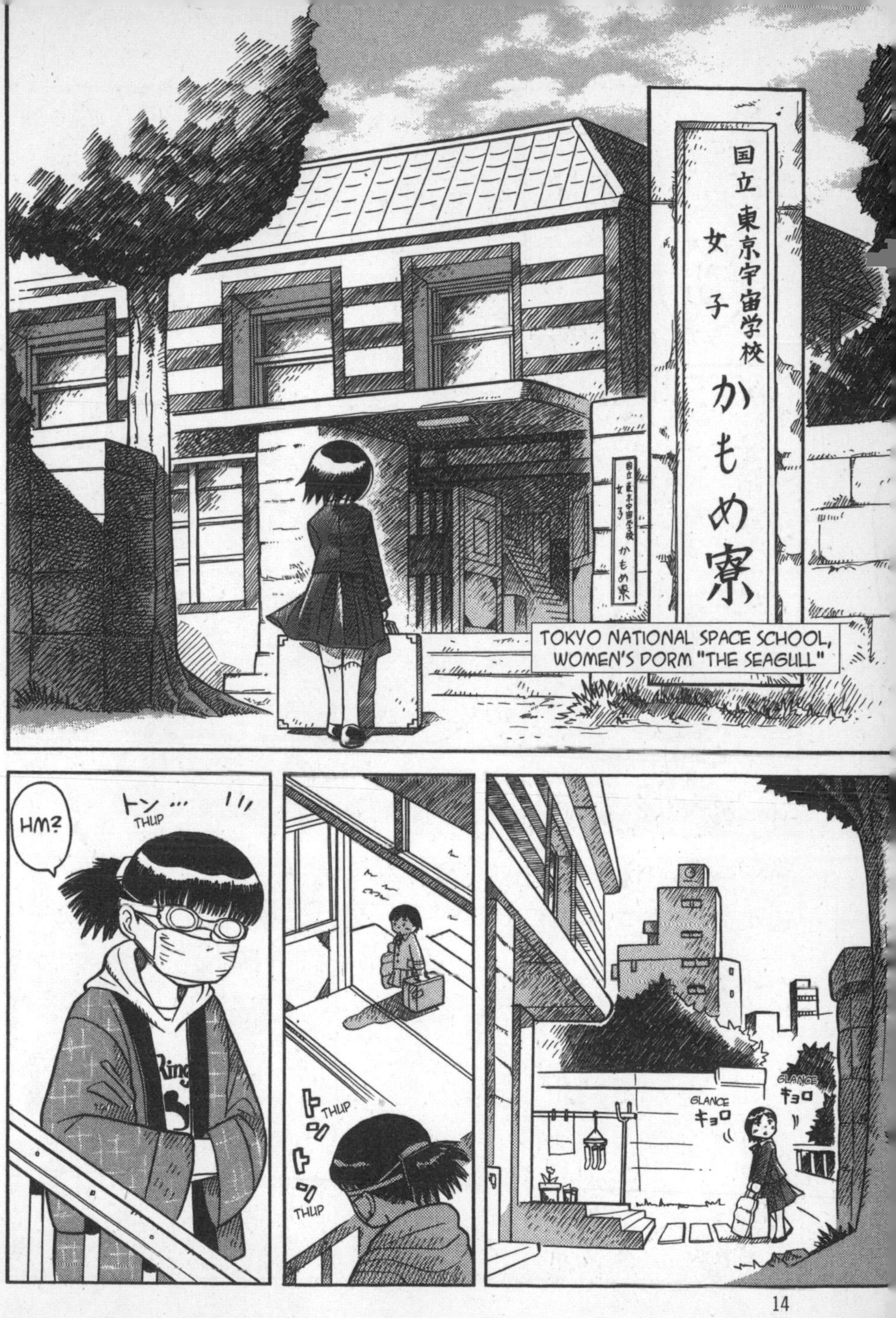
国立東京宇宙学校
女子
かもめ寮
TOKYO NATIONAL SPACE SCHOOL, WOMEN'S DORM "THE SEAGULL"
GLANCE キョロ
GLANCE キョロ
トッ THUP
トッ THUP
HM?
トン… THUP

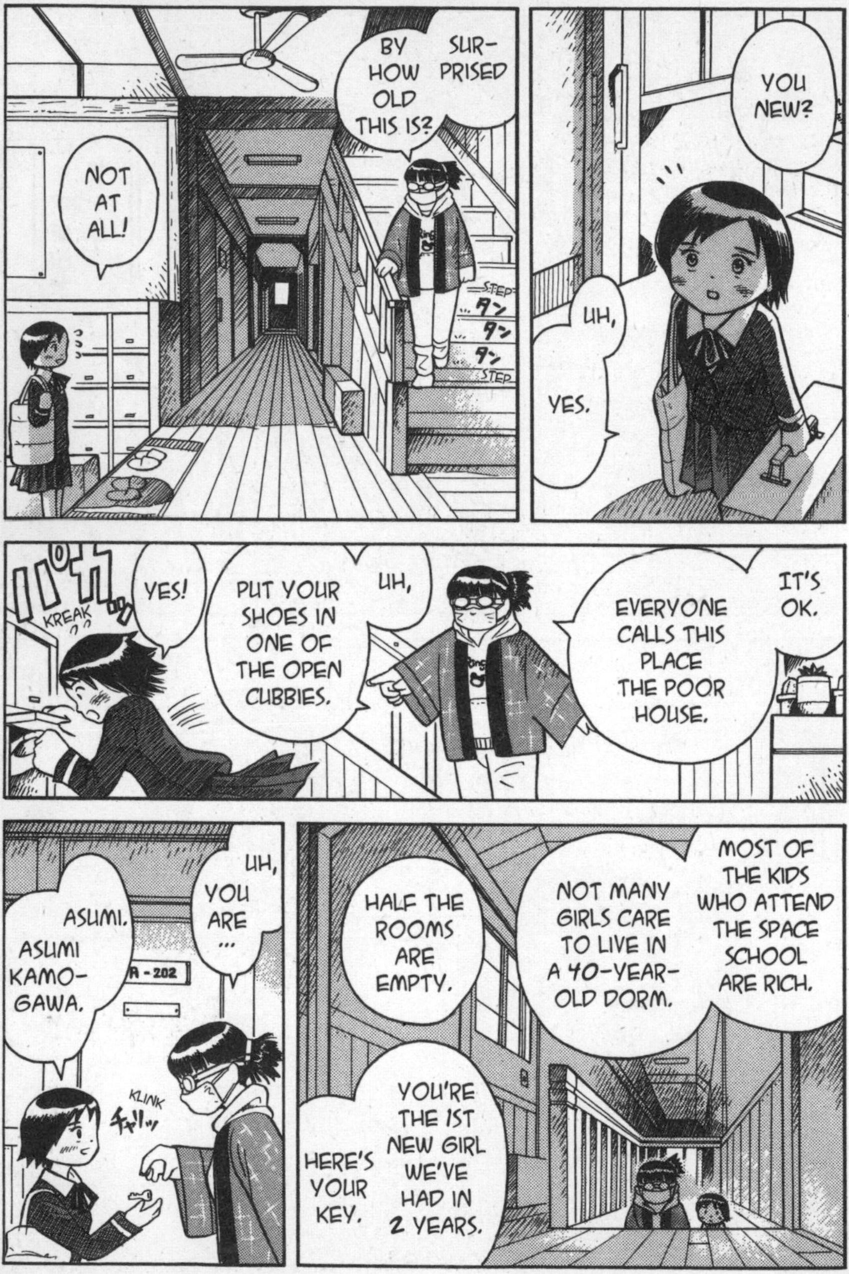
YOU NEW?
UH,
YES.
SUR- PRISED BY HOW OLD THIS IS?
NOT AT ALL!
STEP タン タン タン STEP
IT'S OK.
EVERYONE CALLS THIS PLACE THE POOR HOUSE.
UH,
PUT YOUR SHOES IN ONE OF THE OPEN CUBBIES.
YES!
パカッ KREAK
MOST OF THE KIDS WHO ATTEND THE SPACE SCHOOL ARE RICH.
NOT MANY GIRLS CARE TO LIVE IN A 40-YEAR-OLD DORM.
HALF THE ROOMS ARE EMPTY.
YOU'RE THE 1ST NEW GIRL WE'VE HAD IN 2 YEARS.
HERE'S YOUR KEY.
UH, YOU ARE ...
ASUMI. ASUMI KAMO-GAWA.
A - 202
KLINK チャリッ

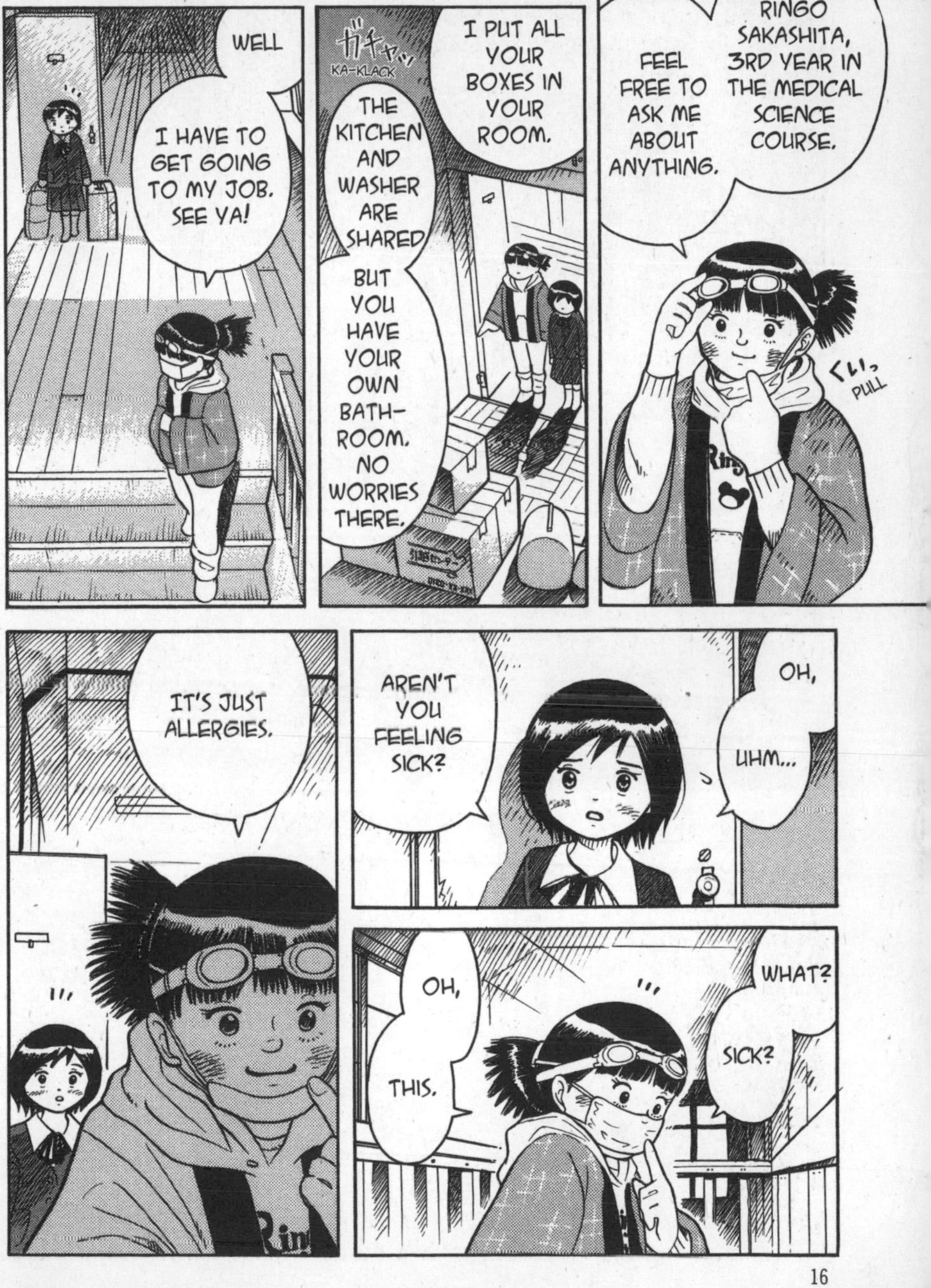
I'M RINGO SAKASHITA, 3RD YEAR IN THE MEDICAL SCIENCE COURSE.
FEEL FREE TO ASK ME ABOUT ANYTHING.
くいっ PULL
ガチャッ KA-KLACK
I PUT ALL YOUR BOXES IN YOUR ROOM.
THE KITCHEN AND WASHER ARE SHARED
BUT YOU HAVE YOUR OWN BATH-ROOM. NO WORRIES THERE.
WELL
I HAVE TO GET GOING TO MY JOB. SEE YA!
OH,
UHM...
AREN'T YOU FEELING SICK?
WHAT?
SICK?
OH,
THIS.
IT'S JUST ALLERGIES.

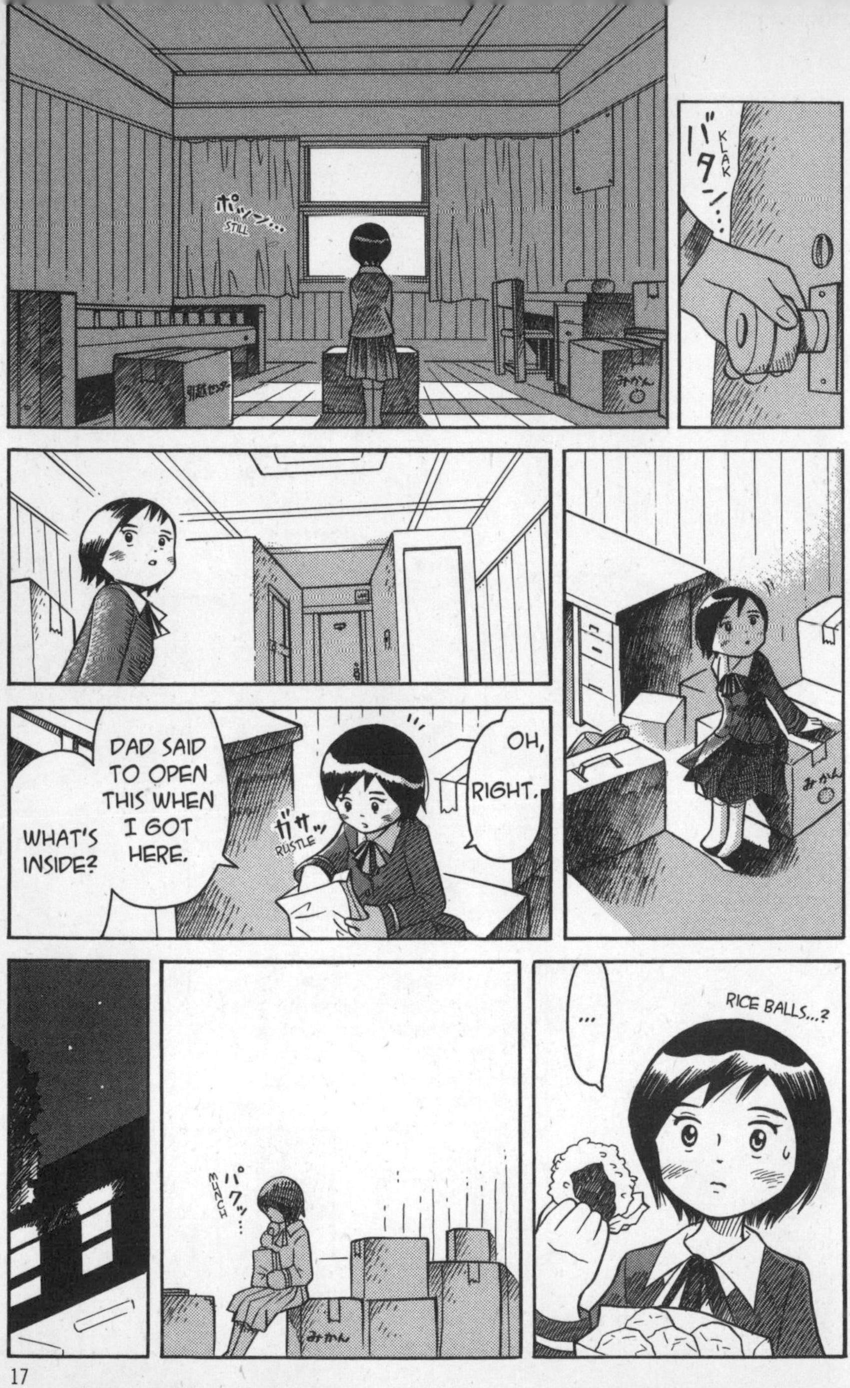

バタン…
KLAK
ポッン…
STILL
OH, RIGHT.
ガサッ
RUSTLE
DAD SAID TO OPEN THIS WHEN I GOT HERE.
WHAT'S INSIDE?
RICE BALLS...?
...
パクッ…
MUNCH

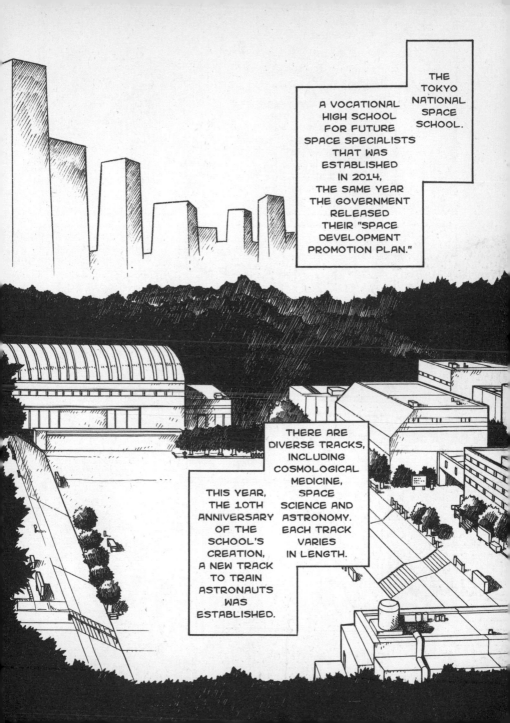

THE TOKYO NATIONAL SPACE SCHOOL.

A VOCATIONAL HIGH SCHOOL FOR FUTURE SPACE SPECIALISTS THAT WAS ESTABLISHED IN 2014, THE SAME YEAR THE GOVERNMENT RELEASED THEIR "SPACE DEVELOPMENT PROMOTION PLAN."

THERE ARE DIVERSE TRACKS, INCLUDING COSMOLOGICAL MEDICINE, SPACE SCIENCE AND ASTRONOMY. EACH TRACK VARIES IN LENGTH.

THIS YEAR, THE 10TH ANNIVERSARY OF THE SCHOOL'S CREATION, A NEW TRACK TO TRAIN ASTRONAUTS WAS ESTABLISHED.

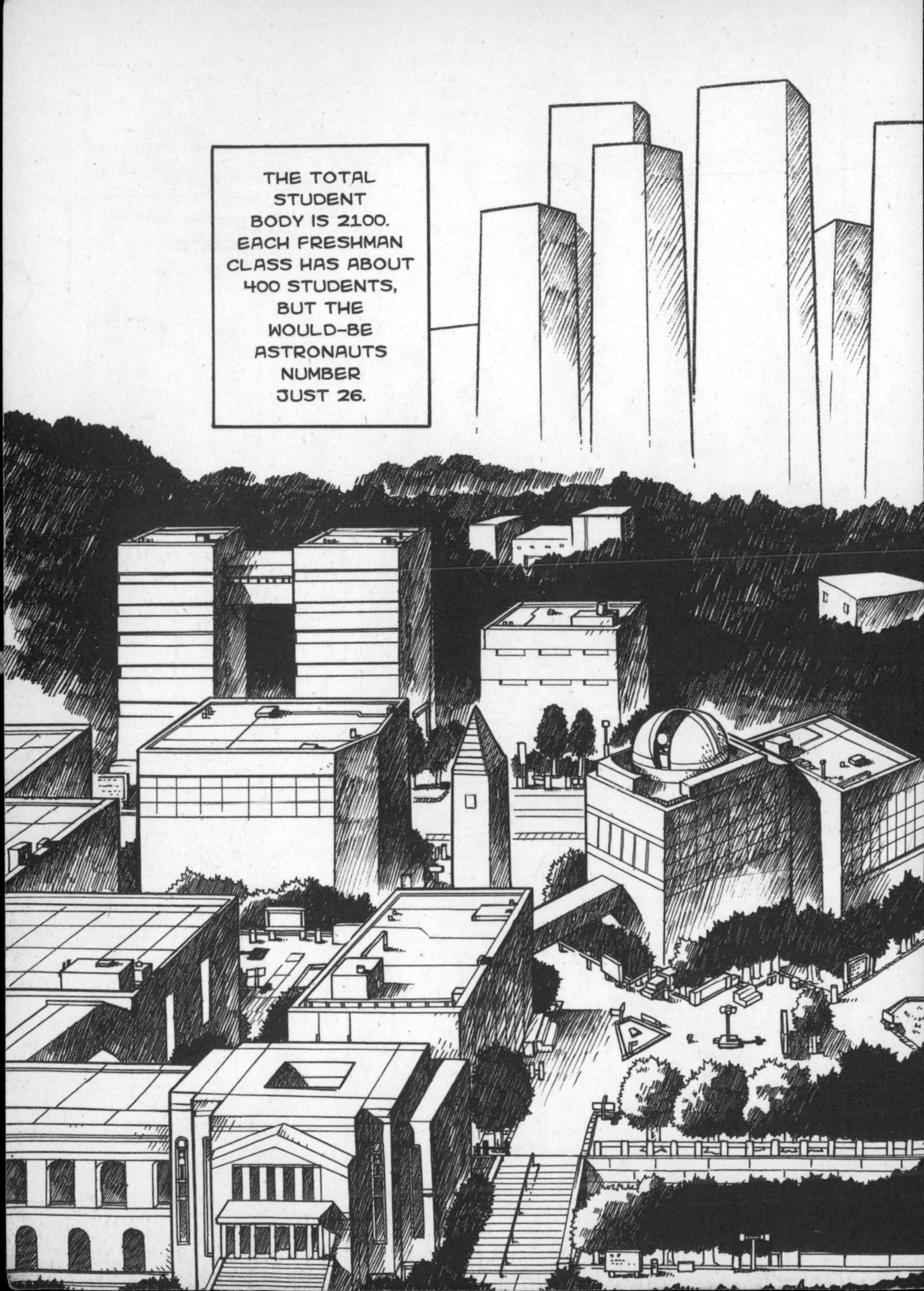
THE TOTAL STUDENT BODY IS 2100. EACH FRESHMAN CLASS HAS ABOUT 400 STUDENTS, BUT THE WOULD-BE ASTRONAUTS NUMBER JUST 26.

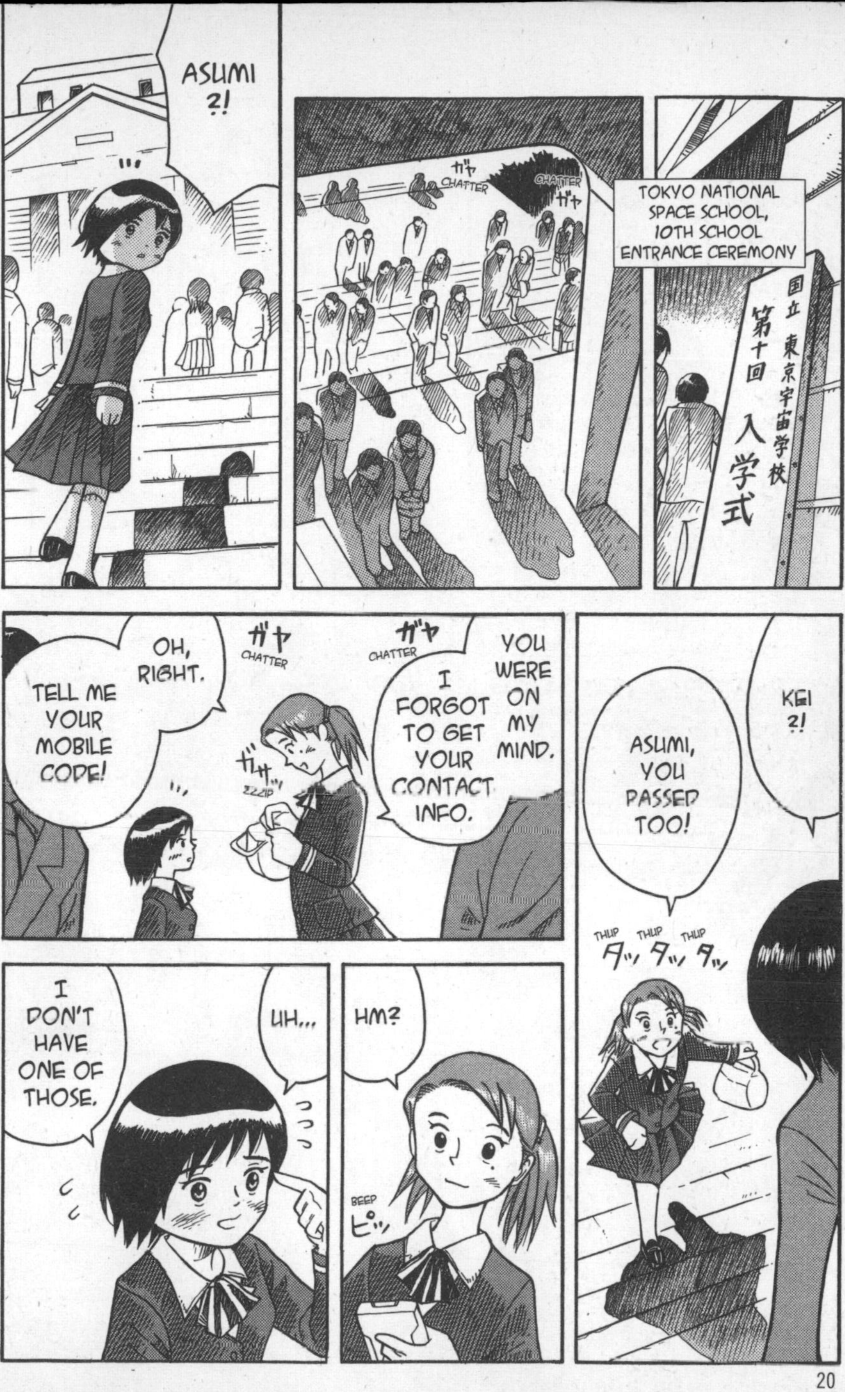
TOKYO NATIONAL SPACE SCHOOL, 10TH SCHOOL ENTRANCE CEREMONY
国立 東京宇宙学校 第十回 入学式
ガヤ CHATTER
CHATTER ガヤ
ASUMI ?!
KEI ?!
ASUMI, YOU PASSED TOO!
THUP タッ THUP タッ THUP タッ
YOU WERE ON MY MIND.
I FORGOT TO GET YOUR CONTACT INFO.
ガヤ CHATTER
ガヤ CHATTER
ガサッ ZZZIP
OH, RIGHT.
TELL ME YOUR MOBILE CODE!
HM?
BEEP ピッ
UH...
I DON'T HAVE ONE OF THOSE.

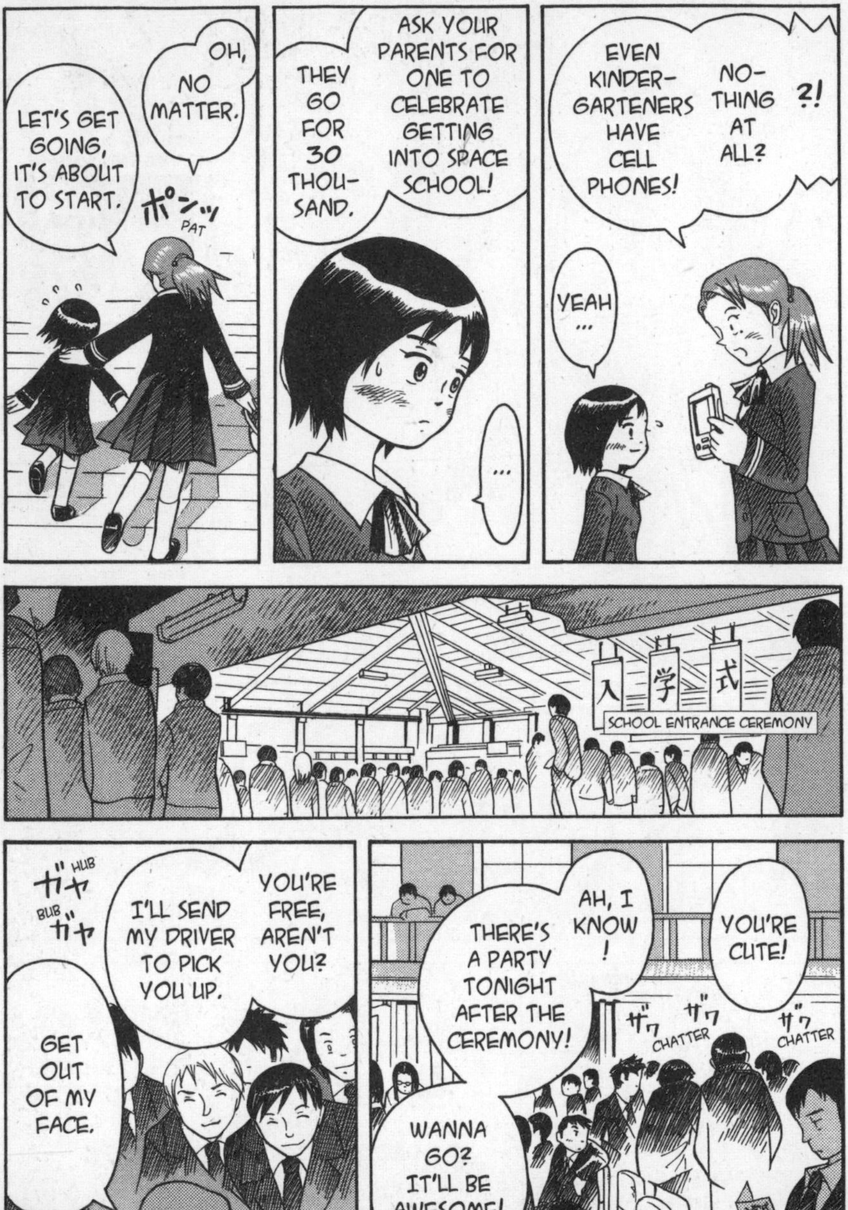
?!
NO-THING AT ALL?
EVEN KINDER-GARTENERS HAVE CELL PHONES!
YEAH ...
ASK YOUR PARENTS FOR ONE TO CELEBRATE GETTING INTO SPACE SCHOOL!
THEY GO FOR 30 THOU-SAND.
...
OH, NO MATTER.
ポンッ PAT
LET'S GET GOING, IT'S ABOUT TO START.
入学式
SCHOOL ENTRANCE CEREMONY
YOU'RE CUTE!
ザワ CHATTER
ザワ CHATTER
AH, I KNOW!
THERE'S A PARTY TONIGHT AFTER THE CEREMONY!
WANNA GO? IT'LL BE AWESOME!
YOU'RE FREE, AREN'T YOU?
I'LL SEND MY DRIVER TO PICK YOU UP.
ガヤ HUB
ガヤ BUB
GET OUT OF MY FACE.

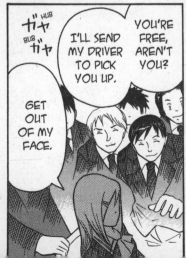

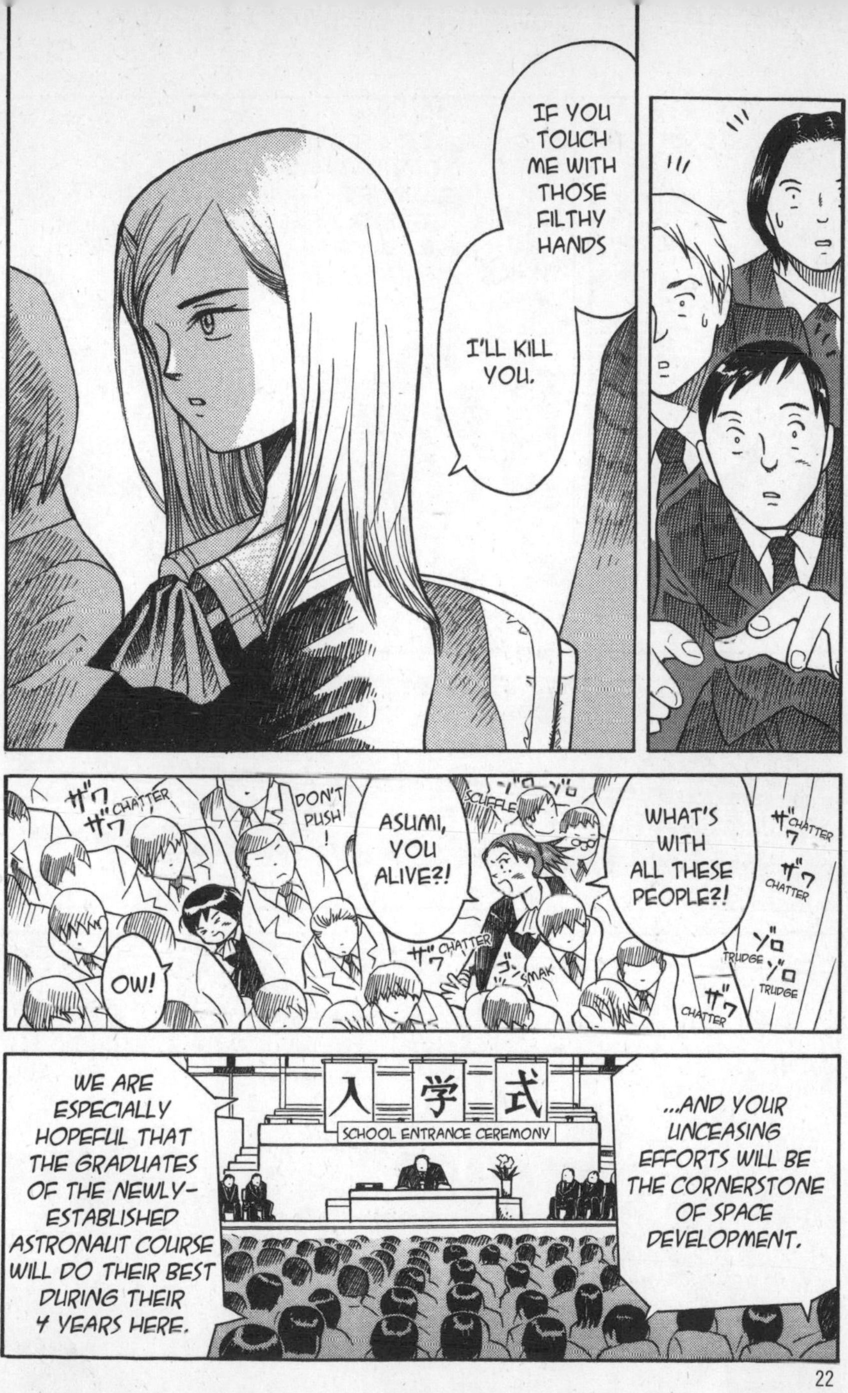
IF YOU TOUCH ME WITH THOSE FILTHY HANDS
I'LL KILL YOU.
ザワ CHATTER
ザワ CHATTER
WHAT'S WITH ALL THESE PEOPLE?!
ゾロ TRUDGE
ゾロ TRUDGE
ザワ CHATTER
ゾロ ゾロ SCUFFLE
ASUMI, YOU ALIVE?!
DON'T PUSH!
ザワ ザワ CHATTER
ザワ CHATTER
ゴン SMAK
OW!
入学式
SCHOOL ENTRANCE CEREMONY
WE ARE ESPECIALLY HOPEFUL THAT THE GRADUATES OF THE NEWLY-ESTABLISHED ASTRONAUT COURSE WILL DO THEIR BEST DURING THEIR 4 YEARS HERE.
...AND YOUR UNCEASING EFFORTS WILL BE THE CORNERSTONE OF SPACE DEVELOPMENT.

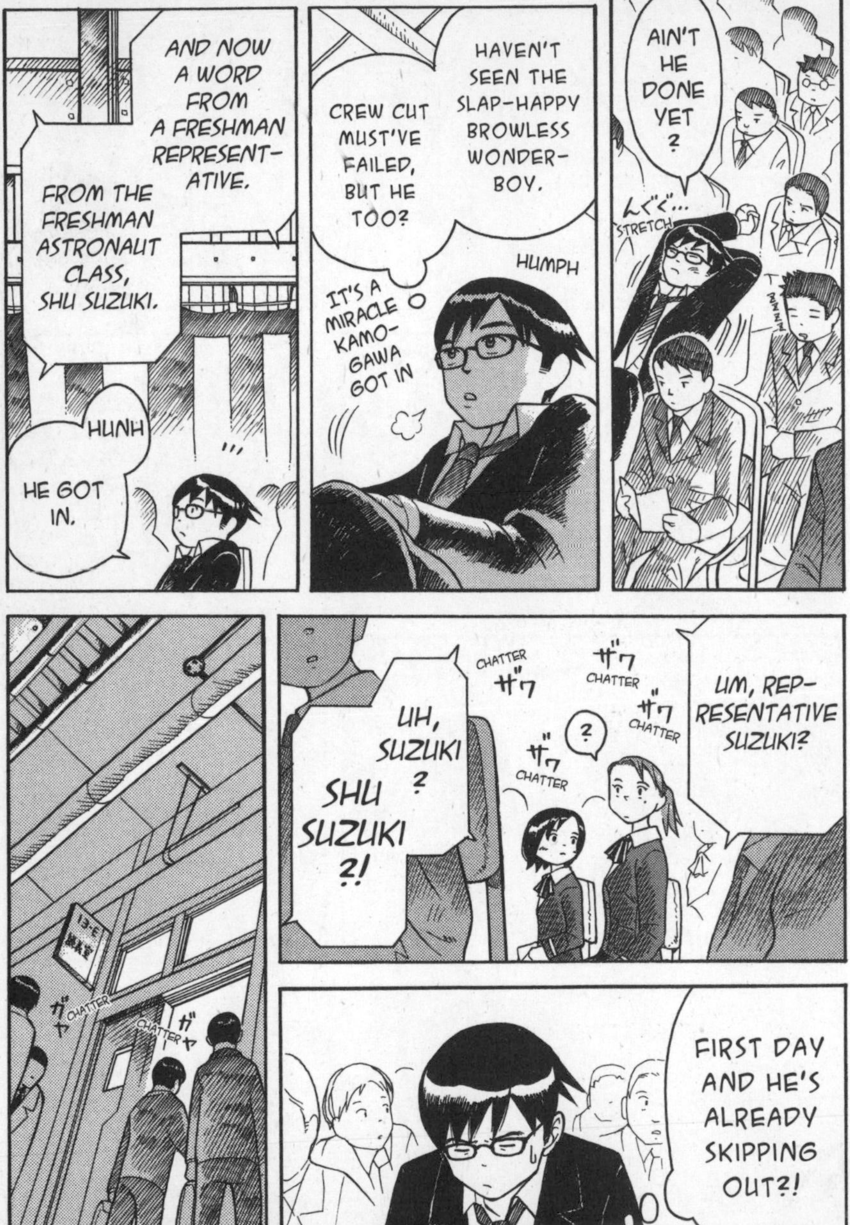

AIN'T HE DONE YET?
んぐぐ…
STRETCH
HAVEN'T SEEN THE SLAP-HAPPY BROWLESS WONDER-BOY.
CREW CUT MUST'VE FAILED, BUT HE TOO?
HUMPH
IT'S A MIRACLE KAMOGAWA GOT IN
AND NOW A WORD FROM A FRESHMAN REPRESENT-ATIVE.
FROM THE FRESHMAN ASTRONAUT CLASS, SHU SUZUKI.
HUNH
HE GOT IN.
UM, REP-RESENTATIVE SUZUKI?
ザワ CHATTER
ザワ CHATTER
?
ザワ CHATTER
ザワ CHATTER
UH, SUZUKI?
SHU SUZUKI?!
FIRST DAY AND HE'S ALREADY SKIPPING OUT?!
ガヤ CHATTER
ガヤ CHATTER

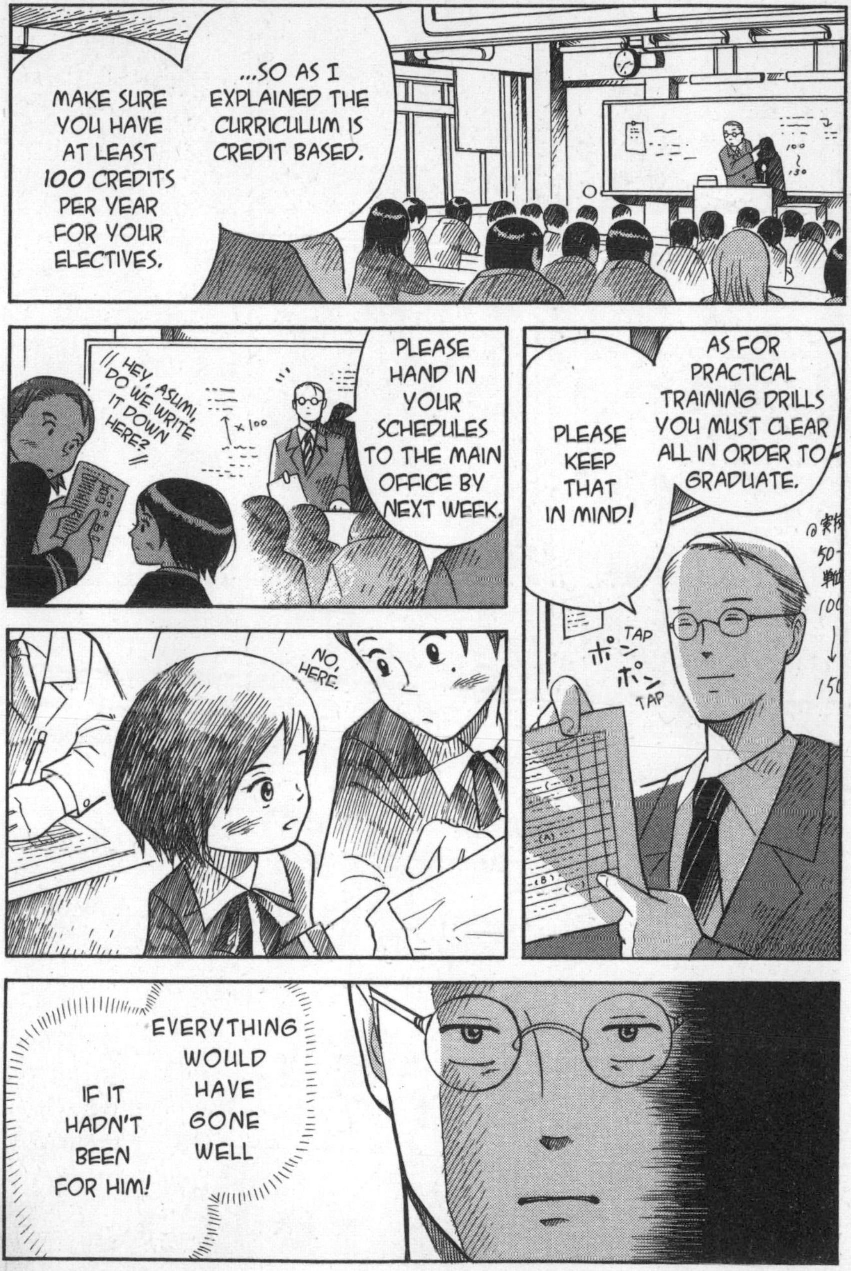
...SO AS I EXPLAINED THE CURRICULUM IS CREDIT BASED.
MAKE SURE YOU HAVE AT LEAST 100 CREDITS PER YEAR FOR YOUR ELECTIVES.
AS FOR PRACTICAL TRAINING DRILLS YOU MUST CLEAR ALL IN ORDER TO GRADUATE.
PLEASE KEEP THAT IN MIND!
ポン TAP
ポン TAP
PLEASE HAND IN YOUR SCHEDULES TO THE MAIN OFFICE BY NEXT WEEK.
HEY, ASUMI, DO WE WRITE IT DOWN HERE?
NO, HERE.
EVERYTHING WOULD HAVE GONE WELL
IF IT HADN'T BEEN FOR HIM!

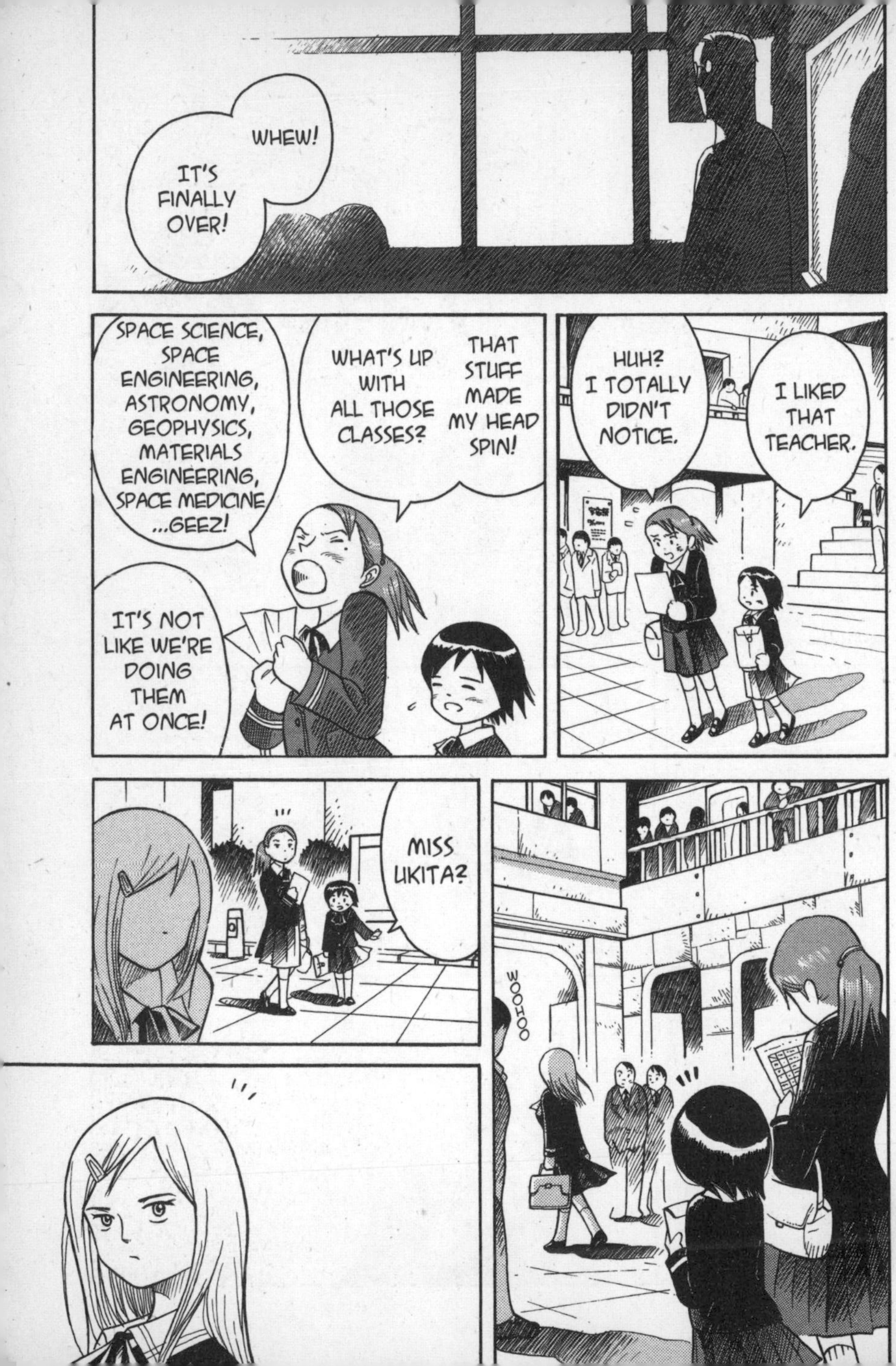
WHEW!
IT'S FINALLY OVER!
I LIKED THAT TEACHER.
HUH? I TOTALLY DIDN'T NOTICE.
THAT STUFF MADE MY HEAD SPIN!
WHAT'S UP WITH ALL THOSE CLASSES?
SPACE SCIENCE, SPACE ENGINEERING, ASTRONOMY, GEOPHYSICS, MATERIALS ENGINEERING, SPACE MEDICINE ...GEEZ!
IT'S NOT LIKE WE'RE DOING THEM AT ONCE!
WOOHOO
MISS UKITA?

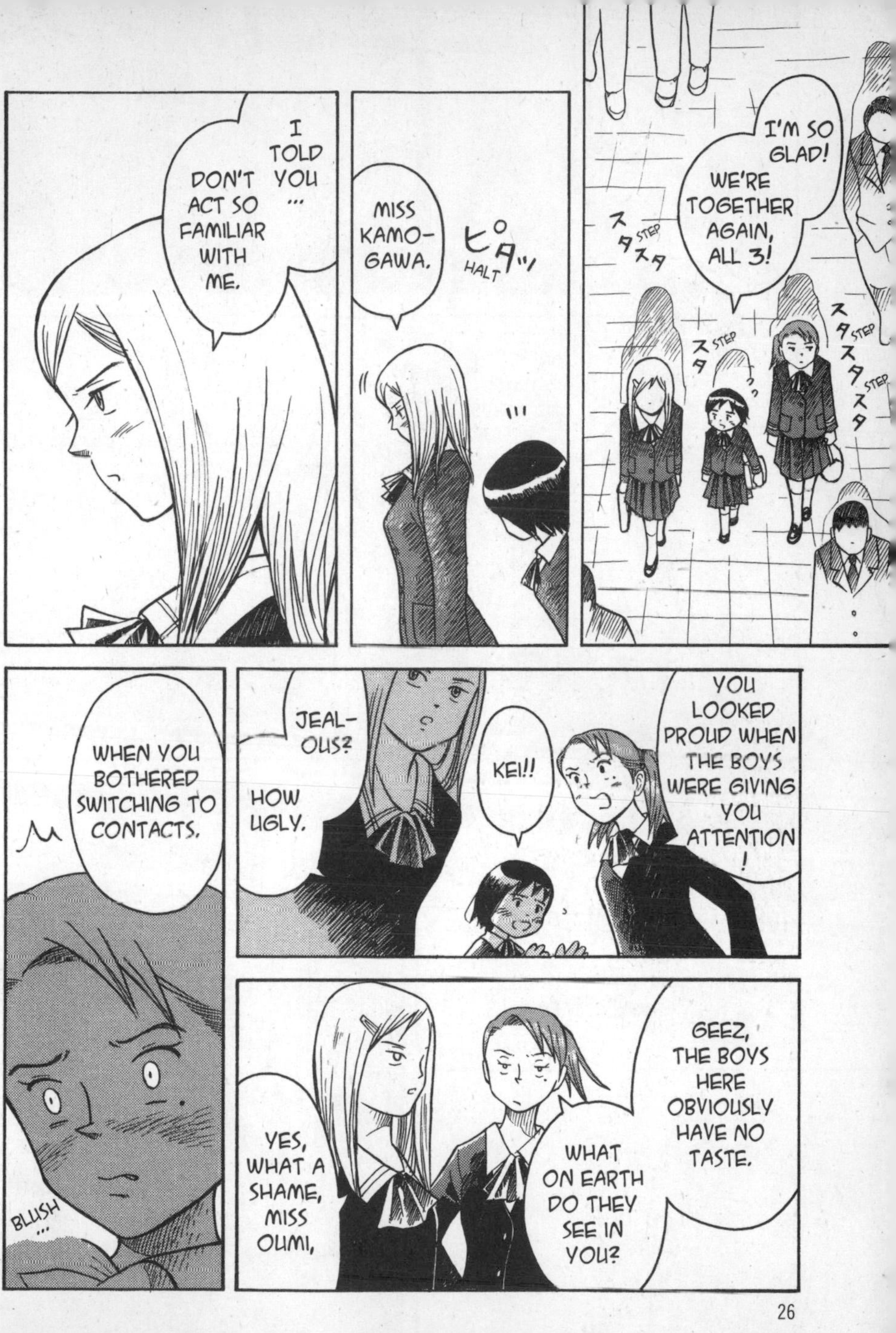

I'M SO GLAD! WE'RE TOGETHER AGAIN, ALL 3!
スタスタ STEP
スタ STEP
スタスタ STEP
スタスタ STEP
MISS KAMO-GAWA.
ピタッ HALT
I TOLD YOU ...
DON'T ACT SO FAMILIAR WITH ME.
YOU LOOKED PROUD WHEN THE BOYS WERE GIVING YOU ATTENTION!
KEI!!
JEAL-OUS?
HOW UGLY.
GEEZ, THE BOYS HERE OBVIOUSLY HAVE NO TASTE.
WHAT ON EARTH DO THEY SEE IN YOU?
YES, WHAT A SHAME, MISS OUMI,
WHEN YOU BOTHERED SWITCHING TO CONTACTS.
ム
BLUSH ...

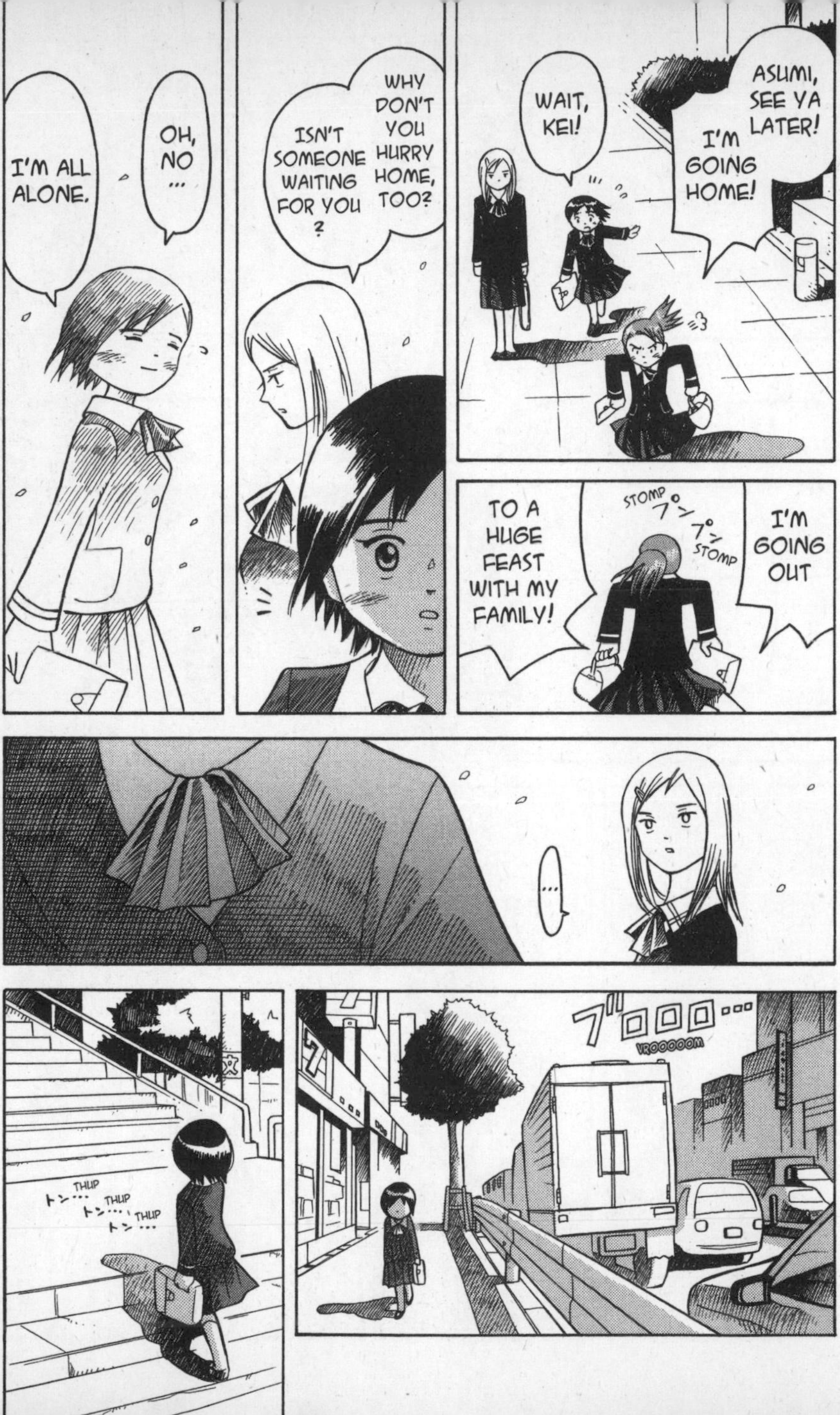
ASUMI, SEE YA LATER!
I'M GOING HOME!
WAIT, KEI!
I'M GOING OUT
STOMP プン プン STOMP
TO A HUGE FEAST WITH MY FAMILY!
WHY DON'T YOU HURRY HOME, TOO?
ISN'T SOMEONE WAITING FOR YOU?
OH, NO ...
I'M ALL ALONE.
...
ブロロロ･･･ VROOOOOM
トン･･･ THUP
トン･･･ THUP
トン･･･ THUP

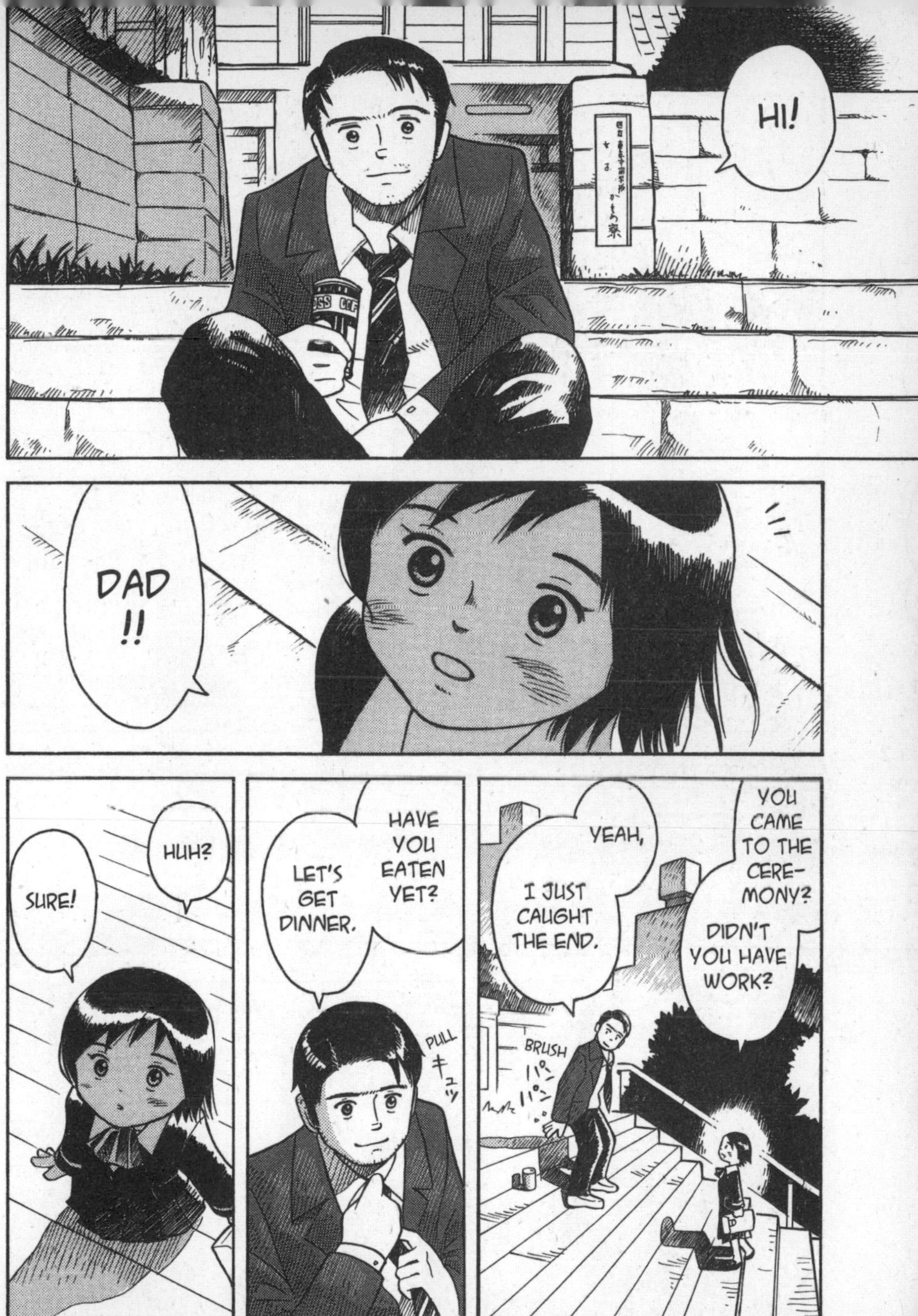
HI!
DAD !!
YOU CAME TO THE CERE-MONY?
DIDN'T YOU HAVE WORK?
YEAH,
I JUST CAUGHT THE END.
BRUSH
パン パン
HAVE YOU EATEN YET?
LET'S GET DINNER.
PULL
キュッ
HUH?
SURE!

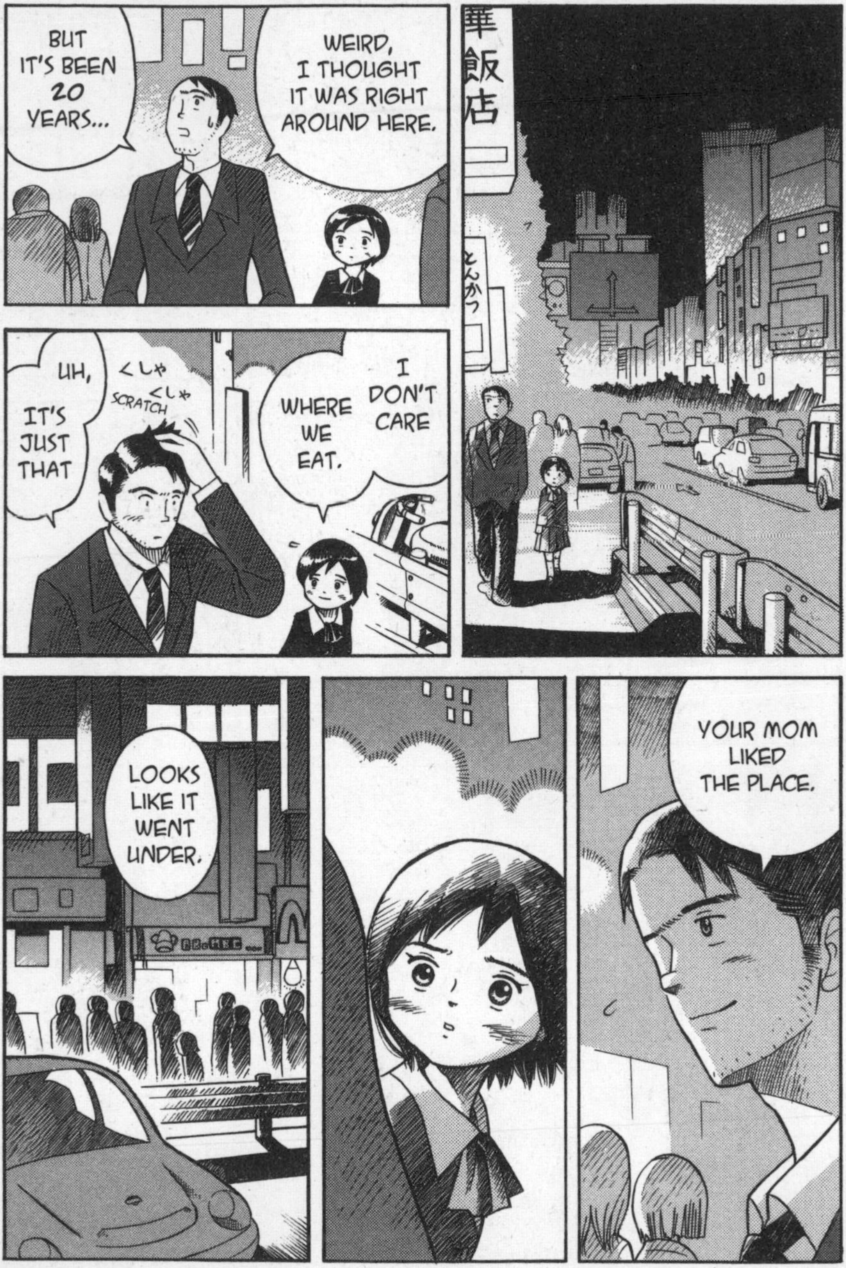
華飯店
とんかつ
WEIRD, I THOUGHT IT WAS RIGHT AROUND HERE.
BUT IT'S BEEN 20 YEARS...
I DON'T CARE WHERE WE EAT.
くしゃ くしゃ
SCRATCH
UH, IT'S JUST THAT
YOUR MOM LIKED THE PLACE.
LOOKS LIKE IT WENT UNDER.

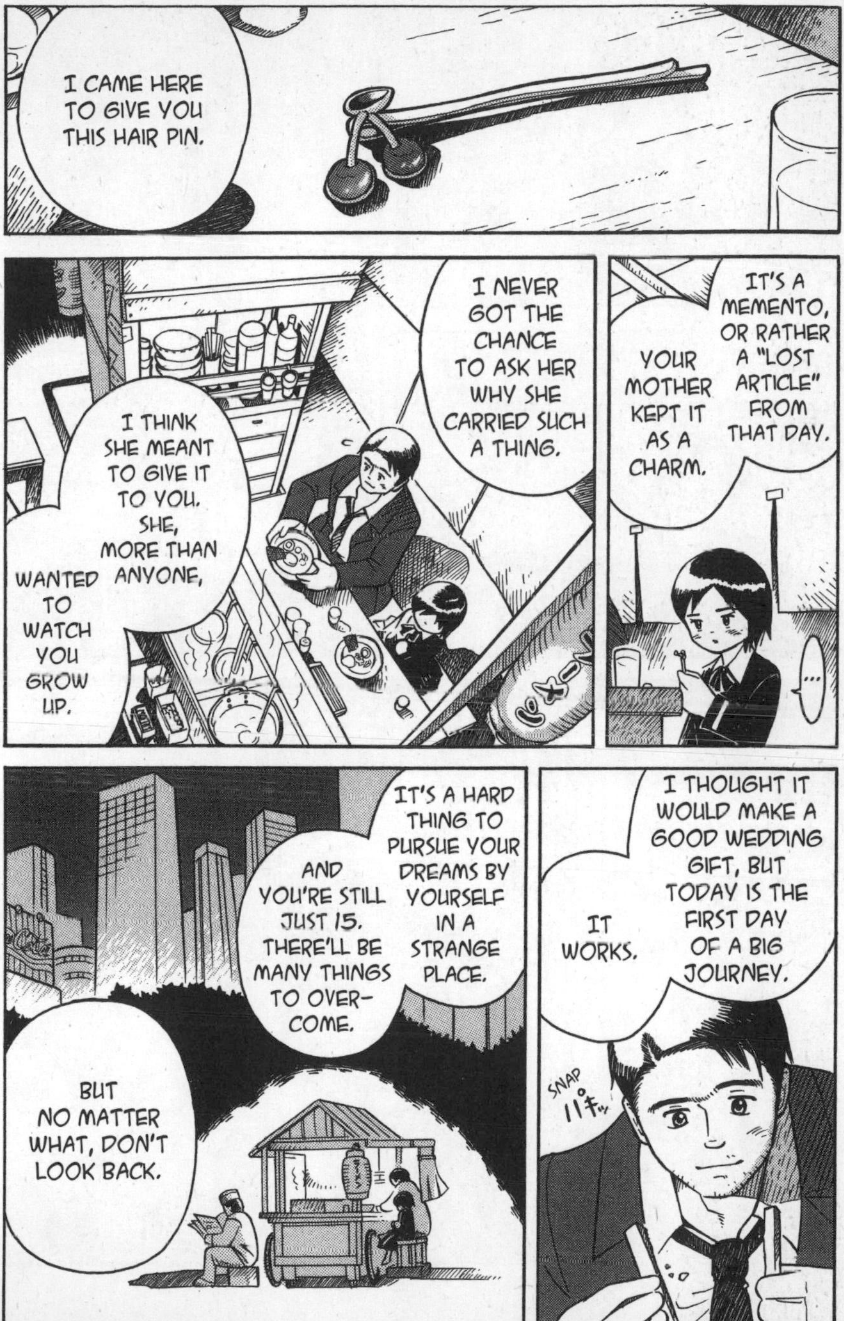
I CAME HERE TO GIVE YOU THIS HAIR PIN.
IT'S A MEMENTO, OR RATHER A "LOST ARTICLE" FROM THAT DAY.
YOUR MOTHER KEPT IT AS A CHARM.
...
I NEVER GOT THE CHANCE TO ASK HER WHY SHE CARRIED SUCH A THING.
I THINK SHE MEANT TO GIVE IT TO YOU.
SHE, MORE THAN ANYONE, WANTED TO WATCH YOU GROW UP.
I THOUGHT IT WOULD MAKE A GOOD WEDDING GIFT, BUT TODAY IS THE FIRST DAY OF A BIG JOURNEY.
IT WORKS.
SNAP
パキッ
IT'S A HARD THING TO PURSUE YOUR DREAMS BY YOURSELF IN A STRANGE PLACE.
AND YOU'RE STILL JUST 15. THERE'LL BE MANY THINGS TO OVERCOME.
BUT NO MATTER WHAT, DON'T LOOK BACK.

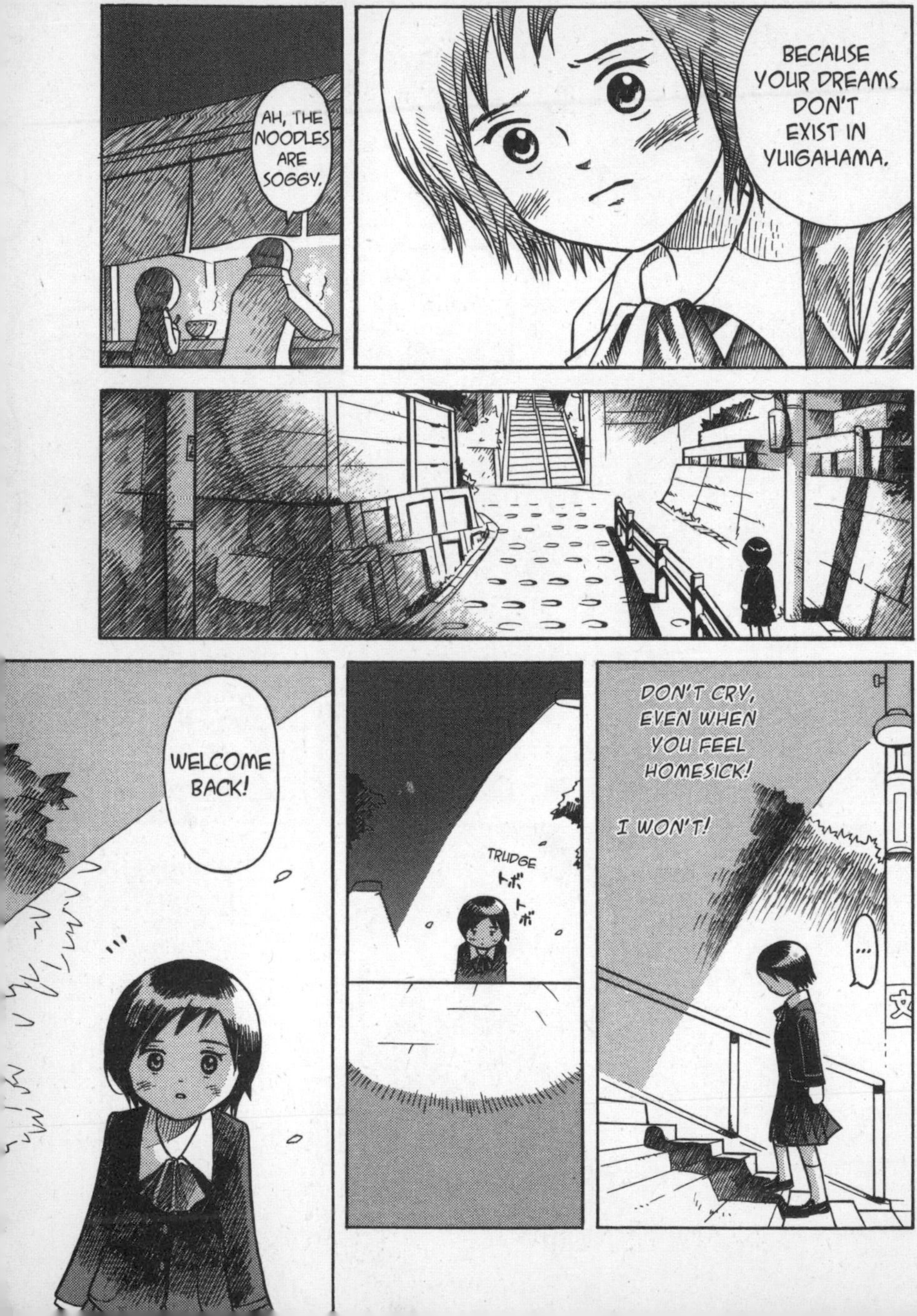
BECAUSE YOUR DREAMS DON'T EXIST IN YUIGAHAMA.
AH, THE NOODLES ARE SOGGY.
DON'T CRY, EVEN WHEN YOU FEEL HOMESICK!
I WON'T!
...
TRUDGE
トボ
トボ
WELCOME BACK!

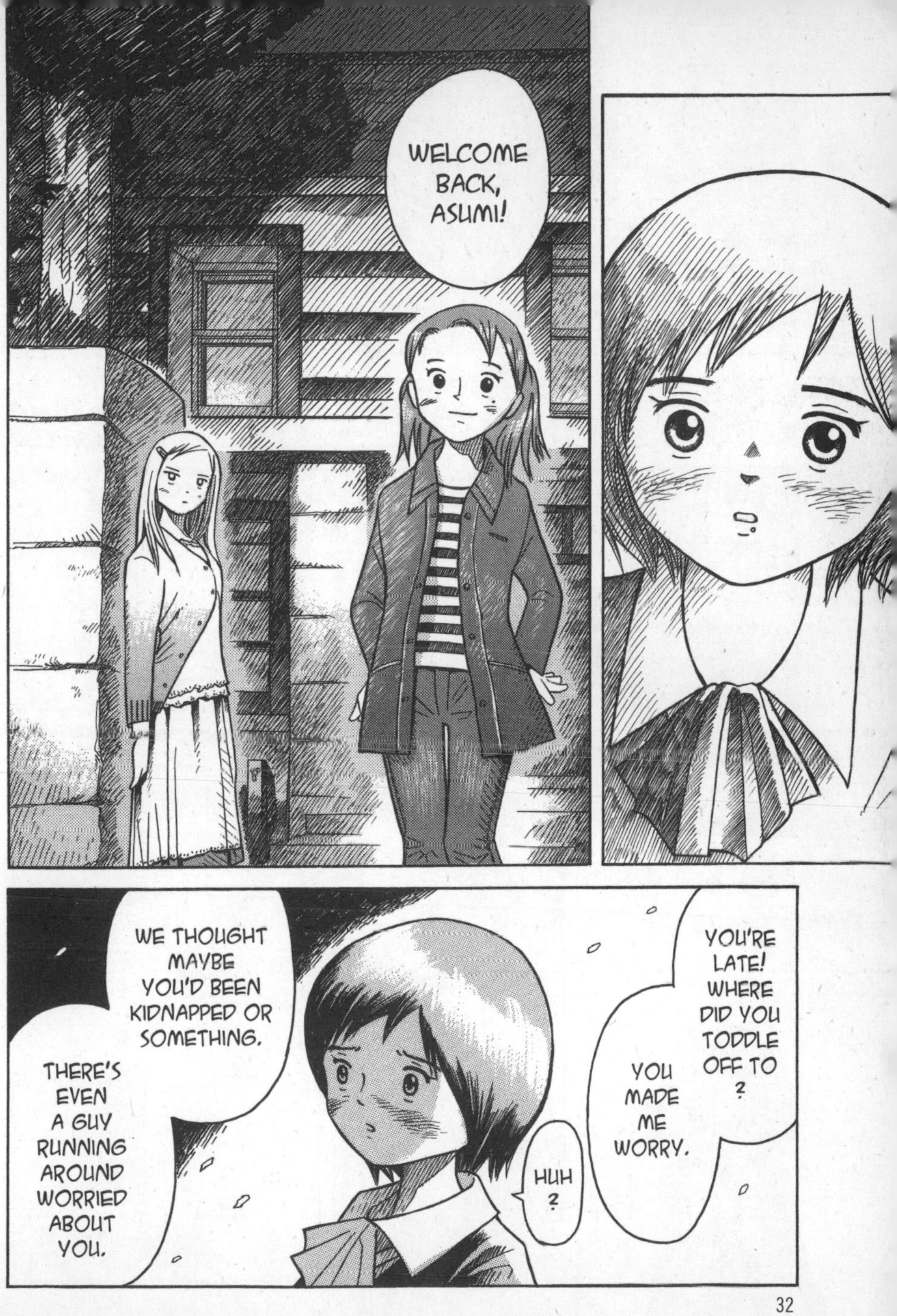
WELCOME BACK, ASUMI!
YOU'RE LATE! WHERE DID YOU TODDLE OFF TO?
YOU MADE ME WORRY.
HUH?
WE THOUGHT MAYBE YOU'D BEEN KIDNAPPED OR SOMETHING.
THERE'S EVEN A GUY RUNNING AROUND WORRIED ABOUT YOU.

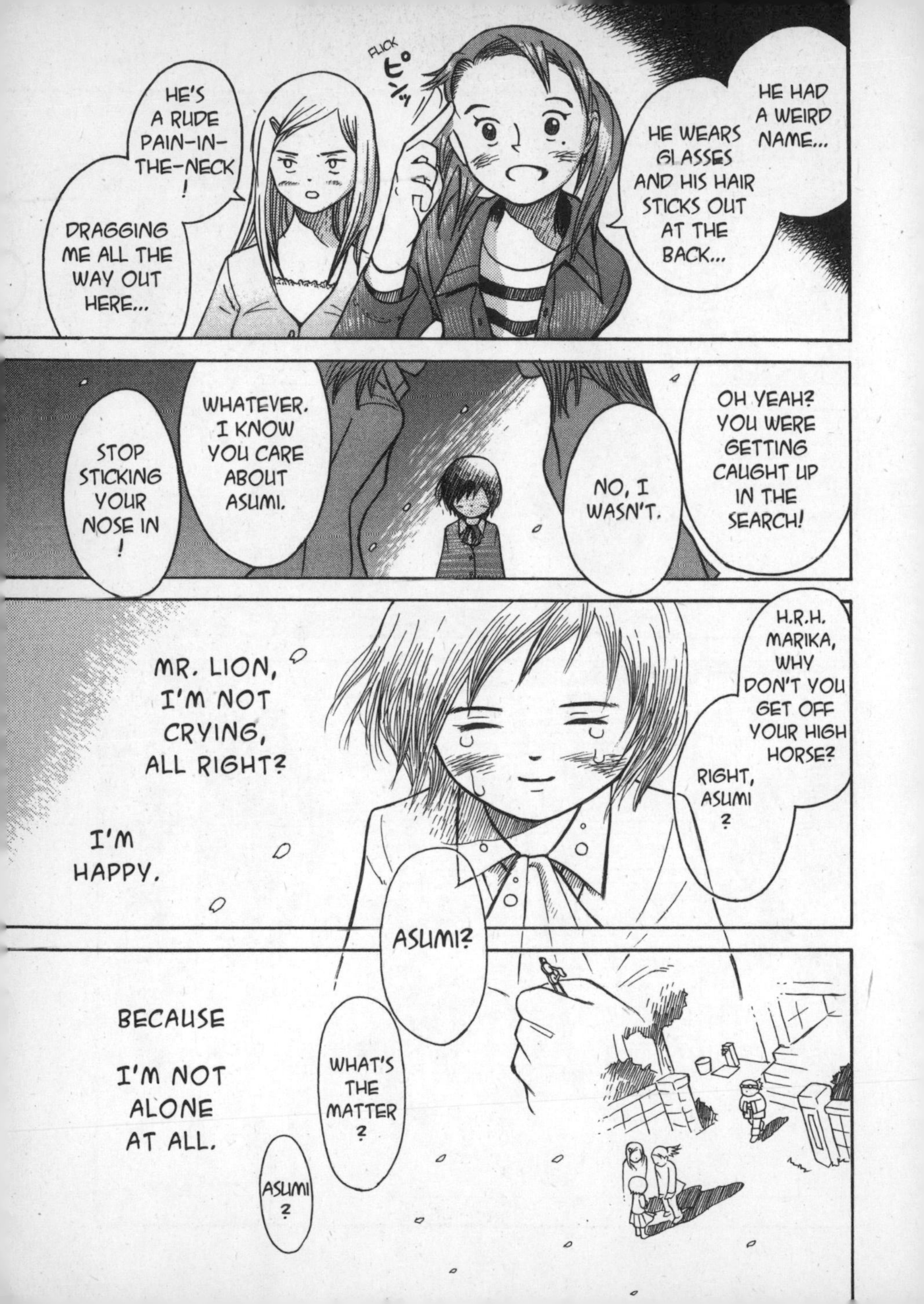
HE HAD A WEIRD NAME...
HE WEARS GLASSES AND HIS HAIR STICKS OUT AT THE BACK...
FLICK
ピッ
HE'S A RUDE PAIN-IN-THE-NECK!
DRAGGING ME ALL THE WAY OUT HERE...
OH YEAH? YOU WERE GETTING CAUGHT UP IN THE SEARCH!
NO, I WASN'T.
WHATEVER. I KNOW YOU CARE ABOUT ASUMI.
STOP STICKING YOUR NOSE IN!
H.R.H. MARIKA, WHY DON'T YOU GET OFF YOUR HIGH HORSE?
RIGHT, ASUMI?
MR. LION, I'M NOT CRYING, ALL RIGHT?
I'M HAPPY.
ASUMI?
WHAT'S THE MATTER?
ASUMI?
BECAUSE
I'M NOT ALONE AT ALL.

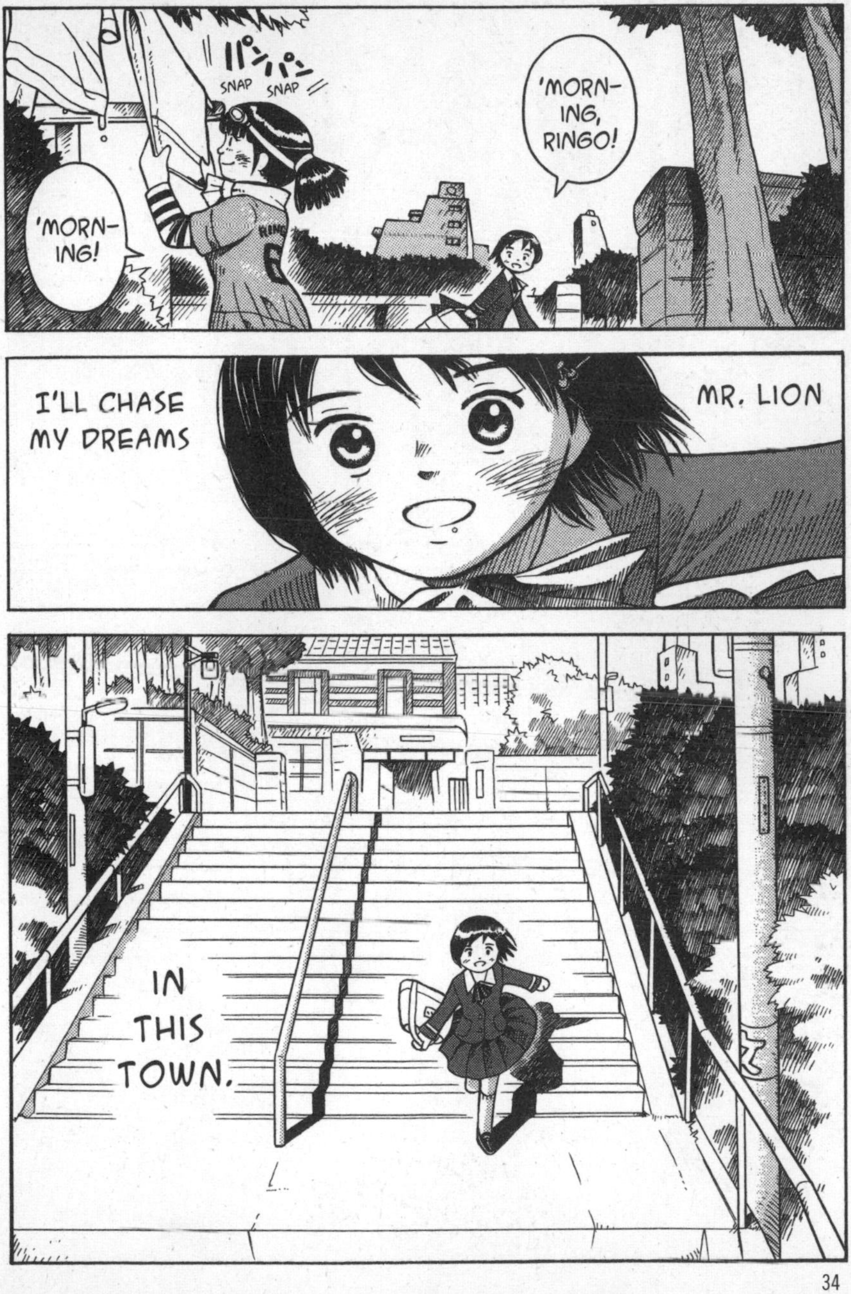
'MORN-ING, RINGO!
パンパン
SNAP SNAP
'MORN-ING!
MR. LION
I'LL CHASE MY DREAMS
IN THIS TOWN.

MISSION:06

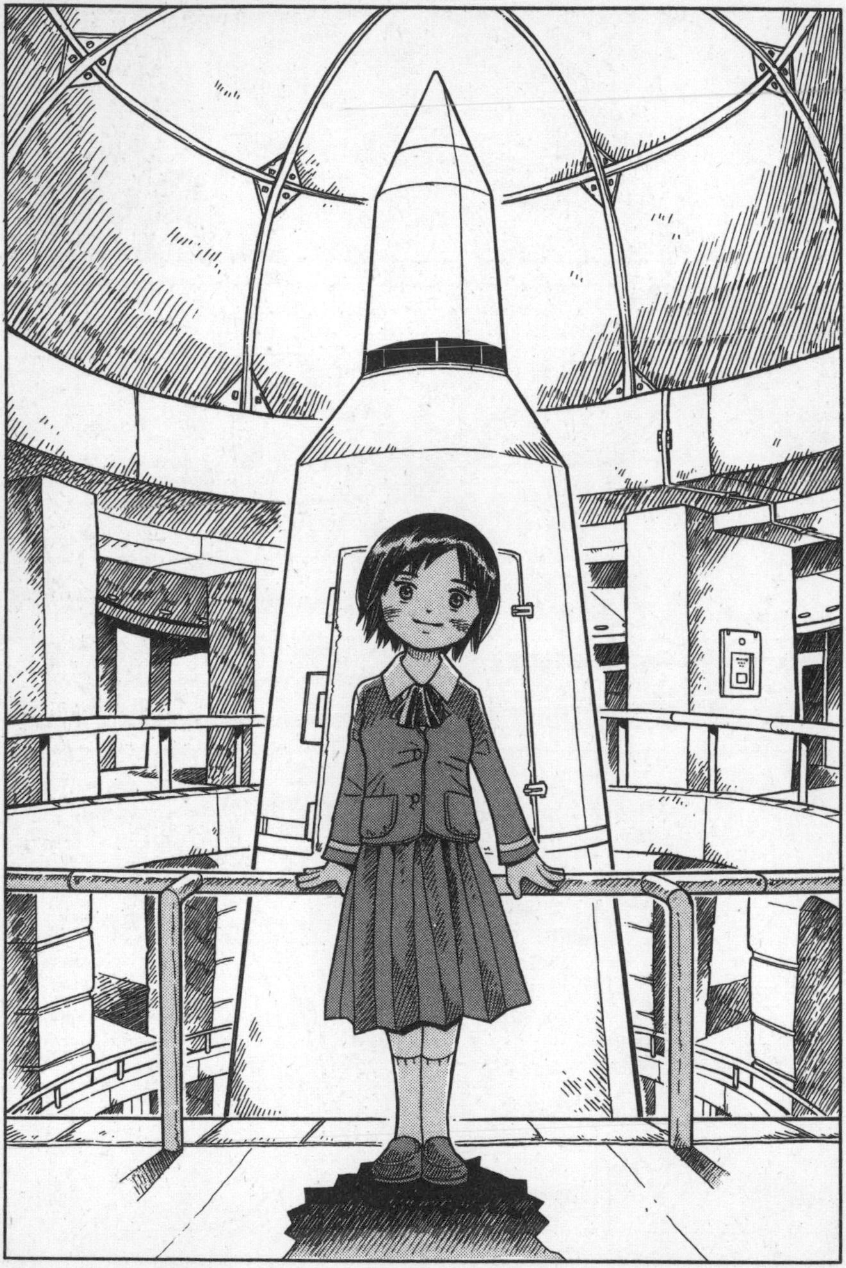

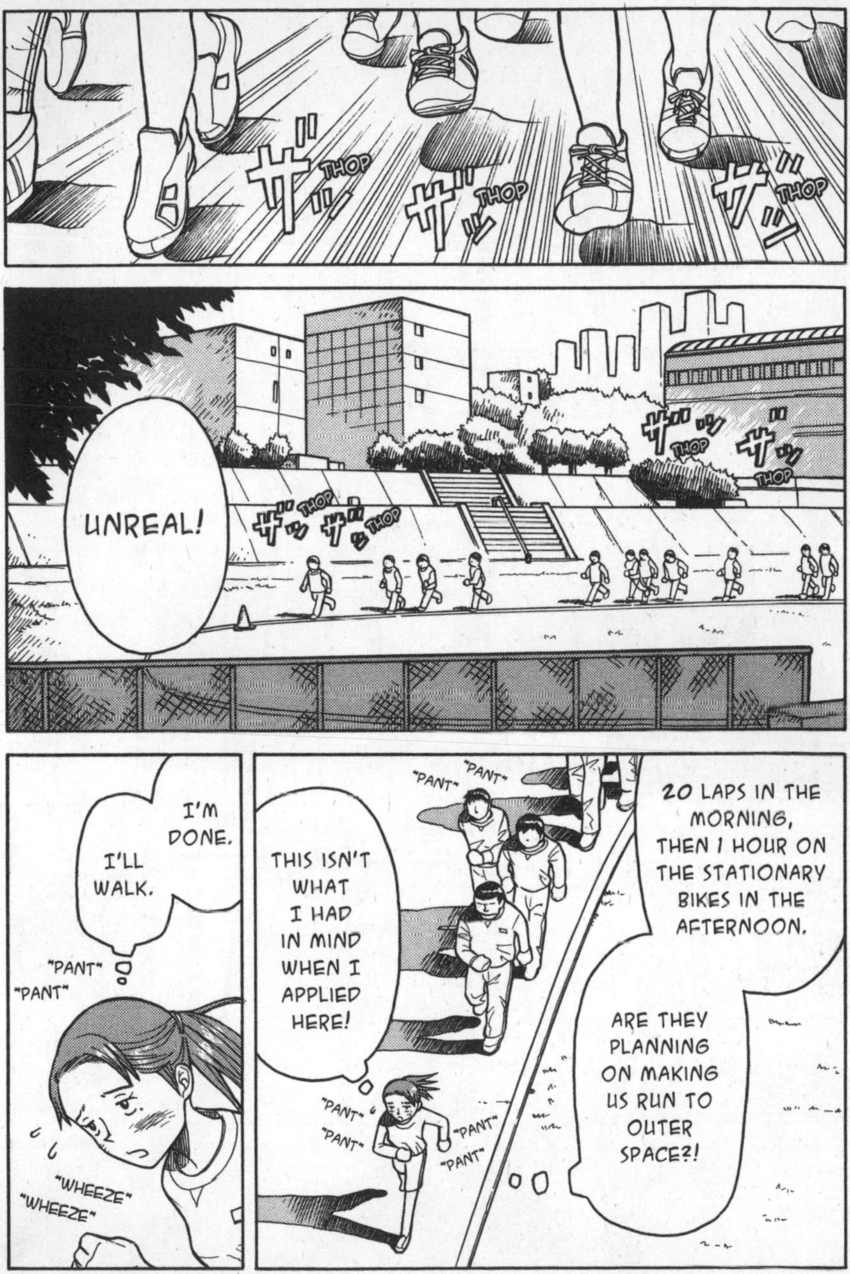
ザッ THOP
ザッ THOP
ザッ THOP
ザッ THOP
ザッ THOP
ザッ THOP
ザッ THOP
UNREAL!
20 LAPS IN THE MORNING, THEN 1 HOUR ON THE STATIONARY BIKES IN THE AFTERNOON.
"PANT" "PANT"
ARE THEY PLANNING ON MAKING US RUN TO OUTER SPACE?!
THIS ISN'T WHAT I HAD IN MIND WHEN I APPLIED HERE!
"PANT" "PANT" "PANT" "PANT"
I'M DONE.
I'LL WALK.
"PANT" "PANT"
"WHEEZE" "WHEEZE"

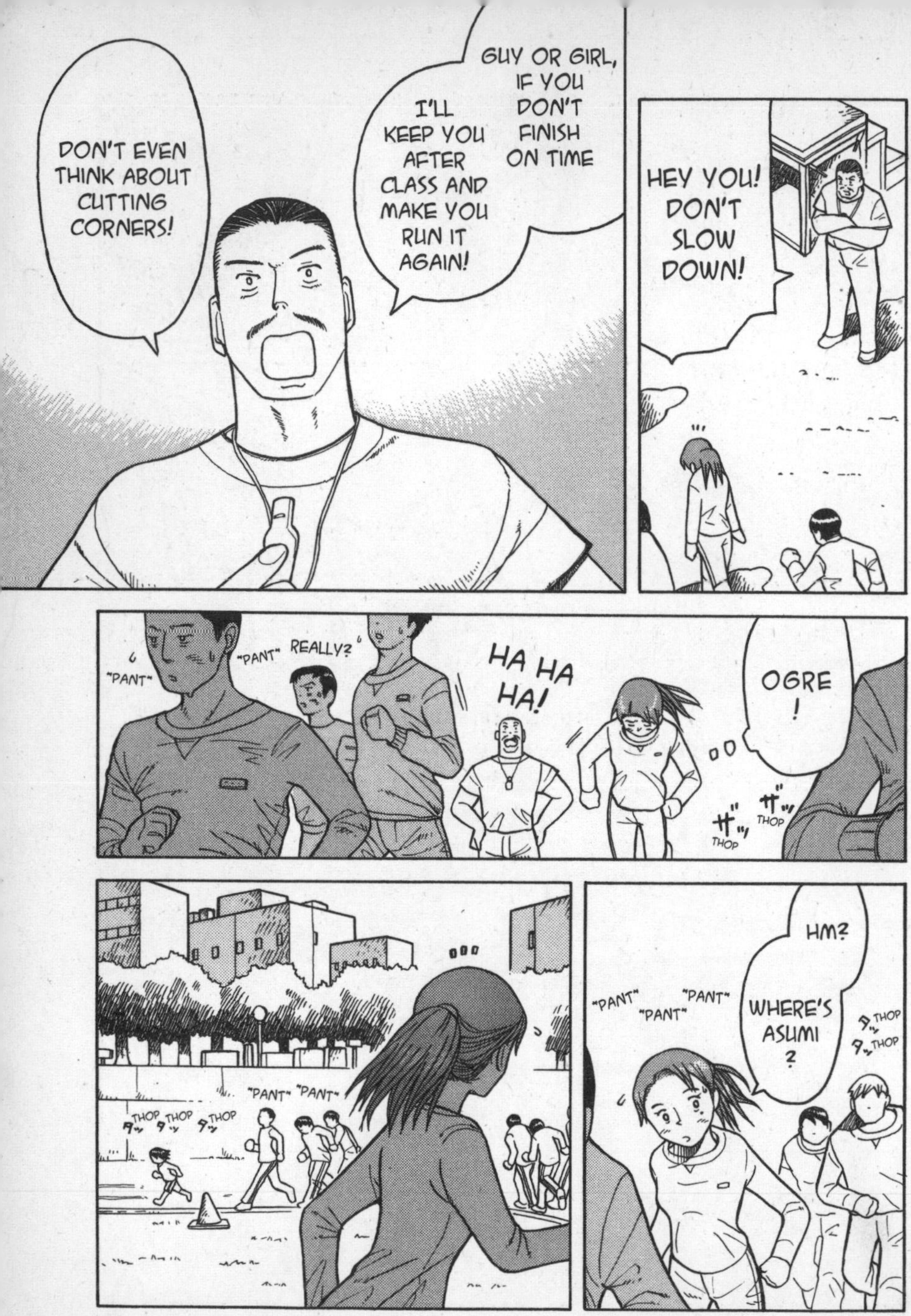
HEY YOU! DON'T SLOW DOWN!
GUY OR GIRL, IF YOU DON'T FINISH ON TIME
I'LL KEEP YOU AFTER CLASS AND MAKE YOU RUN IT AGAIN!
DON'T EVEN THINK ABOUT CUTTING CORNERS!
OGRE!
ザッ THOP
ザッ THOP
HA HA HA!
REALLY?
"PANT"
"PANT"
HM?
WHERE'S ASUMI?
タッ THOP
タッ THOP
"PANT"
"PANT"
"PANT"
"PANT" "PANT"
タッ THOP タッ THOP タッ THOP

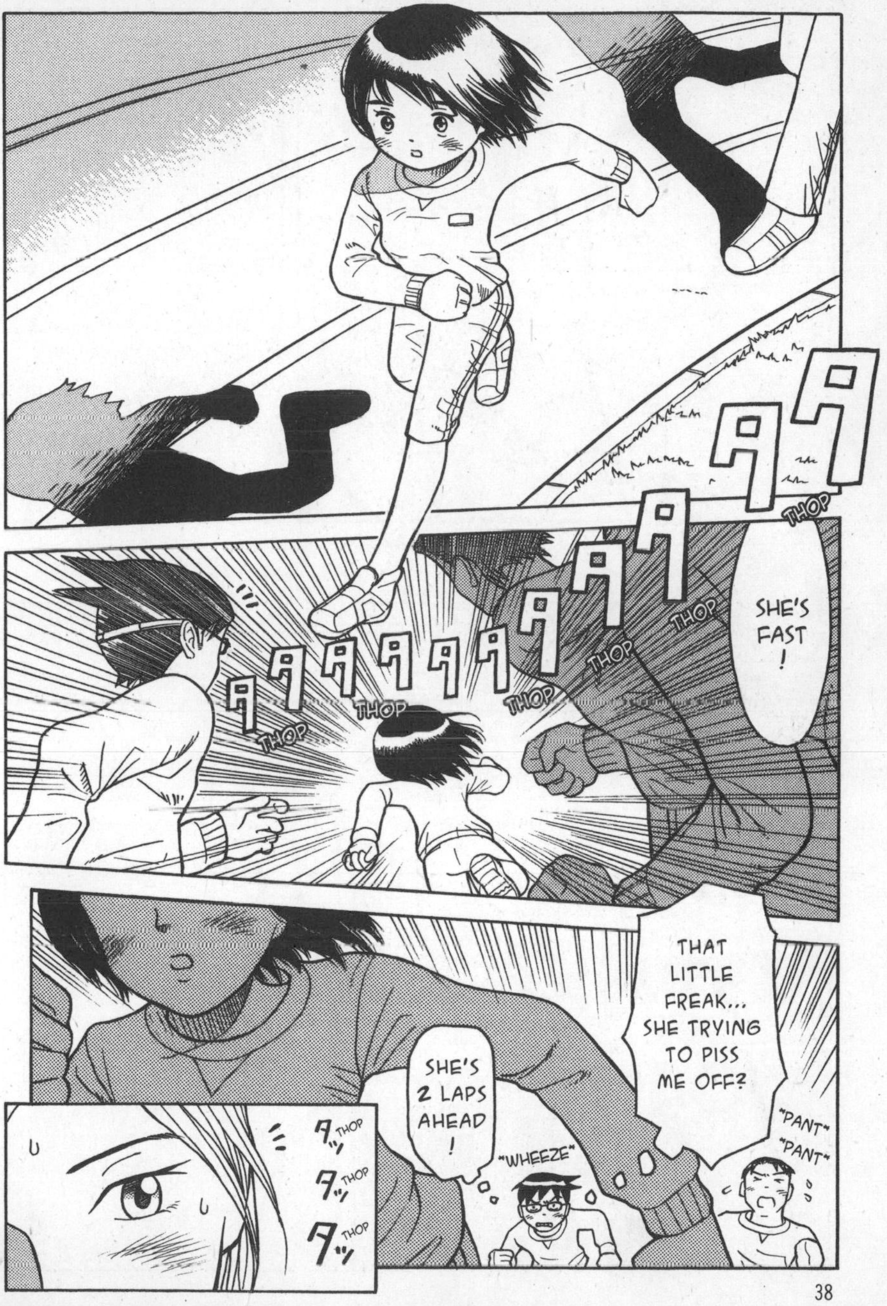
タタ
THOP
SHE'S FAST!
タタタタタタタタタタタ
THOP
THOP
THOP
THOP
THOP
THOP
THAT LITTLE FREAK... SHE TRYING TO PISS ME OFF?
"PANT" "PANT"
"WHEEZE"
SHE'S 2 LAPS AHEAD!
タッ THOP
タッ THOP
タッ THOP

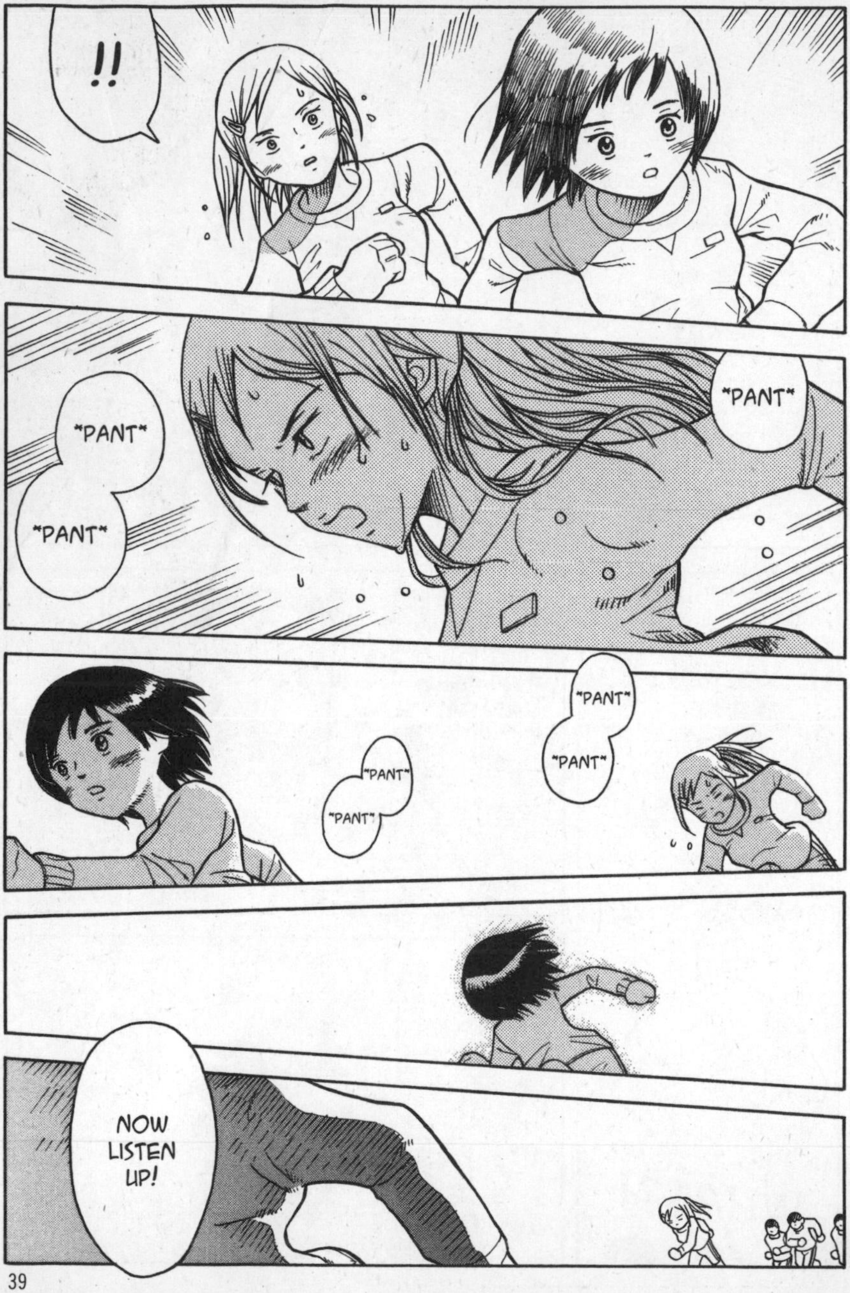
!!
PANT
PANT
PANT
PANT
PANT
PANT
PANT
NOW LISTEN UP!

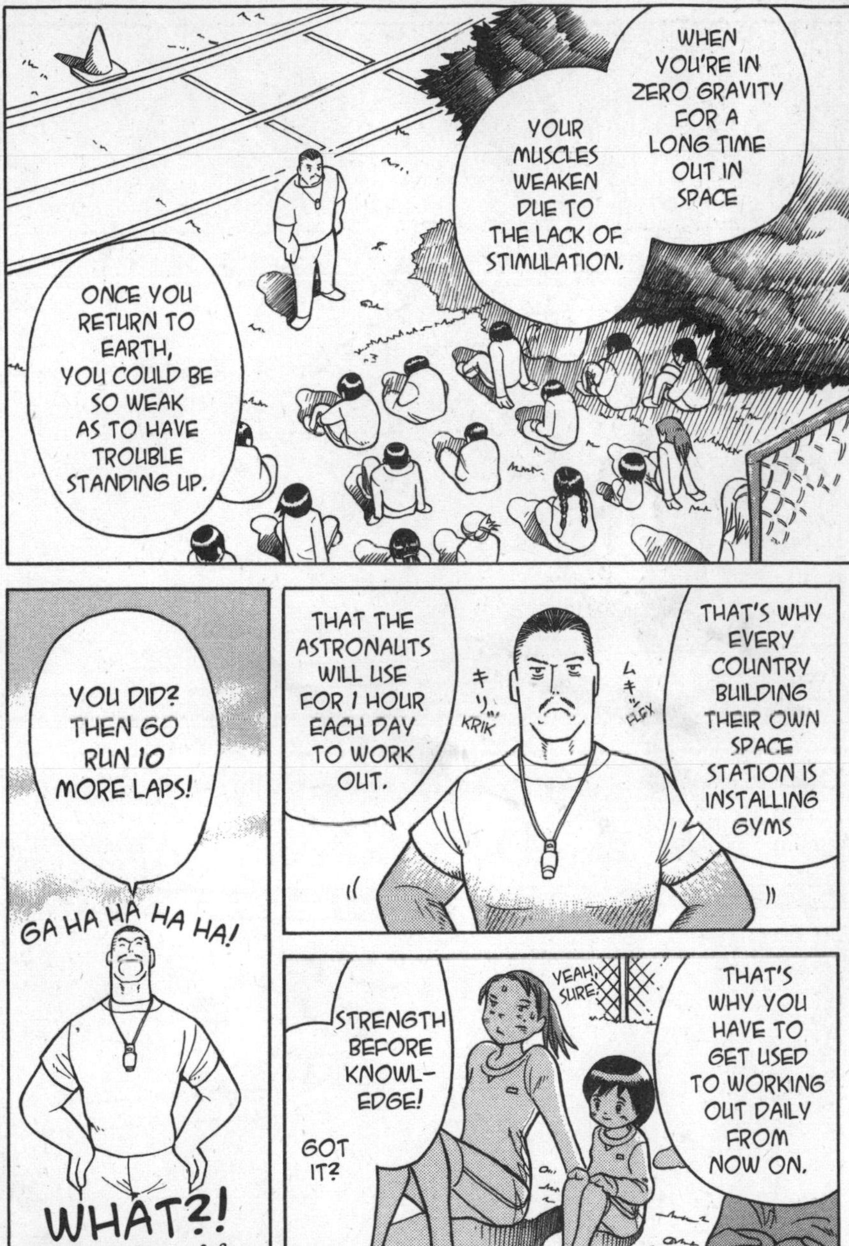
WHEN YOU'RE IN ZERO GRAVITY FOR A LONG TIME OUT IN SPACE
YOUR MUSCLES WEAKEN DUE TO THE LACK OF STIMULATION.
ONCE YOU RETURN TO EARTH, YOU COULD BE SO WEAK AS TO HAVE TROUBLE STANDING UP.
THAT'S WHY EVERY COUNTRY BUILDING THEIR OWN SPACE STATION IS INSTALLING GYMS
ムキッ FLEX
キリッ KRIK
THAT THE ASTRONAUTS WILL USE FOR 1 HOUR EACH DAY TO WORK OUT.
THAT'S WHY YOU HAVE TO GET USED TO WORKING OUT DAILY FROM NOW ON.
YEAH, SURE.
STRENGTH BEFORE KNOWL-EDGE!
GOT IT?
YOU DID? THEN GO RUN 10 MORE LAPS!
GA HA HA HA HA!
WHAT?!

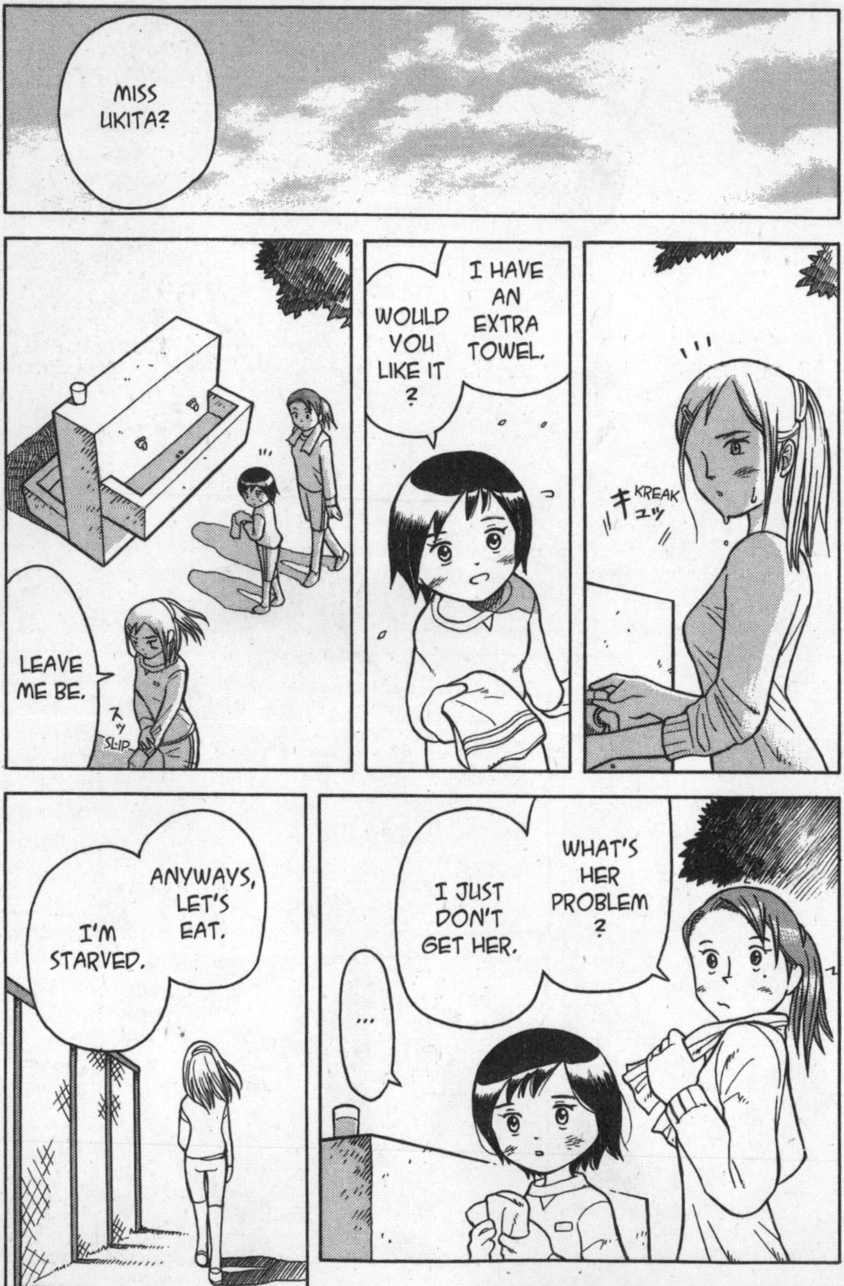
MISS UKITA?
キュッ
KREAK
I HAVE AN EXTRA TOWEL.
WOULD YOU LIKE IT?
LEAVE ME BE.
スッ
SLIP
WHAT'S HER PROBLEM?
I JUST DON'T GET HER.
...
ANYWAYS, LET'S EAT.
I'M STARVED.

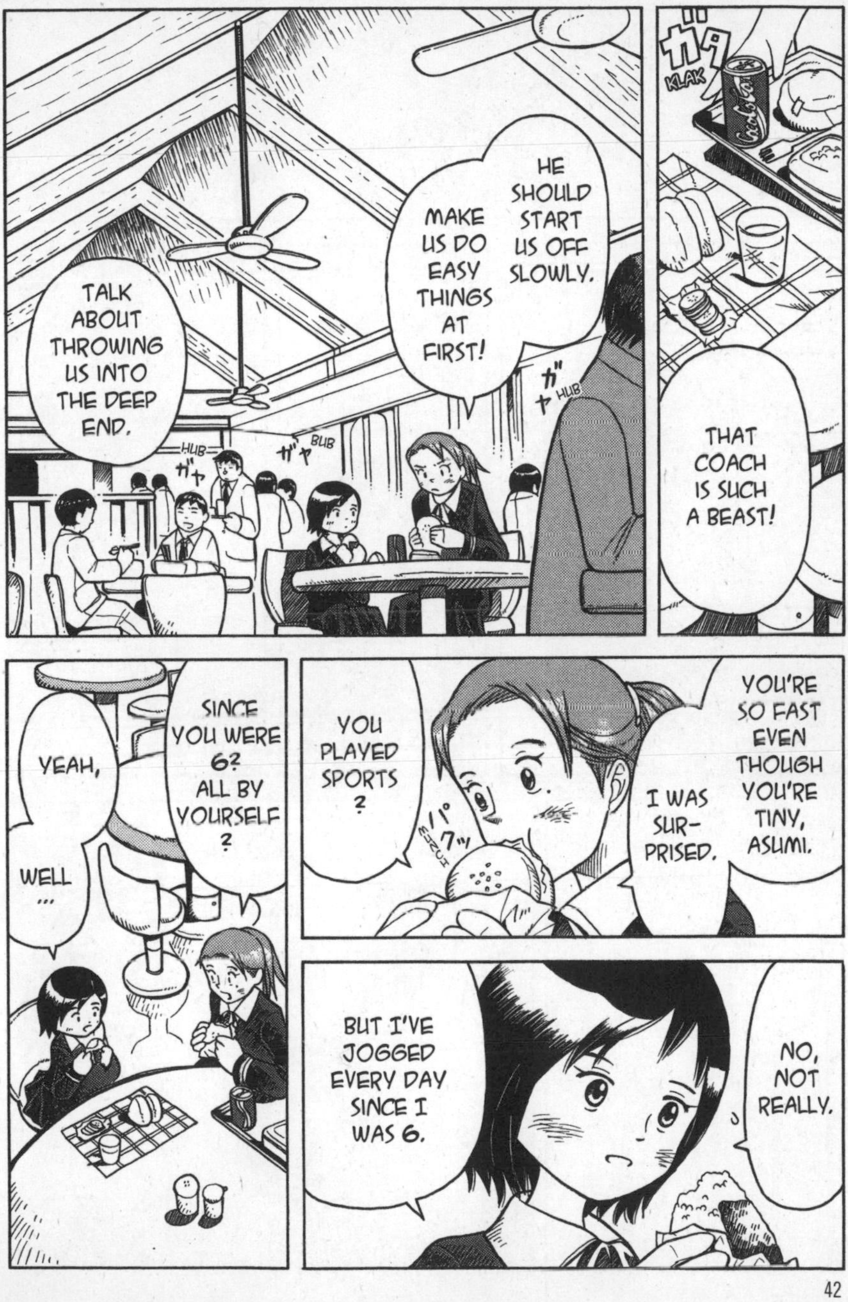
ガタ
KLAK
THAT COACH IS SUCH A BEAST!
HE SHOULD START US OFF SLOWLY.
MAKE US DO EASY THINGS AT FIRST!
ガヤ
HUB
TALK ABOUT THROWING US INTO THE DEEP END.
ガヤ
BUB
HUB
ガヤ
YOU'RE SO FAST EVEN THOUGH YOU'RE TINY, ASUMI.
I WAS SUR-PRISED.
パクッ
YOU PLAYED SPORTS?
NO, NOT REALLY.
BUT I'VE JOGGED EVERY DAY SINCE I WAS 6.
SINCE YOU WERE 6? ALL BY YOURSELF?
YEAH,
WELL ...

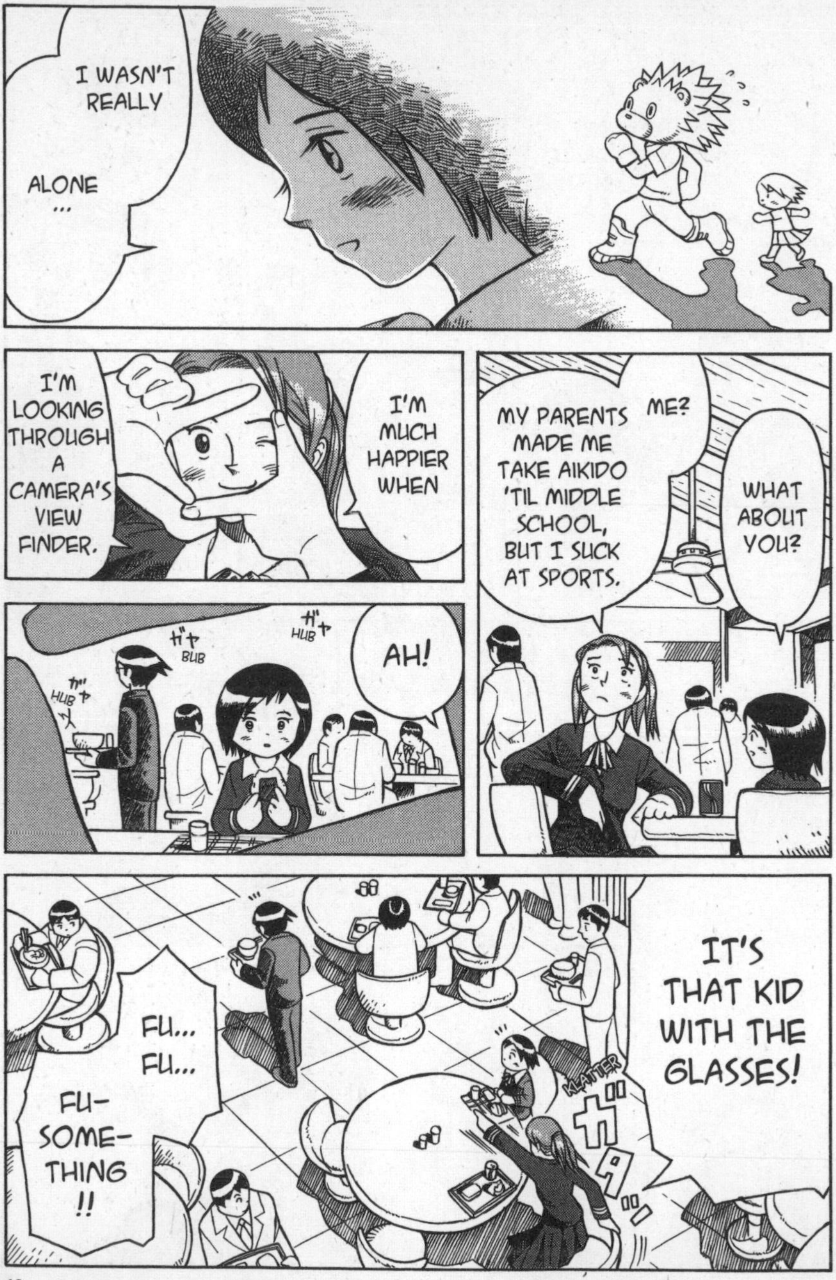
I WASN'T REALLY
ALONE ...
WHAT ABOUT YOU?
ME?
MY PARENTS MADE ME TAKE AIKIDO 'TIL MIDDLE SCHOOL, BUT I SUCK AT SPORTS.
I'M MUCH HAPPIER WHEN
I'M LOOKING THROUGH A CAMERA'S VIEW FINDER.
AH!
ガヤ HUB
ガヤ BUB
ガヤ HUB
IT'S THAT KID WITH THE GLASSES!
ガタ KLATTER
FU... FU...
FU-SOMETHING!!

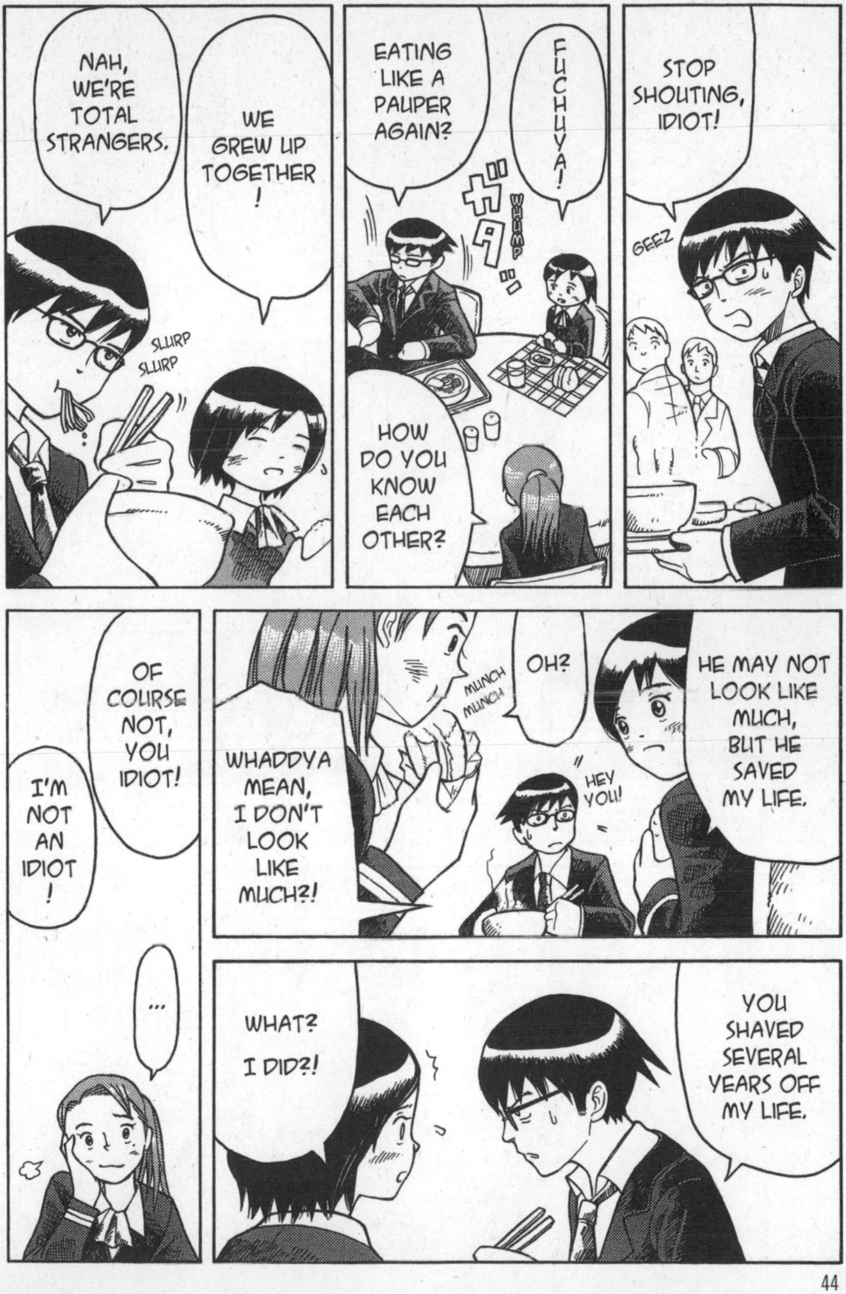
STOP SHOUTING, IDIOT!
GEEZ
FUCHUYA!
WHUMP
EATING LIKE A PAUPER AGAIN?
HOW DO YOU KNOW EACH OTHER?
WE GREW UP TOGETHER!
NAH, WE'RE TOTAL STRANGERS.
SLURP
SLURP
HE MAY NOT LOOK LIKE MUCH, BUT HE SAVED MY LIFE.
OH?
MUNCH
MUNCH
HEY YOU!
WHADDYA MEAN, I DON'T LOOK LIKE MUCH?!
YOU SHAVED SEVERAL YEARS OFF MY LIFE.
WHAT?
I DID?!
OF COURSE NOT, YOU IDIOT!
I'M NOT AN IDIOT!
...

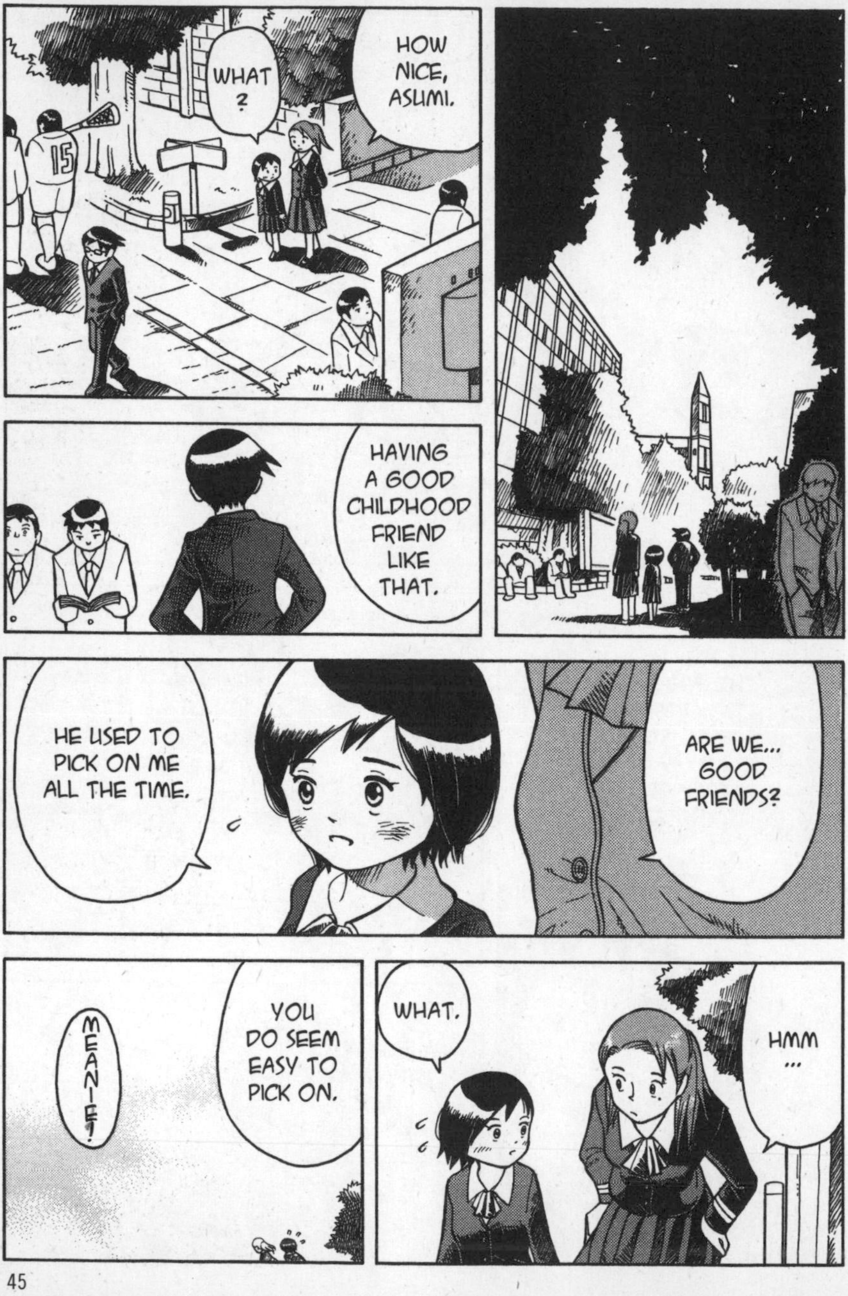
HOW NICE, ASUMI.
WHAT?
HAVING A GOOD CHILDHOOD FRIEND LIKE THAT.
ARE WE... GOOD FRIENDS?
HE USED TO PICK ON ME ALL THE TIME.
HMM ...
WHAT.
YOU DO SEEM EASY TO PICK ON.
MEANIE!

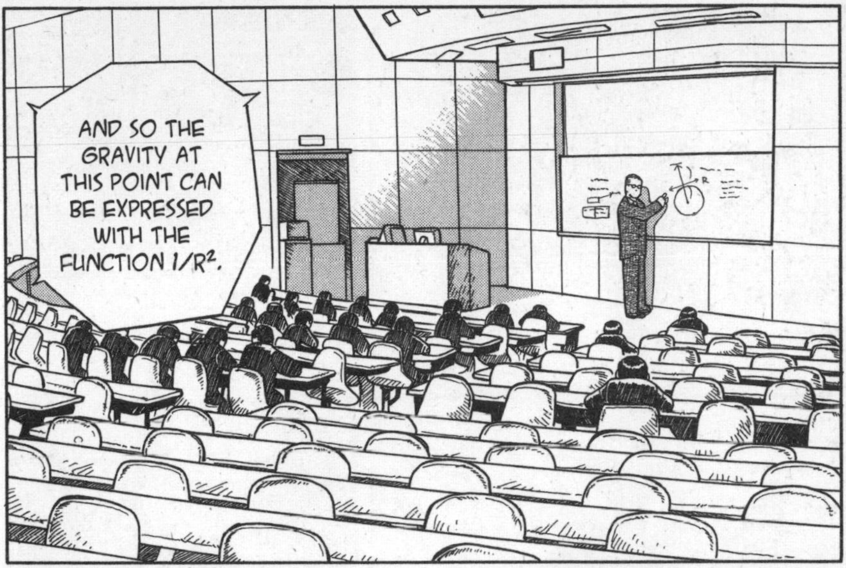
AND SO THE GRAVITY AT THIS POINT CAN BE EXPRESSED WITH THE FUNCTION 1/R².

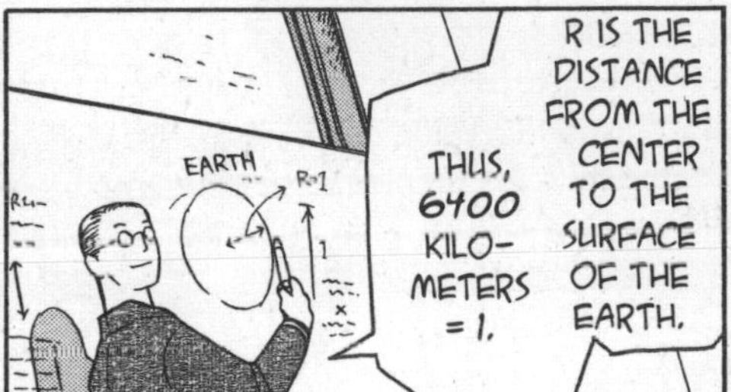
R IS THE DISTANCE FROM THE CENTER TO THE SURFACE OF THE EARTH.
THUS, 6400 KILOMETERS = 1.
EARTH

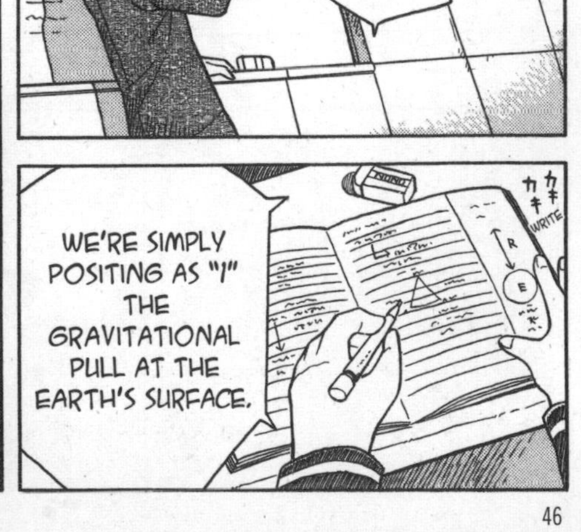
カキ カキ
WRITE
WE'RE SIMPLY POSITING AS "1" THE GRAVITATIONAL PULL AT THE EARTH'S SURFACE.

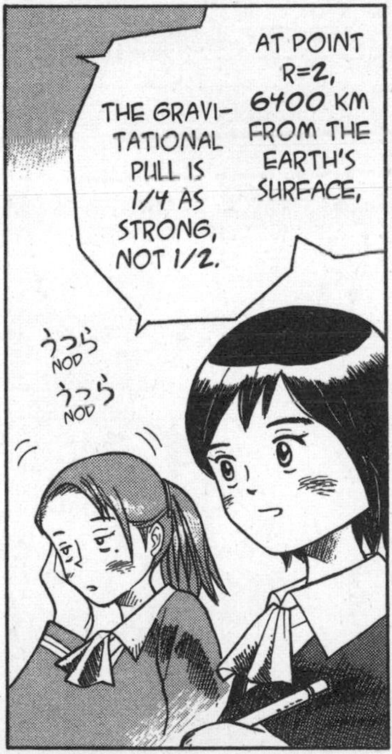
AT POINT R=2, 6400 KM FROM THE EARTH'S SURFACE,
THE GRAVITATIONAL PULL IS 1/4 AS STRONG, NOT 1/2.
うつら
NOD
うつら
NOD

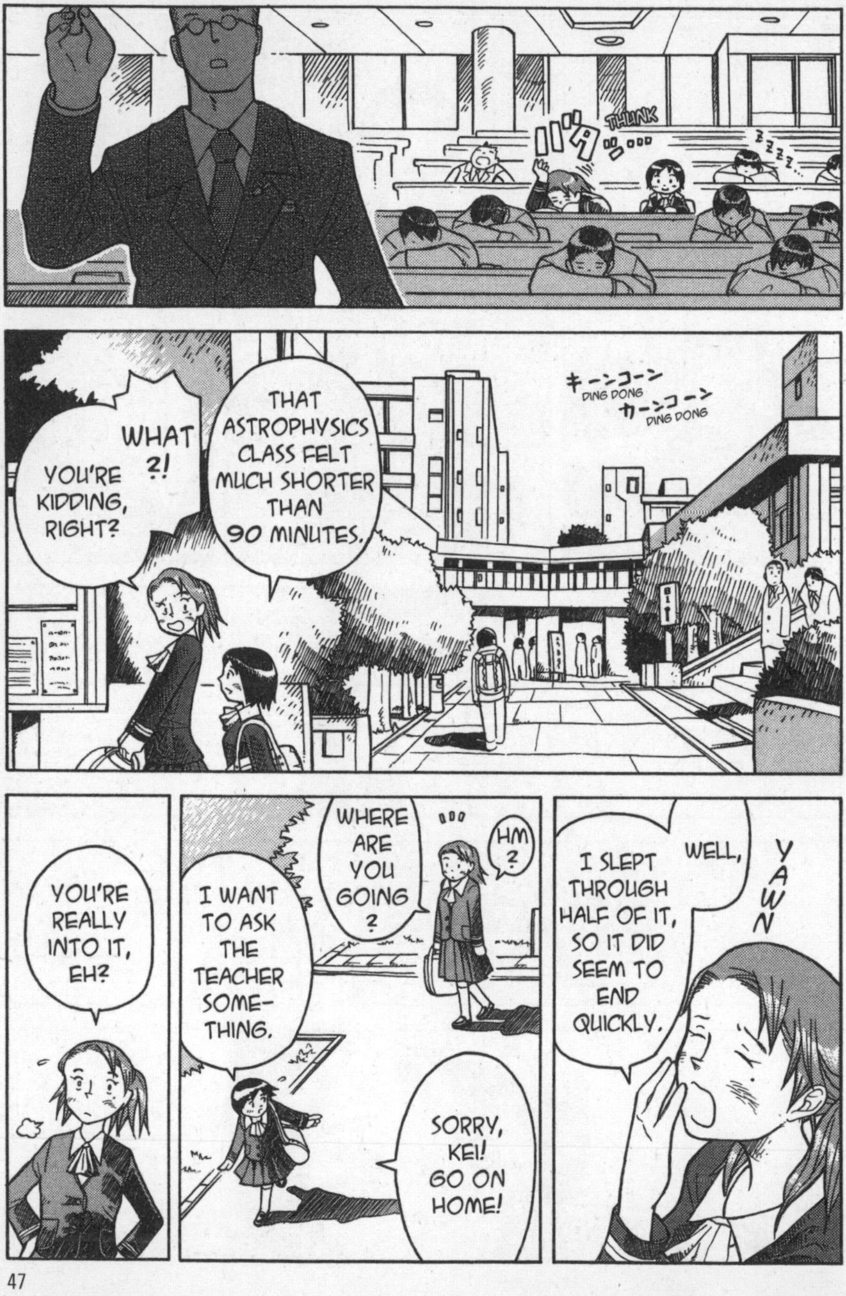

THUNK
ZZZZ...
DING DONG
DING DONG
THAT ASTROPHYSICS CLASS FELT MUCH SHORTER THAN 90 MINUTES.
WHAT?!
YOU'RE KIDDING, RIGHT?
YAWN
WELL,
I SLEPT THROUGH HALF OF IT, SO IT DID SEEM TO END QUICKLY.
SORRY, KEI! GO ON HOME!
HM?
WHERE ARE YOU GOING?
I WANT TO ASK THE TEACHER SOMETHING.
YOU'RE REALLY INTO IT, EH?

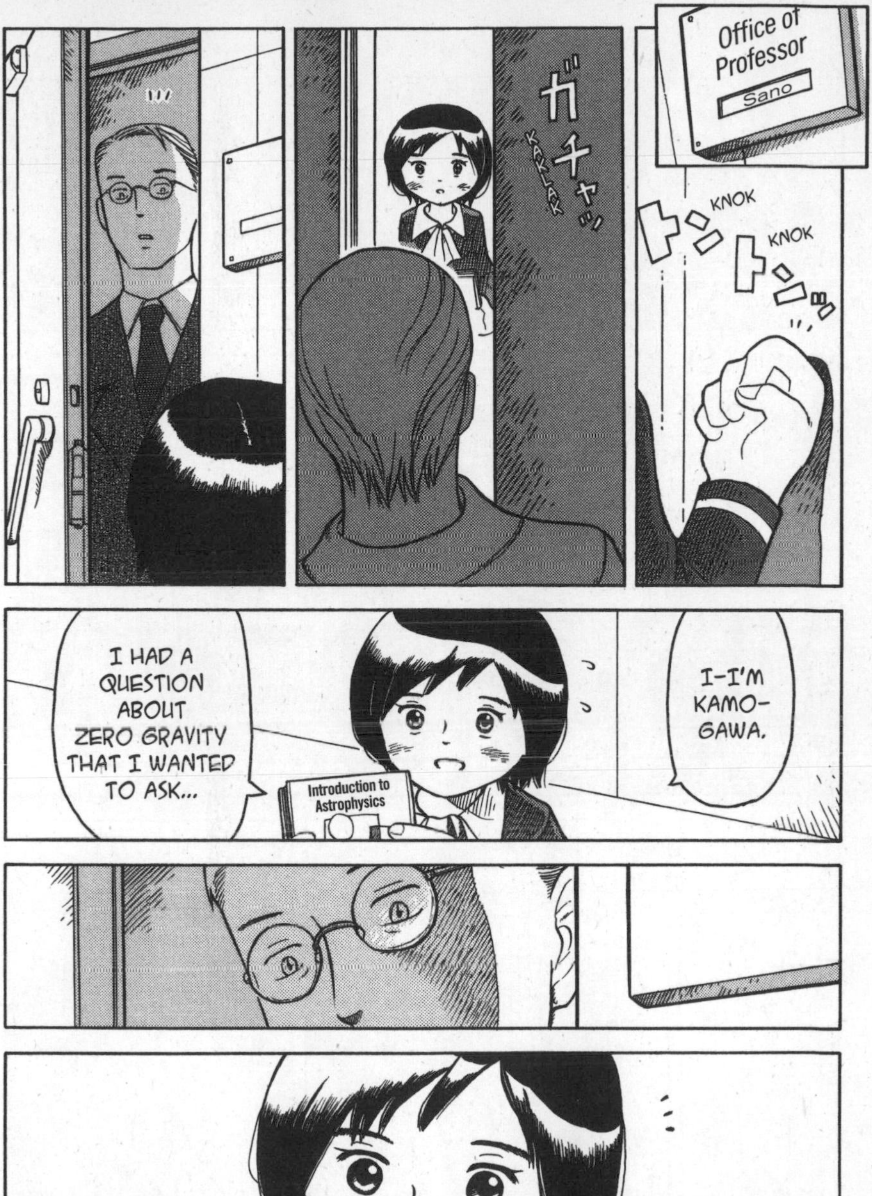
Office of Professor
Sano
トン KNOK
トン KNOK
ガチャッ
KAKLAK
I-I'M KAMO-GAWA.
I HAD A QUESTION ABOUT ZERO GRAVITY THAT I WANTED TO ASK...
Introduction to Astrophysics

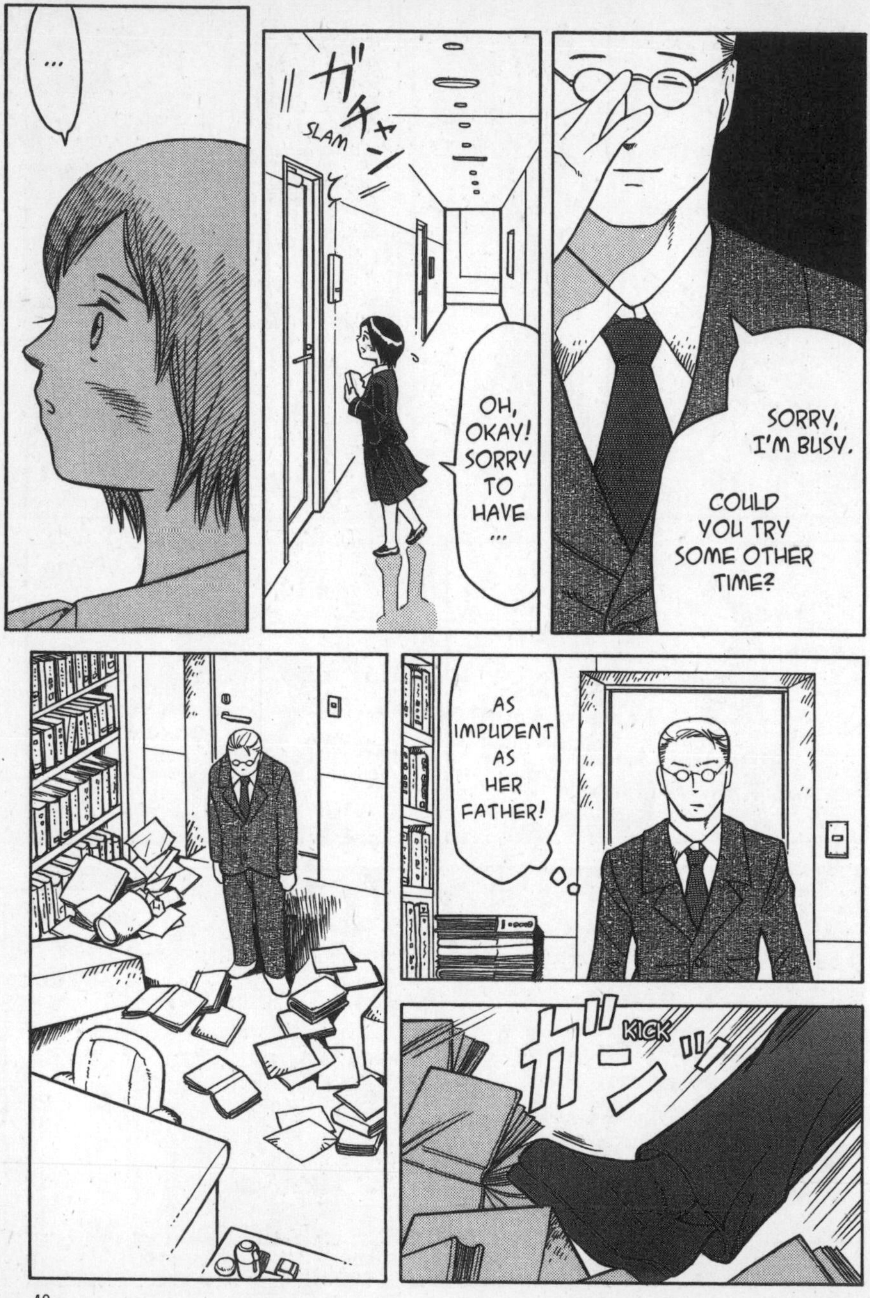
SORRY, I'M BUSY.
COULD YOU TRY SOME OTHER TIME?
ガチャン
SLAM
OH, OKAY! SORRY TO HAVE ...
...
AS IMPUDENT AS HER FATHER!
ガーン
KICK

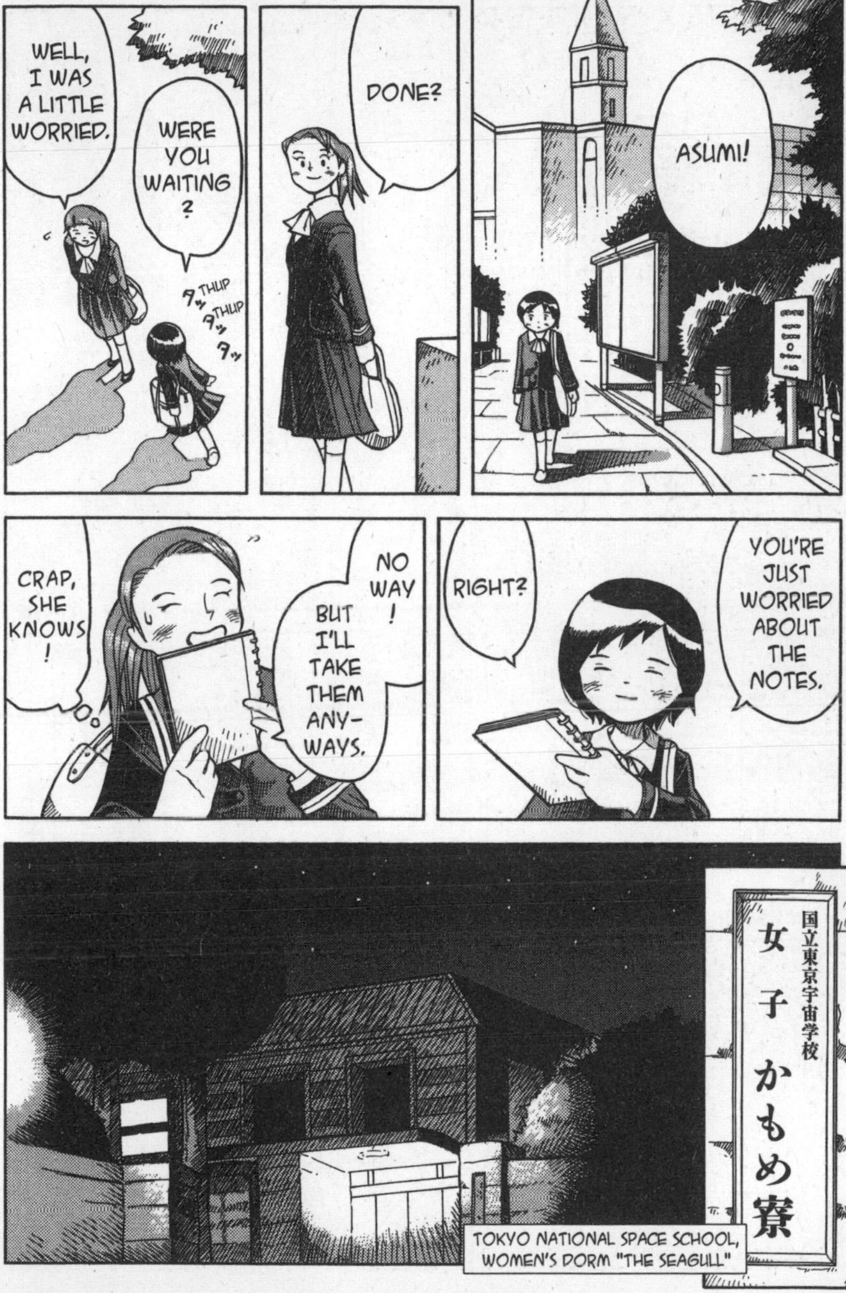
ASUMI!
DONE?
WERE YOU WAITING?
タッ THUP タッ THUP タッ
WELL, I WAS A LITTLE WORRIED.
YOU'RE JUST WORRIED ABOUT THE NOTES.
RIGHT?
NO WAY!
BUT I'LL TAKE THEM ANY-WAYS.
CRAP, SHE KNOWS!
国立東京宇宙学校
女子かもめ寮
TOKYO NATIONAL SPACE SCHOOL, WOMEN'S DORM "THE SEAGULL"

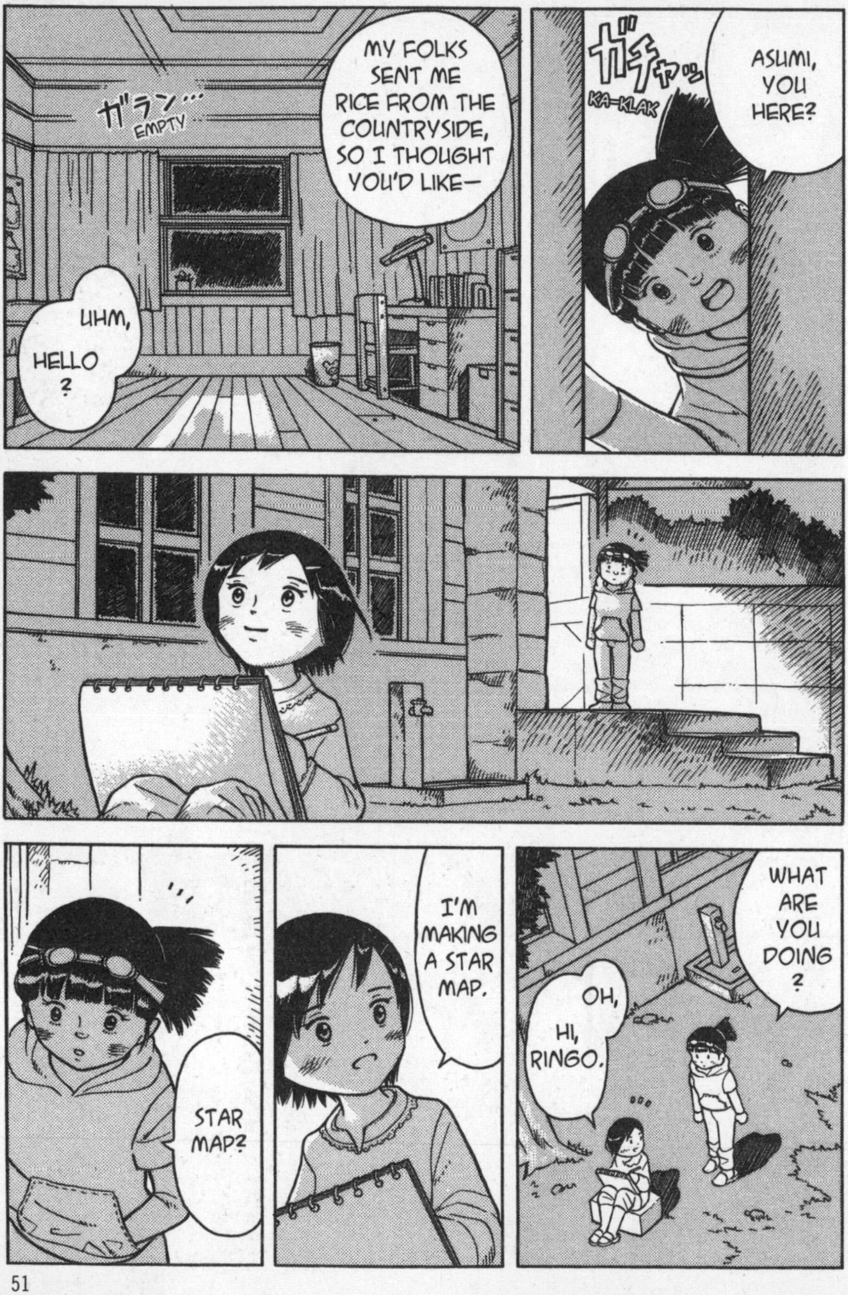
ガチャッ
KA-KLAK
ASUMI, YOU HERE?
ガラン…
EMPTY
MY FOLKS SENT ME RICE FROM THE COUNTRYSIDE, SO I THOUGHT YOU'D LIKE—
UHM, HELLO?
WHAT ARE YOU DOING?
OH, HI, RINGO.
I'M MAKING A STAR MAP.
STAR MAP?

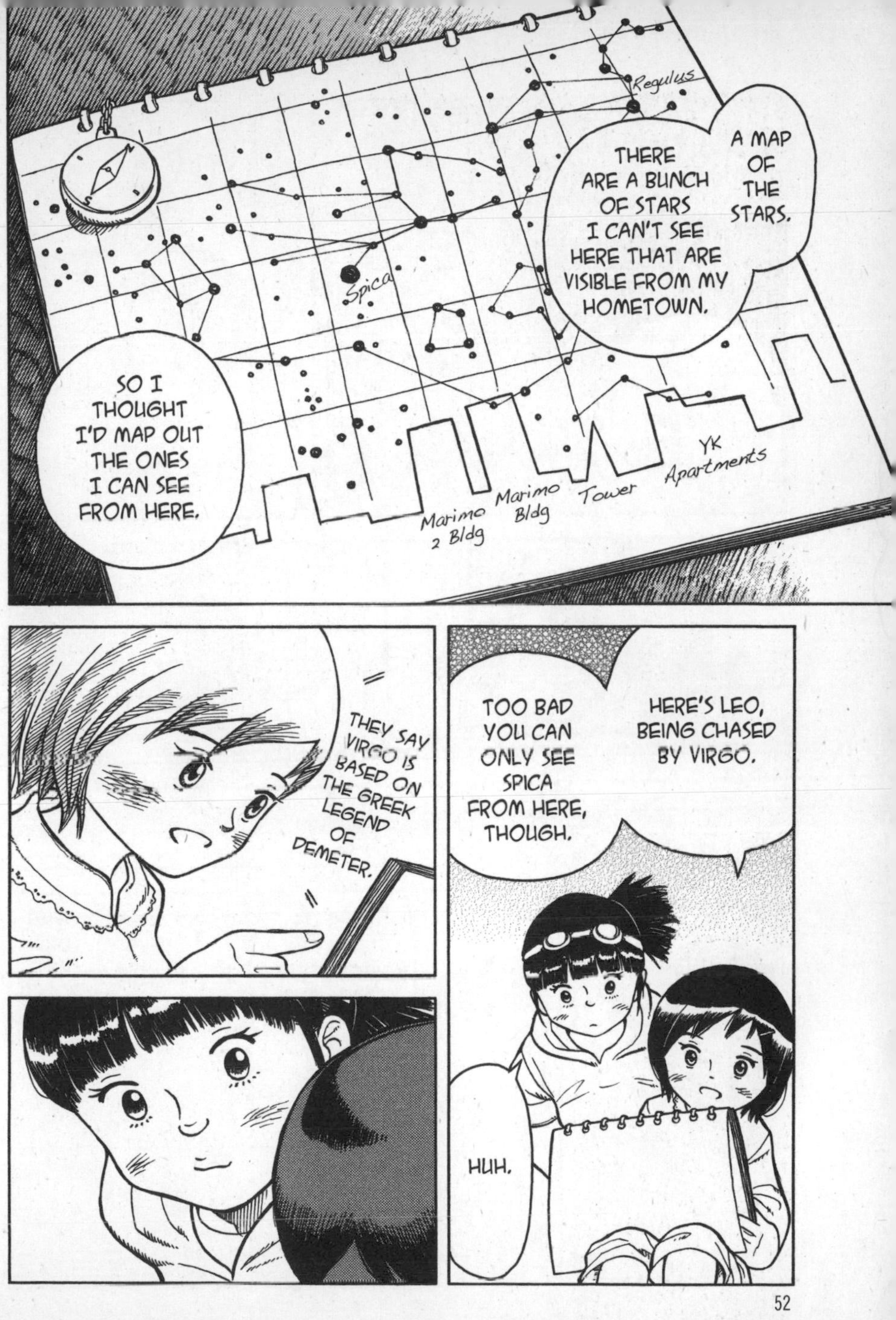
A MAP OF THE STARS.
Regulus
THERE ARE A BUNCH OF STARS I CAN'T SEE HERE THAT ARE VISIBLE FROM MY HOMETOWN.
Spica
YK Apartments
Tower
Marimo Bldg
Marimo 2 Bldg
SO I THOUGHT I'D MAP OUT THE ONES I CAN SEE FROM HERE.
HERE'S LEO, BEING CHASED BY VIRGO.
TOO BAD YOU CAN ONLY SEE SPICA FROM HERE, THOUGH.
HUH.
THEY SAY VIRGO IS BASED ON THE GREEK LEGEND OF DEMETER.

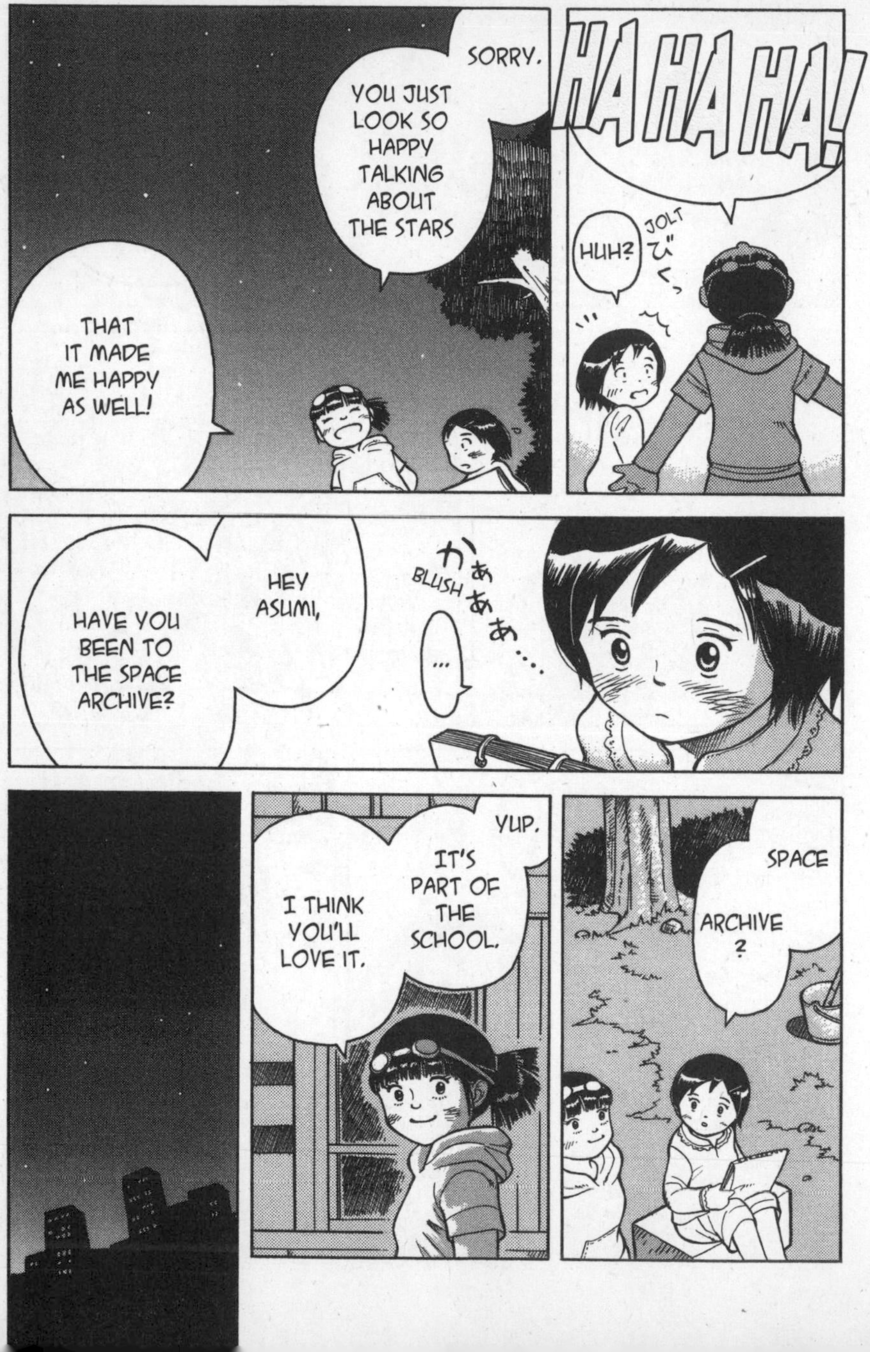
HA HA HA HA!
HUH?
JOLT
びくっ
SORRY.
YOU JUST LOOK SO HAPPY TALKING ABOUT THE STARS
THAT IT MADE ME HAPPY AS WELL!
かあああ…
BLUSH
...
HEY ASUMI,
HAVE YOU BEEN TO THE SPACE ARCHIVE?
SPACE
ARCHIVE ?
YUP.
IT'S PART OF THE SCHOOL.
I THINK YOU'LL LOVE IT.

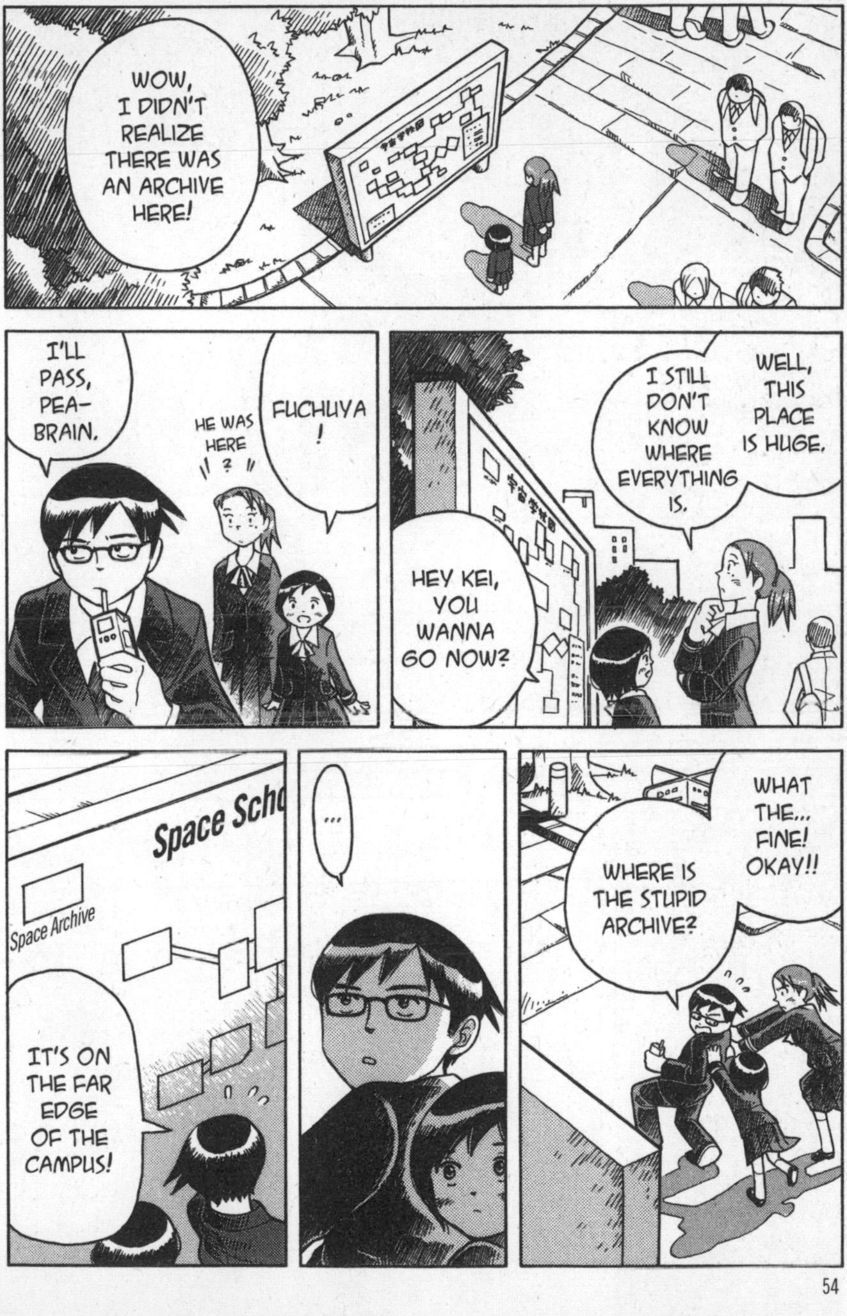
WOW, I DIDN'T REALIZE THERE WAS AN ARCHIVE HERE!
WELL, THIS PLACE IS HUGE.
I STILL DON'T KNOW WHERE EVERYTHING IS.
HEY KEI, YOU WANNA GO NOW?
FUCHUYA!
HE WAS HERE ?
I'LL PASS, PEA-BRAIN.
WHAT THE... FINE! OKAY!!
WHERE IS THE STUPID ARCHIVE?
...
Space Scho
Space Archive
IT'S ON THE FAR EDGE OF THE CAMPUS!

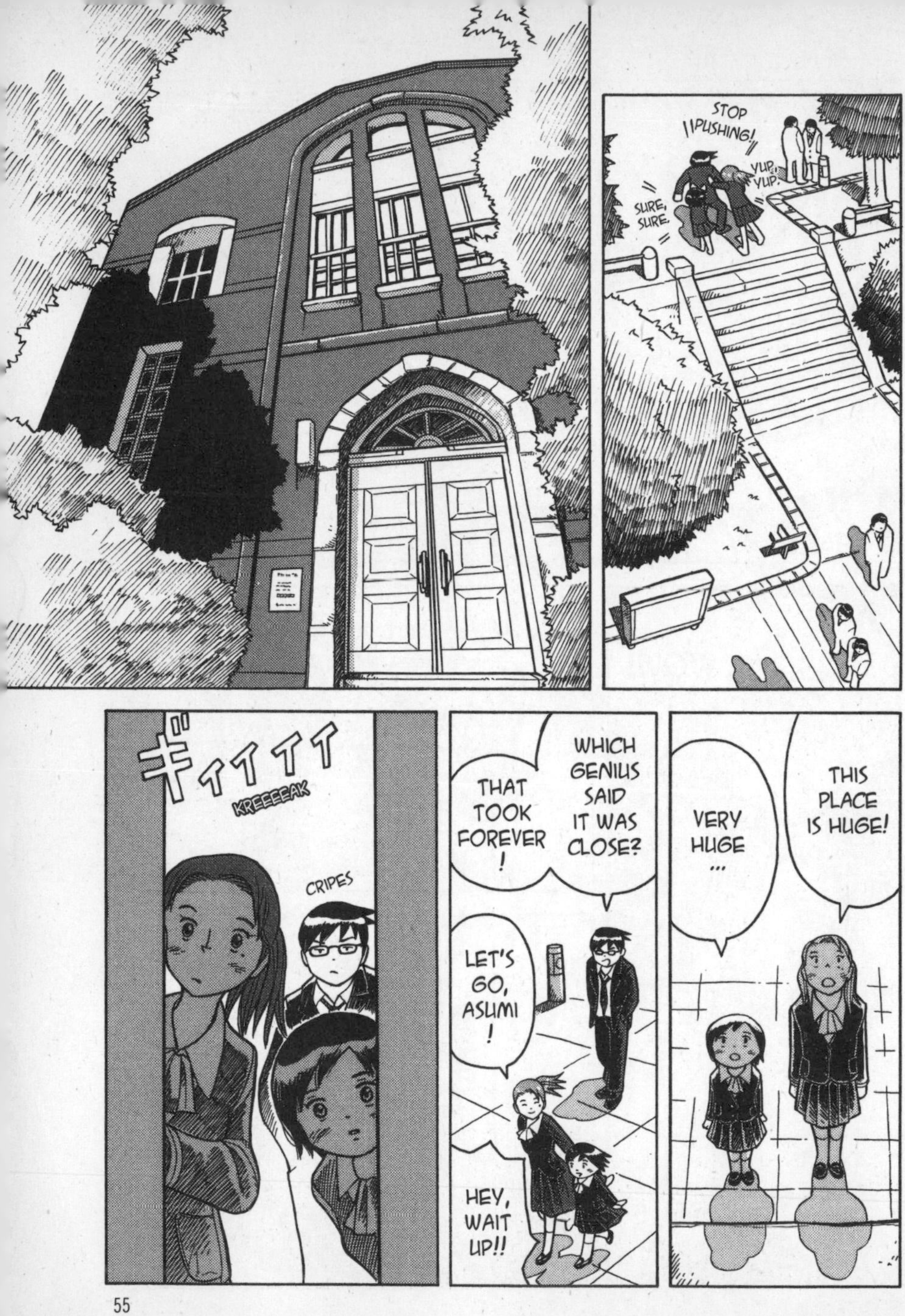

STOP PUSHING!
YUP, YUP.
SURE, SURE.
THIS PLACE IS HUGE!
VERY HUGE ...
WHICH GENIUS SAID IT WAS CLOSE?
THAT TOOK FOREVER!
LET'S GO, ASUMI!
HEY, WAIT UP!!
ギィィイイ
KREEEEAK
CRIPES

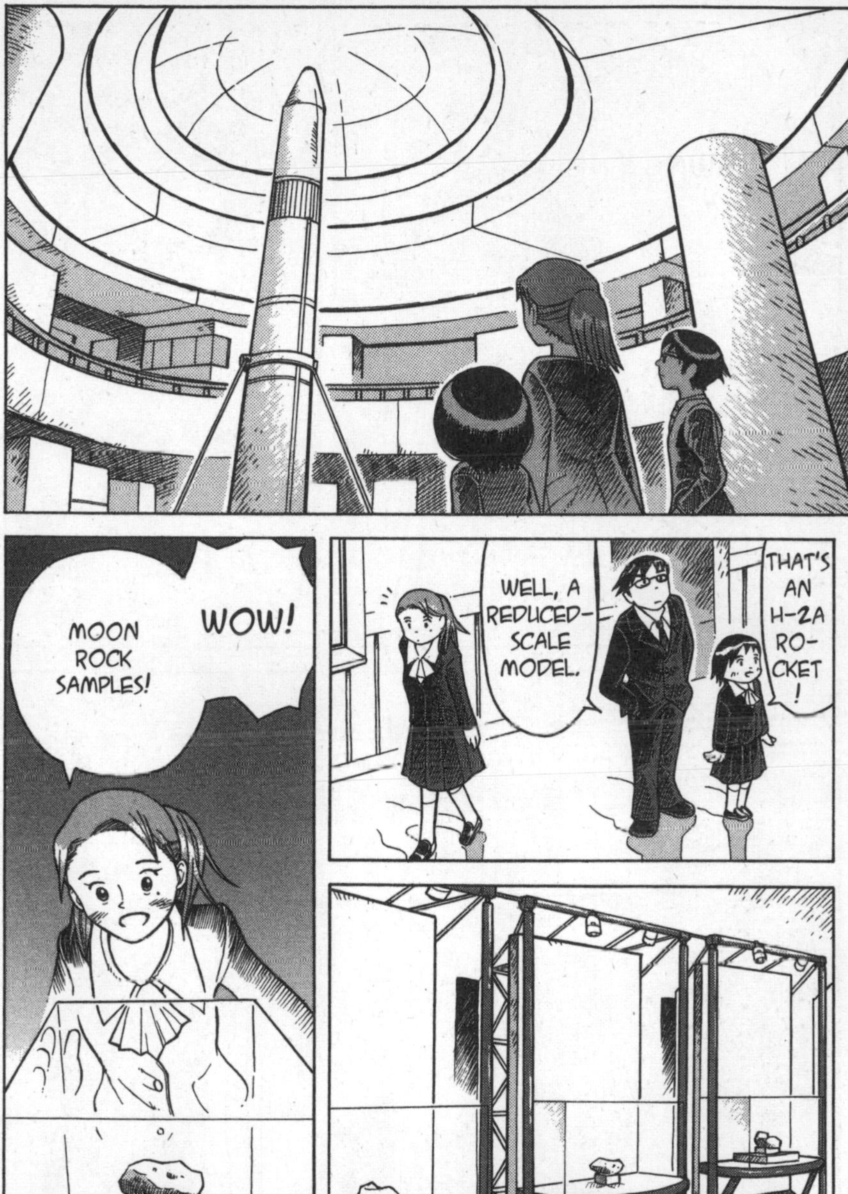
THAT'S AN H-2A ROCKET!
WELL, A REDUCED-SCALE MODEL.
WOW!
MOON ROCK SAMPLES!

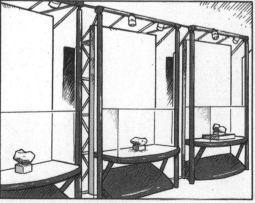

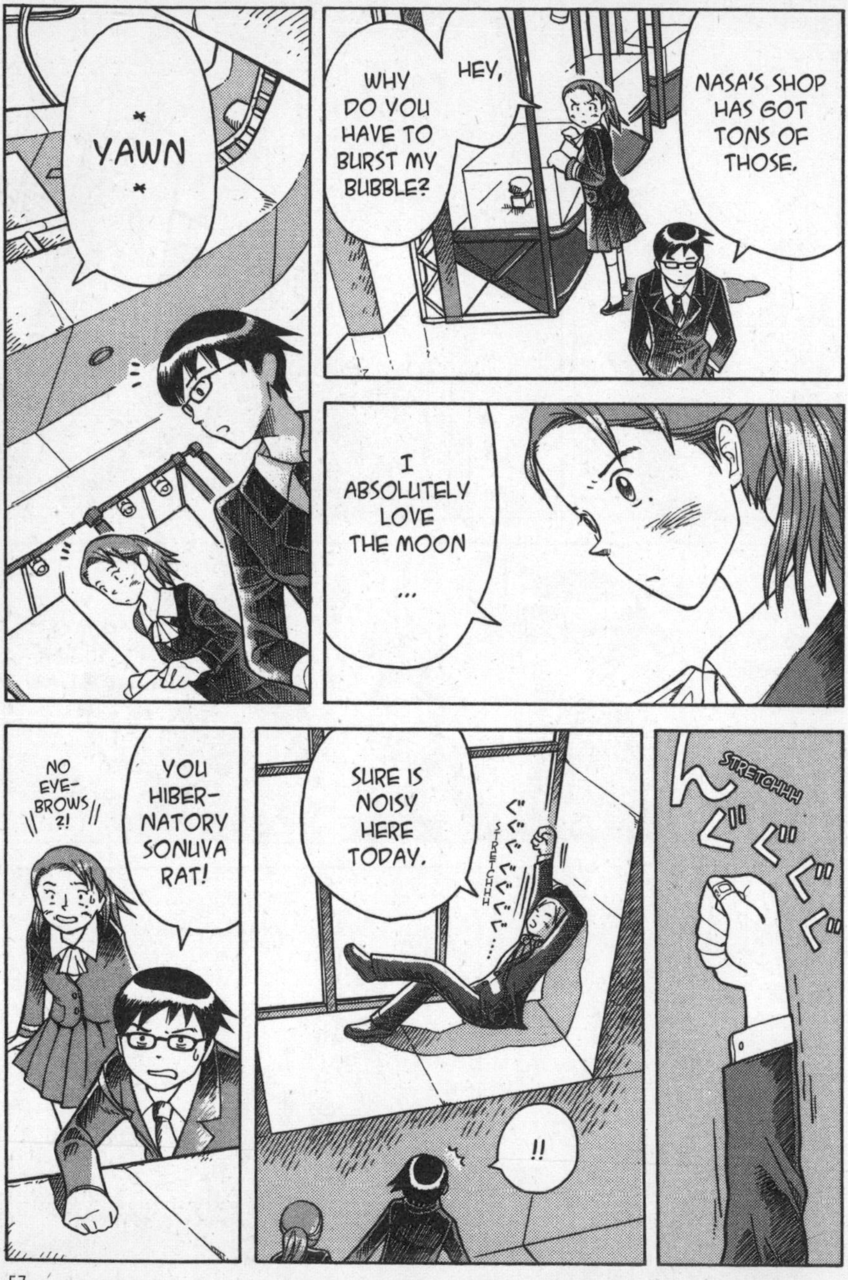

NASA'S SHOP HAS GOT TONS OF THOSE.
HEY,
WHY DO YOU HAVE TO BURST MY BUBBLE?
I ABSOLUTELY LOVE THE MOON
...
* YAWN *
STRETCHHH
んぐぐぐぐ
SURE IS NOISY HERE TODAY.
STRETCHHH
ぐぐぐぐぐぐぐ…
!!
YOU HIBERNATORY SONUVA RAT!
NO EYE-BROWS?!

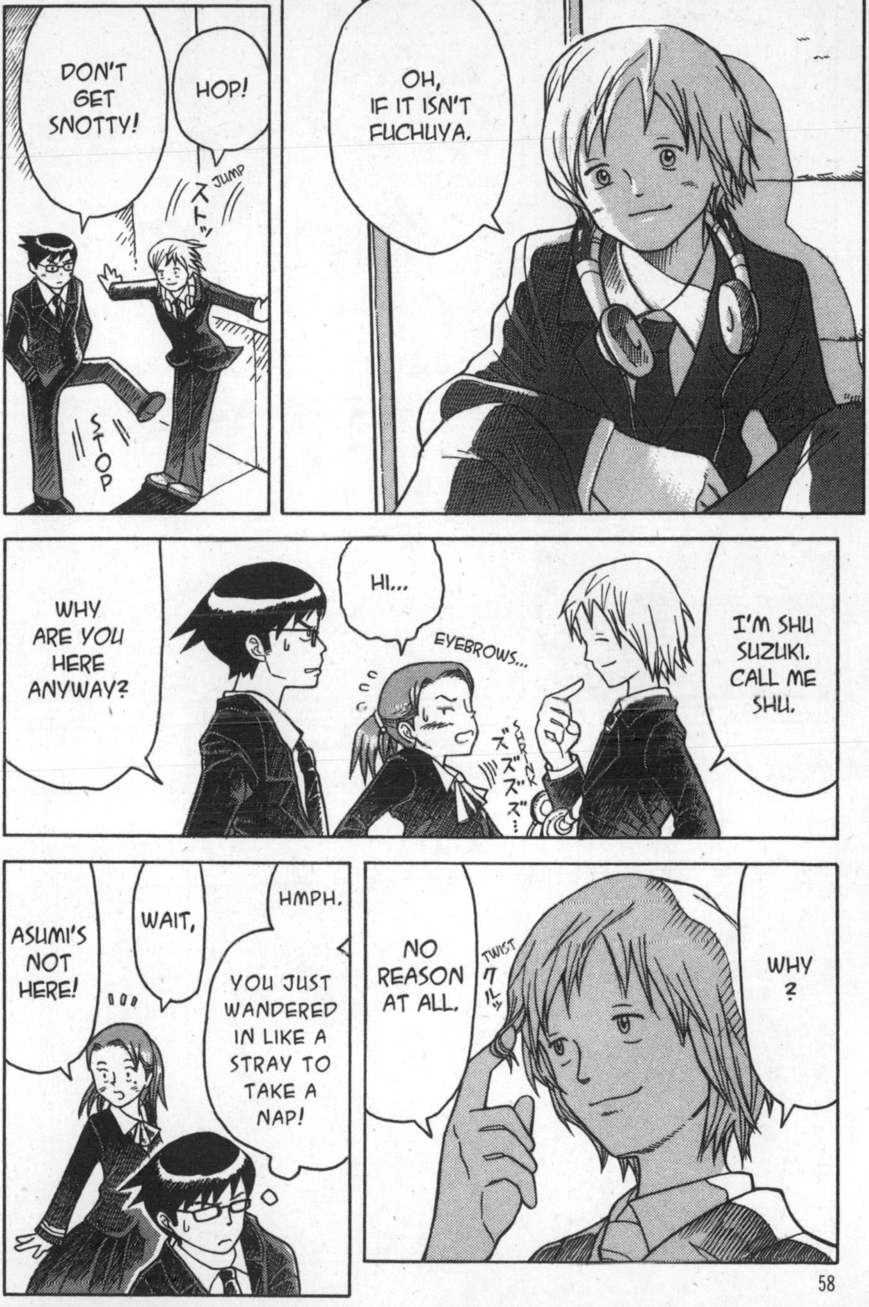
OH, IF IT ISN'T FUCHUYA.
HOP!
JUMP
ストッ
DON'T GET SNOTTY!
STOP
I'M SHU SUZUKI. CALL ME SHU.
SHRINK
ズズズズ...
EYEBROWS...
HI...
WHY ARE YOU HERE ANYWAY?
WHY?
NO REASON AT ALL.
TWIST
クルッ
HMPH.
YOU JUST WANDERED IN LIKE A STRAY TO TAKE A NAP!
WAIT,
ASUMI'S NOT HERE!
...

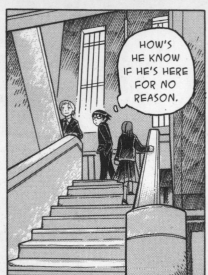

AH, YOU MEAN THE LITTLE GIRL?
SHE WASN'T A ZASHIKI WARASHI?
OF COURSE NOT!
PAM
WELL THEN, I THINK I KNOW WHERE SHE IS.
HOW'S HE KNOW IF HE'S HERE FOR NO REASON.

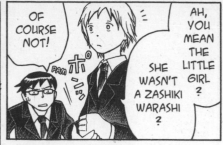

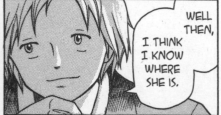

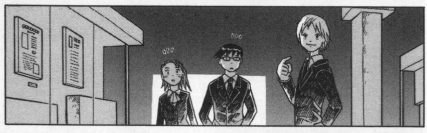

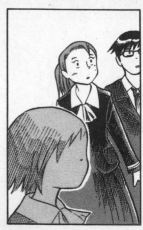

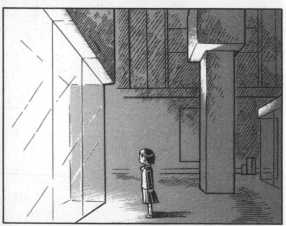

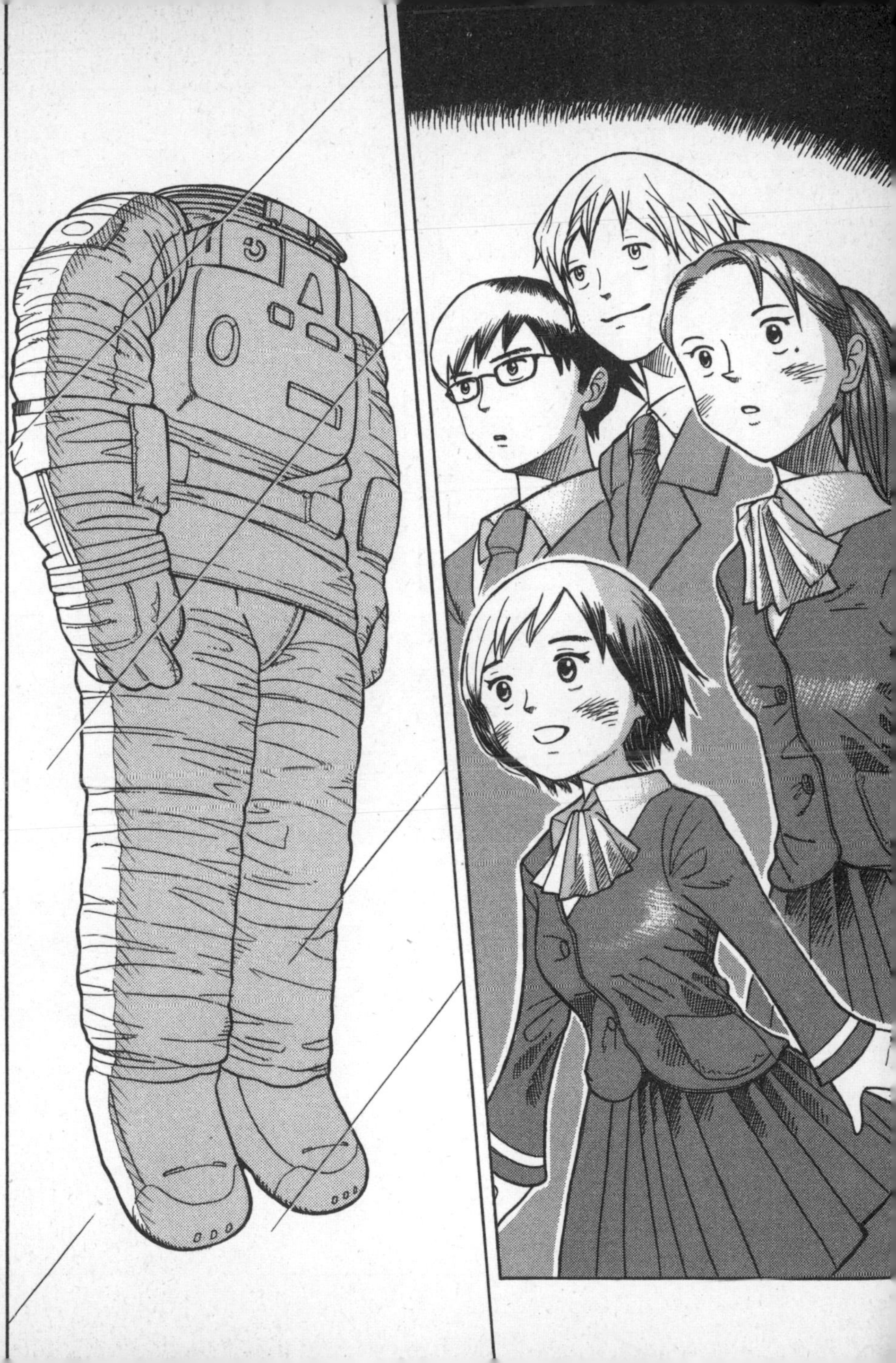

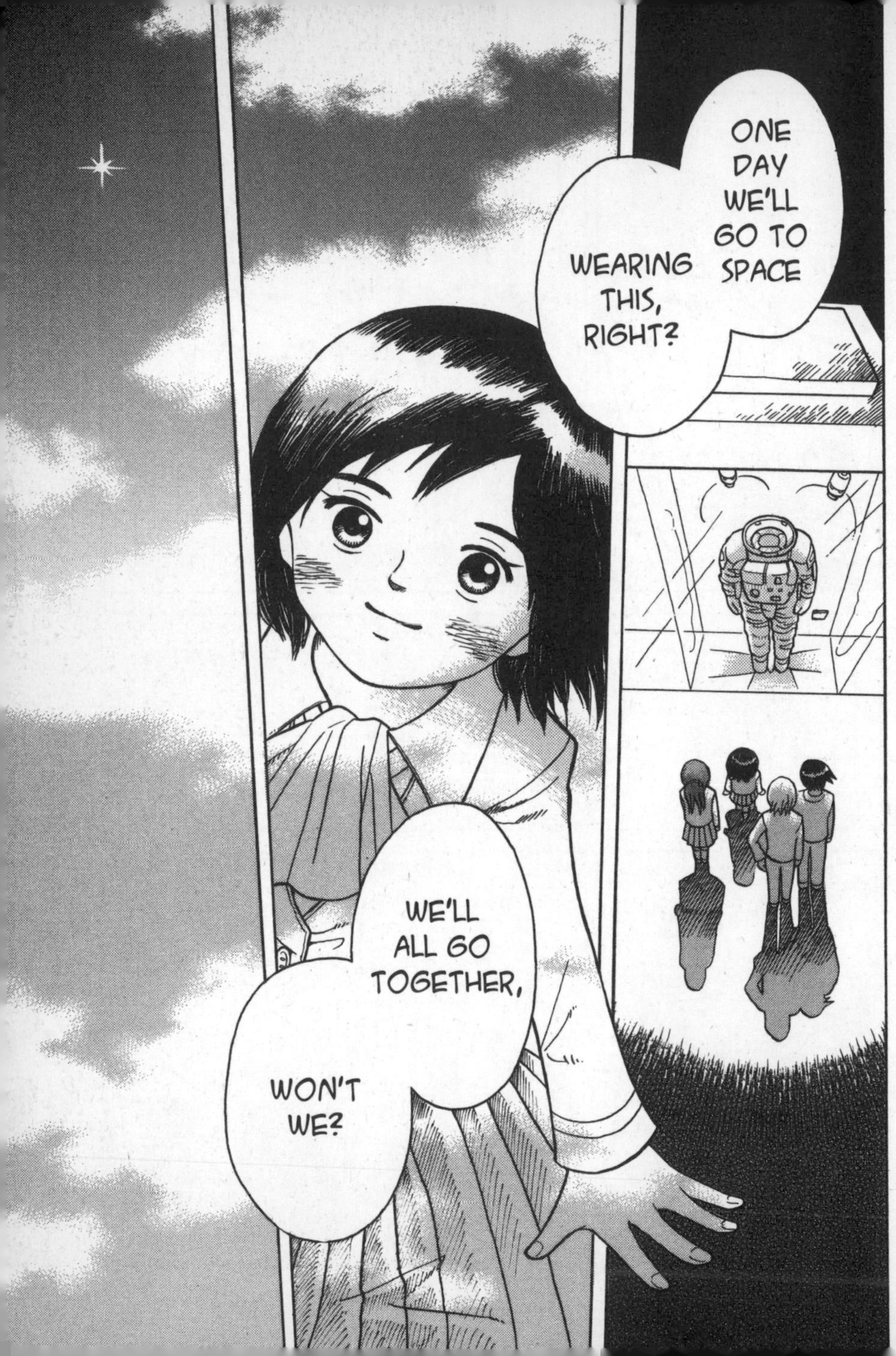
ONE DAY WE'LL GO TO SPACE
WEARING THIS, RIGHT?
WE'LL ALL GO TOGETHER,
WON'T WE?

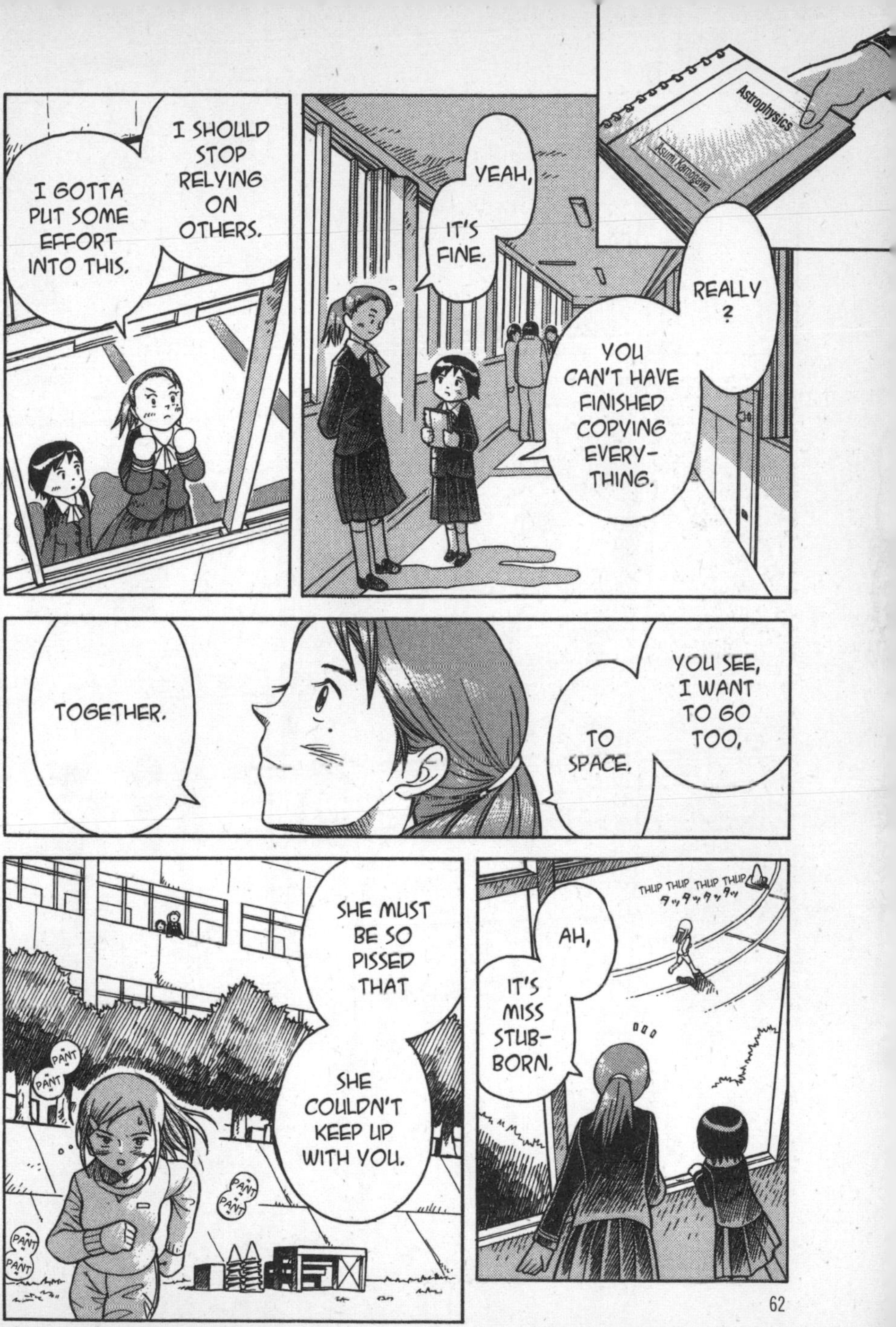
Astrophysics
Asumi Kamogawa
REALLY ?
YOU CAN'T HAVE FINISHED COPYING EVERYTHING.
YEAH,
IT'S FINE.
I SHOULD STOP RELYING ON OTHERS.
I GOTTA PUT SOME EFFORT INTO THIS.
YOU SEE, I WANT TO GO TOO,
TO SPACE.
TOGETHER.
THUP THUP THUP THUP
タッタッタッタッ
AH,
IT'S MISS STUBBORN.
SHE MUST BE SO PISSED THAT
SHE COULDN'T KEEP UP WITH YOU.
PANT
PANT
PANT
PANT
PANT
PANT

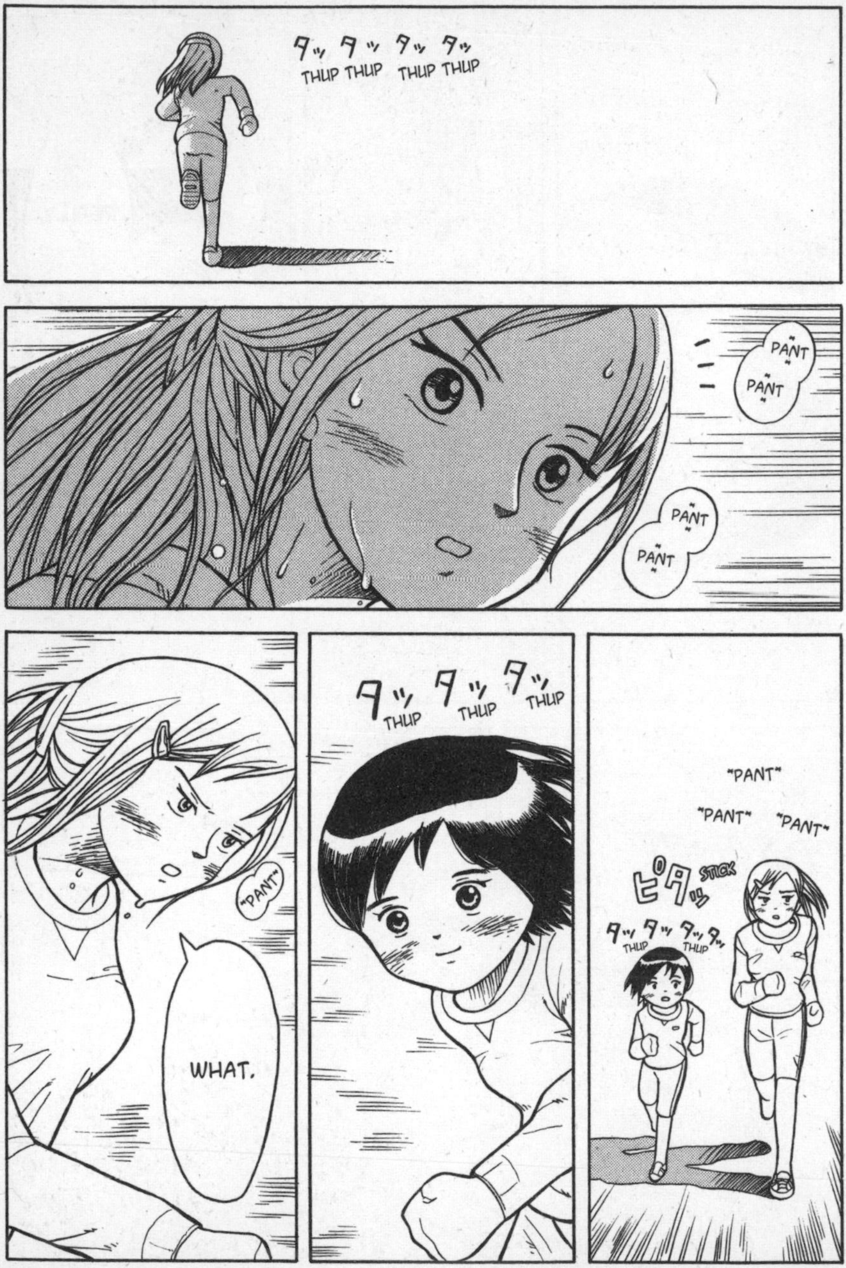
タッタッタッタッ
THUP THUP THUP THUP
PANT
PANT
PANT
PANT
"PANT"
"PANT"
"PANT"
ピタッ
STICK
タッタッタッタッ
THUP THUP
タッタッタッ
THUP THUP THUP
"PANT"
WHAT.

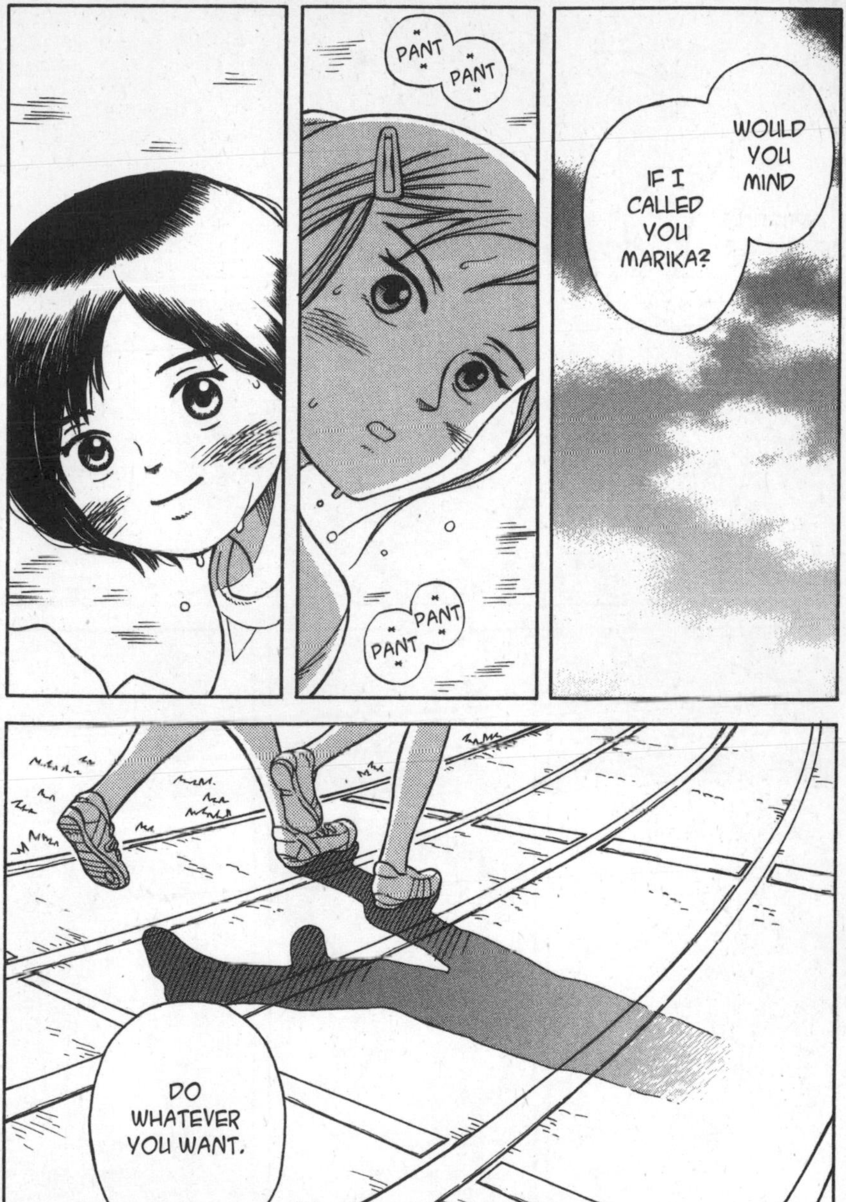
WOULD YOU MIND IF I CALLED YOU MARIKA?
PANT PANT
PANT PANT
DO WHATEVER YOU WANT.

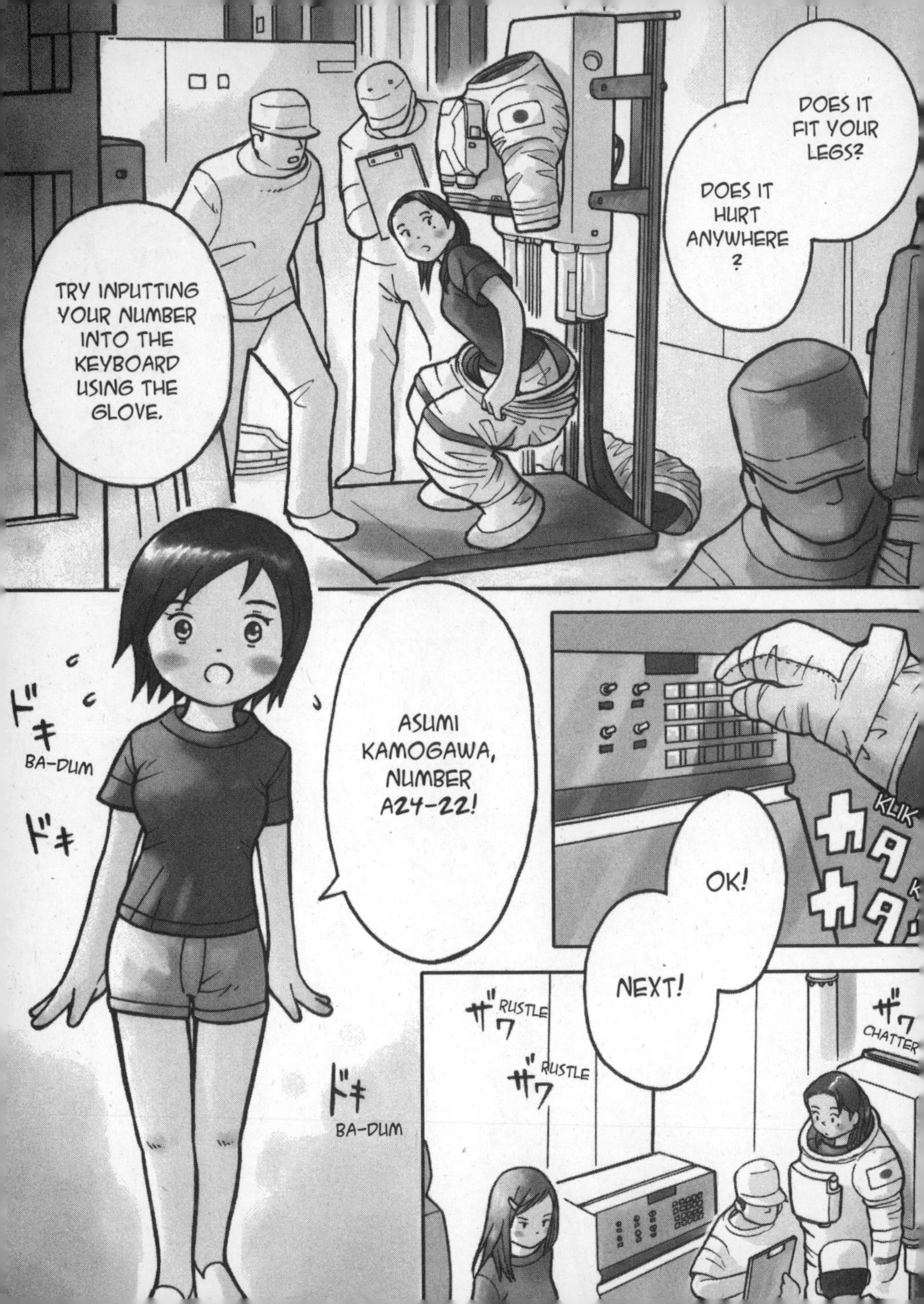

DOES IT FIT YOUR LEGS?
DOES IT HURT ANYWHERE ?
TRY INPUTTING YOUR NUMBER INTO THE KEYBOARD USING THE GLOVE.
KLIK
カタ
カタ
OK!
NEXT!
ザワ
CHATTER
ザワ
RUSTLE
ザワ
RUSTLE
ASUMI KAMOGAWA, NUMBER A24-22!
ドキ
BA-DUM
ドキ
ドキ
BA-DUM

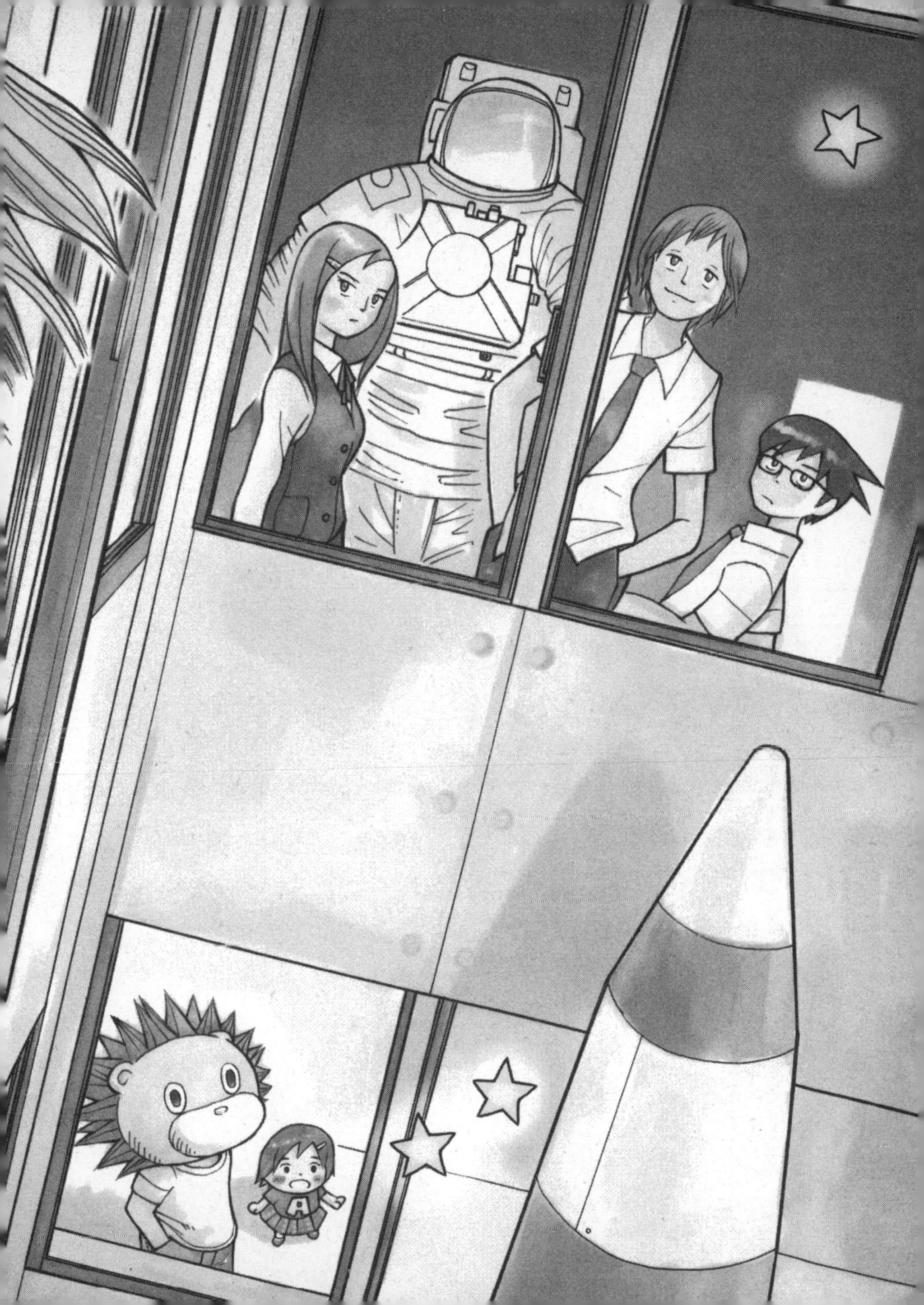

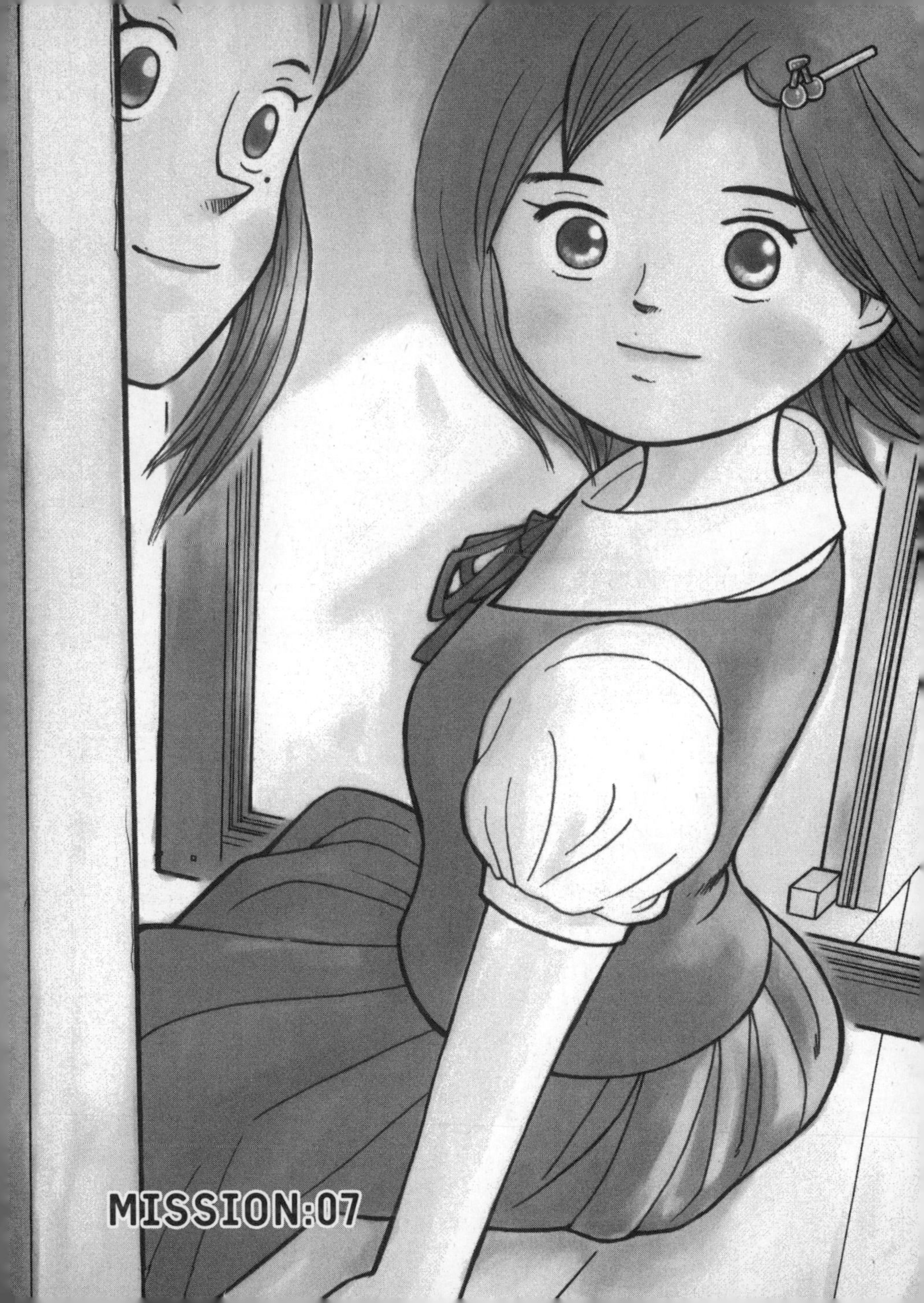
MISSION:07

ドキ
BA-DUM

ドキ
BA-DUM

ドキ
BA-DUM

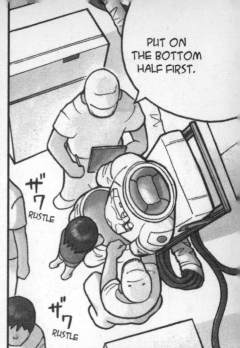

PUT ON THE BOTTOM HALF FIRST.

ザワ
RUSTLE

ザワ
RUSTLE

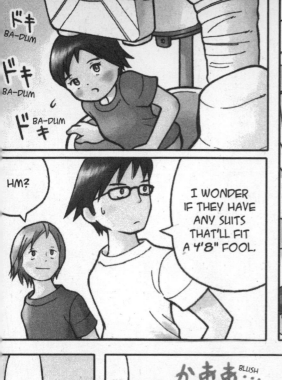

HM?

I WONDER IF THEY HAVE ANY SUITS THAT'LL FIT A 4'8" FOOL.

...

...

かああ...
BLUSH

...

HA HA HA HA HA

YOU LOOK STUPID!

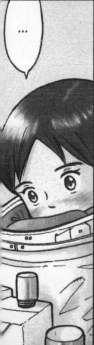

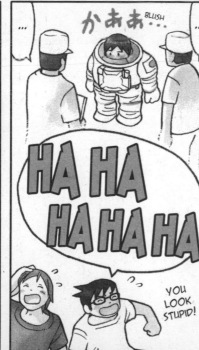

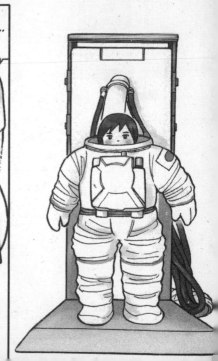

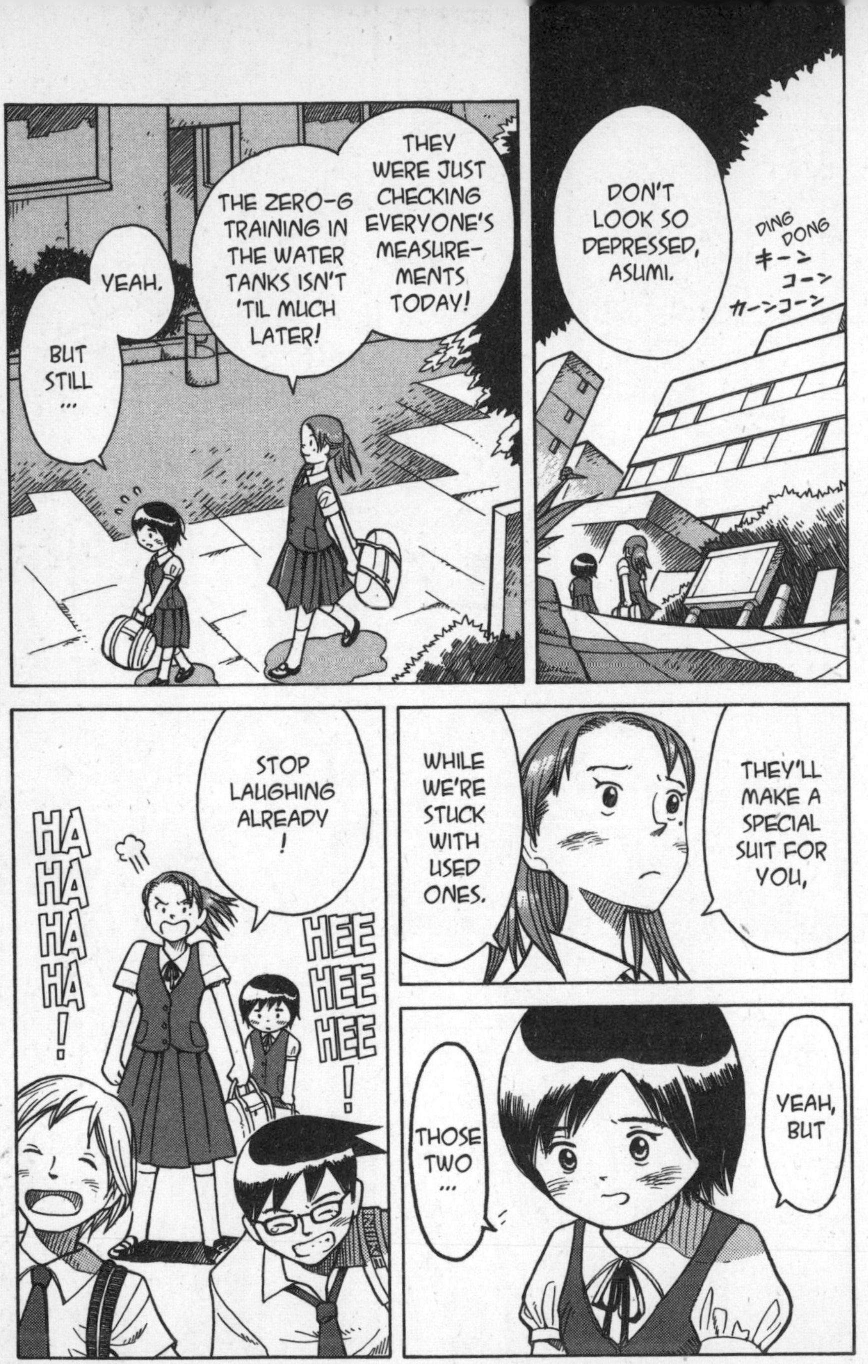
DON'T LOOK SO DEPRESSED, ASUMI.
DING DONG
キーン コーン カーンコーン
THEY WERE JUST CHECKING EVERYONE'S MEASURE-MENTS TODAY!
THE ZERO-G TRAINING IN THE WATER TANKS ISN'T 'TIL MUCH LATER!
YEAH.
BUT STILL ...
THEY'LL MAKE A SPECIAL SUIT FOR YOU,
WHILE WE'RE STUCK WITH USED ONES.
YEAH, BUT
THOSE TWO ...
STOP LAUGHING ALREADY!
HEE HEE HEE!
HA HA HA HA HA!

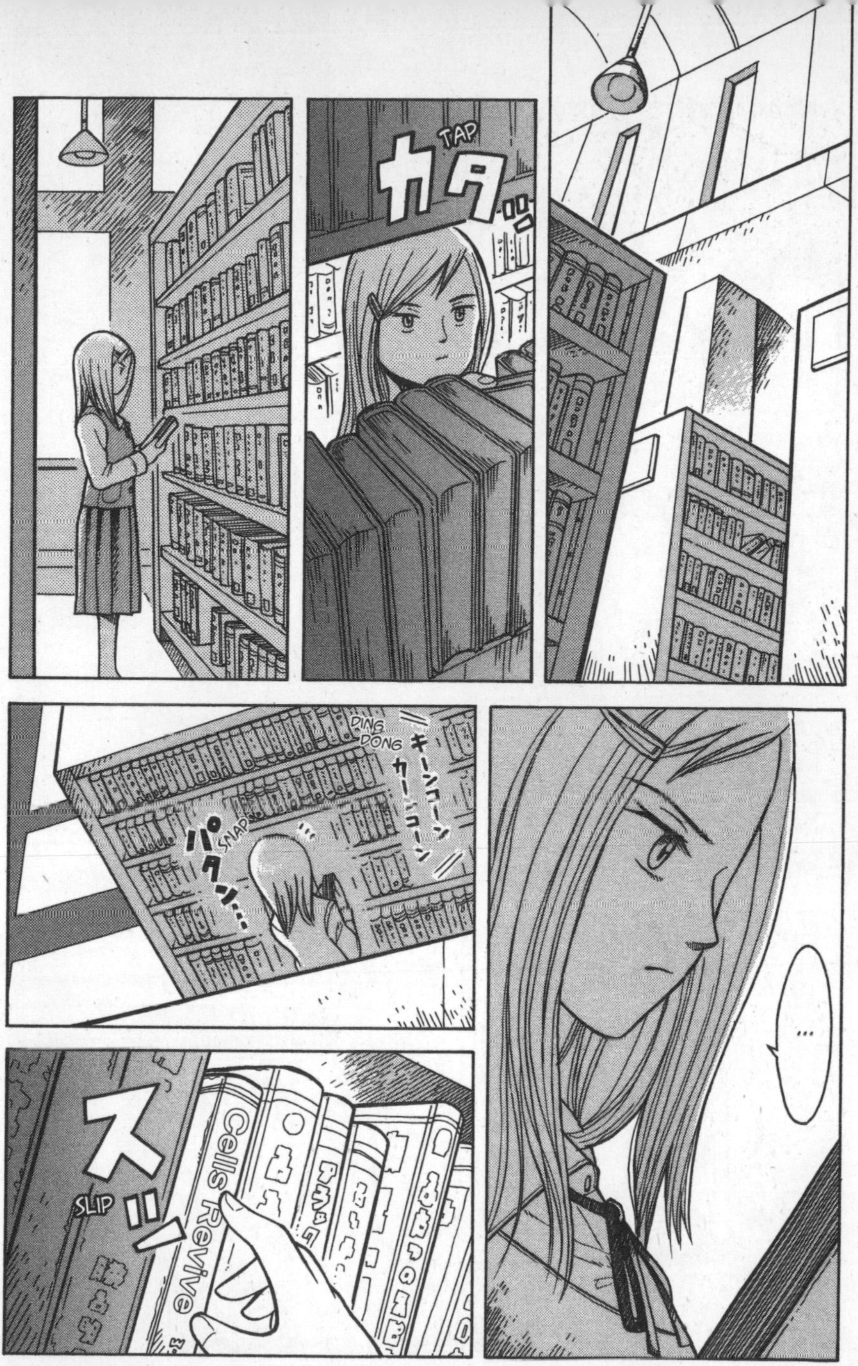
TAP
カタ
…
DING DONG
キーンコーン
カーンコーン
SNAP
パタン…
SLIP
ス!!
Cells Revive

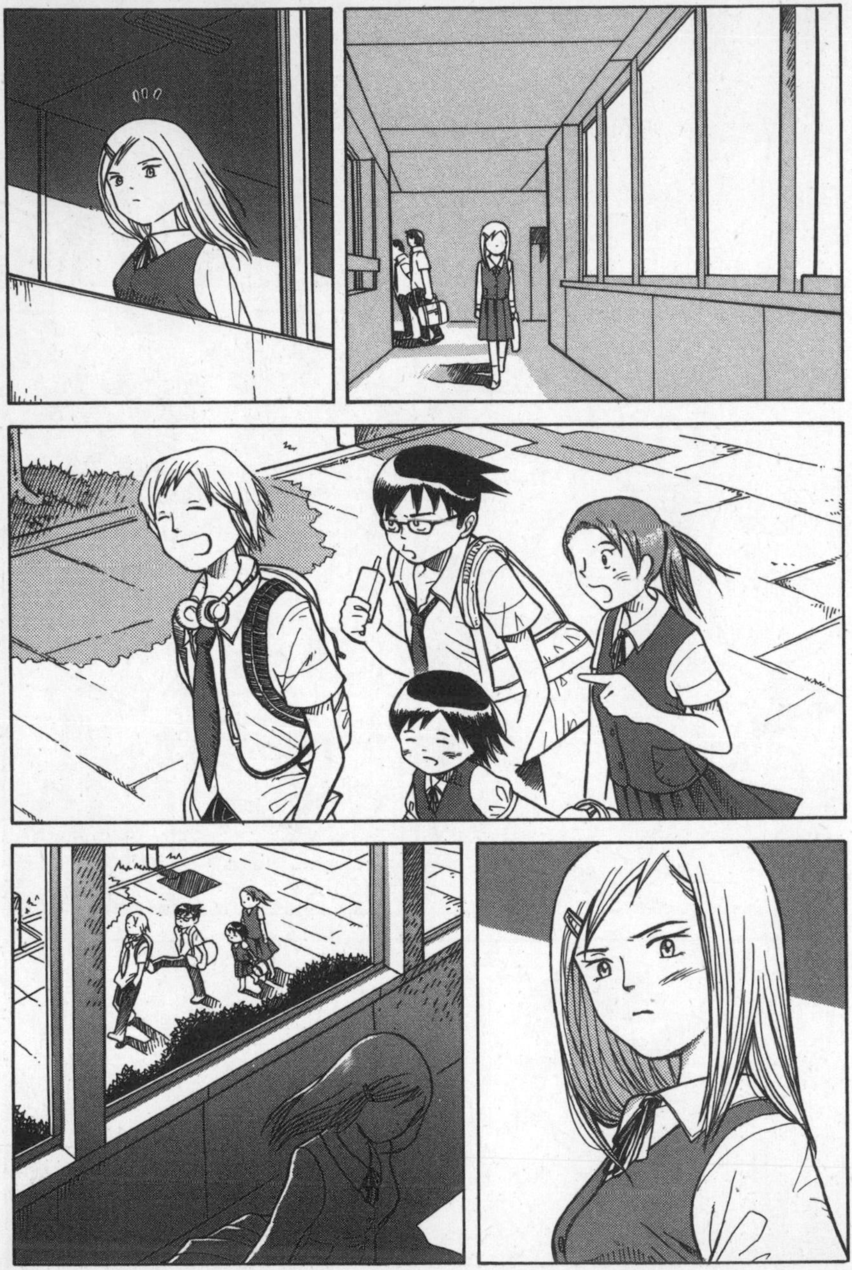

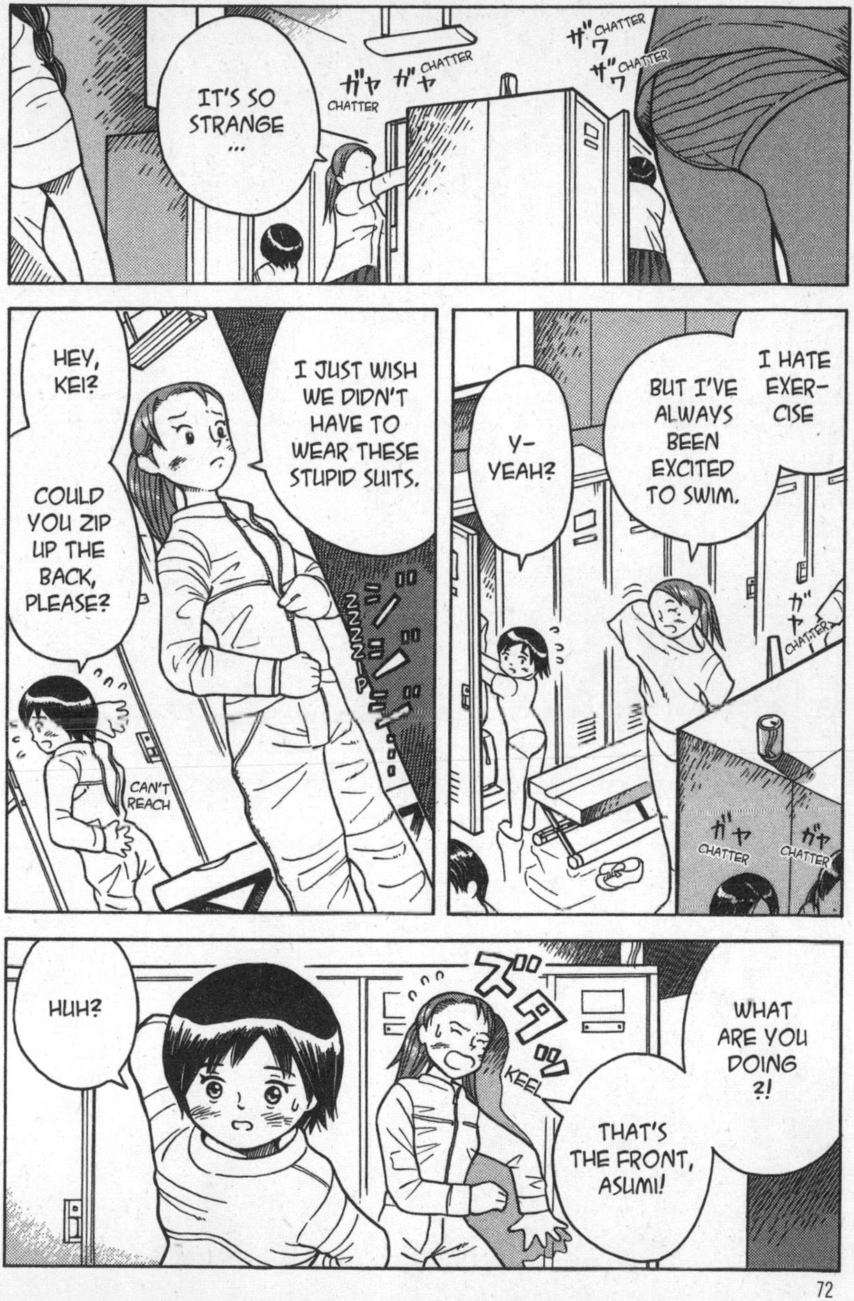

ザワ CHATTER
ザワ CHATTER
ガヤ ガヤ CHATTER
CHATTER
IT'S SO STRANGE ...
I HATE EXER-CISE
BUT I'VE ALWAYS BEEN EXCITED TO SWIM.
Y-YEAH?
ガヤ CHATTER
ガヤ CHATTER
ガヤ CHATTER
I JUST WISH WE DIDN'T HAVE TO WEAR THESE STUPID SUITS.
HEY, KEI?
COULD YOU ZIP UP THE BACK, PLEASE?
ZZZZIP
CAN'T REACH
WHAT ARE YOU DOING ?!
THAT'S THE FRONT, ASUMI!
KEEL
HUH?

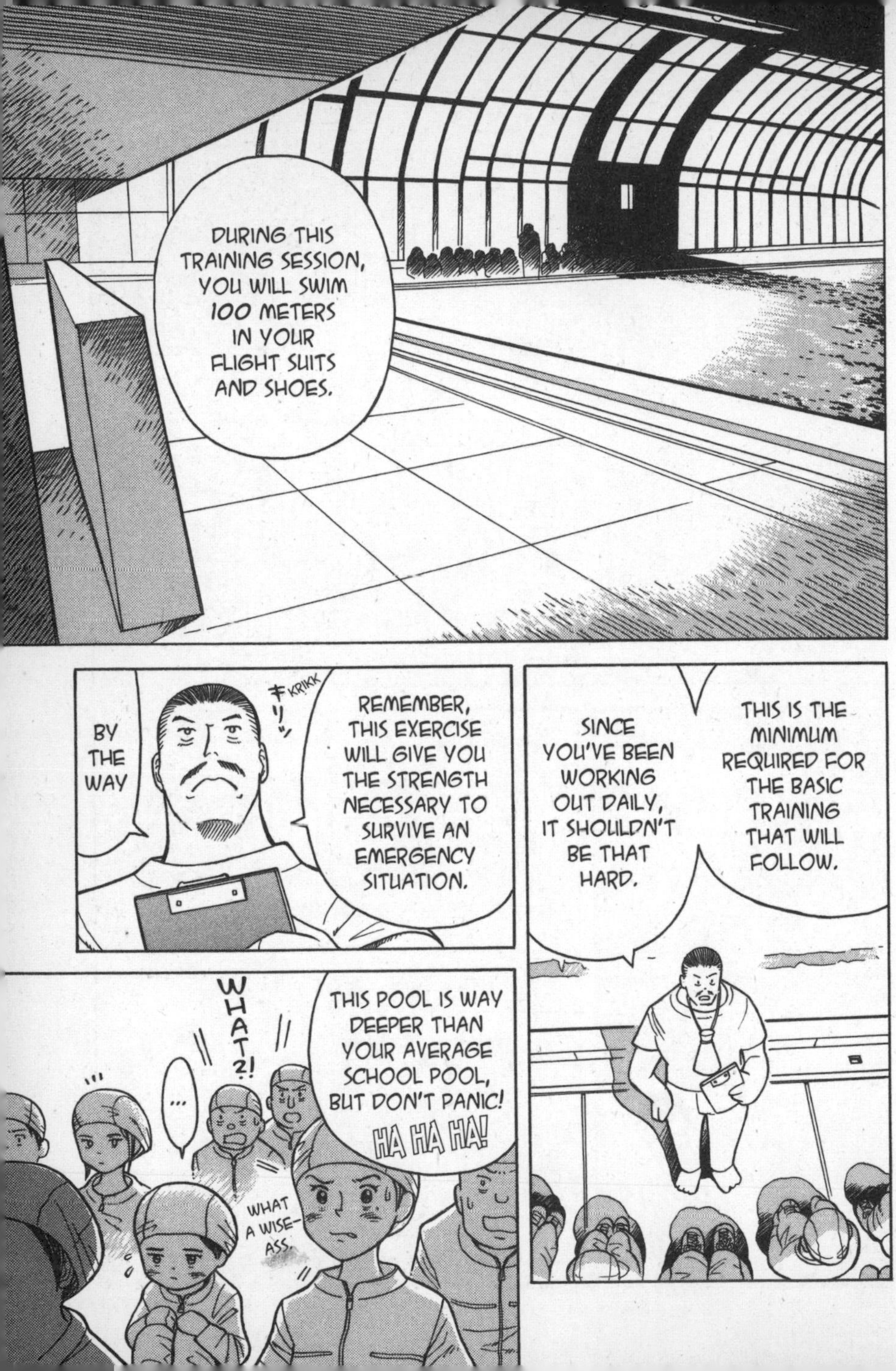
DURING THIS TRAINING SESSION, YOU WILL SWIM 100 METERS IN YOUR FLIGHT SUITS AND SHOES.
THIS IS THE MINIMUM REQUIRED FOR THE BASIC TRAINING THAT WILL FOLLOW.
SINCE YOU'VE BEEN WORKING OUT DAILY, IT SHOULDN'T BE THAT HARD.
KRIKK
REMEMBER, THIS EXERCISE WILL GIVE YOU THE STRENGTH NECESSARY TO SURVIVE AN EMERGENCY SITUATION.
BY THE WAY
THIS POOL IS WAY DEEPER THAN YOUR AVERAGE SCHOOL POOL, BUT DON'T PANIC!
HA HA HA!
WHAT?!
...
WHAT A WISE-ASS.

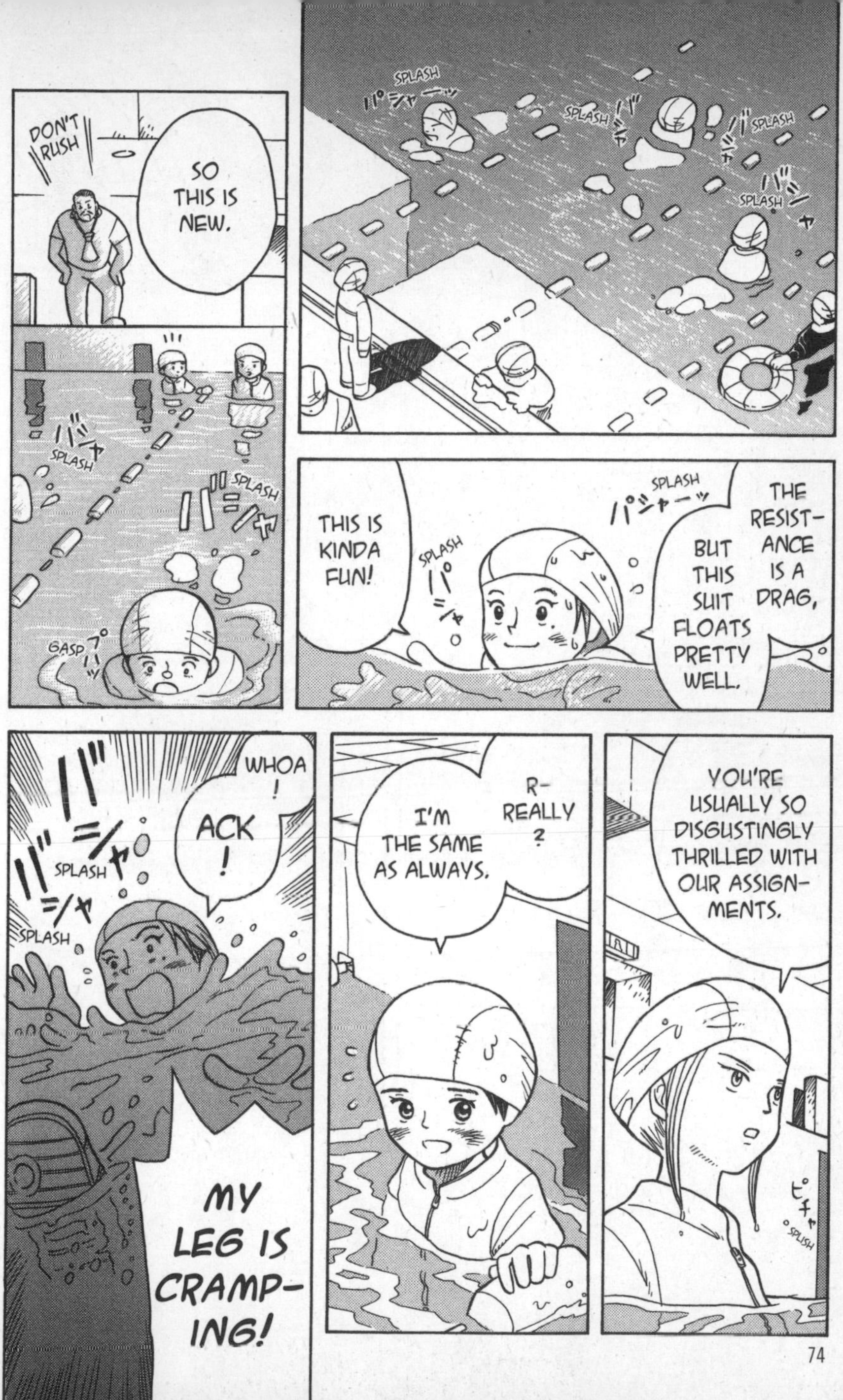
SPLASH
パシャーッ
SPLASH
バシャ
SPLASH
バシャ
SPLASH
バシャ
DON'T RUSH
SO THIS IS NEW.
SPLASH
パシャーッ
THE RESISTANCE IS A DRAG,
BUT THIS SUIT FLOATS PRETTY WELL.
SPLASH
パシャ
THIS IS KINDA FUN!
SPLASH
バシャ
SPLASH
バシャ
GASP
プハッ
YOU'RE USUALLY SO DISGUSTINGLY THRILLED WITH OUR ASSIGNMENTS.
ピチャ
SPLISH
R-REALLY?
I'M THE SAME AS ALWAYS.
WHOA!
ACK!
SPLASH
バシャ
SPLASH
バシャ
MY LEG IS CRAMPING!

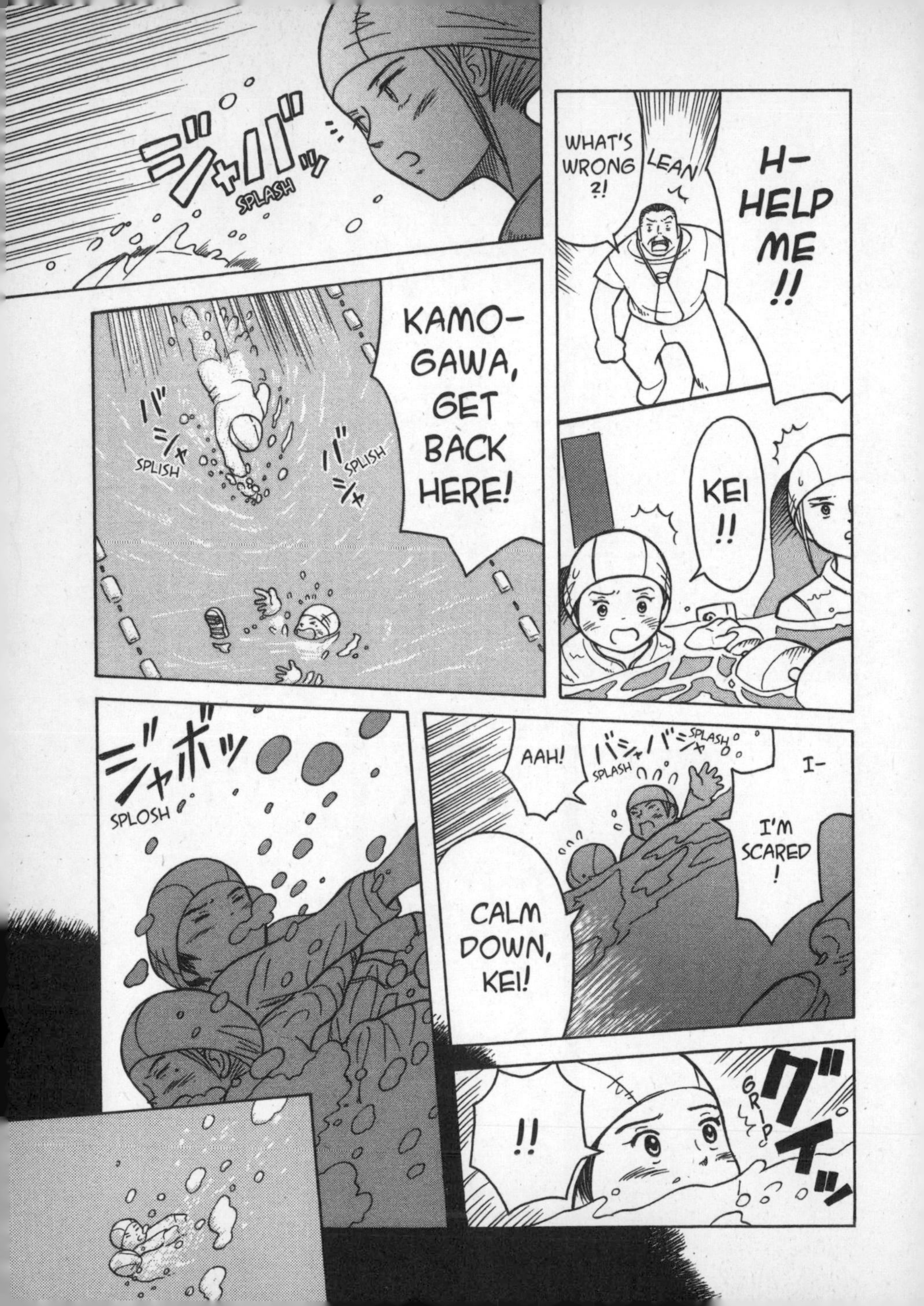
H-HELP ME!!
LEAN
WHAT'S WRONG?!
ジャバッ
SPLASH
...
KEI!!
KAMOGAWA, GET BACK HERE!
バシャ
SPLISH
バシャ
SPLISH
I- I'M SCARED!
バシャバシャ
SPLASH
SPLASH
AAH!
CALM DOWN, KEI!
グイッ
GRIP
!!
ジャボッ
SPLOSH

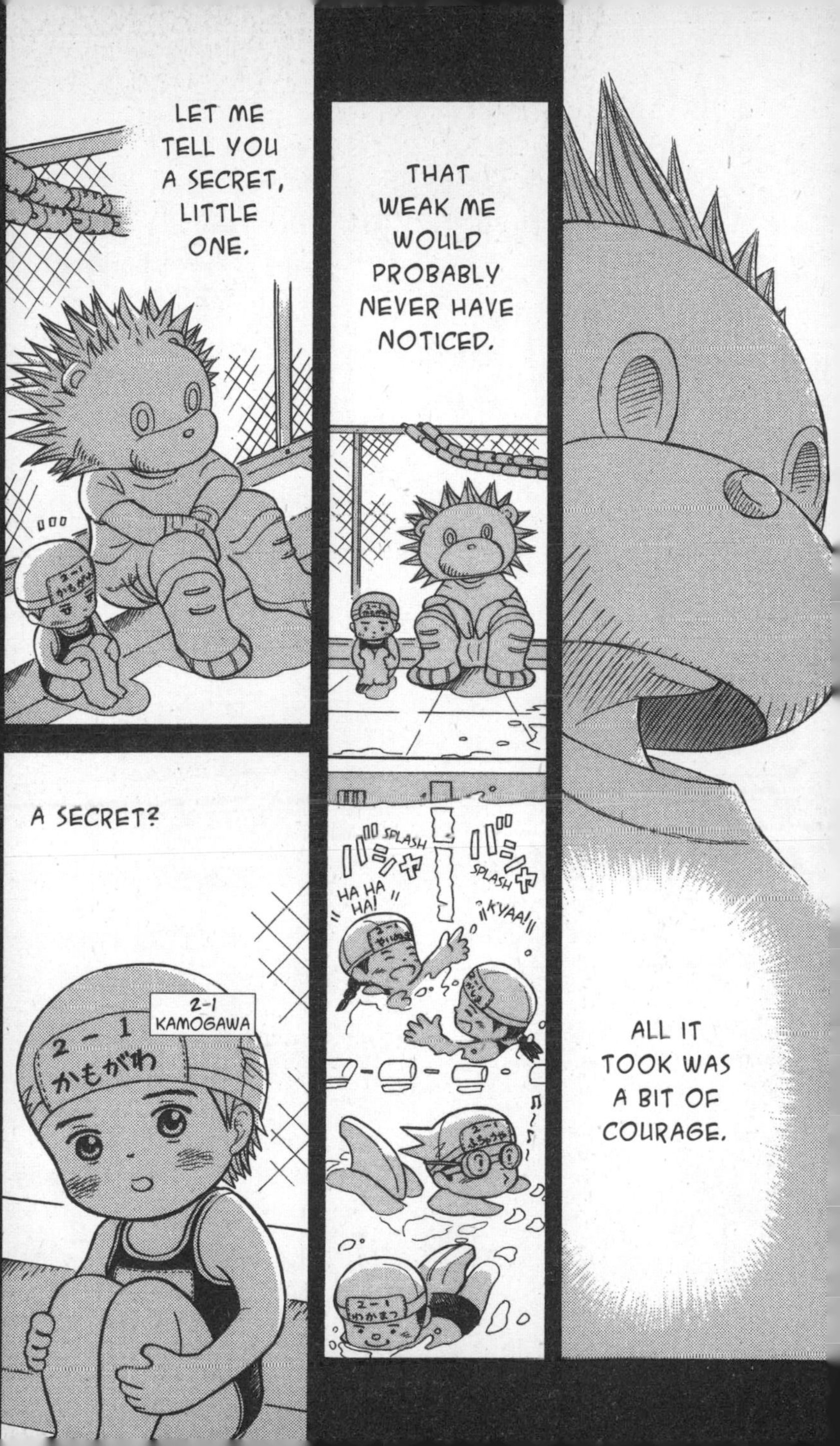
LET ME TELL YOU A SECRET, LITTLE ONE.
A SECRET?
2-1 KAMOGAWA
2-1 かもがわ
THAT WEAK ME WOULD PROBABLY NEVER HAVE NOTICED.
SPLASH
SPLASH
HA HA HA!
KYAA!
2-1 わかまつ
ALL IT TOOK WAS A BIT OF COURAGE.

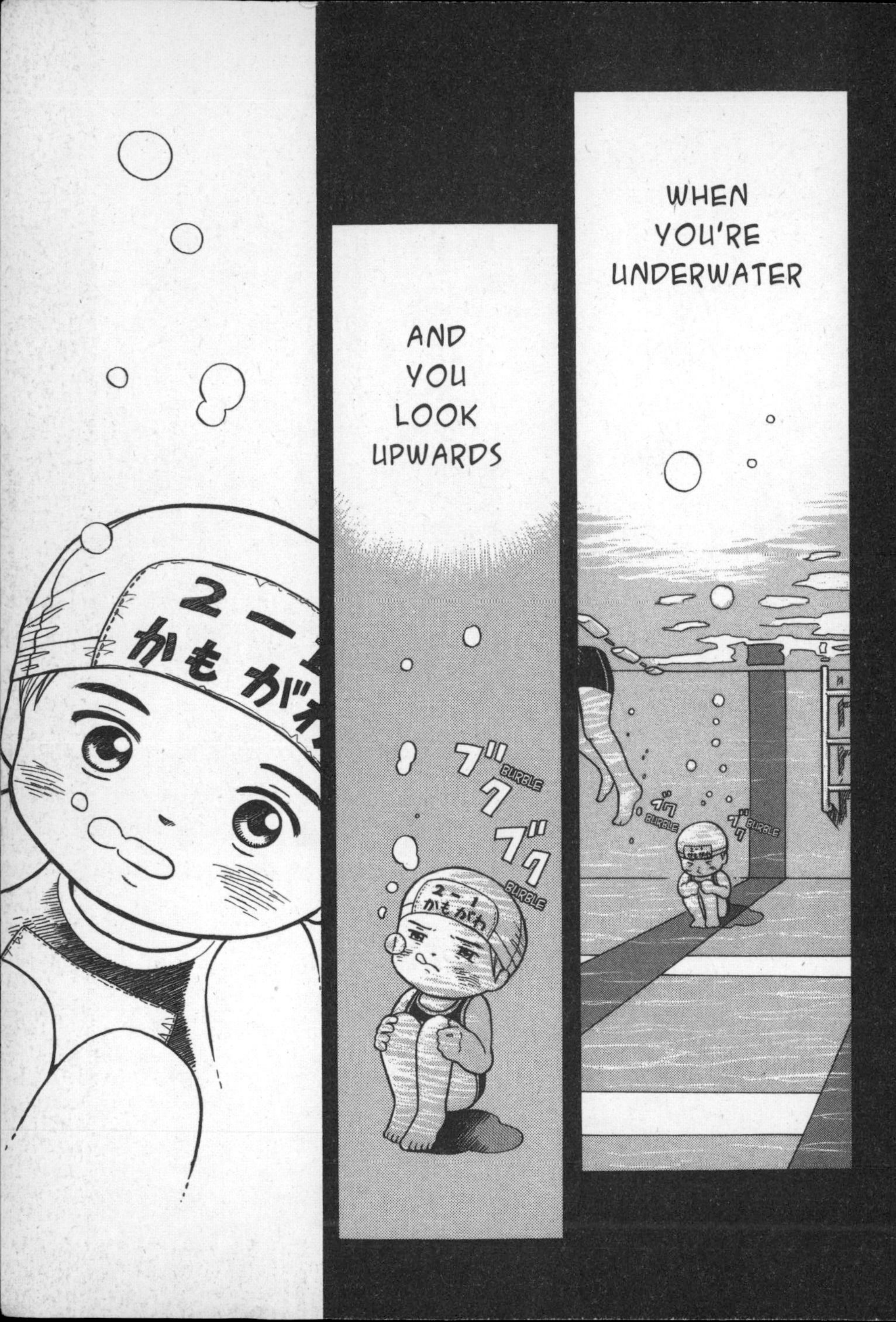
WHEN YOU'RE UNDERWATER
ブク BURBLE
ブク BURBLE
AND YOU LOOK UPWARDS
ブク BURBLE
ブク BURBLE
2-1 かもがわ

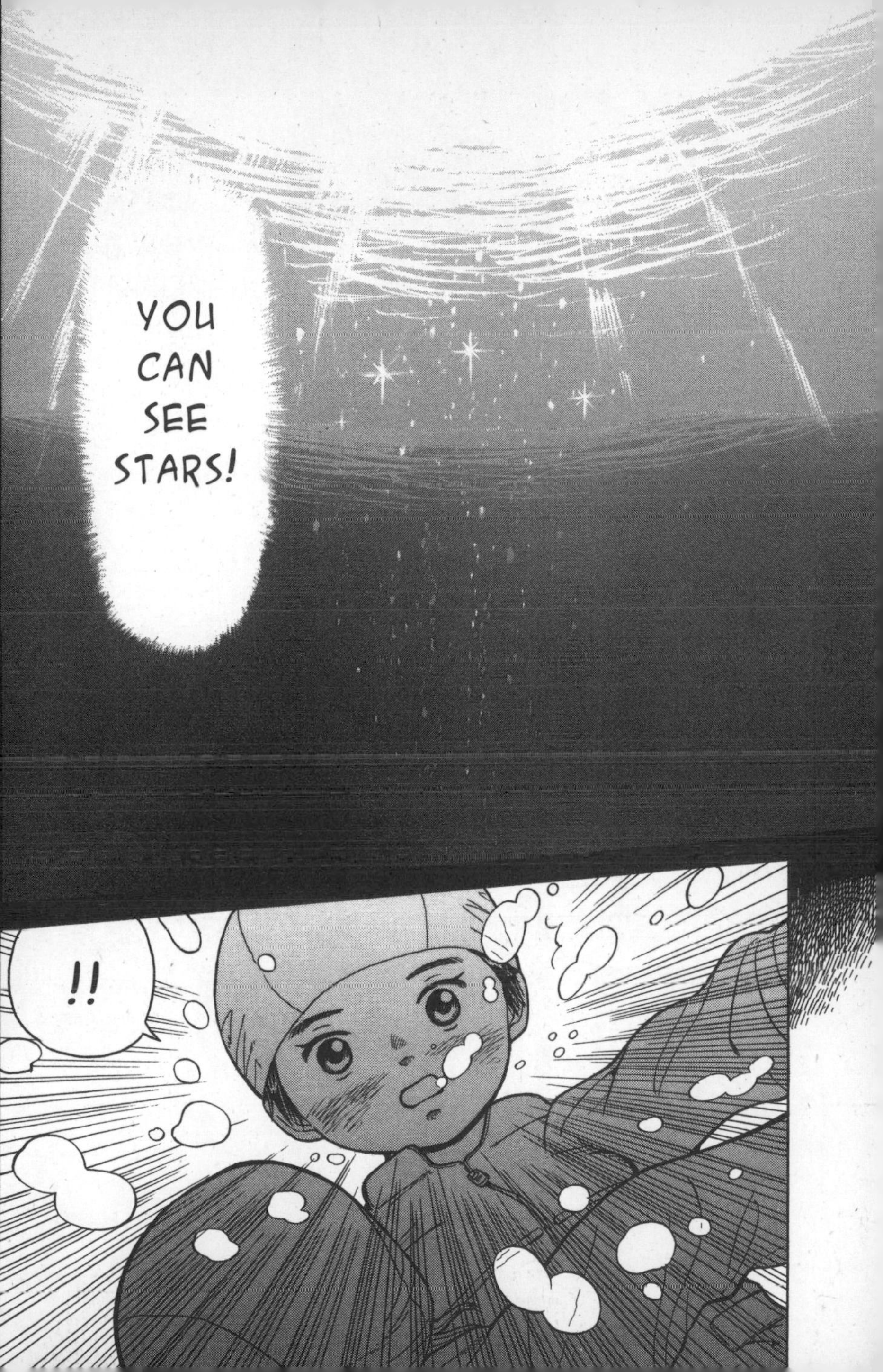
YOU CAN SEE STARS!
!!

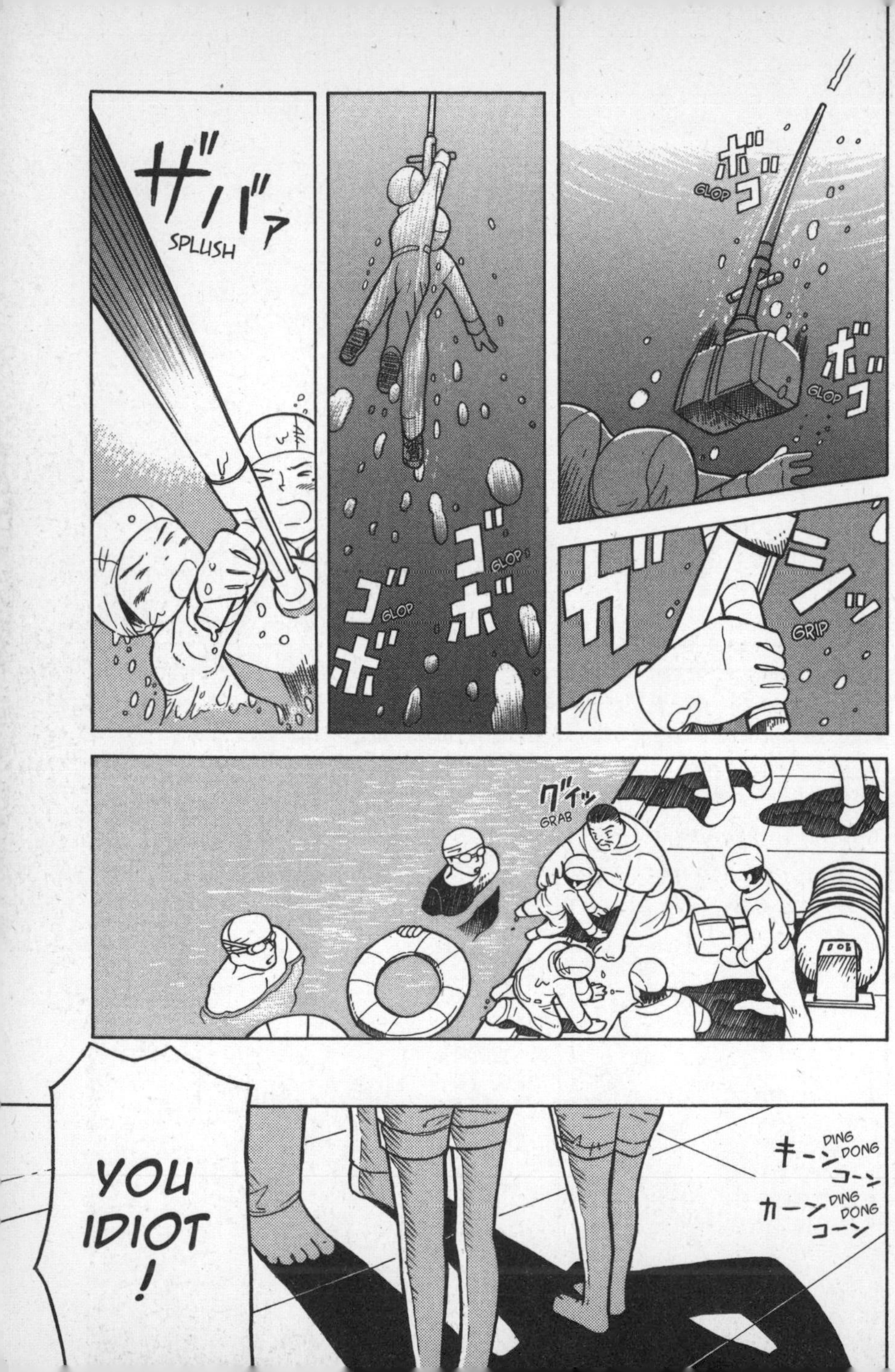
ボゴ
GLOP
ボゴ
GLOP
ガシッ
GRIP
ゴボ
GLOP
ゴボ
GLOP
ザバァ
SPLUSH
グイッ
GRAB
キーン DING
コーン DONG
カーン DING
コーン DONG
YOU IDIOT!

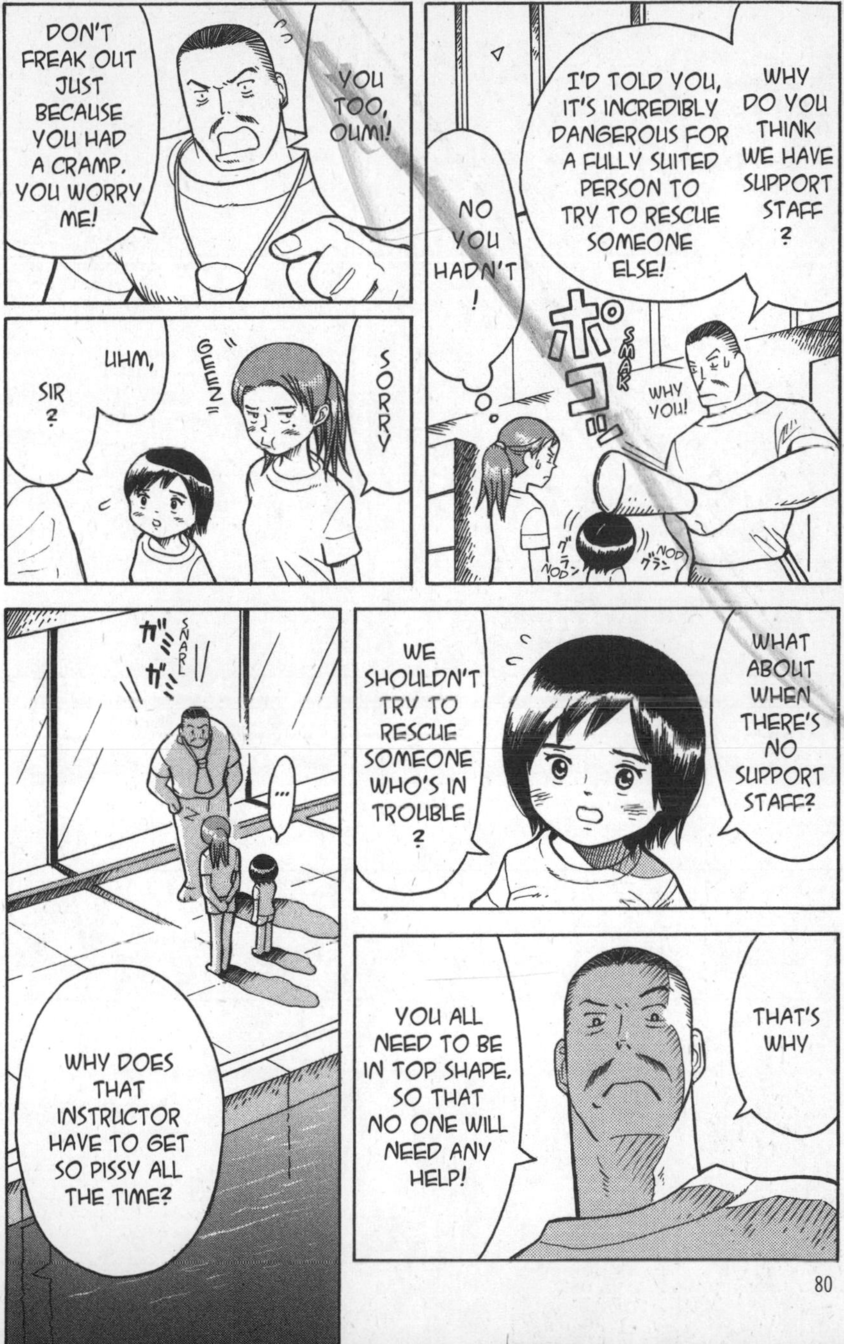
WHY DO YOU THINK WE HAVE SUPPORT STAFF?
I'D TOLD YOU, IT'S INCREDIBLY DANGEROUS FOR A FULLY SUITED PERSON TO TRY TO RESCUE SOMEONE ELSE!
NO YOU HADN'T!
SMAK
WHY YOU!
NOD
NOD
YOU TOO, OUMI!
DON'T FREAK OUT JUST BECAUSE YOU HAD A CRAMP. YOU WORRY ME!
SORRY
GEEZ
UHM, SIR?
WHAT ABOUT WHEN THERE'S NO SUPPORT STAFF?
WE SHOULDN'T TRY TO RESCUE SOMEONE WHO'S IN TROUBLE?
THAT'S WHY
YOU ALL NEED TO BE IN TOP SHAPE, SO THAT NO ONE WILL NEED ANY HELP!
SNARL
...
WHY DOES THAT INSTRUCTOR HAVE TO GET SO PISSY ALL THE TIME?

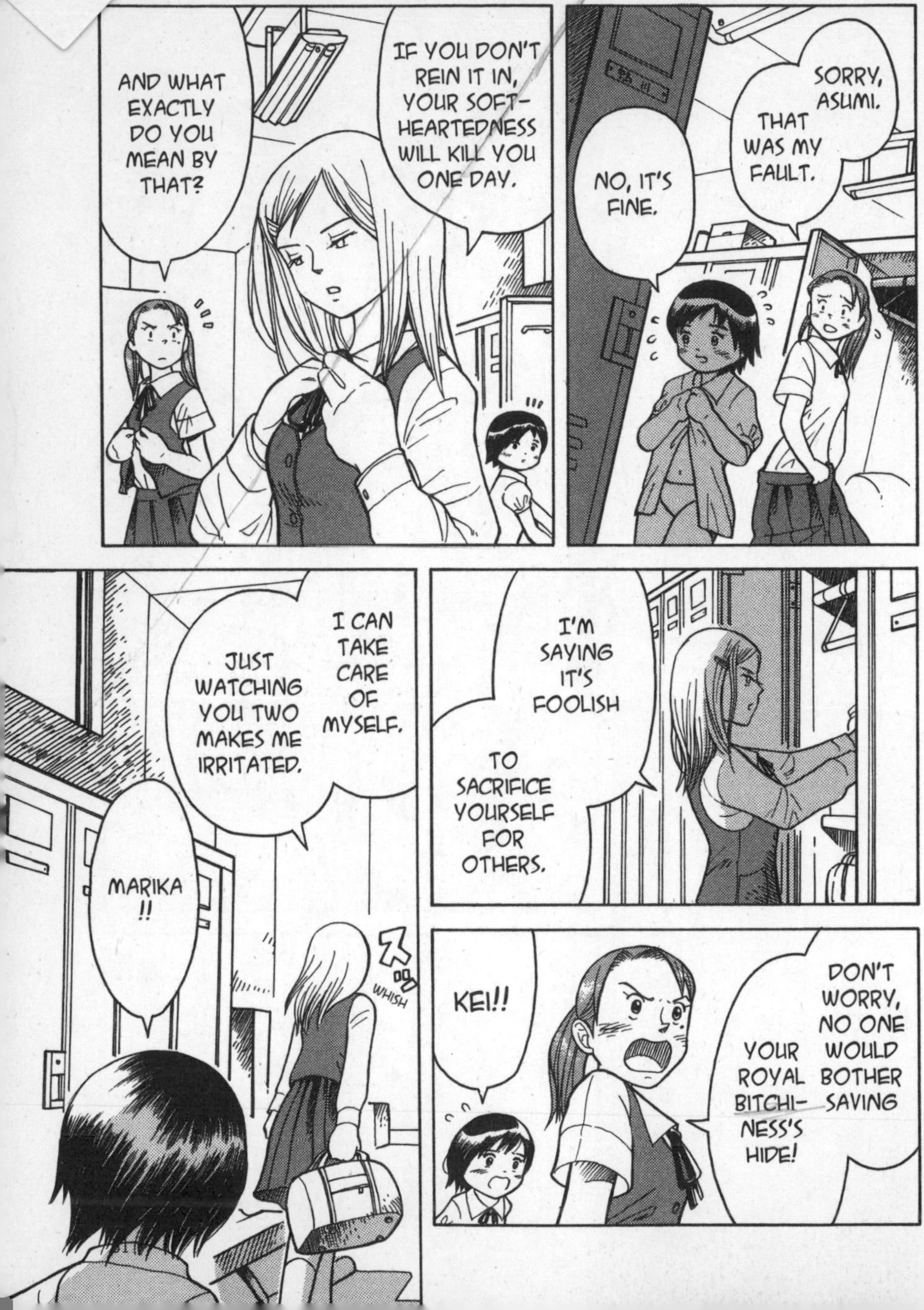
SORRY, ASUMI. THAT WAS MY FAULT.
NO, IT'S FINE.
IF YOU DON'T REIN IT IN, YOUR SOFT-HEARTEDNESS WILL KILL YOU ONE DAY.
AND WHAT EXACTLY DO YOU MEAN BY THAT?
I'M SAYING IT'S FOOLISH
TO SACRIFICE YOURSELF FOR OTHERS.
DON'T WORRY, NO ONE WOULD BOTHER SAVING YOUR ROYAL BITCHI-NESS'S HIDE!
KEI!!
I CAN TAKE CARE OF MYSELF.
JUST WATCHING YOU TWO MAKES ME IRRITATED.
WHISH
MARIKA!!

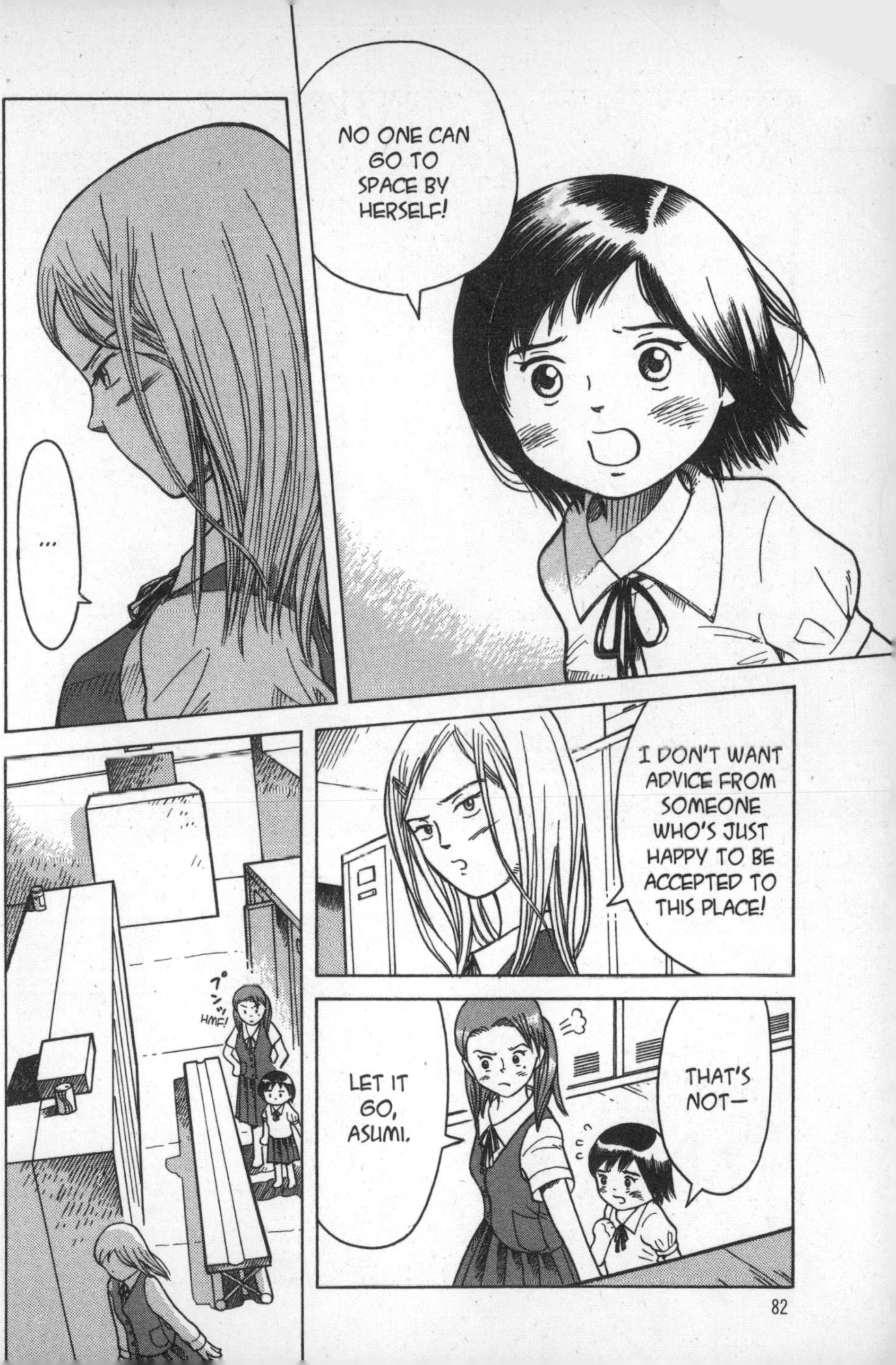
NO ONE CAN GO TO SPACE BY HERSELF!
...
I DON'T WANT ADVICE FROM SOMEONE WHO'S JUST HAPPY TO BE ACCEPTED TO THIS PLACE!
THAT'S NOT—
LET IT GO, ASUMI.
プンッ
HMF!

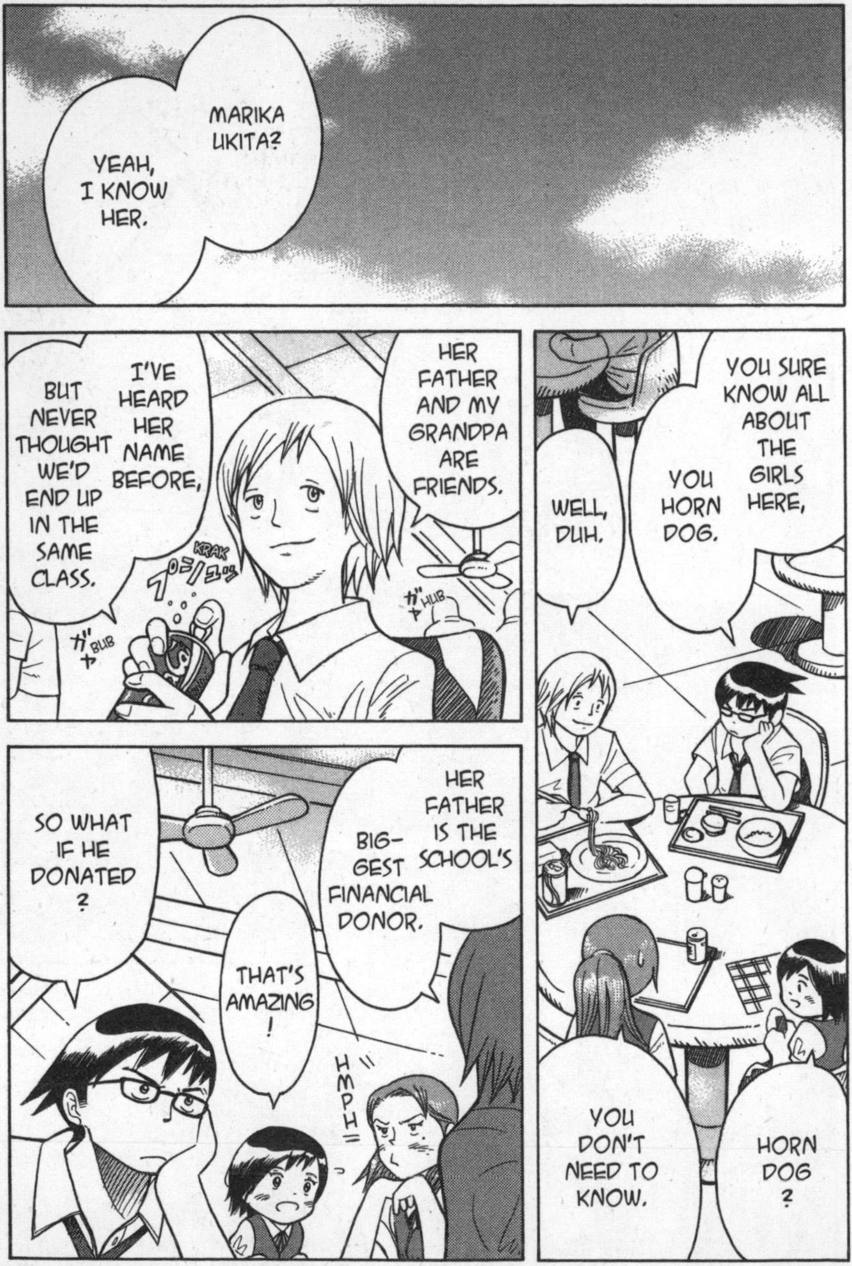
MARIKA UKITA?
YEAH, I KNOW HER.
YOU SURE KNOW ALL ABOUT THE GIRLS HERE,
YOU HORN DOG.
WELL, DUH.
HORN DOG?
YOU DON'T NEED TO KNOW.
HER FATHER AND MY GRANDPA ARE FRIENDS.
I'VE HEARD HER NAME BEFORE,
BUT NEVER THOUGHT WE'D END UP IN THE SAME CLASS.
HUB
KRAK
BUB
HER FATHER IS THE SCHOOL'S BIG-GEST FINANCIAL DONOR.
SO WHAT IF HE DONATED?
THAT'S AMAZING!
HMPH

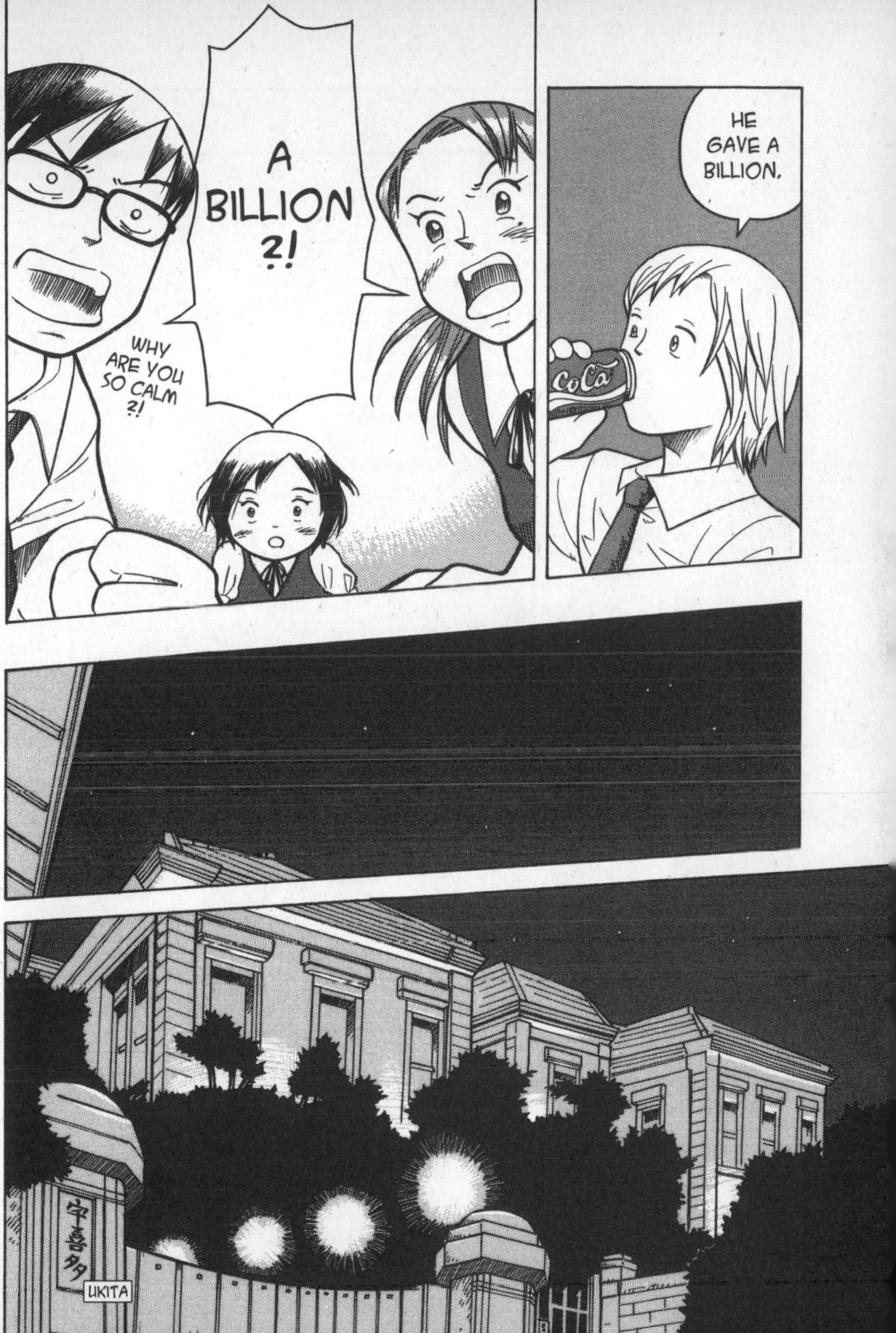
HE GAVE A BILLION.
A BILLION ?!
WHY ARE YOU SO CALM ?!
宇喜多
UKITA

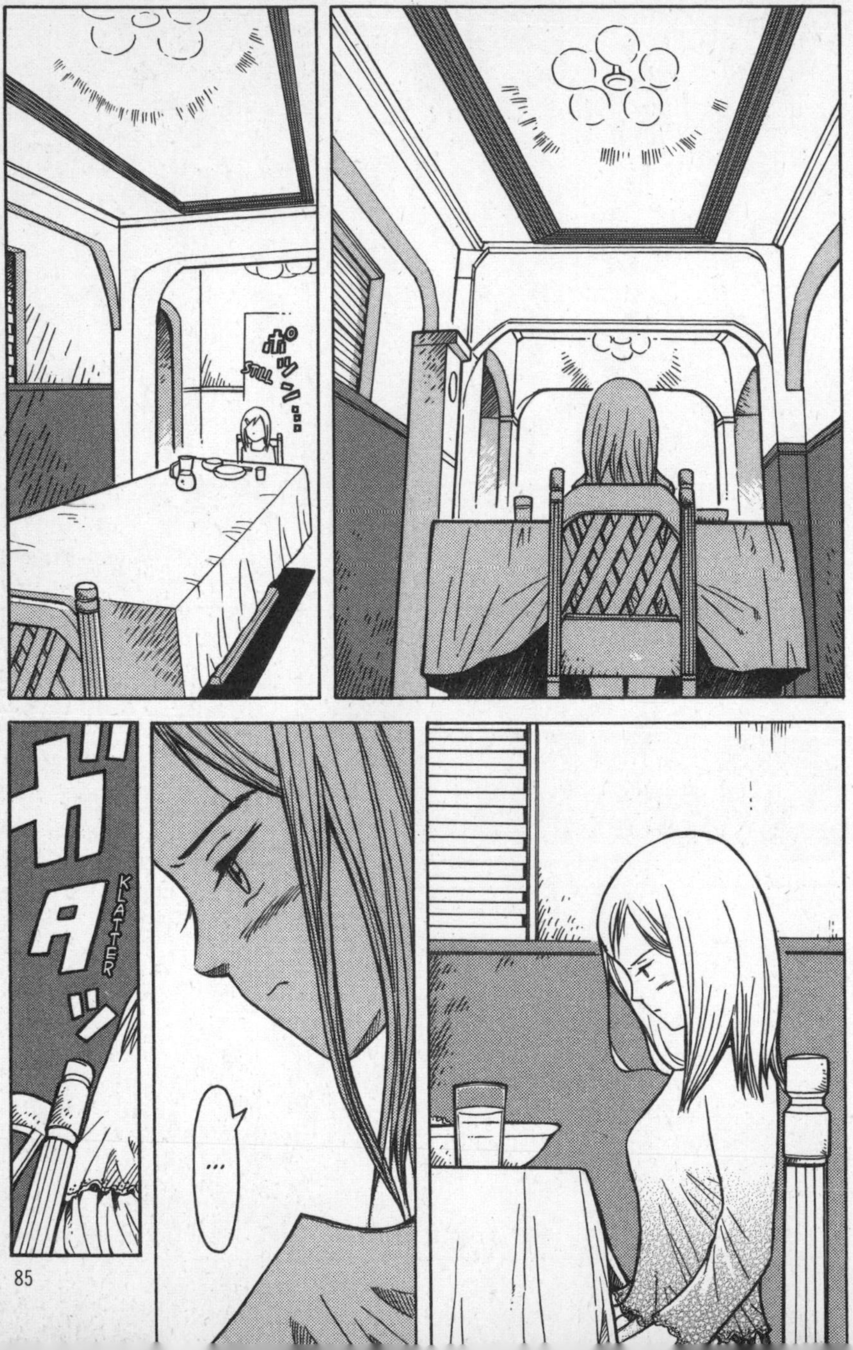
ポツン…
STILL
…
ガタッ
KLATTER

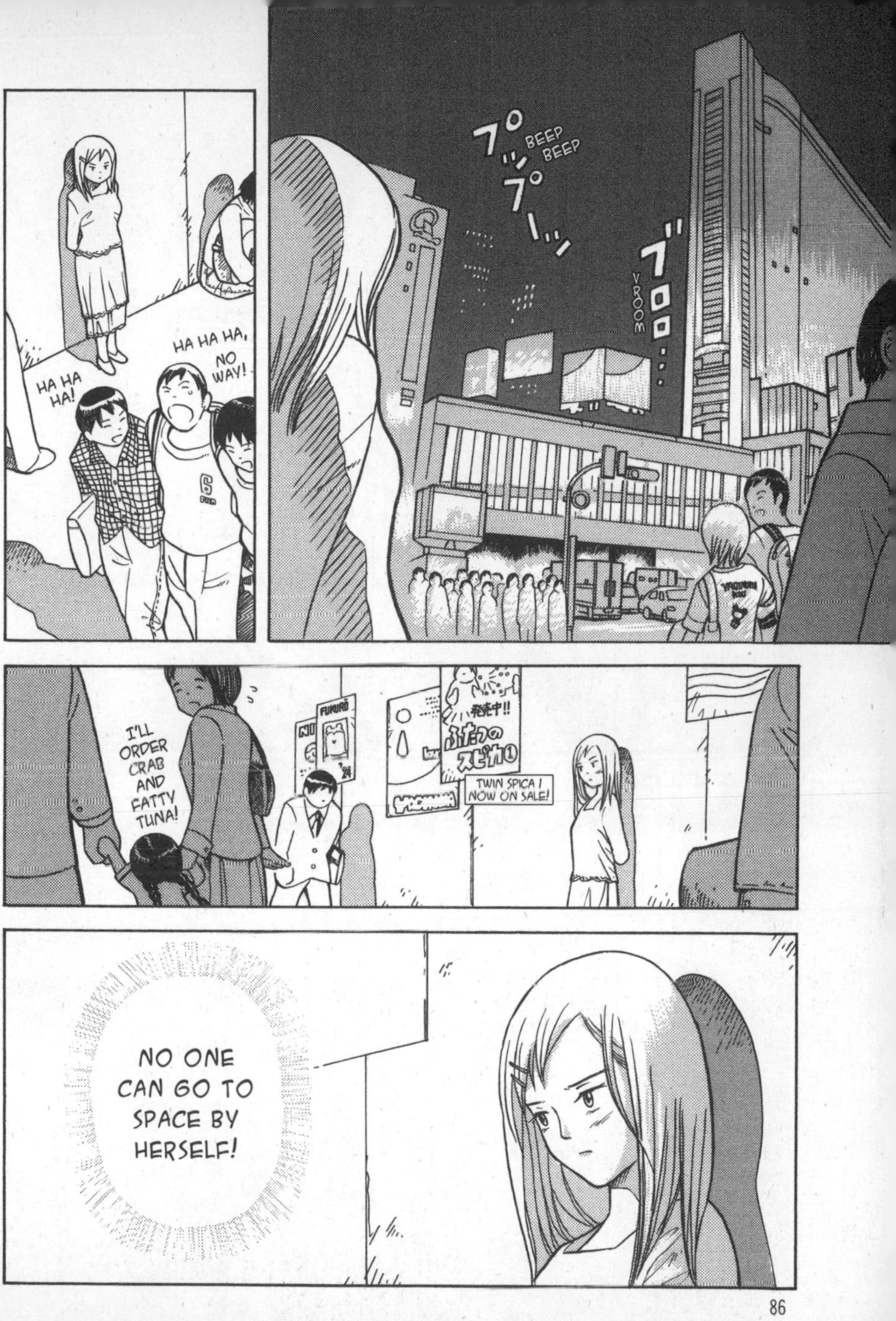
プップーッ
BEEP BEEP
ブロロ…
VROOM
HA HA HA, NO WAY!
HA HA HA!
発売中!! ふたつのスピカ①
TWIN SPICA! NOW ON SALE!
FUKURO
I'LL ORDER CRAB AND FATTY TUNA!
NO ONE CAN GO TO SPACE BY HERSELF!

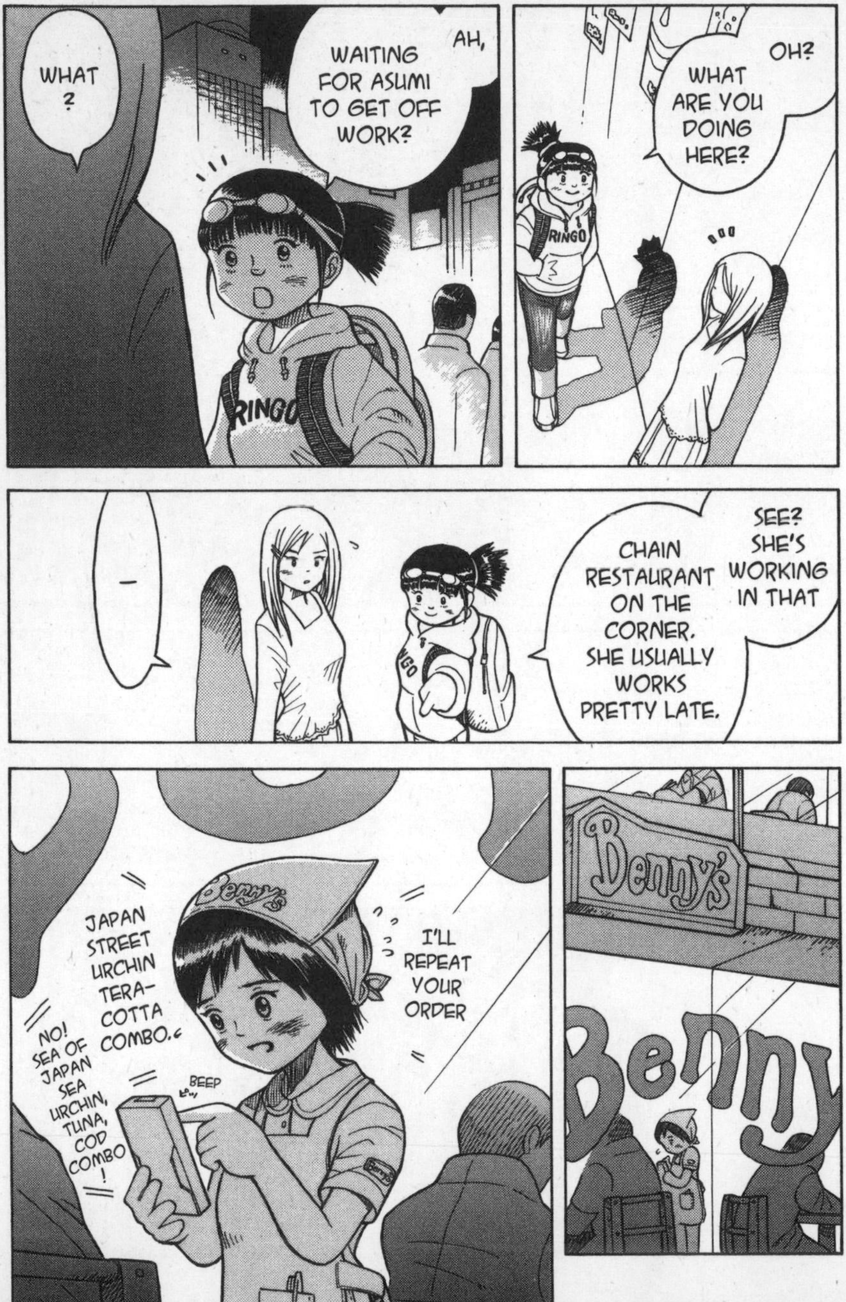
OH? WHAT ARE YOU DOING HERE?
AH, WAITING FOR ASUMI TO GET OFF WORK?
WHAT ?
SEE? SHE'S WORKING IN THAT CHAIN RESTAURANT ON THE CORNER. SHE USUALLY WORKS PRETTY LATE.
—
Benny's
Benny
I'LL REPEAT YOUR ORDER
JAPAN STREET URCHIN TERA-COTTA COMBO.
BEEP ピッ
NO! SEA OF JAPAN SEA URCHIN, TUNA, COD COMBO!
Benny's

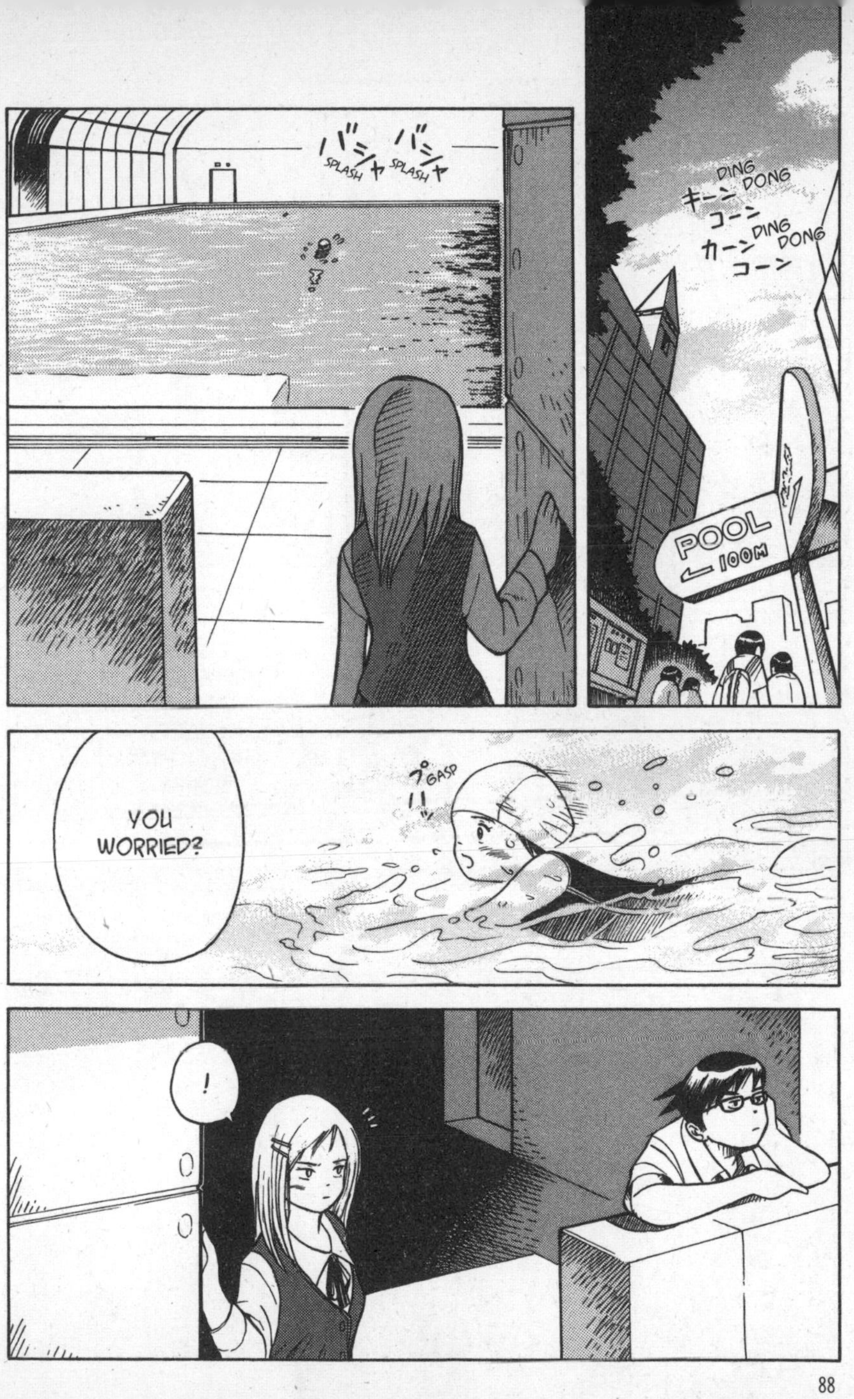

キーン DING
コーン DONG
カーン DING
コーン DONG
POOL
100M
バシャ SPLASH
バシャ SPLASH
プハッ GASP
YOU WORRIED?
!

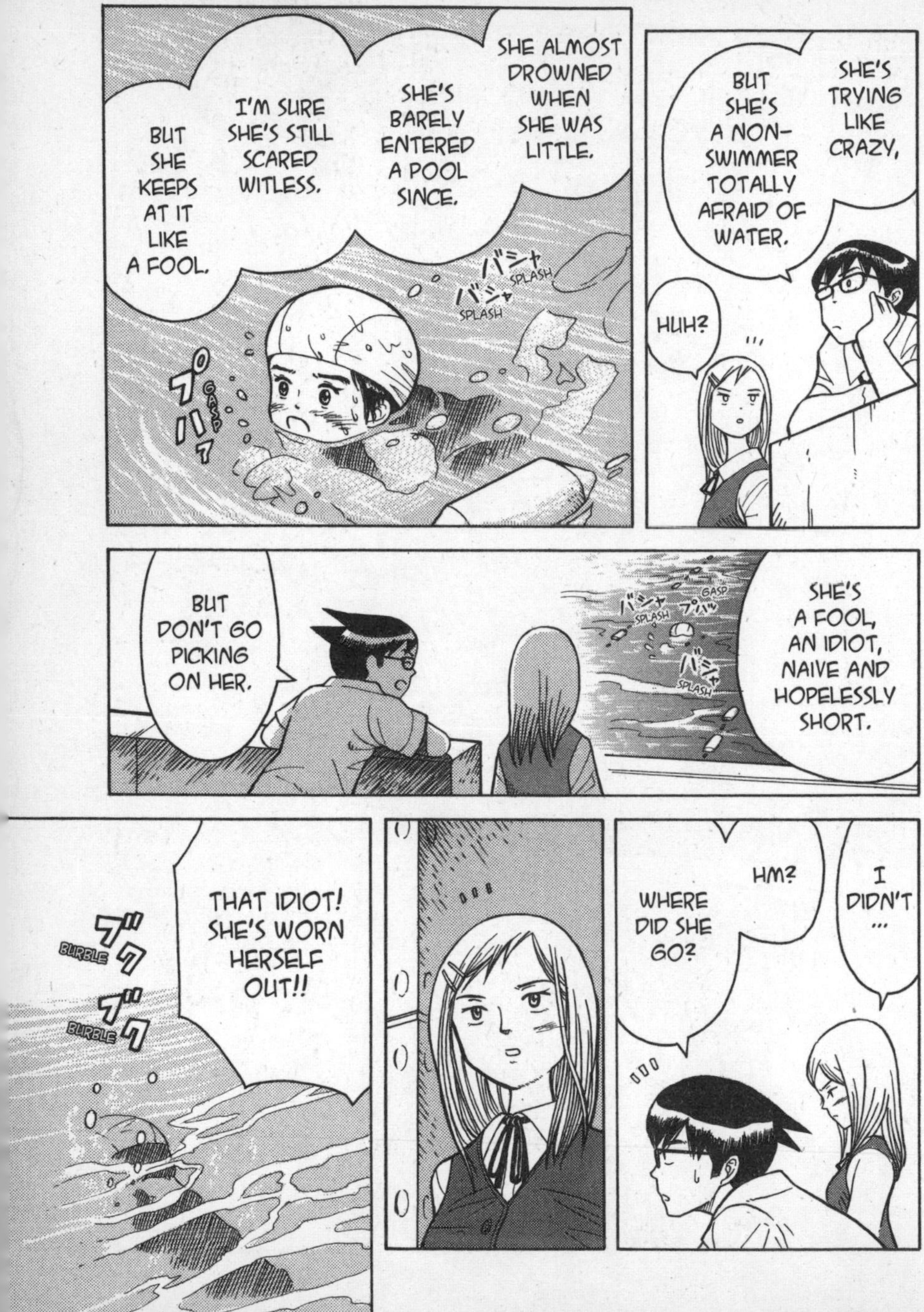
SHE'S TRYING LIKE CRAZY,
BUT SHE'S A NON-SWIMMER TOTALLY AFRAID OF WATER.
HUH?
SHE ALMOST DROWNED WHEN SHE WAS LITTLE.
SHE'S BARELY ENTERED A POOL SINCE.
I'M SURE SHE'S STILL SCARED WITLESS.
BUT SHE KEEPS AT IT LIKE A FOOL.
バシャ SPLASH
バシャ SPLASH
プハァ GASP
SHE'S A FOOL, AN IDIOT, NAIVE AND HOPELESSLY SHORT.
バシャ SPLASH
プハッ GASP
バシャ SPLASH
BUT DON'T GO PICKING ON HER.
I DIDN'T ...
HM?
WHERE DID SHE GO?
THAT IDIOT! SHE'S WORN HERSELF OUT!!
ブク BURBLE
ブク BURBLE

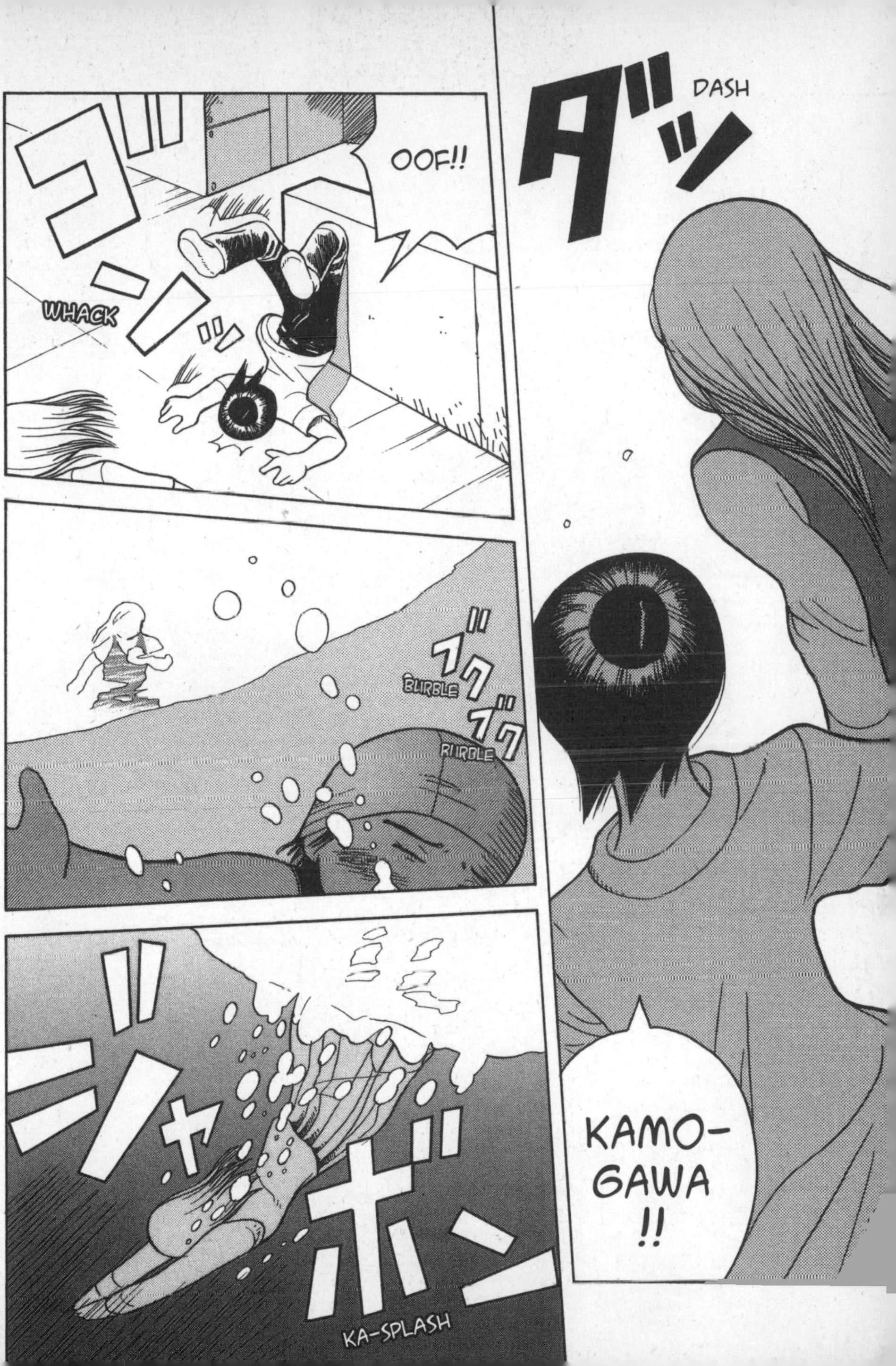
DASH
KAMO-
GAWA
!!
OOF!!
WHACK
BURBLE
BURBLE
KA-SPLASH

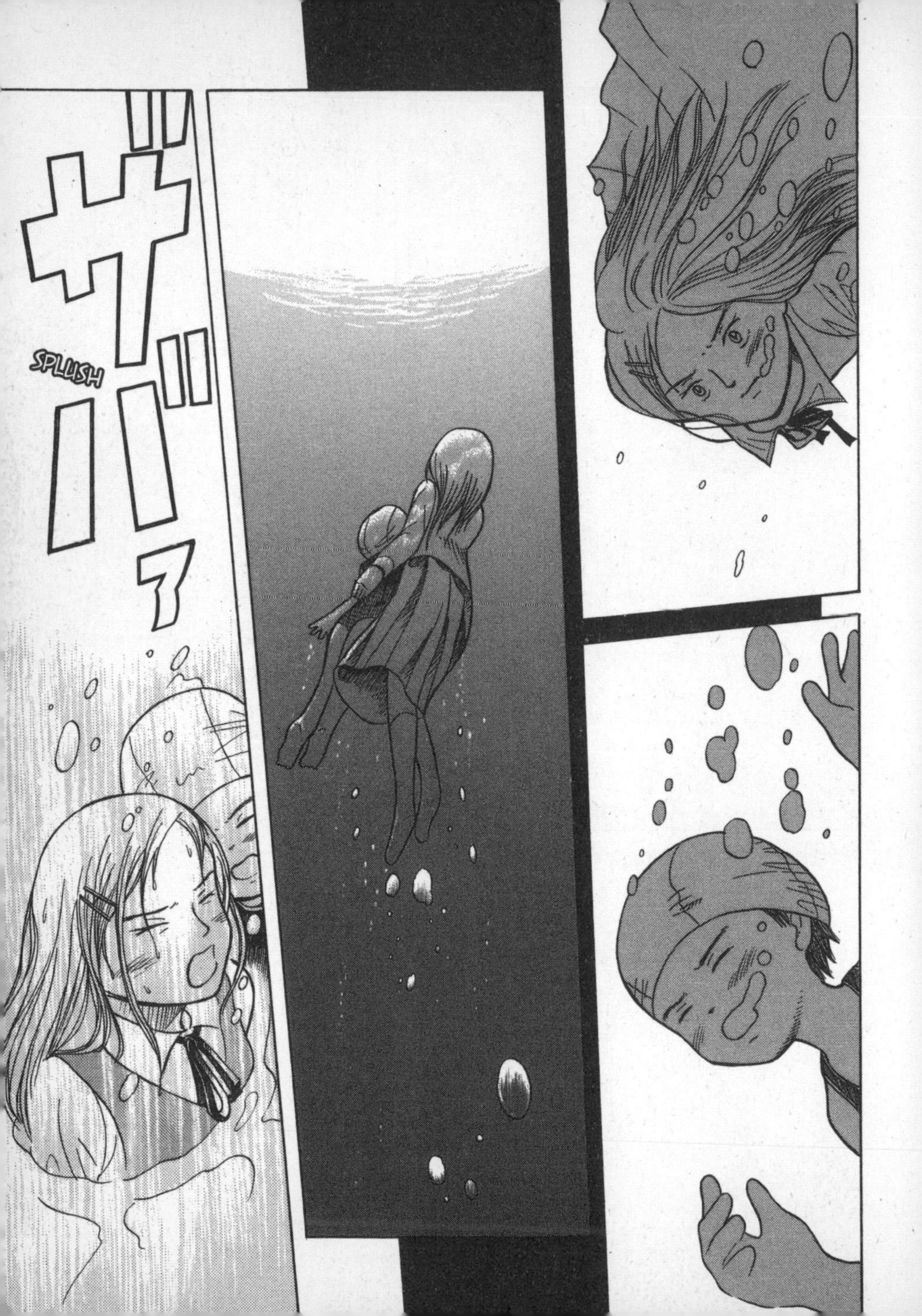
ザバーッ
SPLUSH

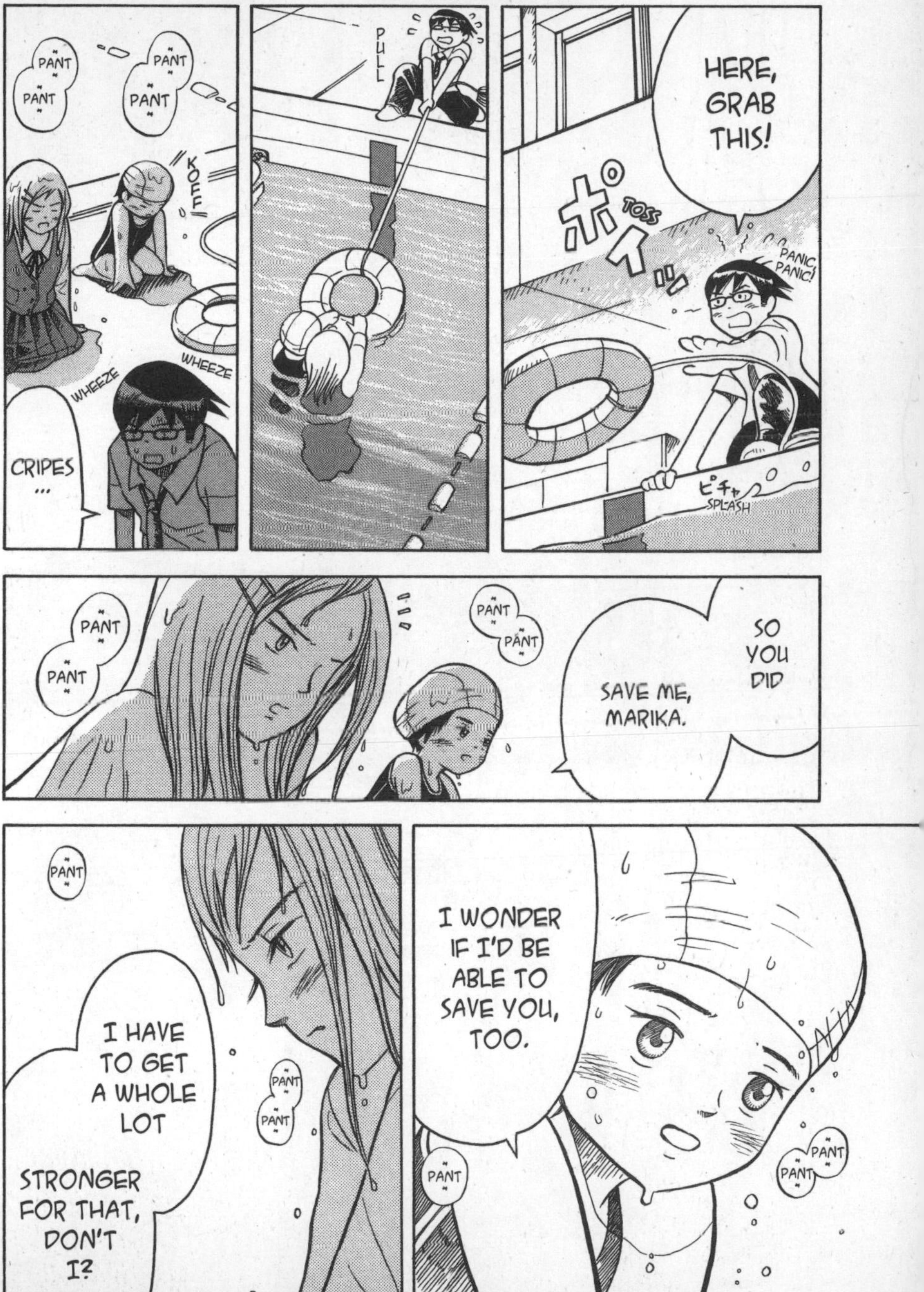
HERE, GRAB THIS!
ポイ
TOSS
PANIC, PANIC!
ピチャ
SPLASH
PULL
PANT PANT
PANT PANT
KOFF
WHEEZE WHEEZE
CRIPES ...
SO YOU DID SAVE ME, MARIKA.
PANT PANT
PANT PANT
I WONDER IF I'D BE ABLE TO SAVE YOU, TOO.
PANT PANT
PANT
PANT
I HAVE TO GET A WHOLE LOT STRONGER FOR THAT, DON'T I?
PANT PANT

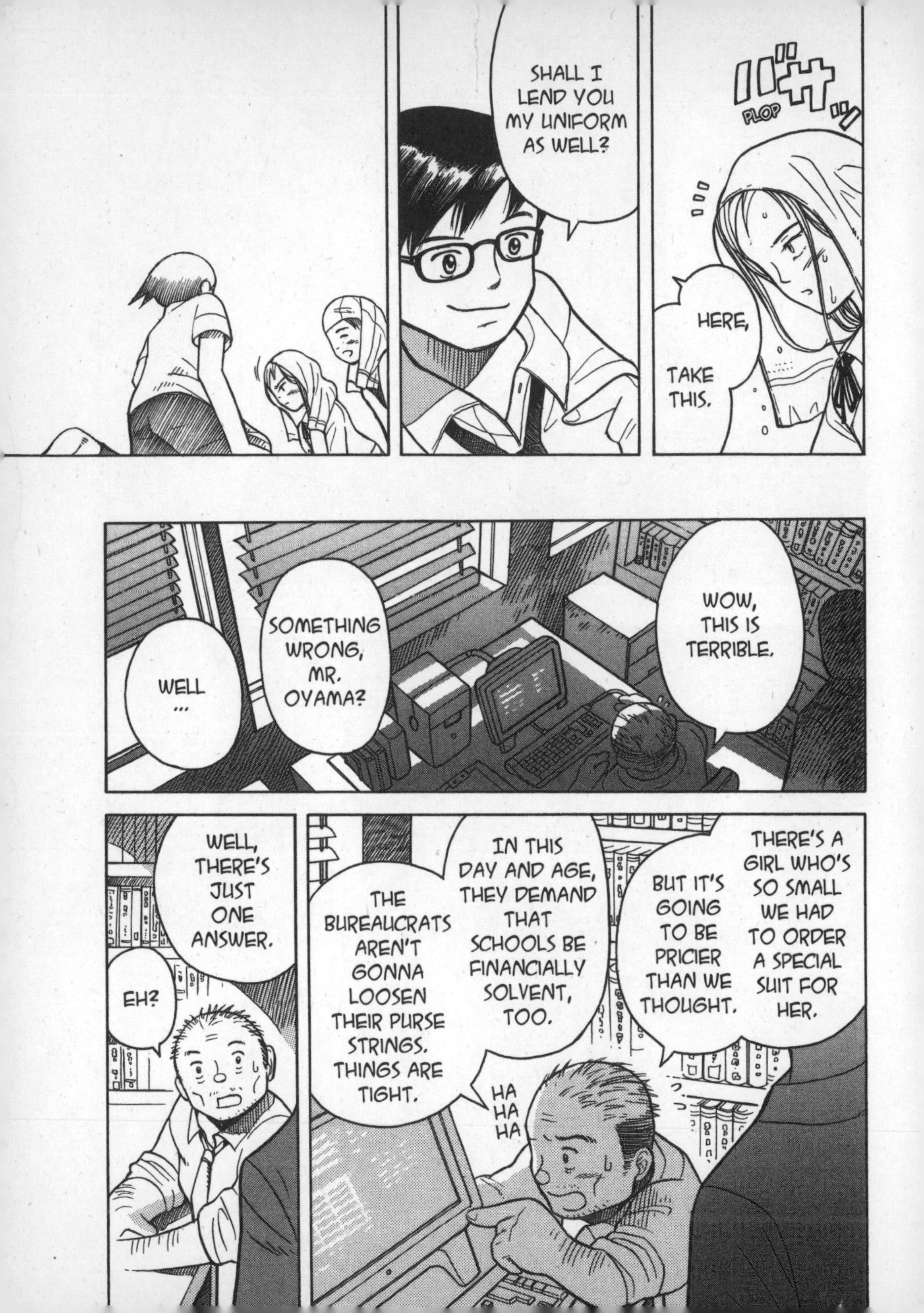
PLOP
HERE, TAKE THIS.
SHALL I LEND YOU MY UNIFORM AS WELL?
WOW, THIS IS TERRIBLE.
SOMETHING WRONG, MR. OYAMA?
WELL ...
THERE'S A GIRL WHO'S SO SMALL WE HAD TO ORDER A SPECIAL SUIT FOR HER.
BUT IT'S GOING TO BE PRICIER THAN WE THOUGHT.
IN THIS DAY AND AGE, THEY DEMAND THAT SCHOOLS BE FINANCIALLY SOLVENT, TOO.
THE BUREAUCRATS AREN'T GONNA LOOSEN THEIR PURSE STRINGS. THINGS ARE TIGHT.
HA HA HA
WELL, THERE'S JUST ONE ANSWER.
EH?

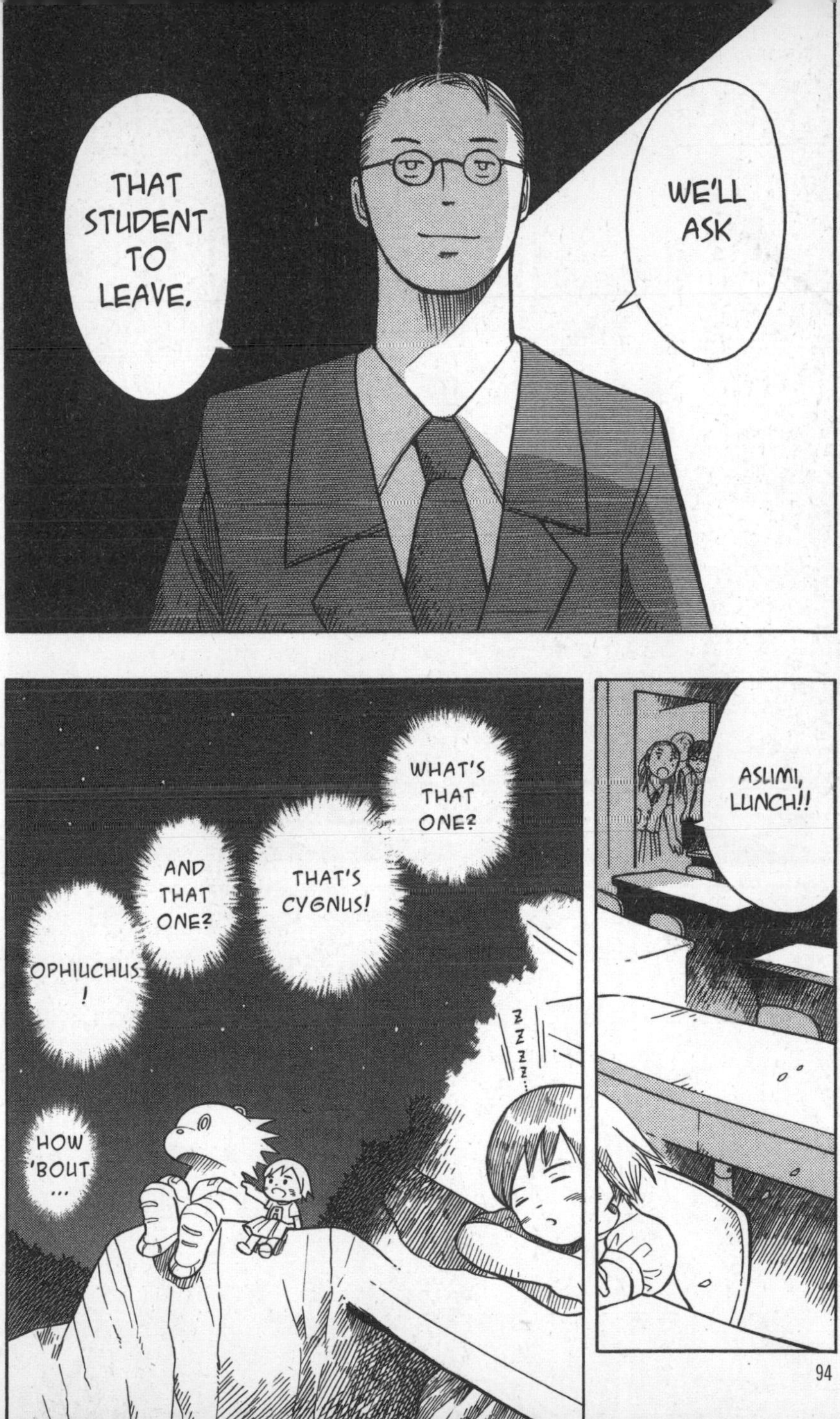
WE'LL ASK
THAT STUDENT TO LEAVE.
ASUMI, LUNCH!!
WHAT'S THAT ONE?
THAT'S CYGNUS!
AND THAT ONE?
OPHIUCHUS!
Z Z Z Z Z...
HOW 'BOUT...

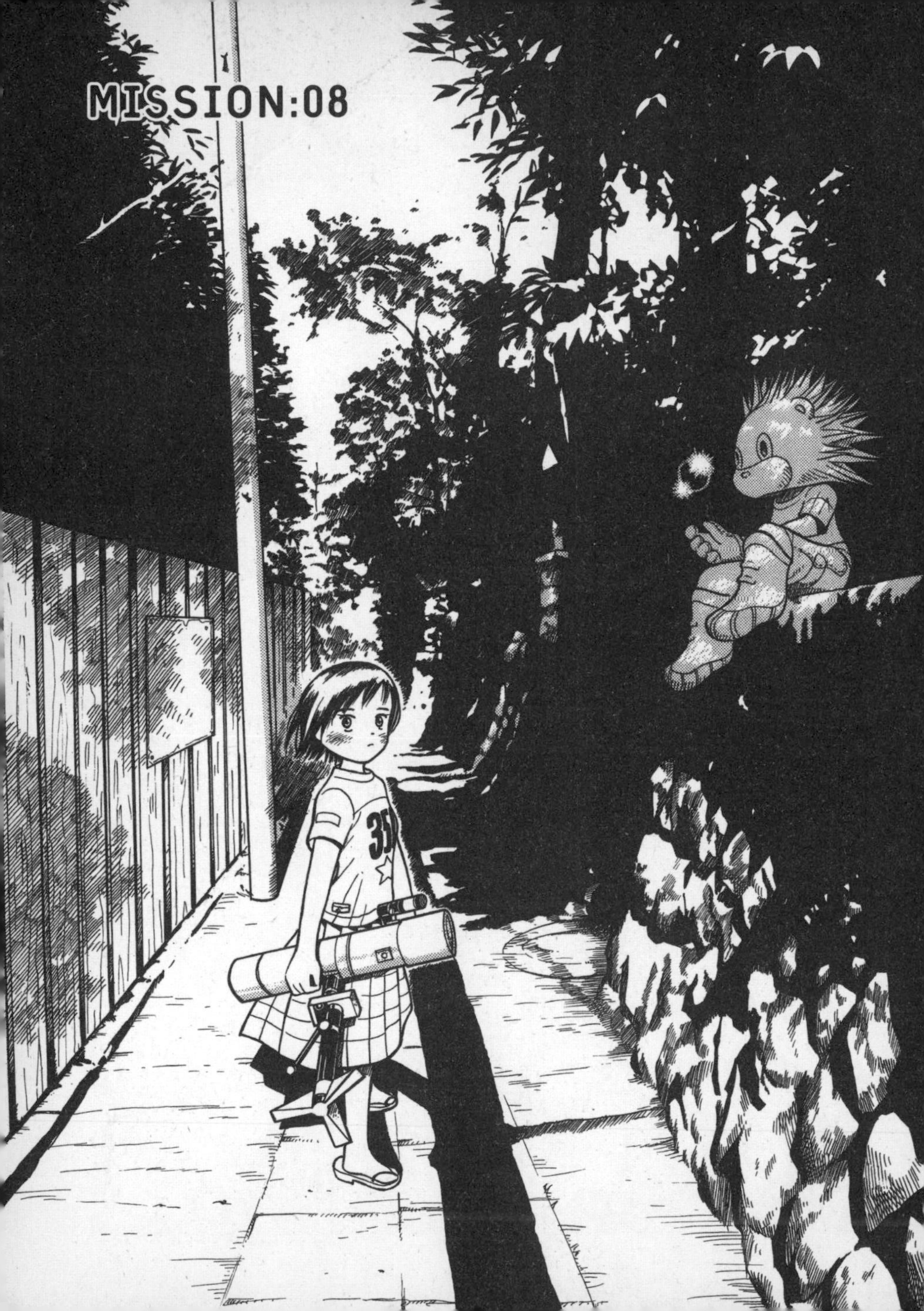
MISSION:08

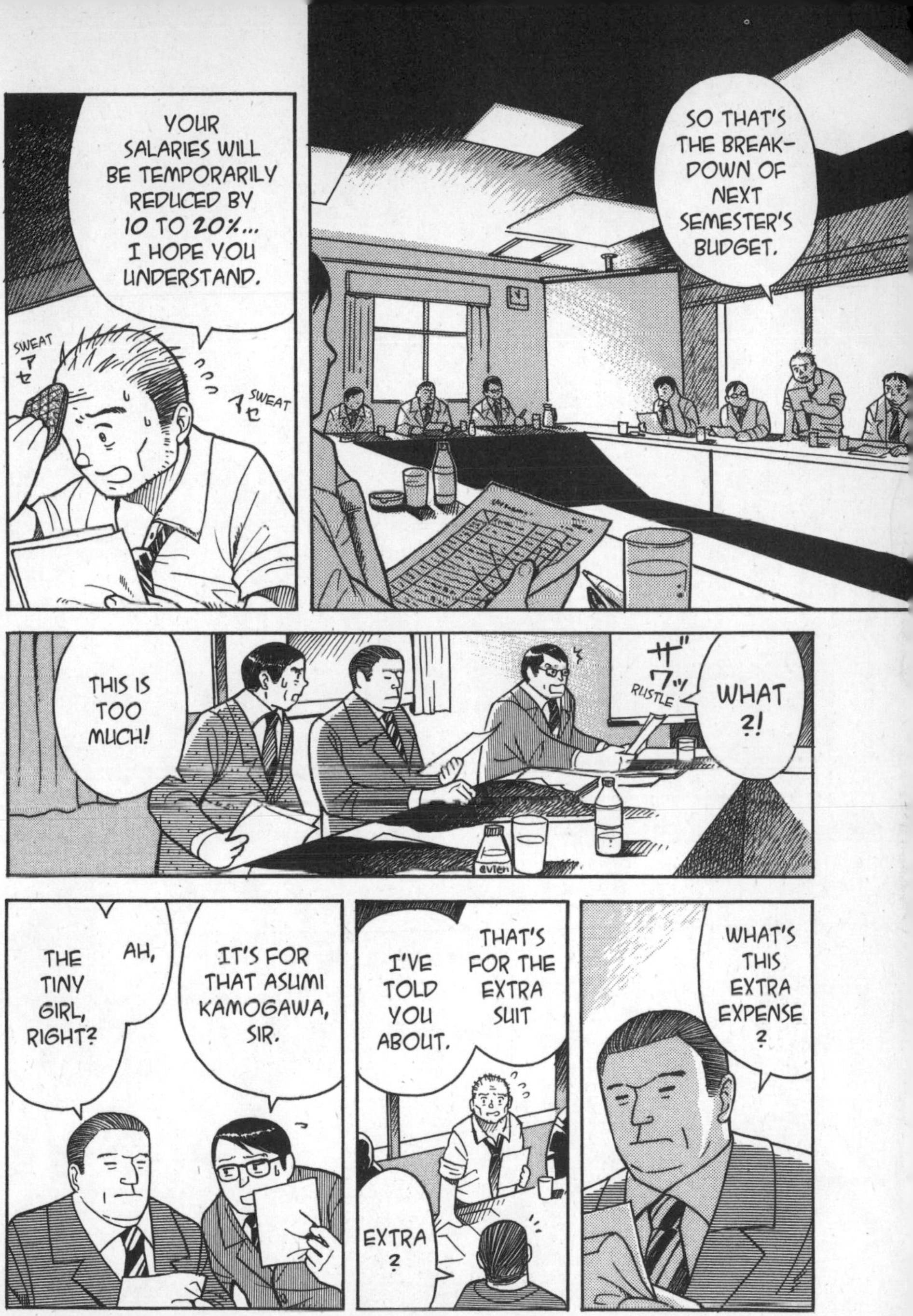
SO THAT'S THE BREAK-DOWN OF NEXT SEMESTER'S BUDGET.
YOUR SALARIES WILL BE TEMPORARILY REDUCED BY 10 TO 20%... I HOPE YOU UNDERSTAND.
SWEAT
SWEAT
WHAT?!
ザワッ
RUSTLE
THIS IS TOO MUCH!
WHAT'S THIS EXTRA EXPENSE?
THAT'S FOR THE EXTRA SUIT
I'VE TOLD YOU ABOUT.
EXTRA?
IT'S FOR THAT ASUMI KAMOGAWA, SIR.
AH,
THE TINY GIRL, RIGHT?

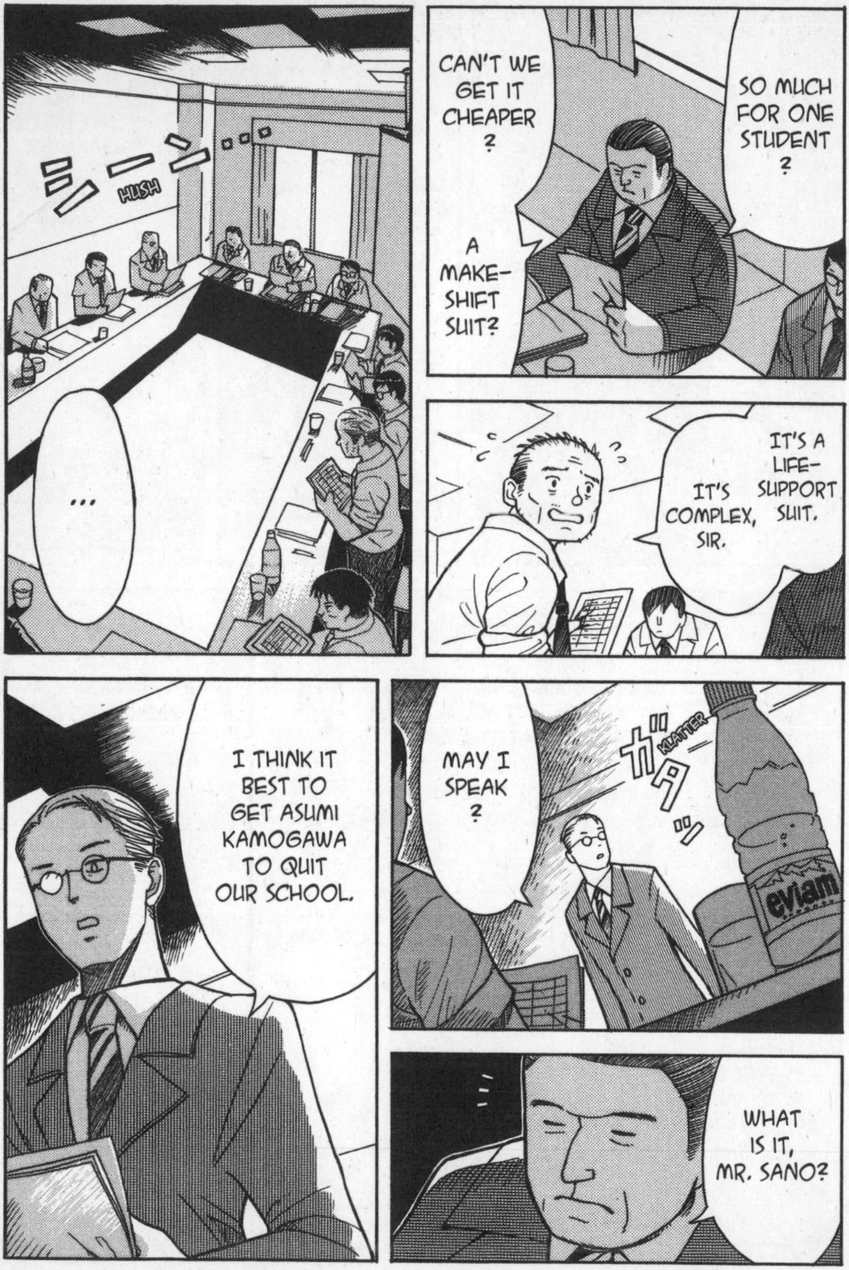
SO MUCH FOR ONE STUDENT?
CAN'T WE GET IT CHEAPER?
A MAKE-SHIFT SUIT?
IT'S A LIFE-SUPPORT SUIT.
IT'S COMPLEX, SIR.
HUSH
...
KLATTER
MAY I SPEAK?
WHAT IS IT, MR. SANO?
I THINK IT BEST TO GET ASUMI KAMOGAWA TO QUIT OUR SCHOOL.

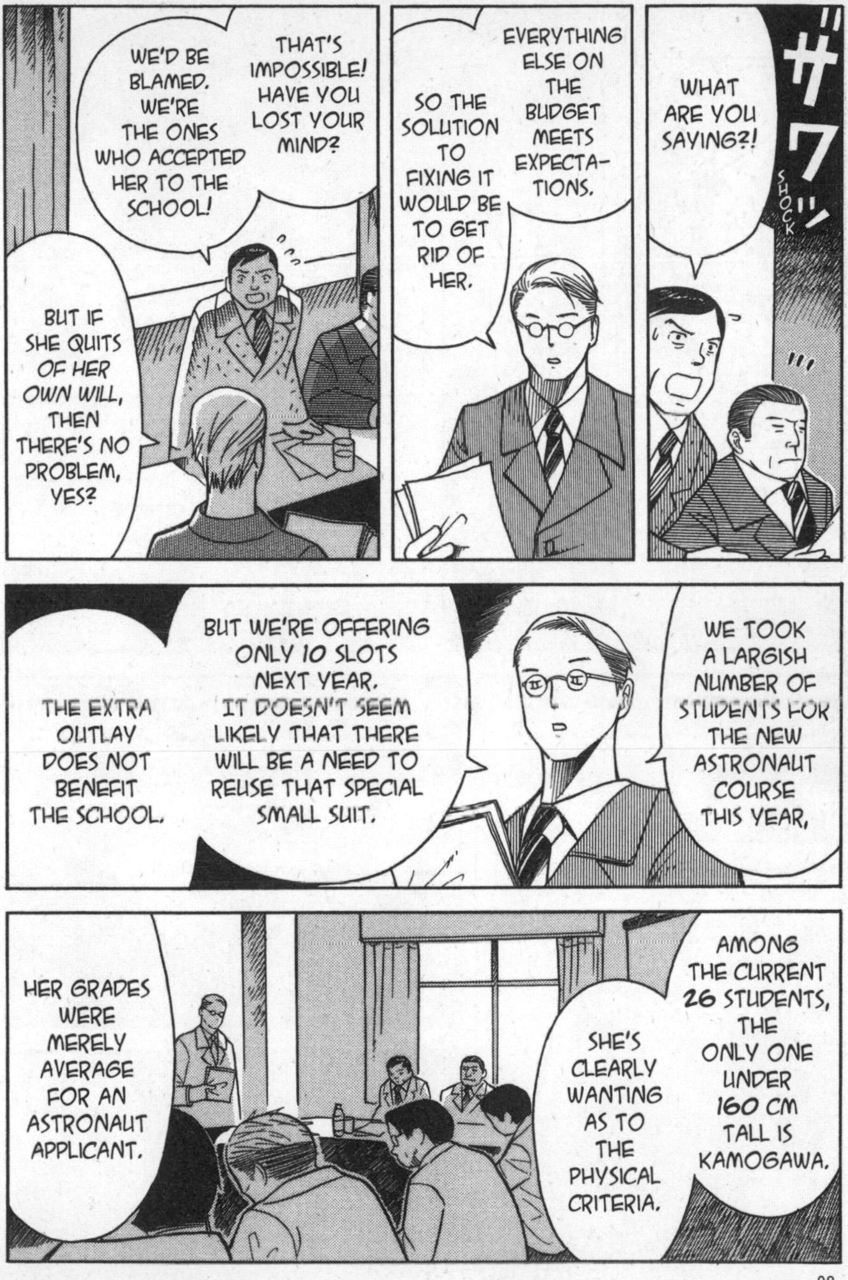

WHAT ARE YOU SAYING?!
ザワッ
SHOCK
EVERYTHING ELSE ON THE BUDGET MEETS EXPECTATIONS.
SO THE SOLUTION TO FIXING IT WOULD BE TO GET RID OF HER.
THAT'S IMPOSSIBLE! HAVE YOU LOST YOUR MIND?
WE'D BE BLAMED. WE'RE THE ONES WHO ACCEPTED HER TO THE SCHOOL!
BUT IF SHE QUITS OF HER OWN WILL, THEN THERE'S NO PROBLEM, YES?
WE TOOK A LARGISH NUMBER OF STUDENTS FOR THE NEW ASTRONAUT COURSE THIS YEAR,
BUT WE'RE OFFERING ONLY 10 SLOTS NEXT YEAR. IT DOESN'T SEEM LIKELY THAT THERE WILL BE A NEED TO REUSE THAT SPECIAL SMALL SUIT.
THE EXTRA OUTLAY DOES NOT BENEFIT THE SCHOOL.
AMONG THE CURRENT 26 STUDENTS, THE ONLY ONE UNDER 160 CM TALL IS KAMOGAWA.
SHE'S CLEARLY WANTING AS TO THE PHYSICAL CRITERIA.
HER GRADES WERE MERELY AVERAGE FOR AN ASTRONAUT APPLICANT.

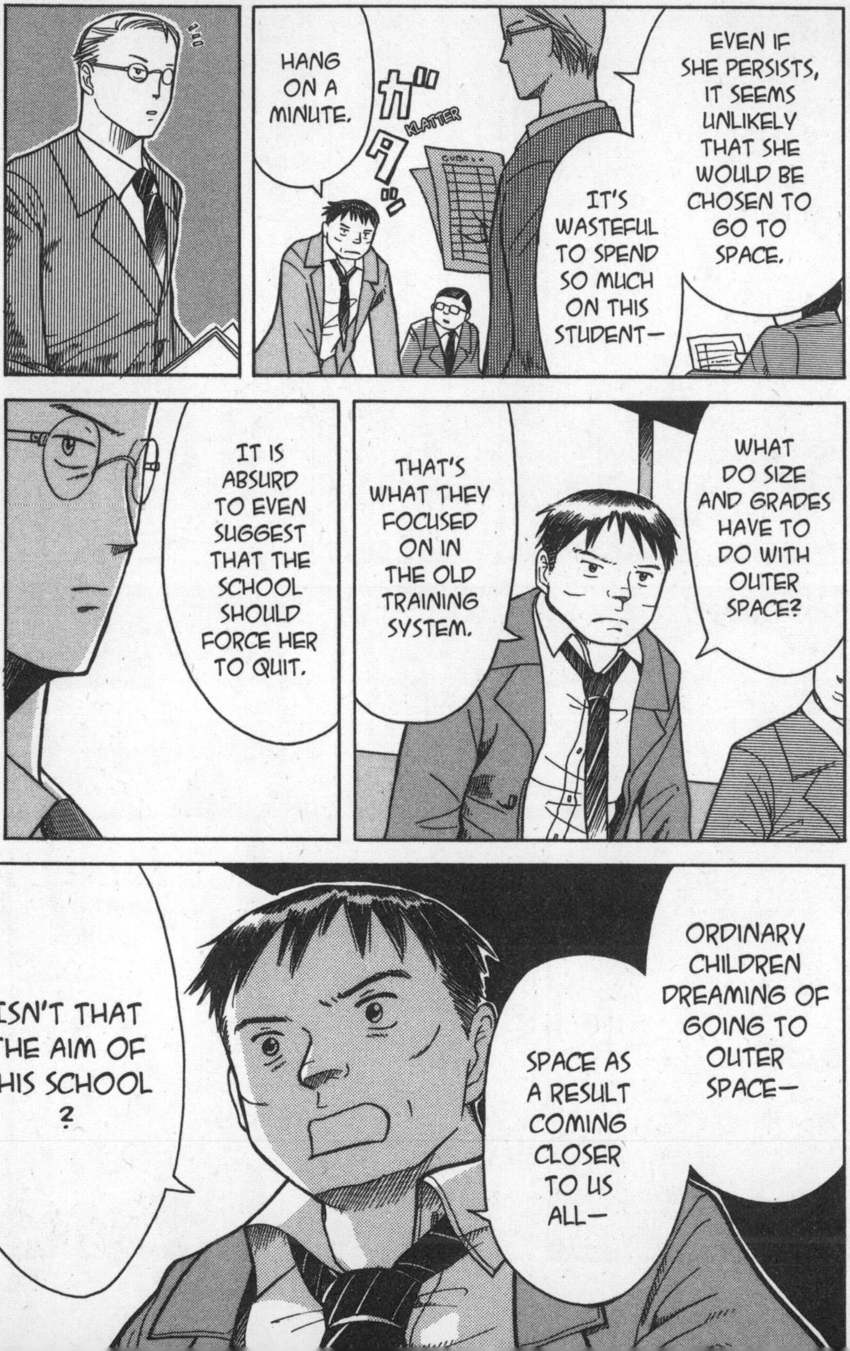
EVEN IF SHE PERSISTS, IT SEEMS UNLIKELY THAT SHE WOULD BE CHOSEN TO GO TO SPACE.
IT'S WASTEFUL TO SPEND SO MUCH ON THIS STUDENT—
ガタッ
KLATTER
HANG ON A MINUTE.
WHAT DO SIZE AND GRADES HAVE TO DO WITH OUTER SPACE?
THAT'S WHAT THEY FOCUSED ON IN THE OLD TRAINING SYSTEM.
IT IS ABSURD TO EVEN SUGGEST THAT THE SCHOOL SHOULD FORCE HER TO QUIT.
ORDINARY CHILDREN DREAMING OF GOING TO OUTER SPACE—
SPACE AS A RESULT COMING CLOSER TO US ALL—
ISN'T THAT THE AIM OF THIS SCHOOL?

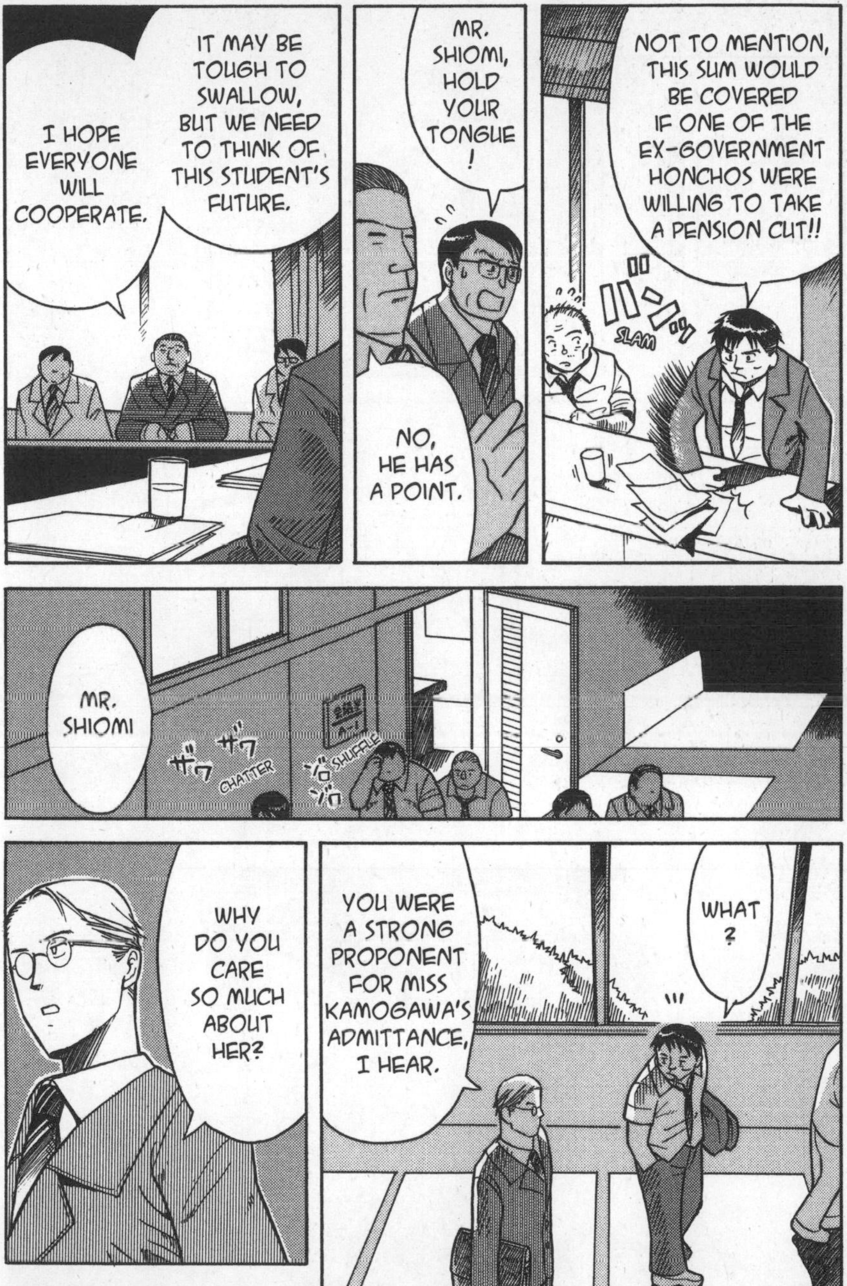
NOT TO MENTION, THIS SUM WOULD BE COVERED IF ONE OF THE EX-GOVERNMENT HONCHOS WERE WILLING TO TAKE A PENSION CUT!!
SLAM
MR. SHIOMI, HOLD YOUR TONGUE!
NO, HE HAS A POINT.
IT MAY BE TOUGH TO SWALLOW, BUT WE NEED TO THINK OF THIS STUDENT'S FUTURE.
I HOPE EVERYONE WILL COOPERATE.
SHUFFLE
CHATTER
MR. SHIOMI
WHAT?
YOU WERE A STRONG PROPONENT FOR MISS KAMOGAWA'S ADMITTANCE, I HEAR.
WHY DO YOU CARE SO MUCH ABOUT HER?

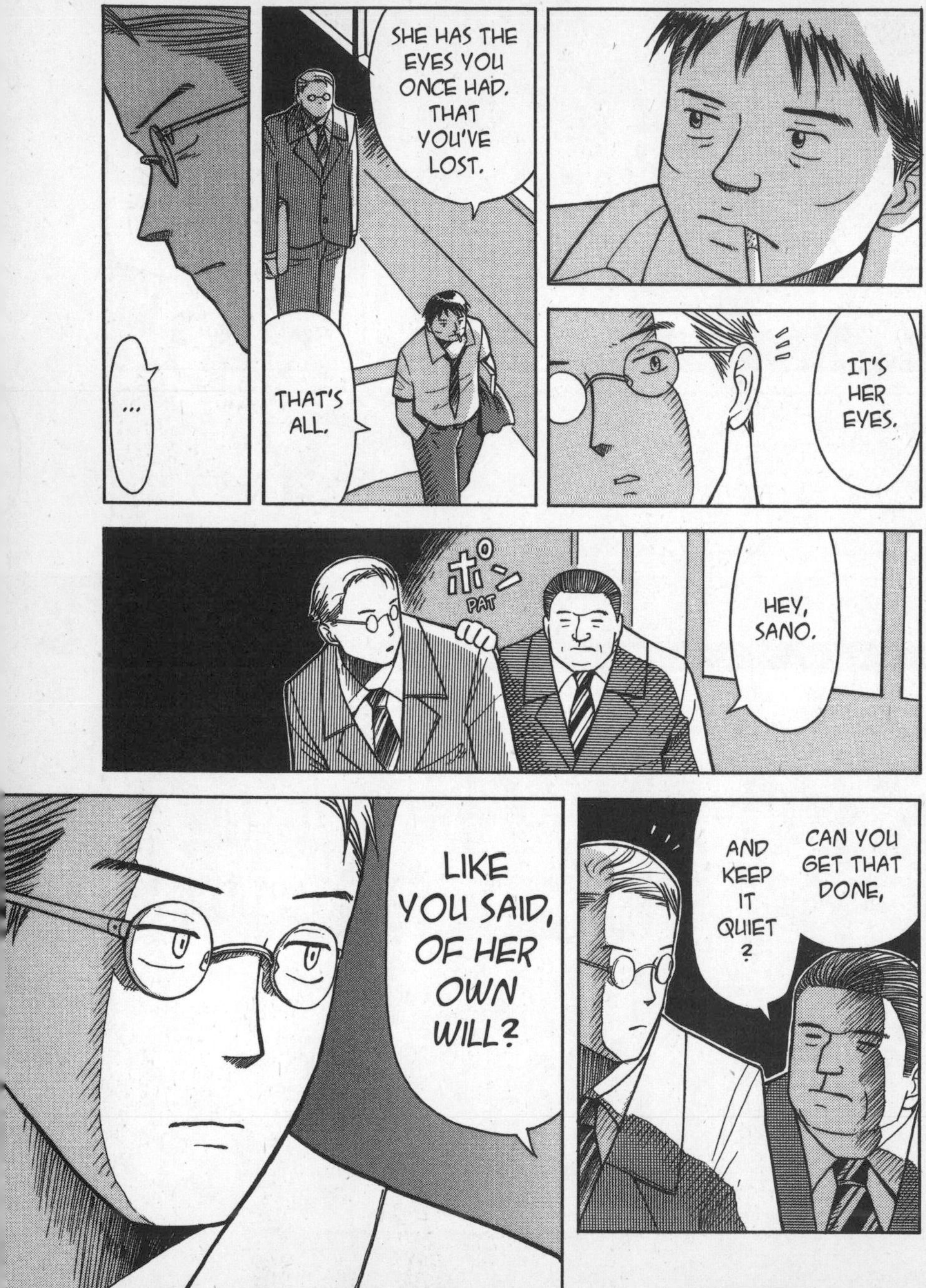
IT'S HER EYES.
SHE HAS THE EYES YOU ONCE HAD. THAT YOU'VE LOST.
THAT'S ALL.
...
HEY, SANO.
ポン
PAT
CAN YOU GET THAT DONE,
AND KEEP IT QUIET?
LIKE YOU SAID, OF HER OWN WILL?

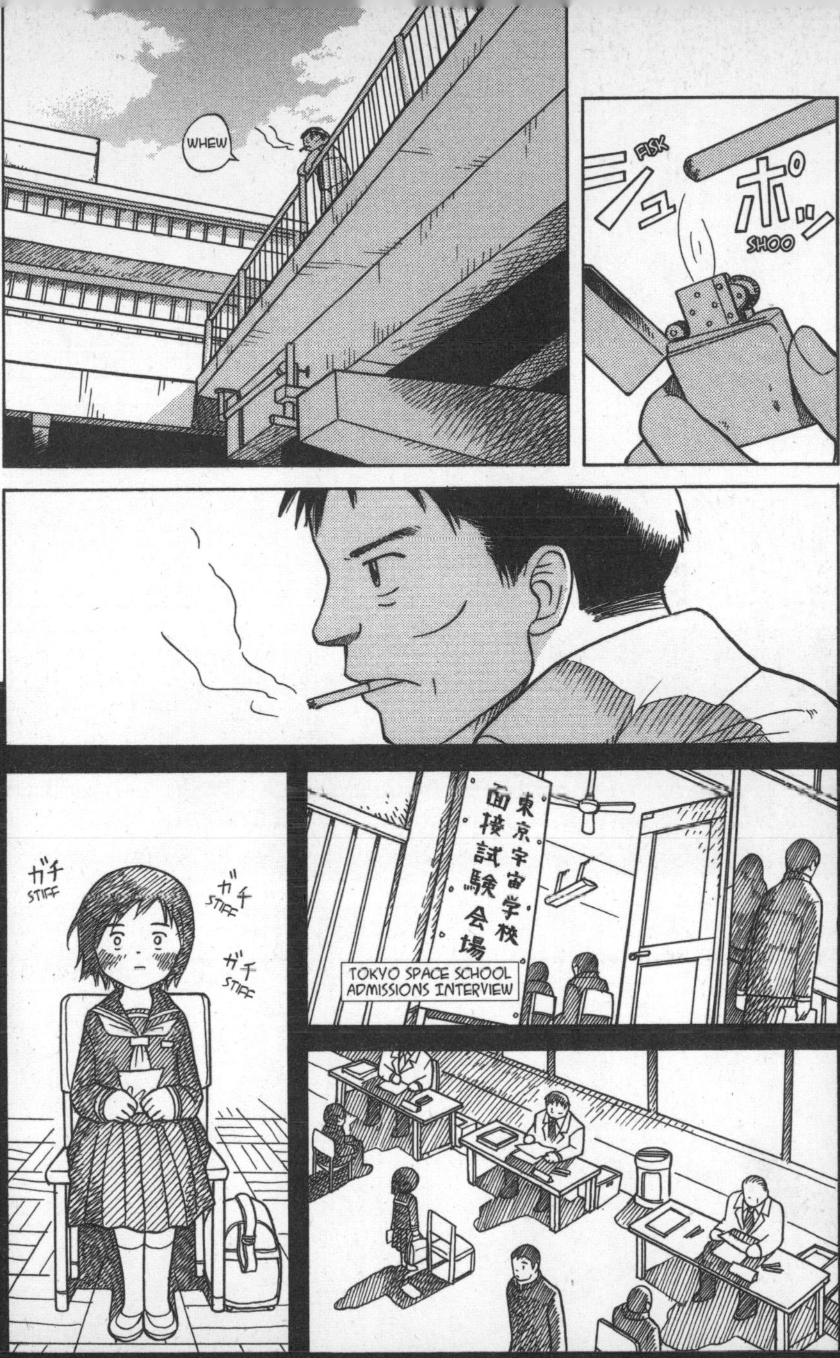

シュ
FSK
ポッ
SHOO
WHEW
東京宇宙学校面接試験会場
TOKYO SPACE SCHOOL ADMISSIONS INTERVIEW
ガチ
STIFF
ガチ
STIFF
ガチ
STIFF

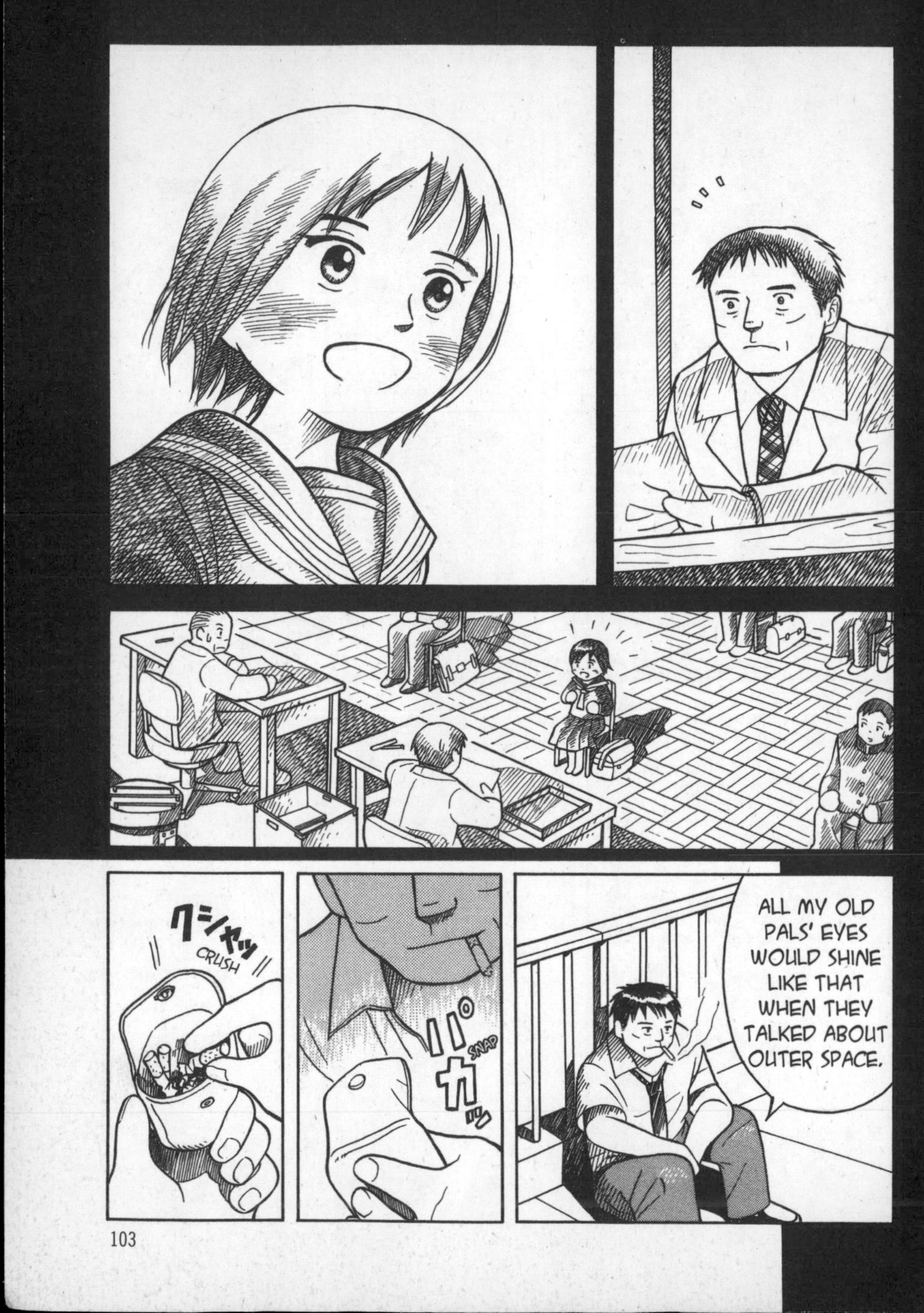
ALL MY OLD PALS' EYES WOULD SHINE LIKE THAT WHEN THEY TALKED ABOUT OUTER SPACE.
パカッ
SNAP
クシャッ
CRUSH

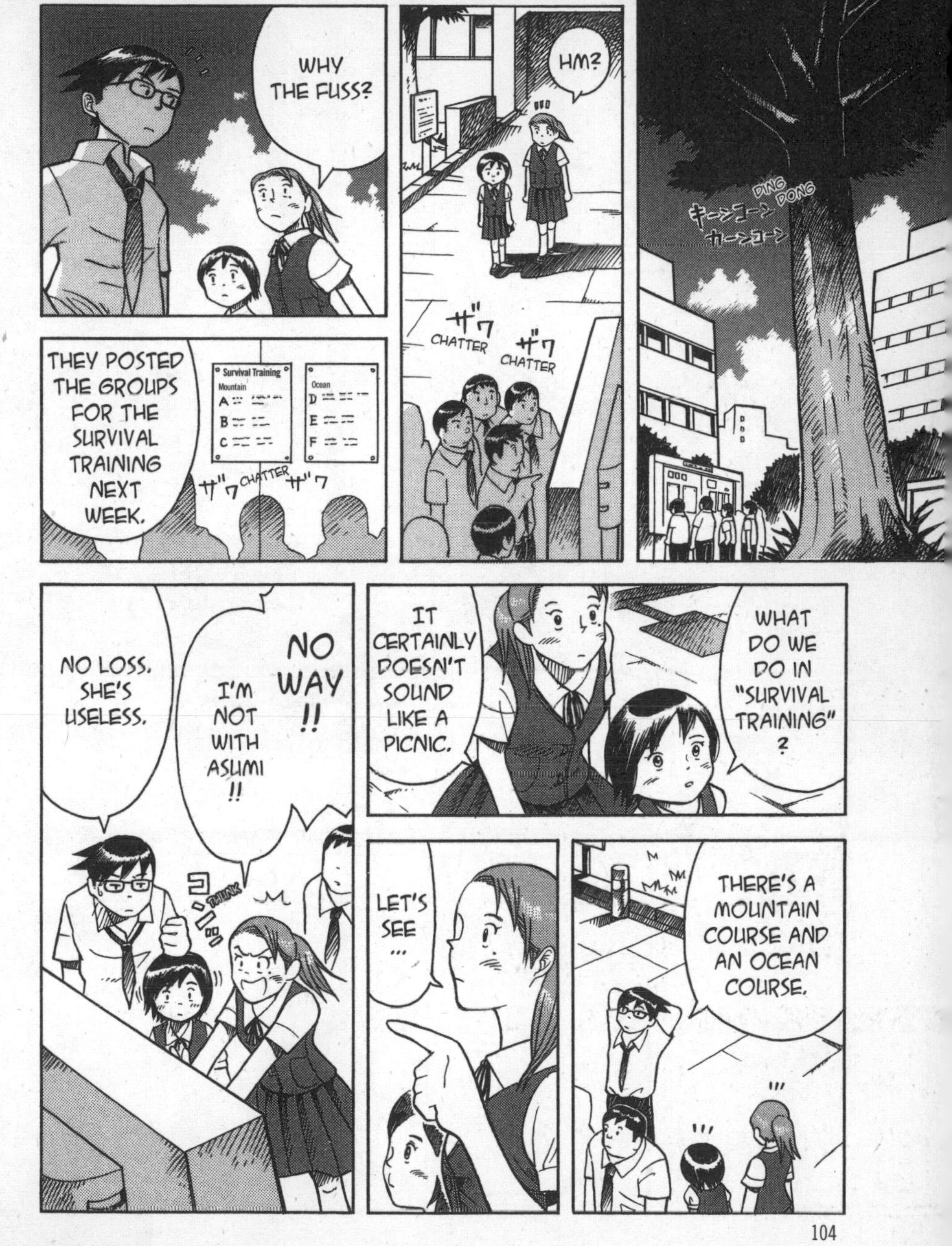

キーンコーン
カーンコーン
DING DONG
HM?
ザワ CHATTER
ザワ CHATTER
WHY THE FUSS?
THEY POSTED THE GROUPS FOR THE SURVIVAL TRAINING NEXT WEEK.
Survival Training
Mountain
A
B
C
Ocean
D
E
F
ザワ CHATTER ザワ
WHAT DO WE DO IN "SURVIVAL TRAINING"?
IT CERTAINLY DOESN'T SOUND LIKE A PICNIC.
THERE'S A MOUNTAIN COURSE AND AN OCEAN COURSE.
LET'S SEE...
NO WAY!!
I'M NOT WITH ASUMI!!
NO LOSS. SHE'S USELESS.
THUNK

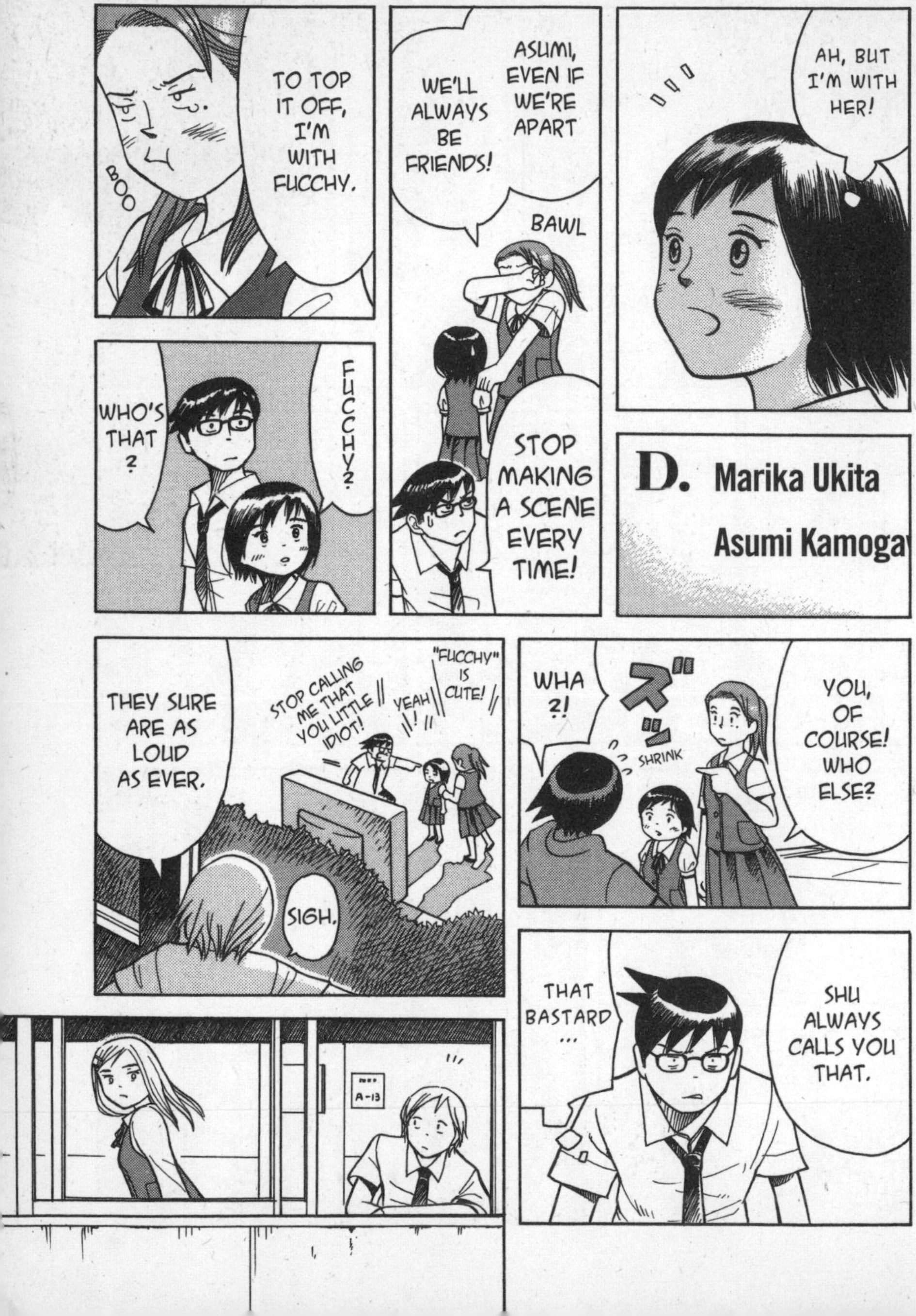
AH, BUT I'M WITH HER!
ASUMI, EVEN IF WE'RE APART
WE'LL ALWAYS BE FRIENDS!
BAWL
TO TOP IT OFF, I'M WITH FUCCHY.
BOO
D. Marika Ukita
Asumi Kamoga
STOP MAKING A SCENE EVERY TIME!
FUCCHY?
WHO'S THAT?
YOU, OF COURSE! WHO ELSE?
SHRINK
WHA?!
"FUCCHY" IS CUTE!
YEAH!
STOP CALLING ME THAT YOU LITTLE IDIOT!
THEY SURE ARE AS LOUD AS EVER.
SIGH.
SHU ALWAYS CALLS YOU THAT.
THAT BASTARD...
A-13

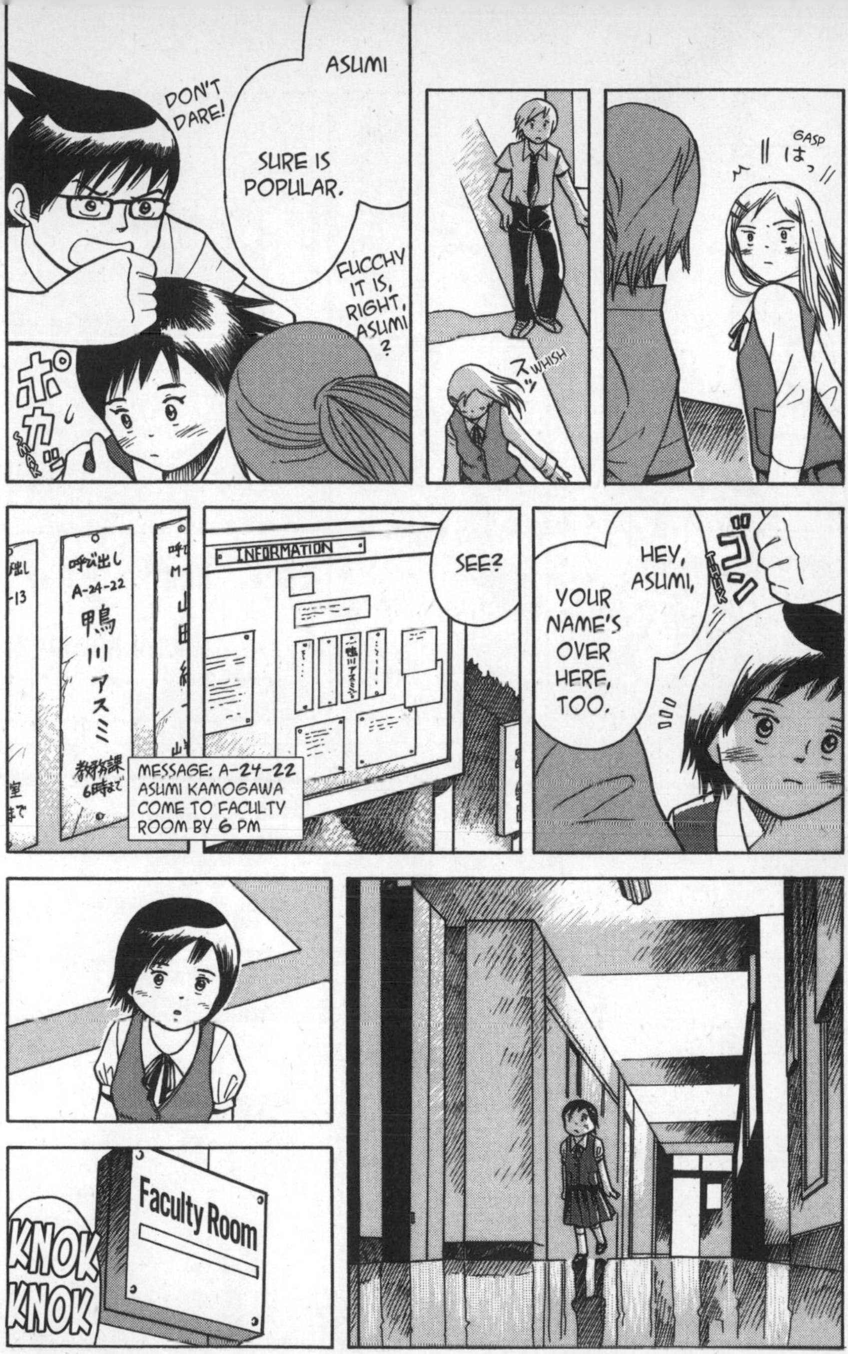
GASP
はっ
スッ
WHISH
ASUMI
SURE IS POPULAR.
DON'T DARE!
FUCCHY IT IS, RIGHT, ASUMI?
ポカッ
SMACK
ゴン
THUNK
HEY, ASUMI,
YOUR NAME'S OVER HERE, TOO.
SEE?
INFORMATION
MESSAGE: A-24-22
ASUMI KAMOGAWA
COME TO FACULTY
ROOM BY 6 PM
Faculty Room
KNOK KNOK

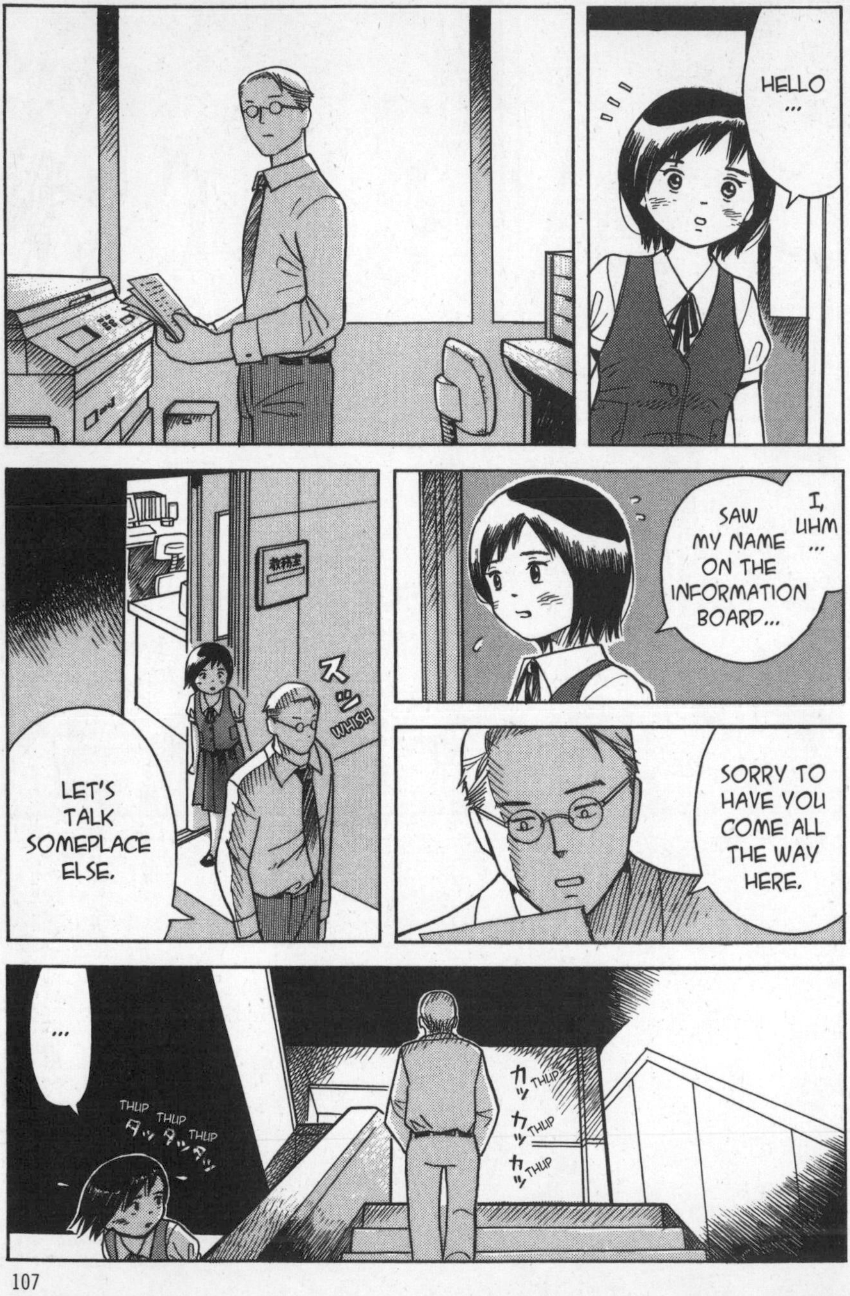
HELLO …
I, UHM …
SAW MY NAME ON THE INFORMATION BOARD…
SORRY TO HAVE YOU COME ALL THE WAY HERE.
LET'S TALK SOMEPLACE ELSE.
スッ WHISH
…
カッ THUP
カッ THUP
カッ THUP
タッ タッ タッ THUP THUP THUP

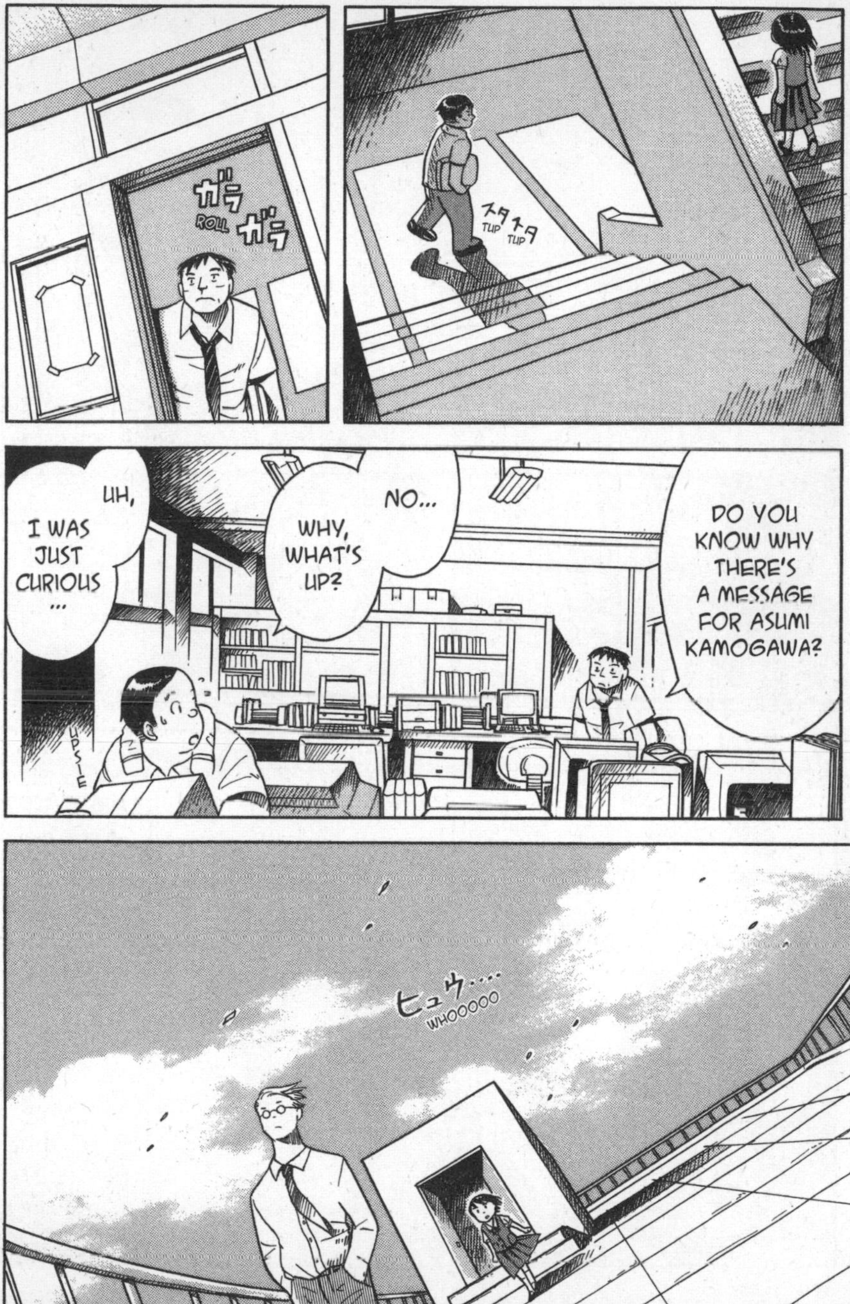
スタスタ
TUP TUP
ガラガラ
ROLL
DO YOU KNOW WHY THERE'S A MESSAGE FOR ASUMI KAMOGAWA?
NO...
WHY, WHAT'S UP?
UH, I WAS JUST CURIOUS ...
UPSIE
ヒュウ....
WHOOOOO

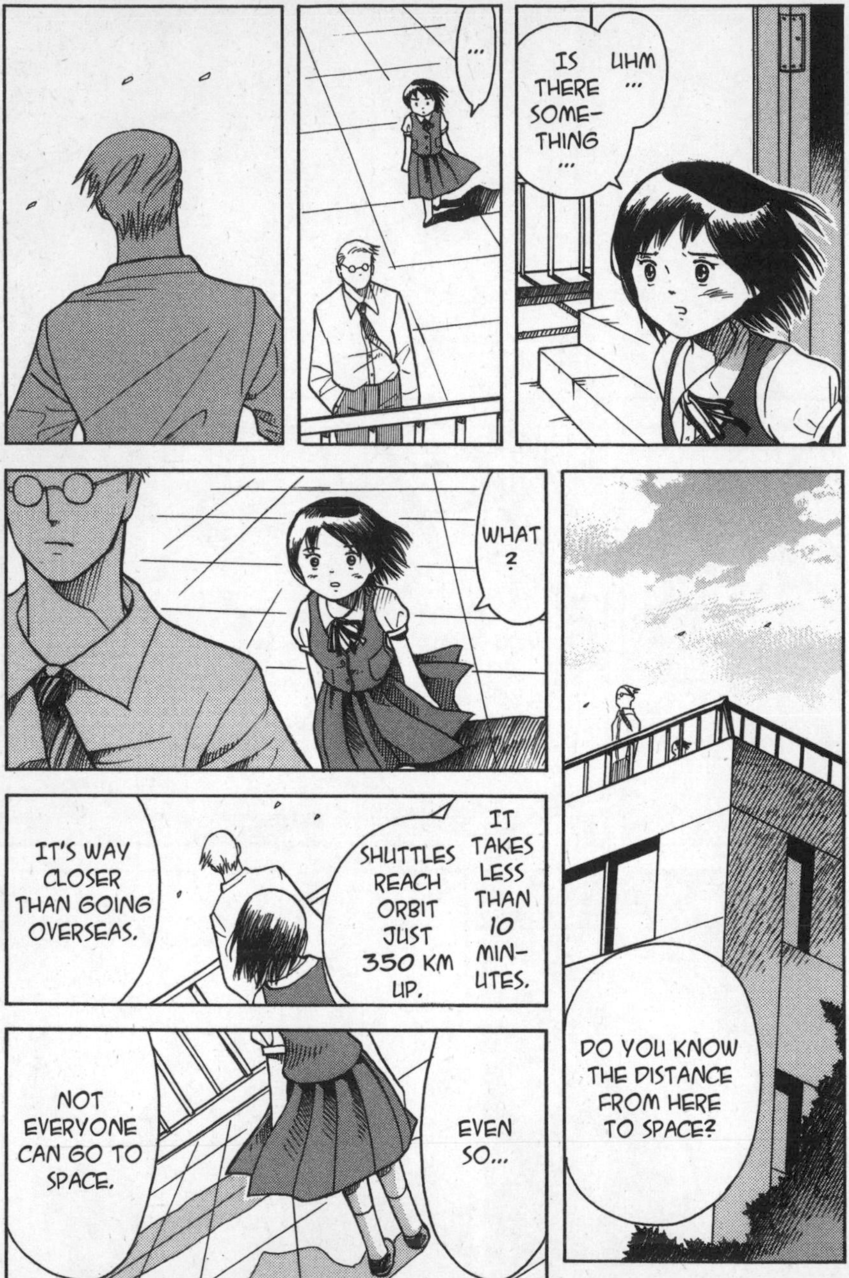
UHM ...
IS THERE SOMETHING ...
...
DO YOU KNOW THE DISTANCE FROM HERE TO SPACE?
WHAT?
IT TAKES LESS THAN 10 MINUTES.
SHUTTLES REACH ORBIT JUST 350 KM UP.
IT'S WAY CLOSER THAN GOING OVERSEAS.
EVEN SO...
NOT EVERYONE CAN GO TO SPACE.

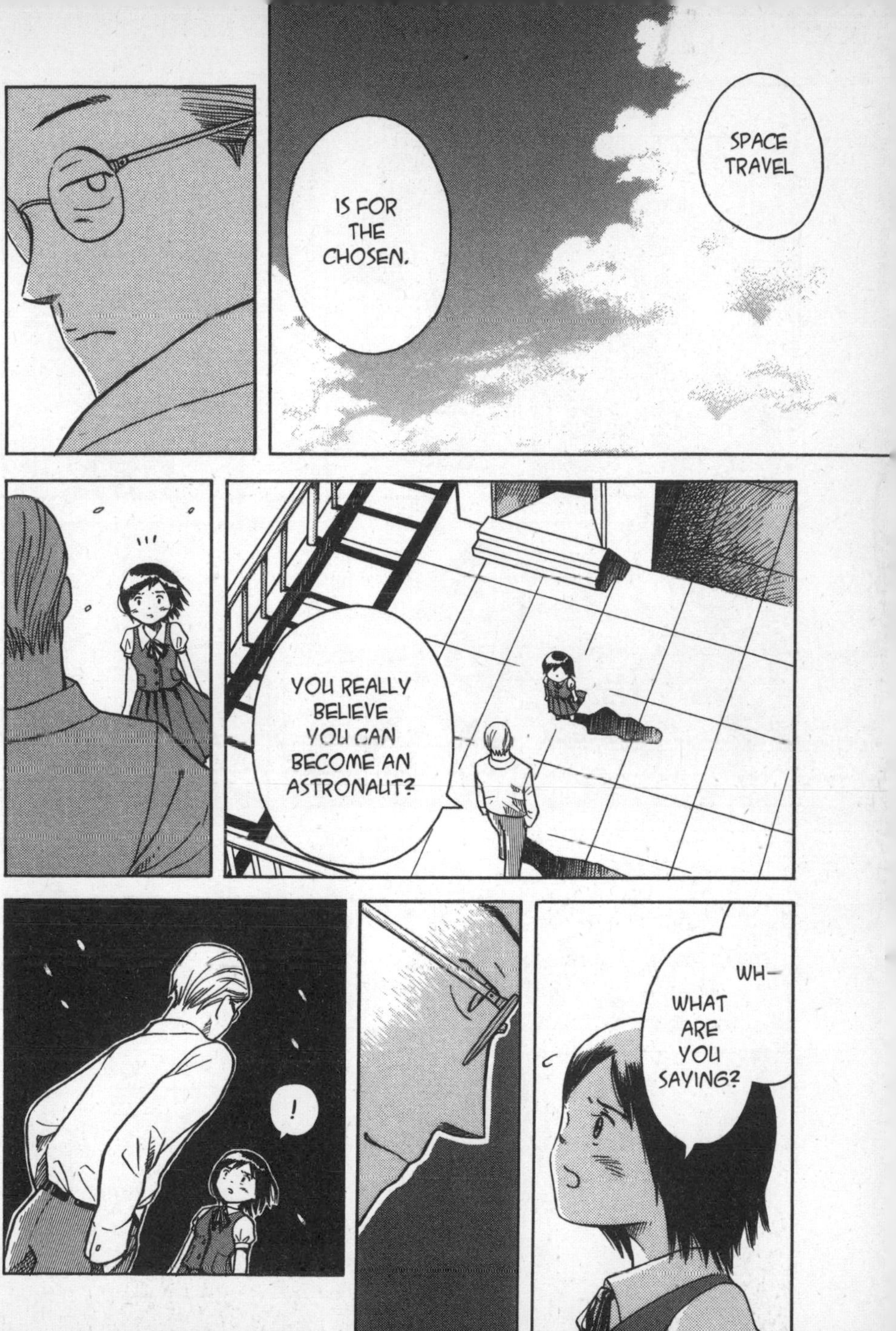
SPACE TRAVEL
IS FOR THE CHOSEN.
YOU REALLY BELIEVE YOU CAN BECOME AN ASTRONAUT?
WH— WHAT ARE YOU SAYING?
!

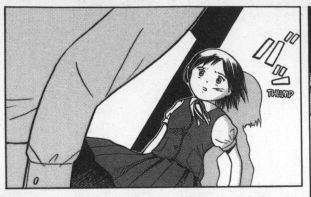

THUMP

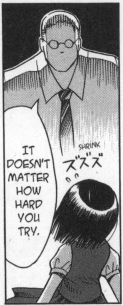

SHRINK
ズズズ

IT DOESN'T MATTER HOW HARD YOU TRY.

THERE IS NO WAY YOU WILL BE CHOSEN TO BECOME AN ASTRONAUT.

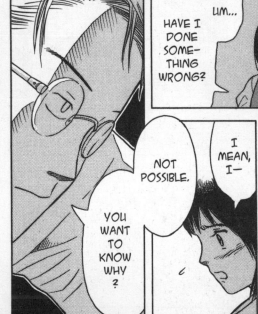

UM...

HAVE I DONE SOMETHING WRONG?

W— WHY ARE YOU SAYING THIS?

NOT POSSIBLE.

YOU WANT TO KNOW WHY?

I MEAN, I—

"FIX IT"? HOW?

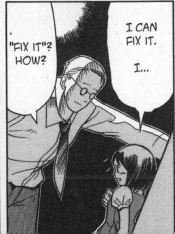

I CAN FIX IT.

I...

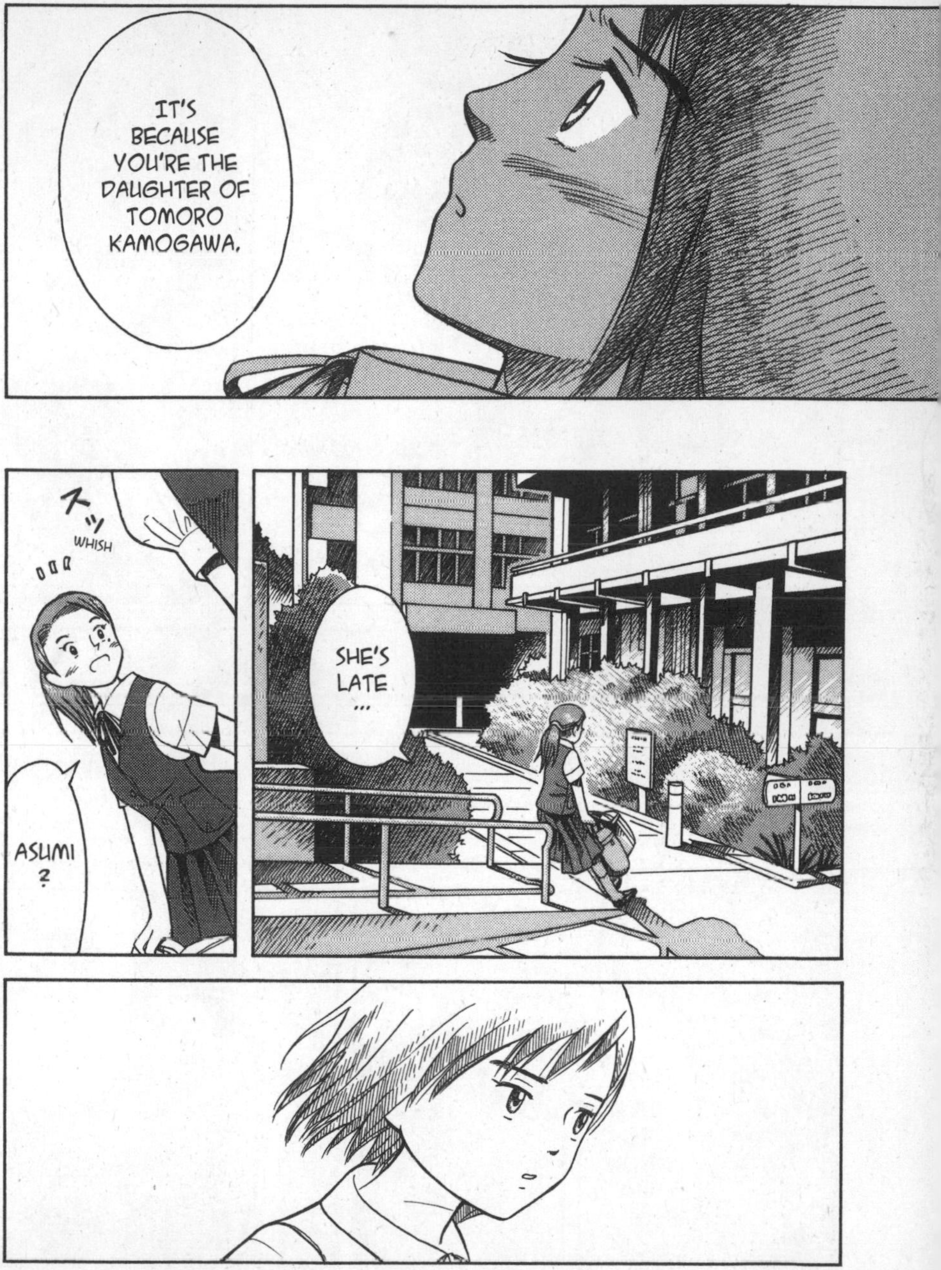
IT'S BECAUSE YOU'RE THE DAUGHTER OF TOMORO KAMOGAWA.
SHE'S LATE ...
スッ
WHISH
ASUMI ?

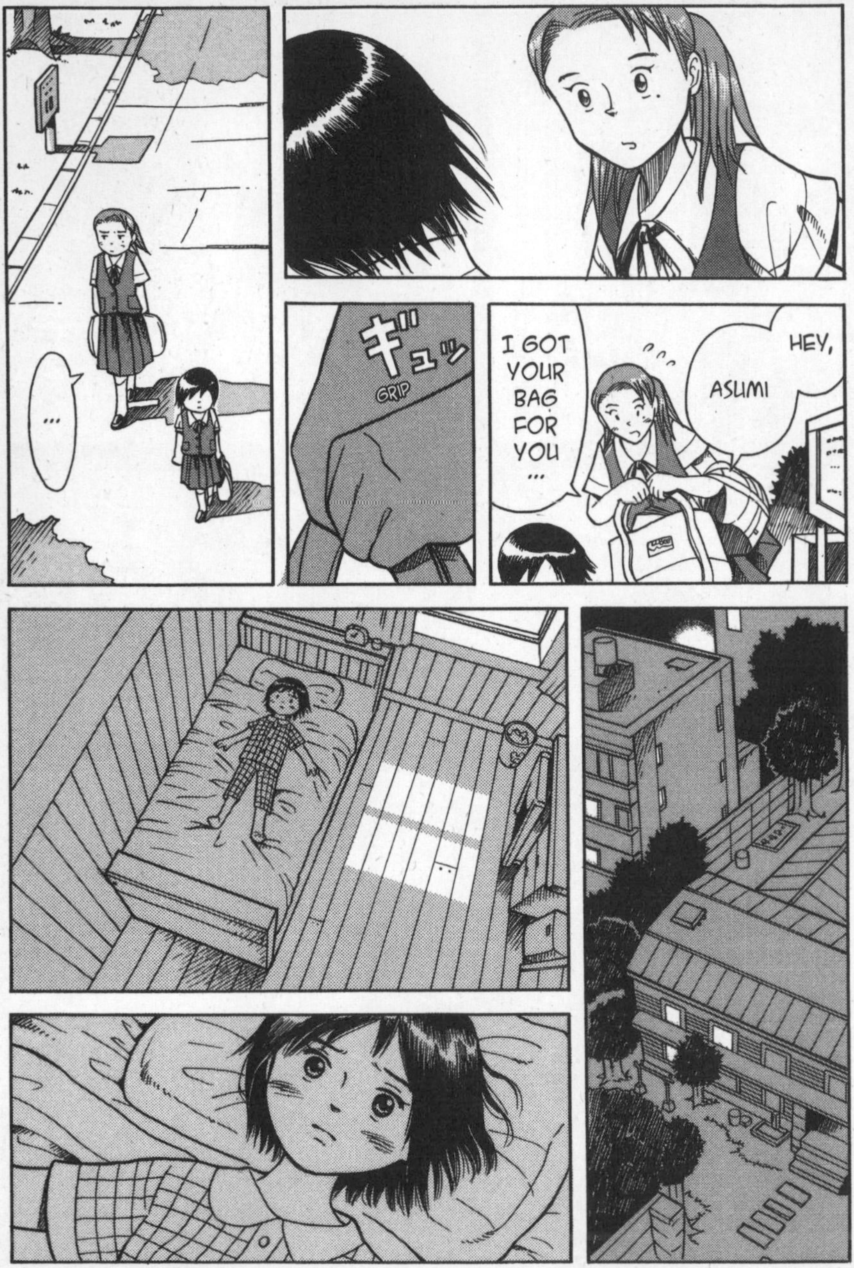
HEY, ASUMI
I GOT YOUR BAG FOR YOU ...
ギュッ
GRIP
...

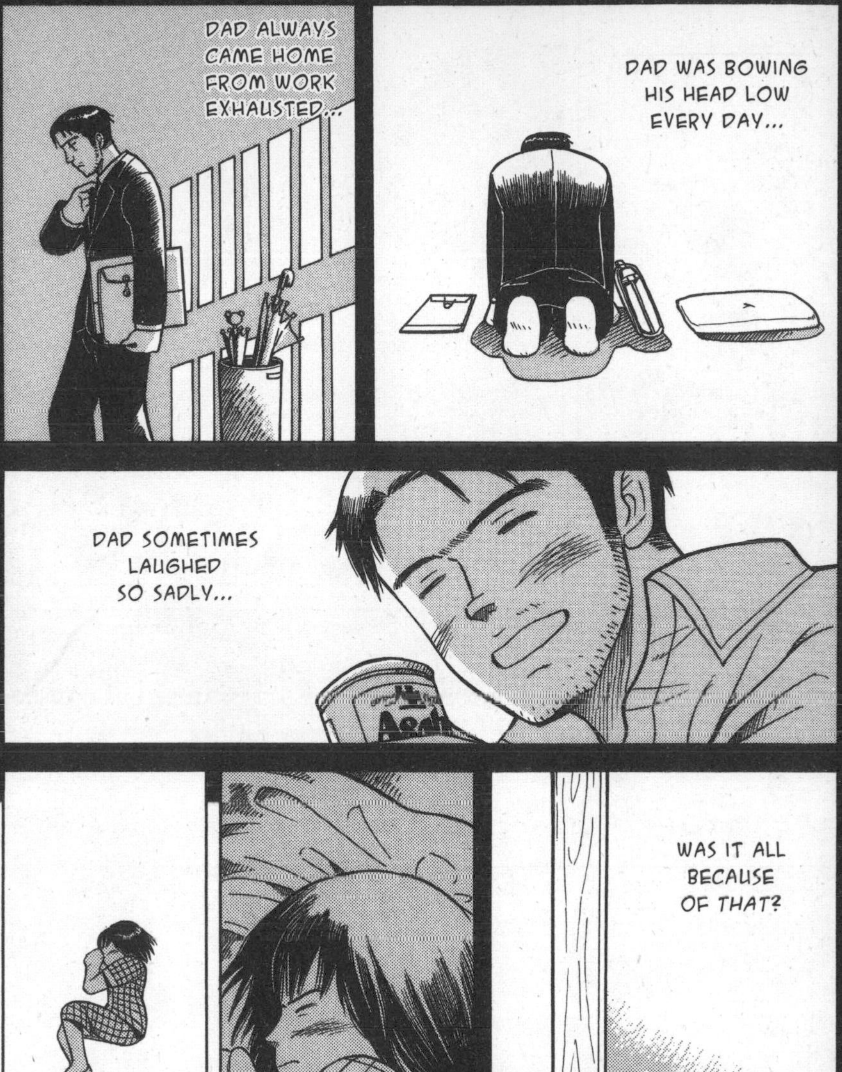
DAD WAS BOWING HIS HEAD LOW EVERY DAY...
DAD ALWAYS CAME HOME FROM WORK EXHAUSTED...
DAD SOMETIMES LAUGHED SO SADLY...
WAS IT ALL BECAUSE OF THAT?

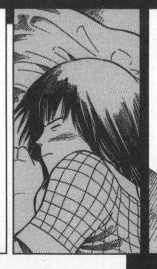

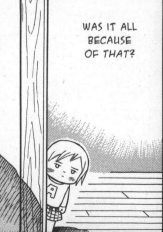

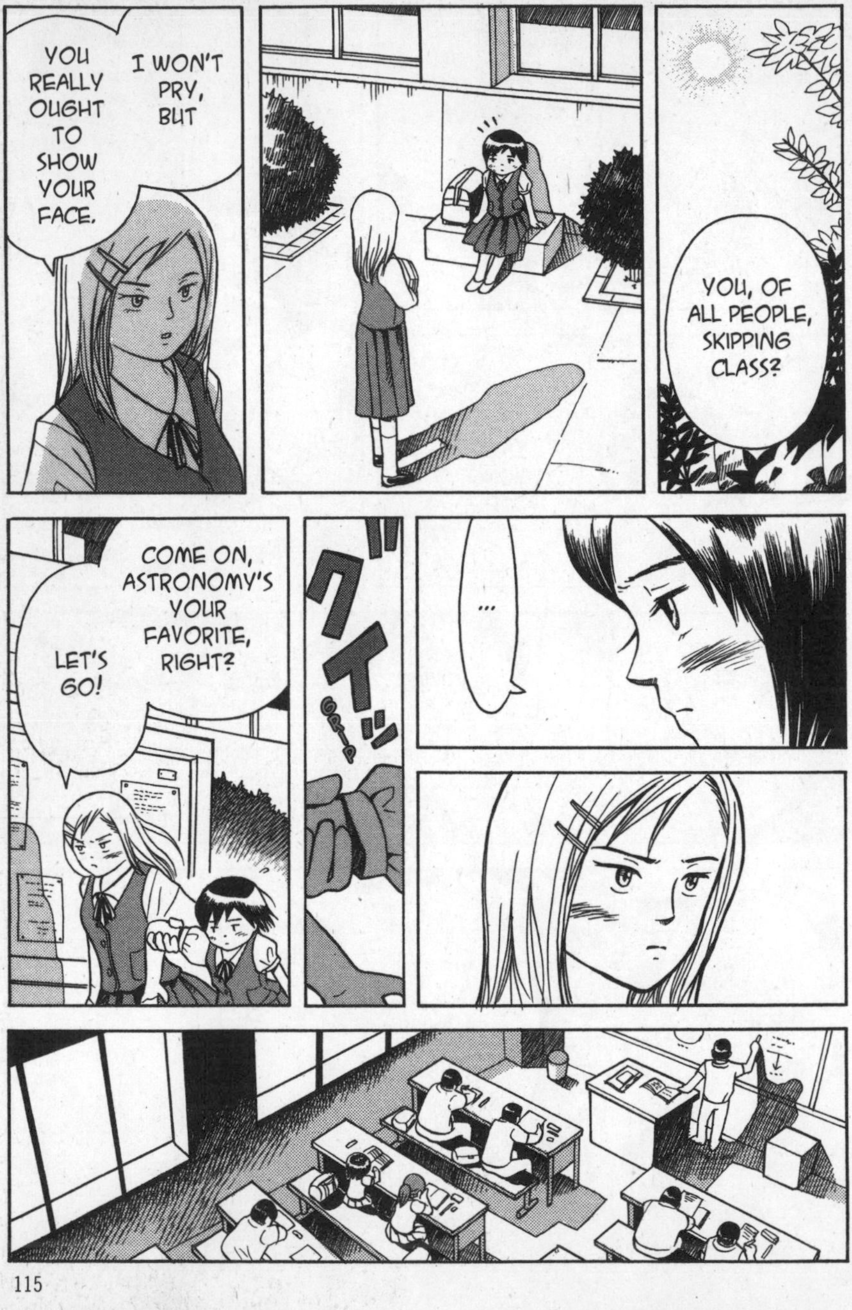
YOU, OF ALL PEOPLE, SKIPPING CLASS?
I WON'T PRY, BUT
YOU REALLY OUGHT TO SHOW YOUR FACE.
...
クイッ
GRIP
COME ON, ASTRONOMY'S YOUR FAVORITE, RIGHT?
LET'S GO!

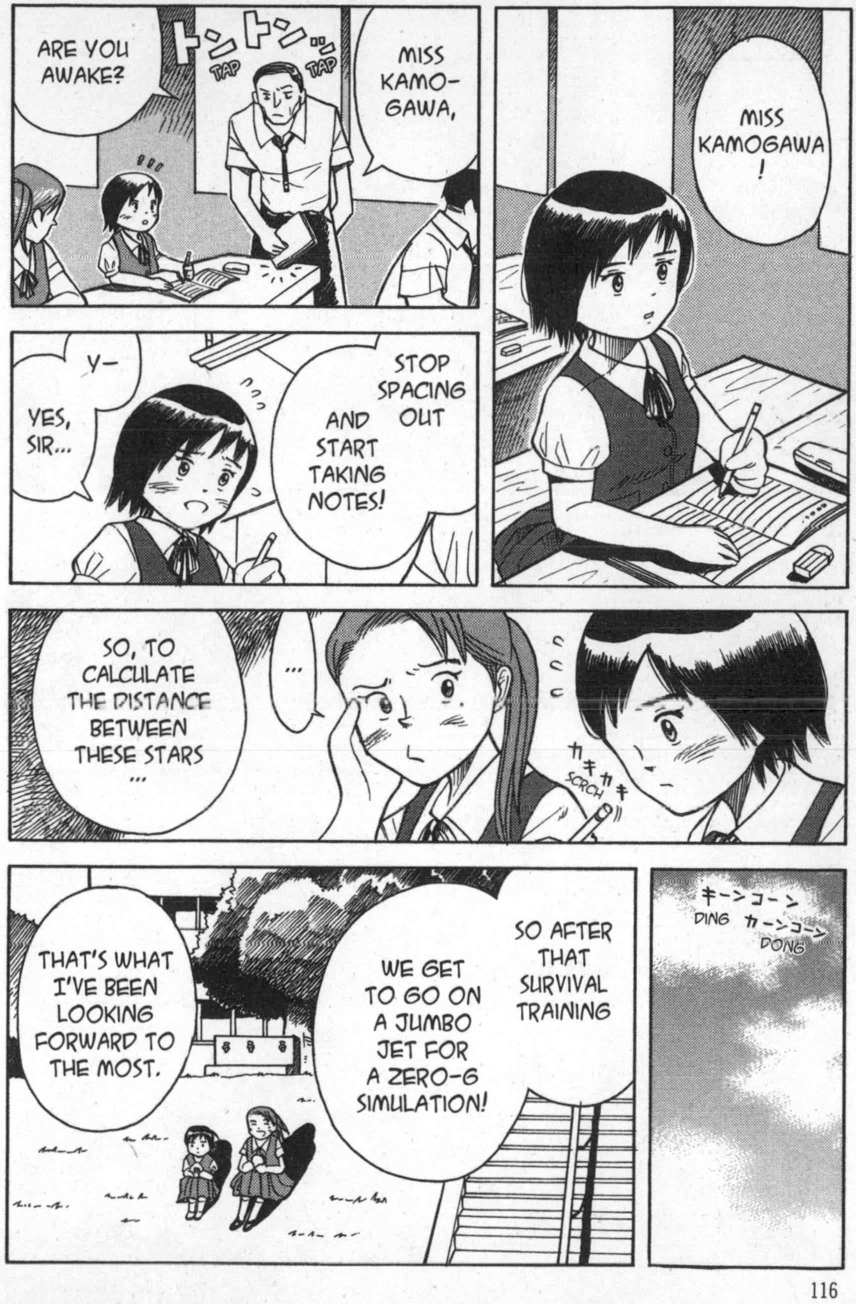
MISS KAMOGAWA!
MISS KAMO-GAWA,
トントン
TAP TAP
ARE YOU AWAKE?
STOP SPACING OUT AND START TAKING NOTES!
Y— YES, SIR...
カキカキ
SCRCH
...
SO, TO CALCULATE THE DISTANCE BETWEEN THESE STARS ...
キーンコーン
DING
カーンコーン
DONG
SO AFTER THAT SURVIVAL TRAINING
WE GET TO GO ON A JUMBO JET FOR A ZERO-G SIMULATION!
THAT'S WHAT I'VE BEEN LOOKING FORWARD TO THE MOST.

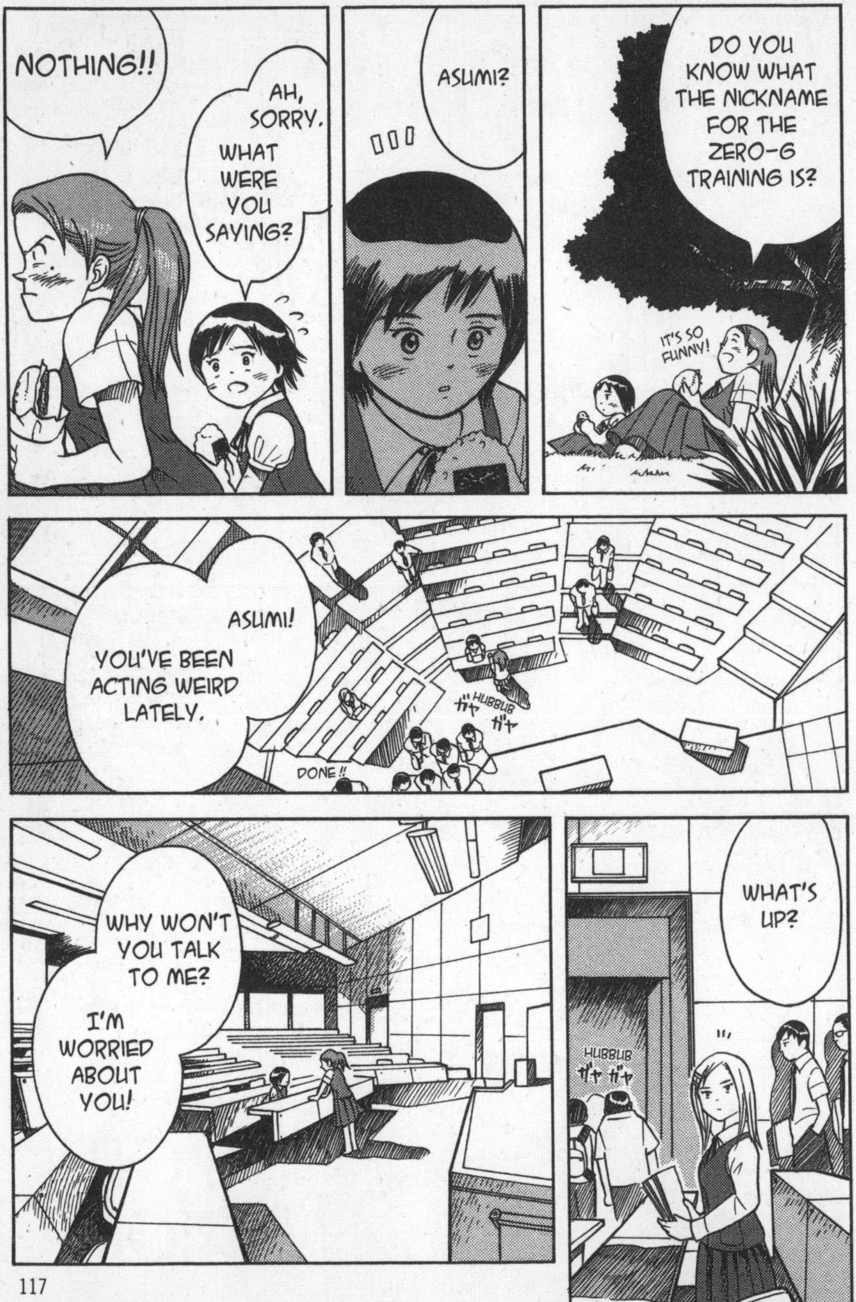
DO YOU KNOW WHAT THE NICKNAME FOR THE ZERO-6 TRAINING IS?
IT'S SO FUNNY!
ASUMI?
AH, SORRY.
WHAT WERE YOU SAYING?
NOTHING!!
ASUMI!
YOU'VE BEEN ACTING WEIRD LATELY.
HUBBUB
ガヤ ガヤ
DONE!!
WHAT'S UP?
HUBBUB
ガヤ ガヤ
WHY WON'T YOU TALK TO ME?
I'M WORRIED ABOUT YOU!

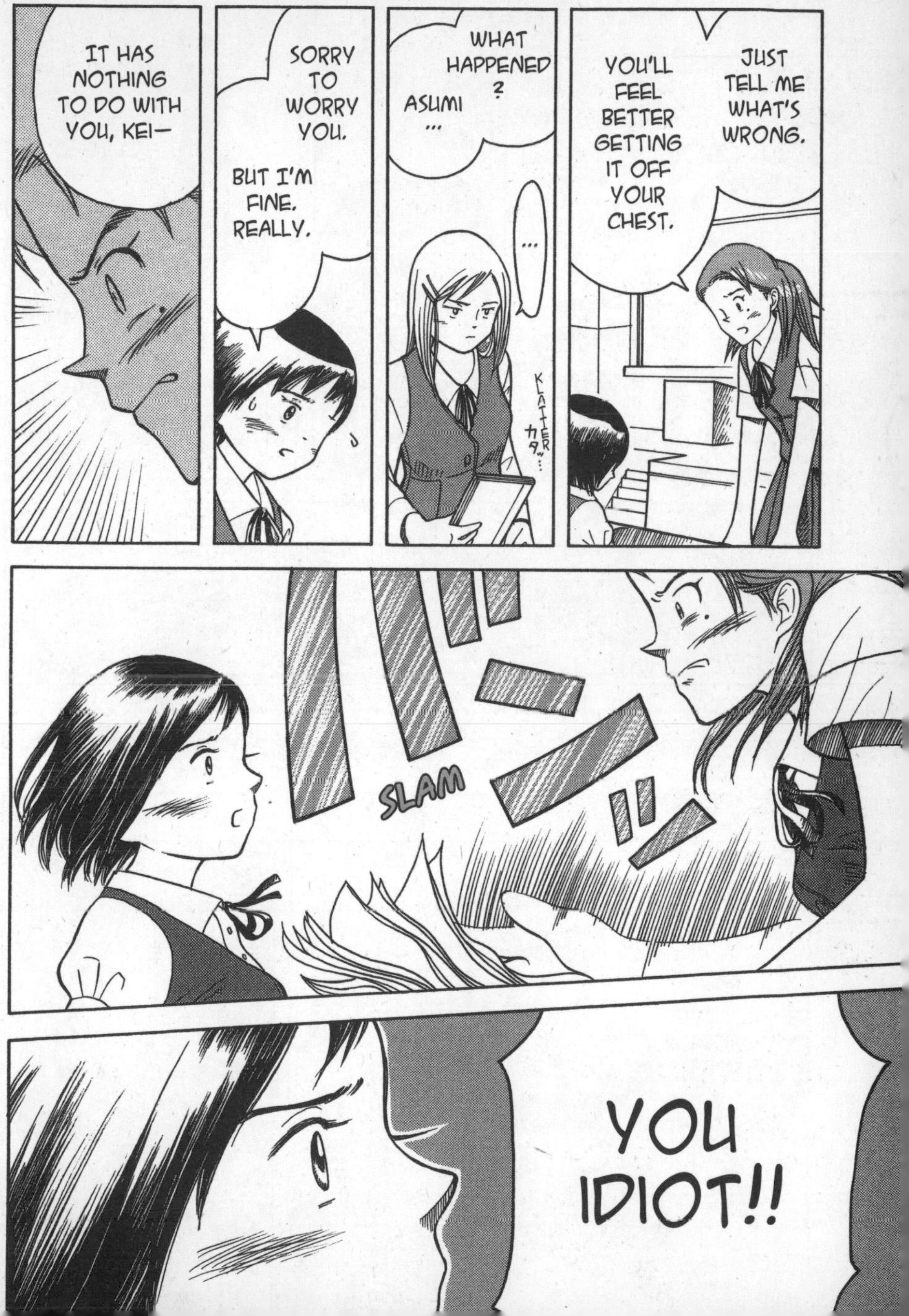

JUST TELL ME WHAT'S WRONG.
YOU'LL FEEL BETTER GETTING IT OFF YOUR CHEST.
WHAT HAPPENED?
ASUMI...
...
KLATTER カタッ...
SORRY TO WORRY YOU.
BUT I'M FINE. REALLY.
IT HAS NOTHING TO DO WITH YOU, KEI—
SLAM
YOU IDIOT!!

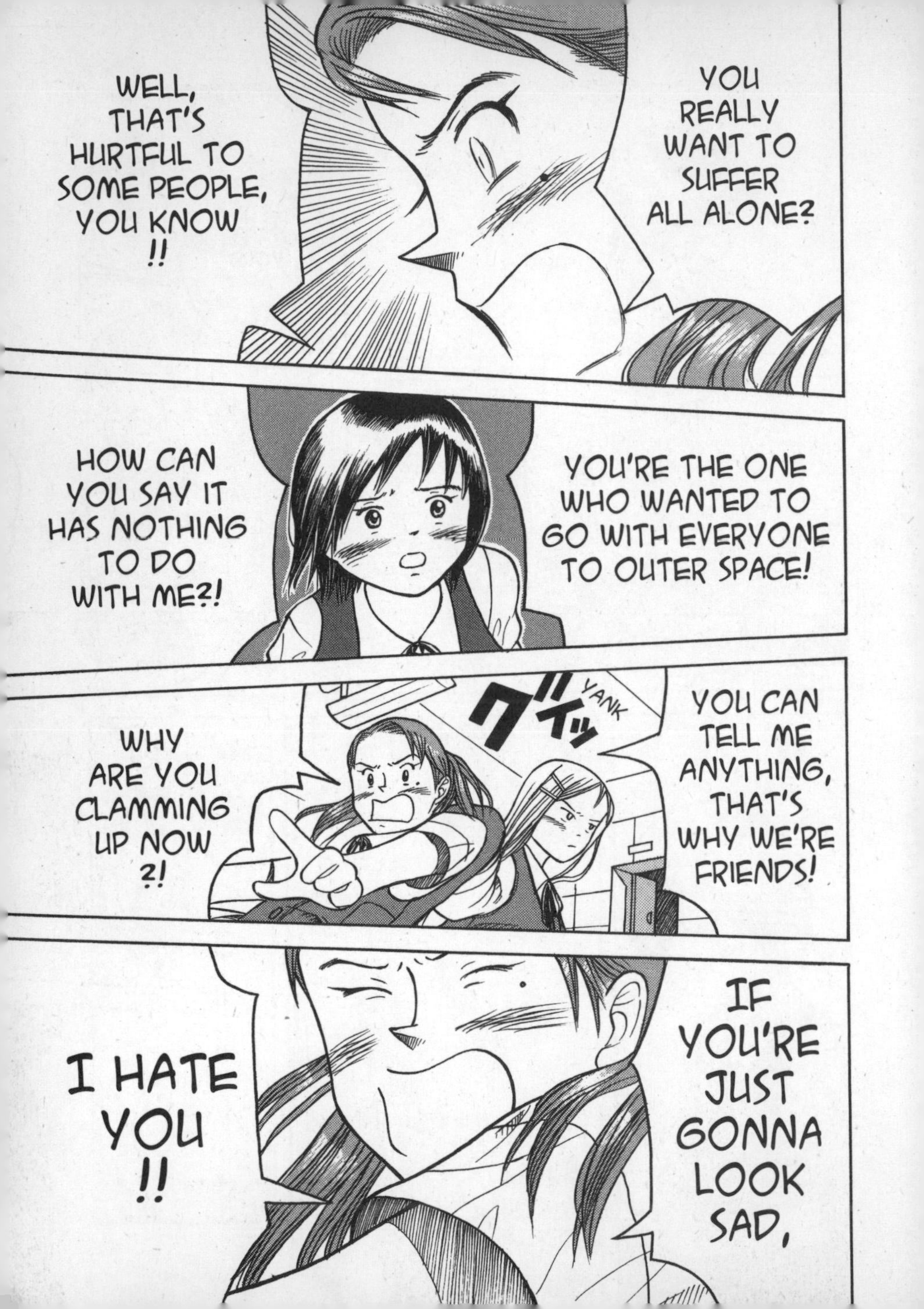
YOU REALLY WANT TO SUFFER ALL ALONE?
WELL, THAT'S HURTFUL TO SOME PEOPLE, YOU KNOW!!
YOU'RE THE ONE WHO WANTED TO GO WITH EVERYONE TO OUTER SPACE!
HOW CAN YOU SAY IT HAS NOTHING TO DO WITH ME?!
YOU CAN TELL ME ANYTHING, THAT'S WHY WE'RE FRIENDS!
グイッ
YANK
WHY ARE YOU CLAMMING UP NOW?!
IF YOU'RE JUST GONNA LOOK SAD,
I HATE YOU!!

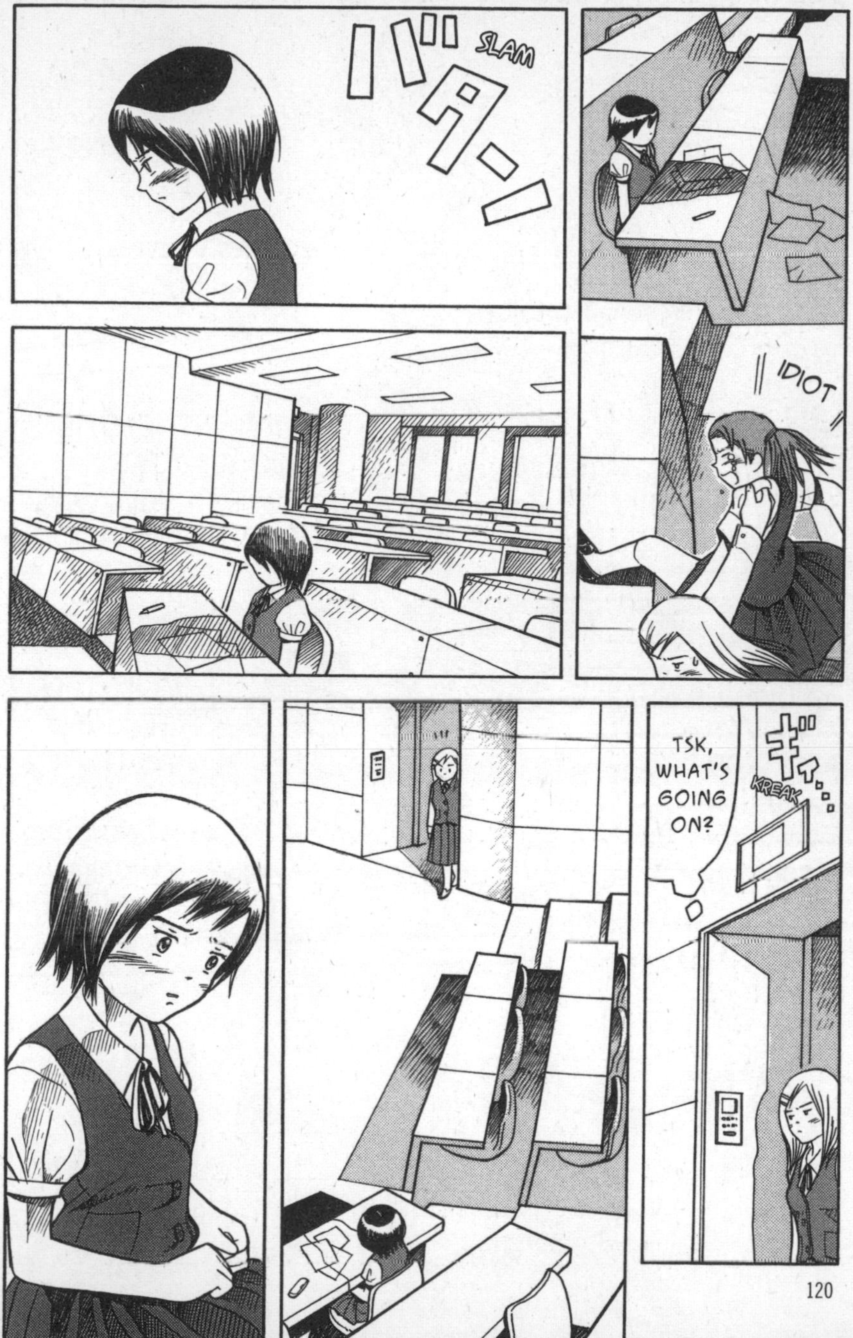
バターン
SLAM
IDIOT
TSK, WHAT'S GOING ON?
ギィ...
KREAK

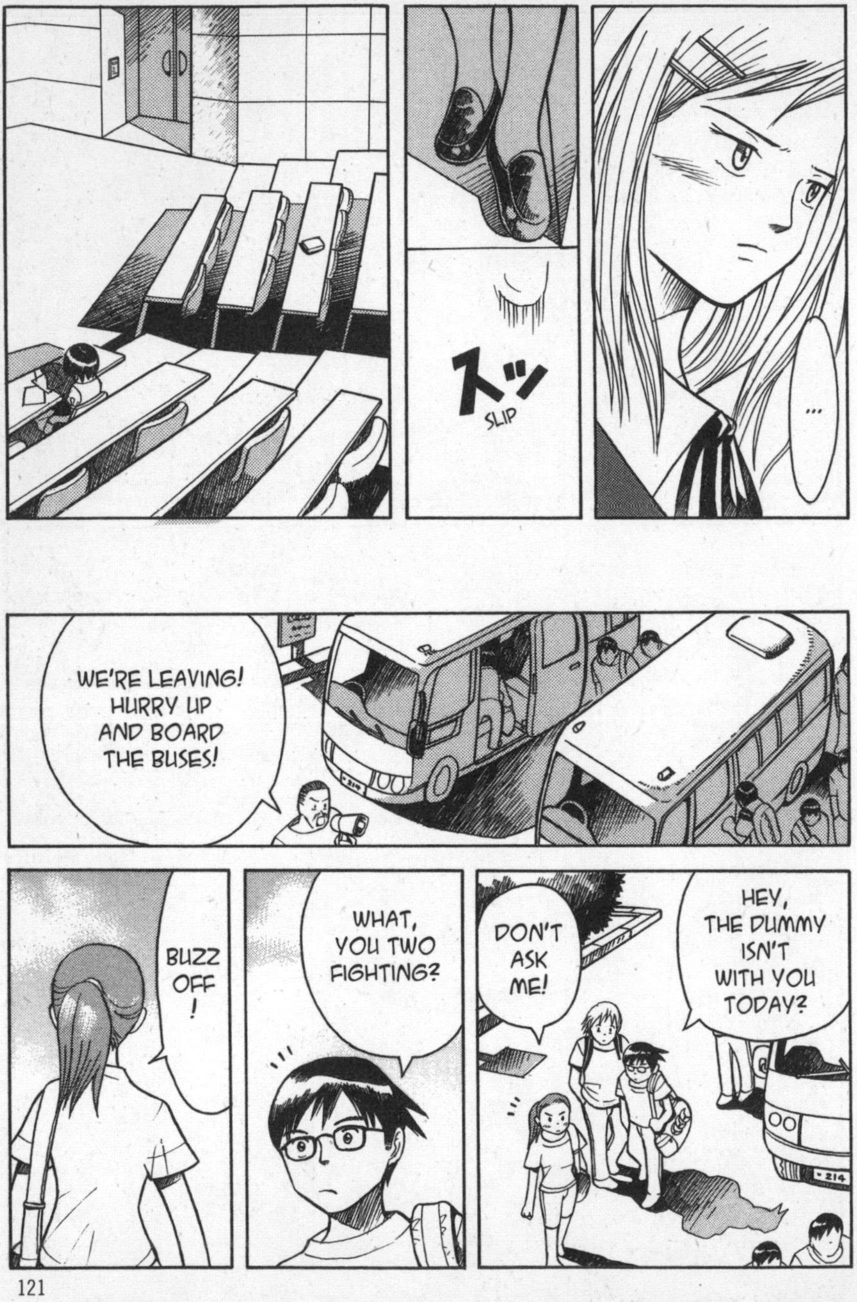
...
スッ
SLIP
WE'RE LEAVING! HURRY UP AND BOARD THE BUSES!
HEY, THE DUMMY ISN'T WITH YOU TODAY?
DON'T ASK ME!
WHAT, YOU TWO FIGHTING?
BUZZ OFF!

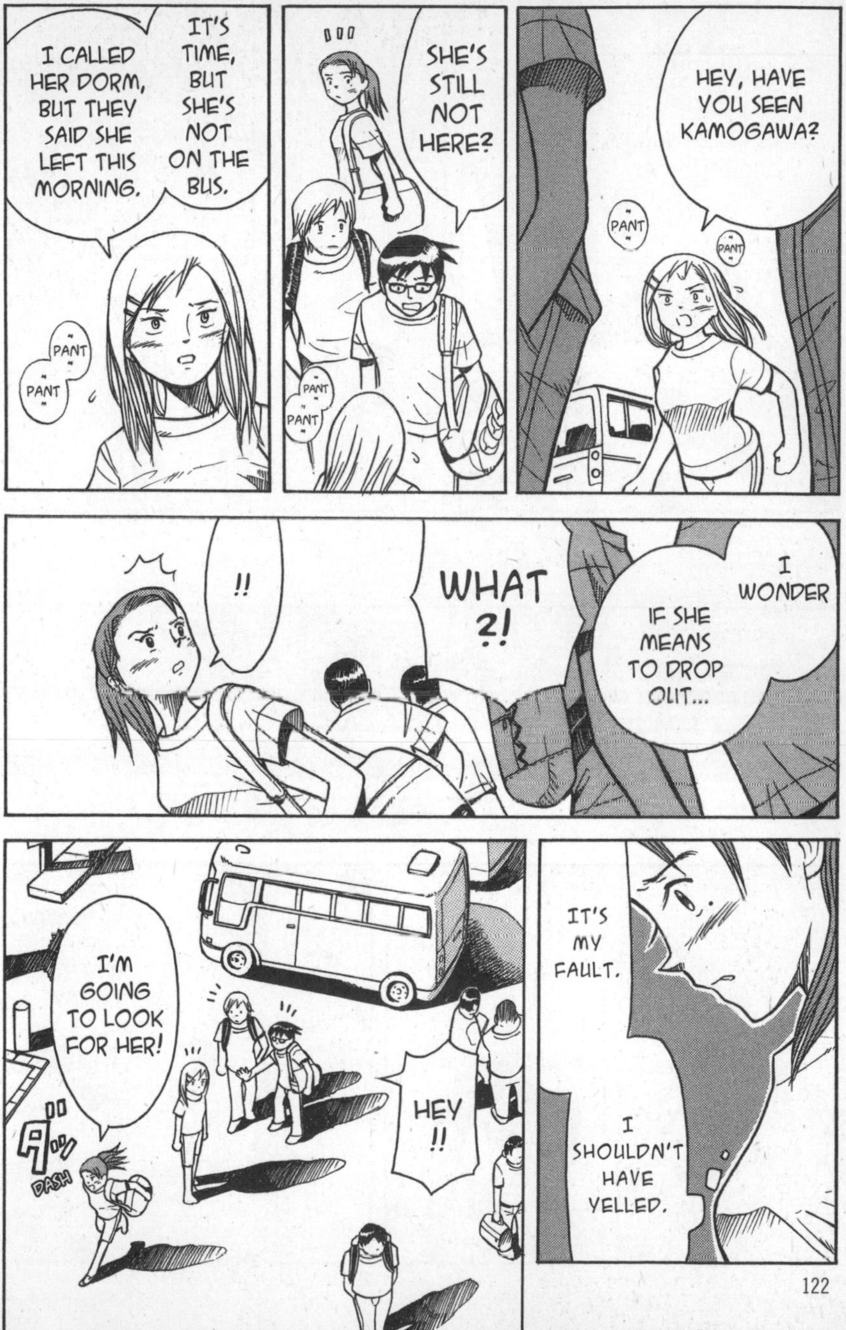

HEY, HAVE YOU SEEN KAMOGAWA?
PANT
PANT
SHE'S STILL NOT HERE?
PANT
PANT
IT'S TIME, BUT SHE'S NOT ON THE BUS.
I CALLED HER DORM, BUT THEY SAID SHE LEFT THIS MORNING.
PANT
PANT
I WONDER IF SHE MEANS TO DROP OUT...
WHAT ?!
!!
IT'S MY FAULT.
I SHOULDN'T HAVE YELLED.
I'M GOING TO LOOK FOR HER!
HEY !!
DASH

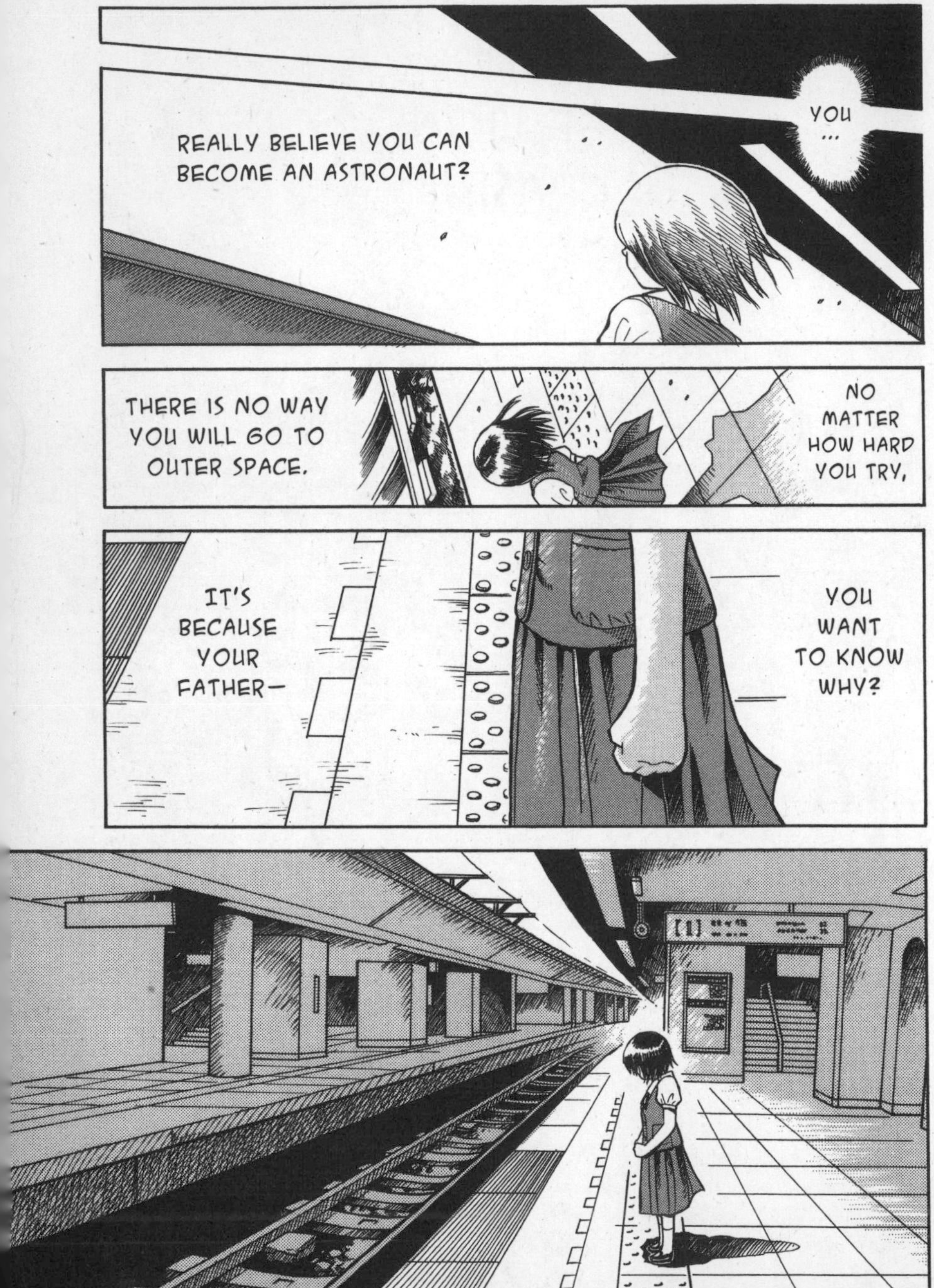
YOU ...
REALLY BELIEVE YOU CAN BECOME AN ASTRONAUT?
NO MATTER HOW HARD YOU TRY,
THERE IS NO WAY YOU WILL GO TO OUTER SPACE.
YOU WANT TO KNOW WHY?
IT'S BECAUSE YOUR FATHER—

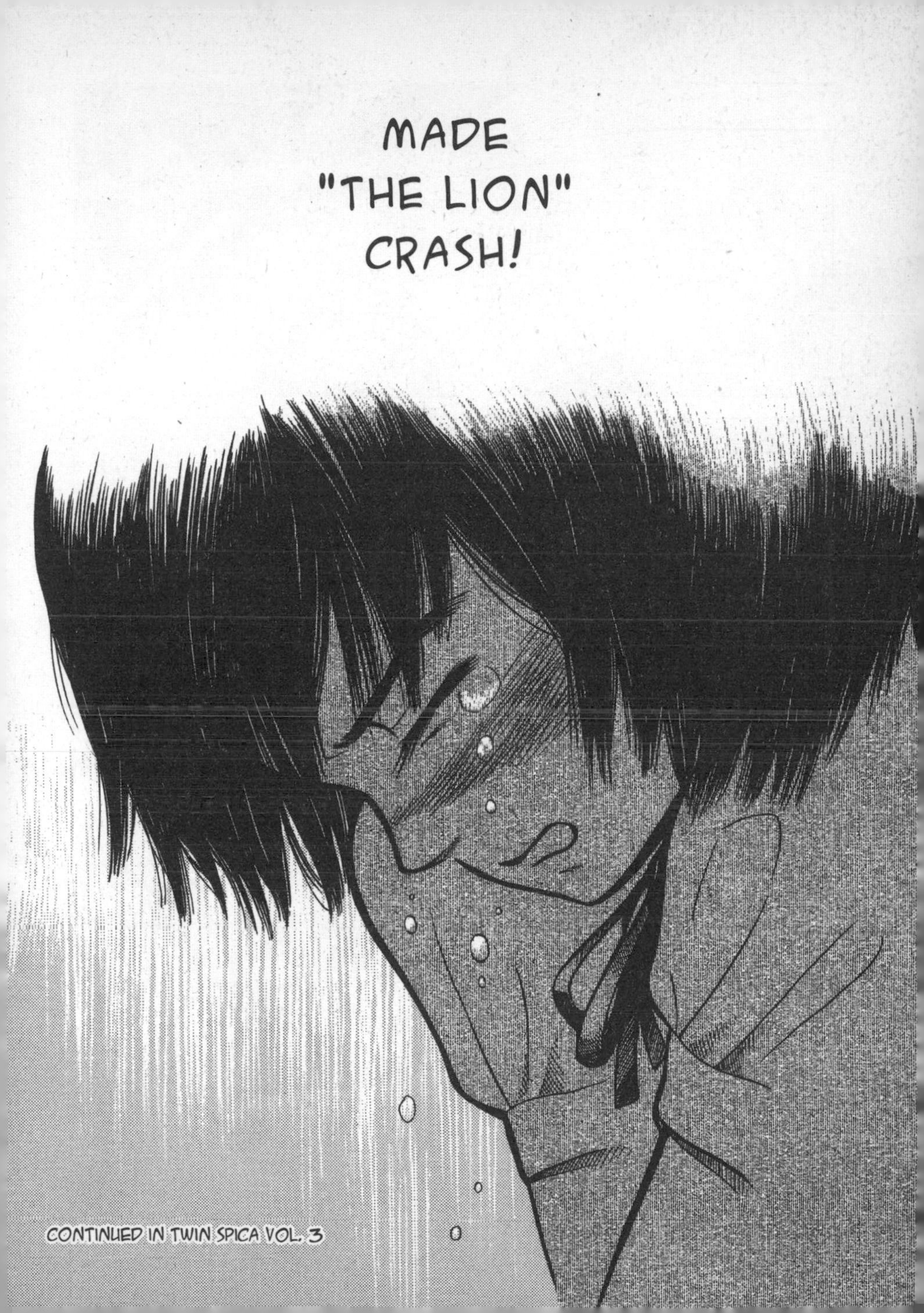
MADE
"THE LION"
CRASH!
CONTINUED IN TWIN SPICA VOL. 3

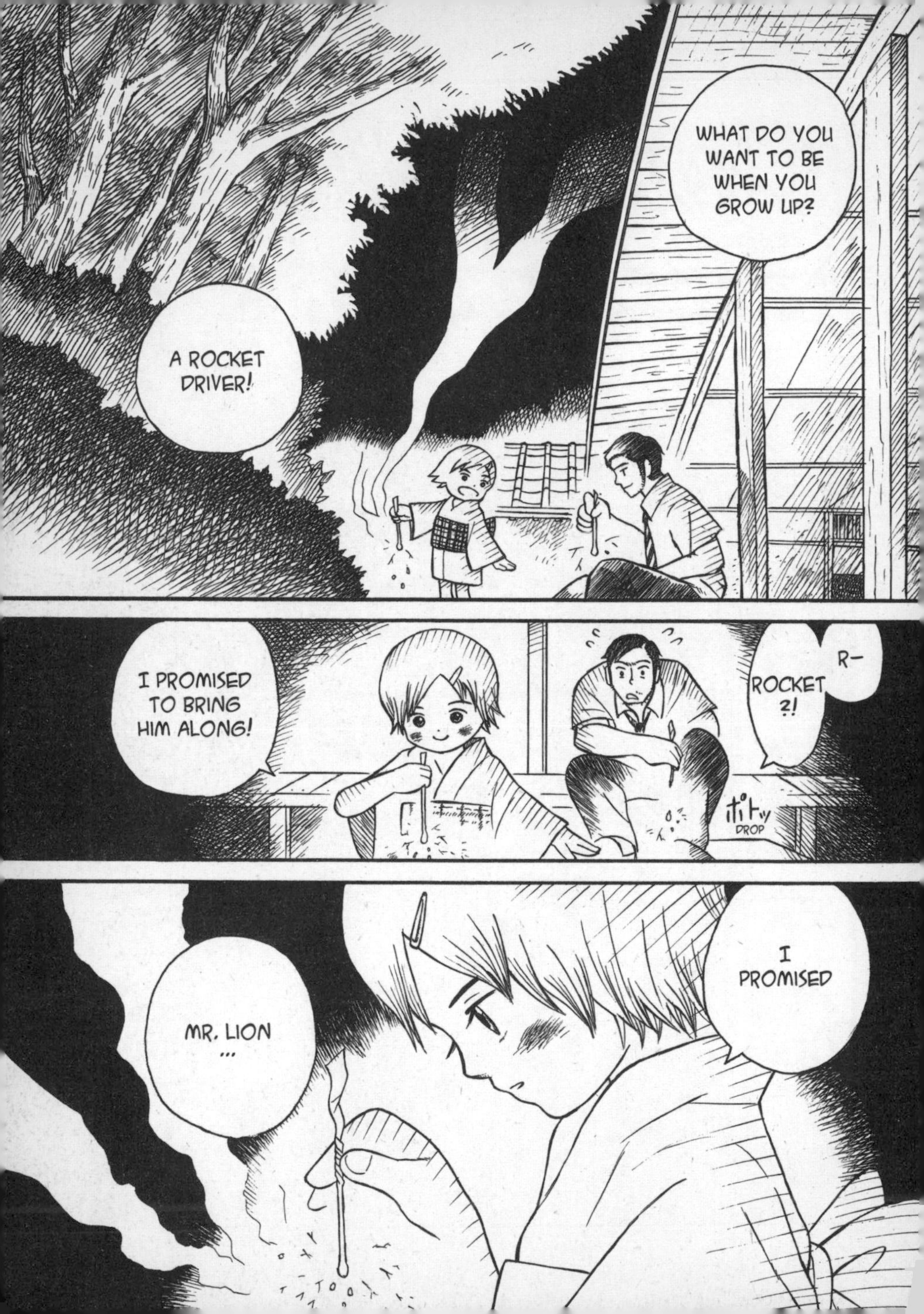
WHAT DO YOU WANT TO BE WHEN YOU GROW UP?
A ROCKET DRIVER!
R- ROCKET ?!
ポトッ
DROP
I PROMISED TO BRING HIM ALONG!
I PROMISED
MR. LION ...

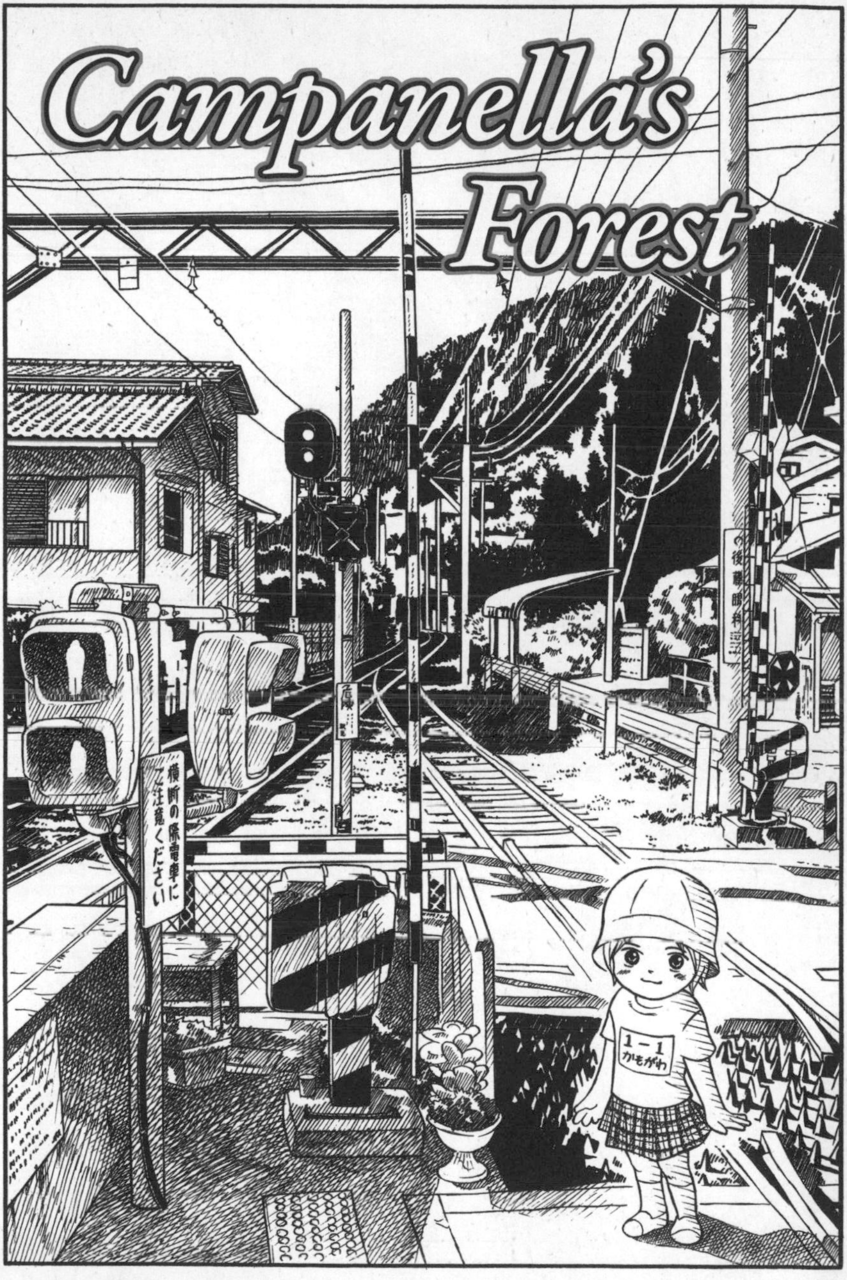
Campanella's Forest
横断の際電車に
ご注意ください
1－1
かもがわ

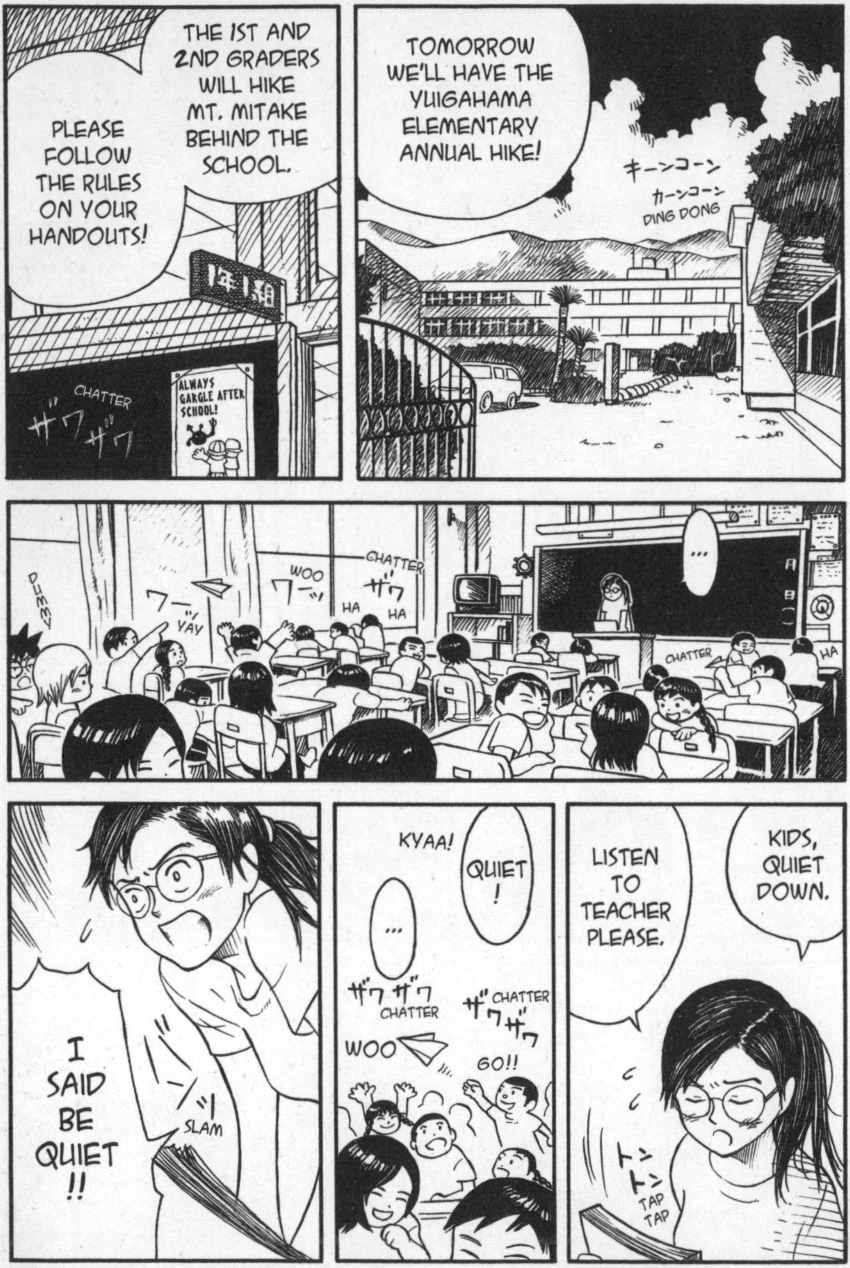
TOMORROW WE'LL HAVE THE YUIGAHAMA ELEMENTARY ANNUAL HIKE!
キーンコーン
カーンコーン
DING DONG
THE 1ST AND 2ND GRADERS WILL HIKE MT. MITAKE BEHIND THE SCHOOL.
PLEASE FOLLOW THE RULES ON YOUR HANDOUTS!
1年1組
ALWAYS GARGLE AFTER SCHOOL!
ザワザワ
CHATTER
...
HA
CHATTER
ザワ
CHATTER
HA
HA
ワーッ
WOO
ワーッ
YAY
DUMMY
KIDS, QUIET DOWN.
LISTEN TO TEACHER PLEASE.
トントン
TAP TAP
QUIET!
KYAA!
...
ザワザワ
CHATTER
ザワザワ
CHATTER
WOO
GO!!
I SAID BE QUIET!!
SLAM

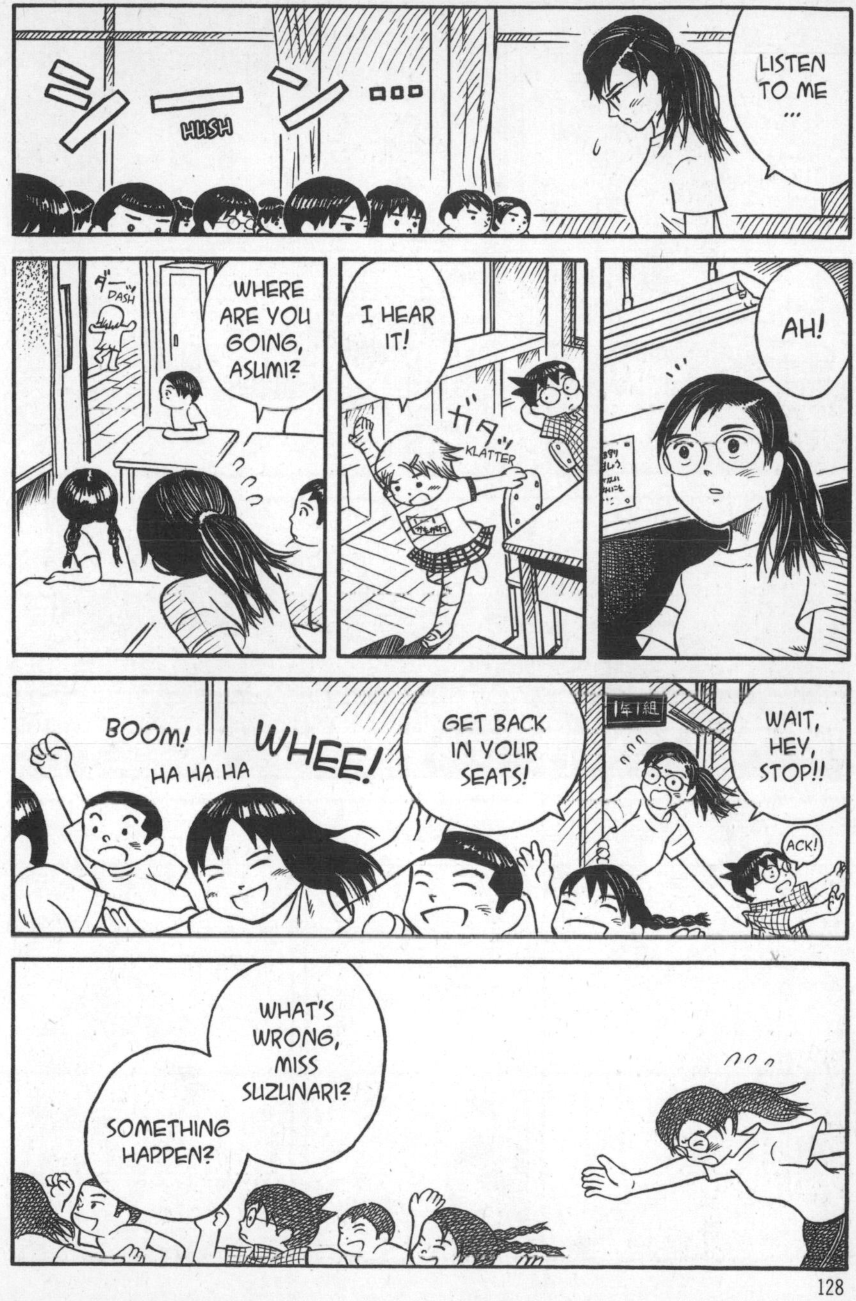
LISTEN TO ME ...
シーーン
HUSH
AH!
I HEAR IT!
ガタッ
KLATTER
WHERE ARE YOU GOING, ASUMI?
ダーッ
DASH
WAIT, HEY, STOP!!
ACK!
1年1組
GET BACK IN YOUR SEATS!
WHEE!
BOOM!
HA HA HA
WHAT'S WRONG, MISS SUZUNARI?
SOMETHING HAPPEN?

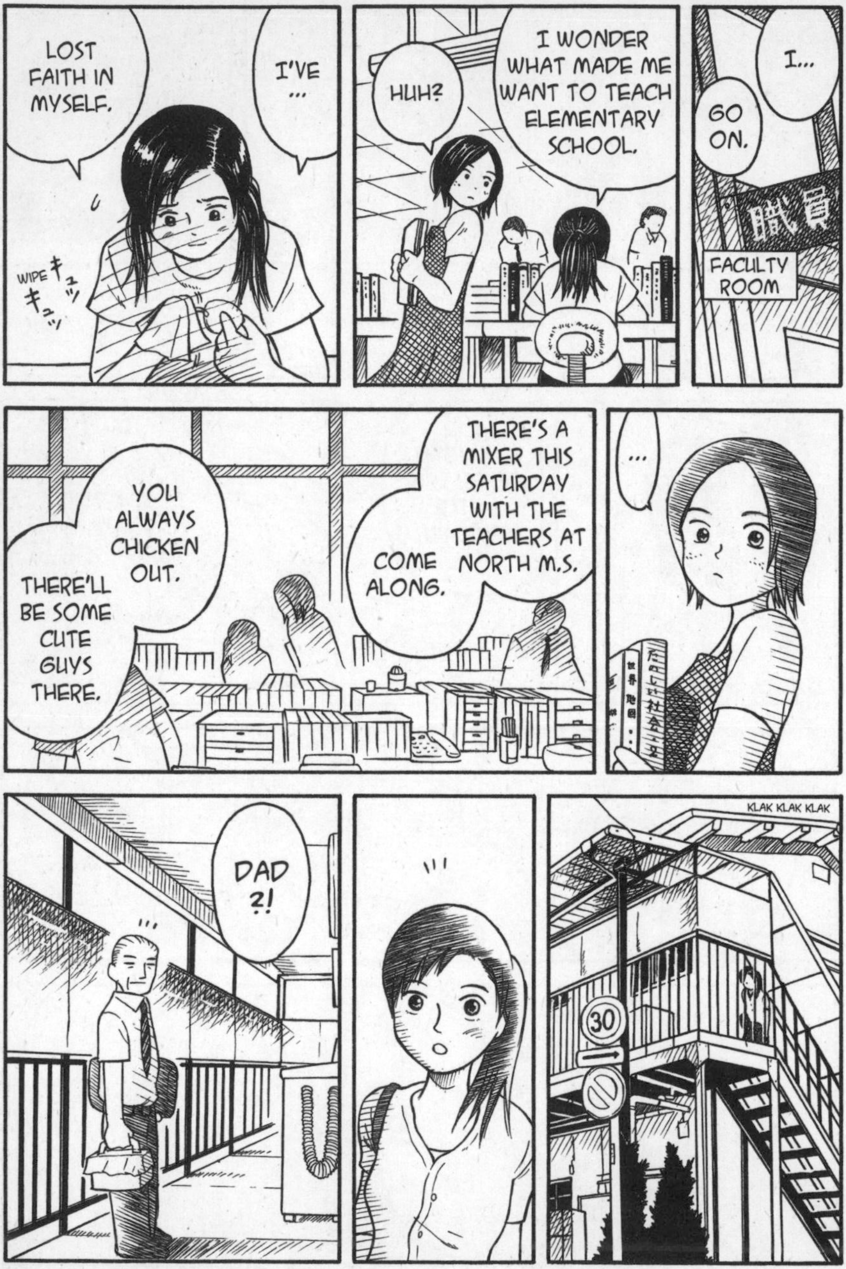
I...
GO ON.
職員
FACULTY ROOM
I WONDER WHAT MADE ME WANT TO TEACH ELEMENTARY SCHOOL.
HUH?
I'VE ...
LOST FAITH IN MYSELF.
WIPE キュッ キュッ
...
THERE'S A MIXER THIS SATURDAY WITH THE TEACHERS AT NORTH M.S.
COME ALONG.
YOU ALWAYS CHICKEN OUT.
THERE'LL BE SOME CUTE GUYS THERE.
KLAK KLAK KLAK
30
DAD ?!

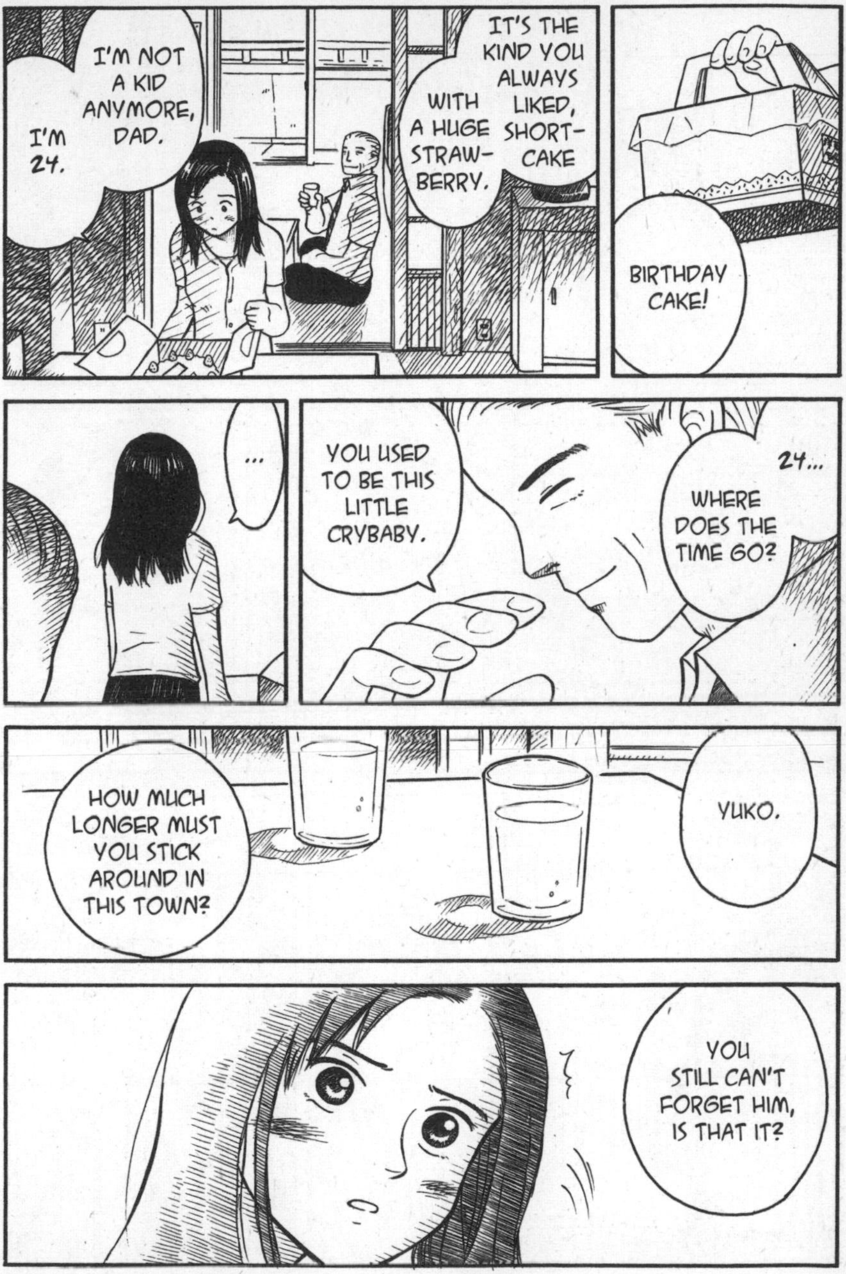
BIRTHDAY CAKE!
IT'S THE KIND YOU ALWAYS LIKED, SHORT-CAKE WITH A HUGE STRAW-BERRY.
I'M NOT A KID ANYMORE, DAD.
I'M 24.
24...
WHERE DOES THE TIME GO?
YOU USED TO BE THIS LITTLE CRYBABY.
...
YUKO.
HOW MUCH LONGER MUST YOU STICK AROUND IN THIS TOWN?
YOU STILL CAN'T FORGET HIM, IS THAT IT?

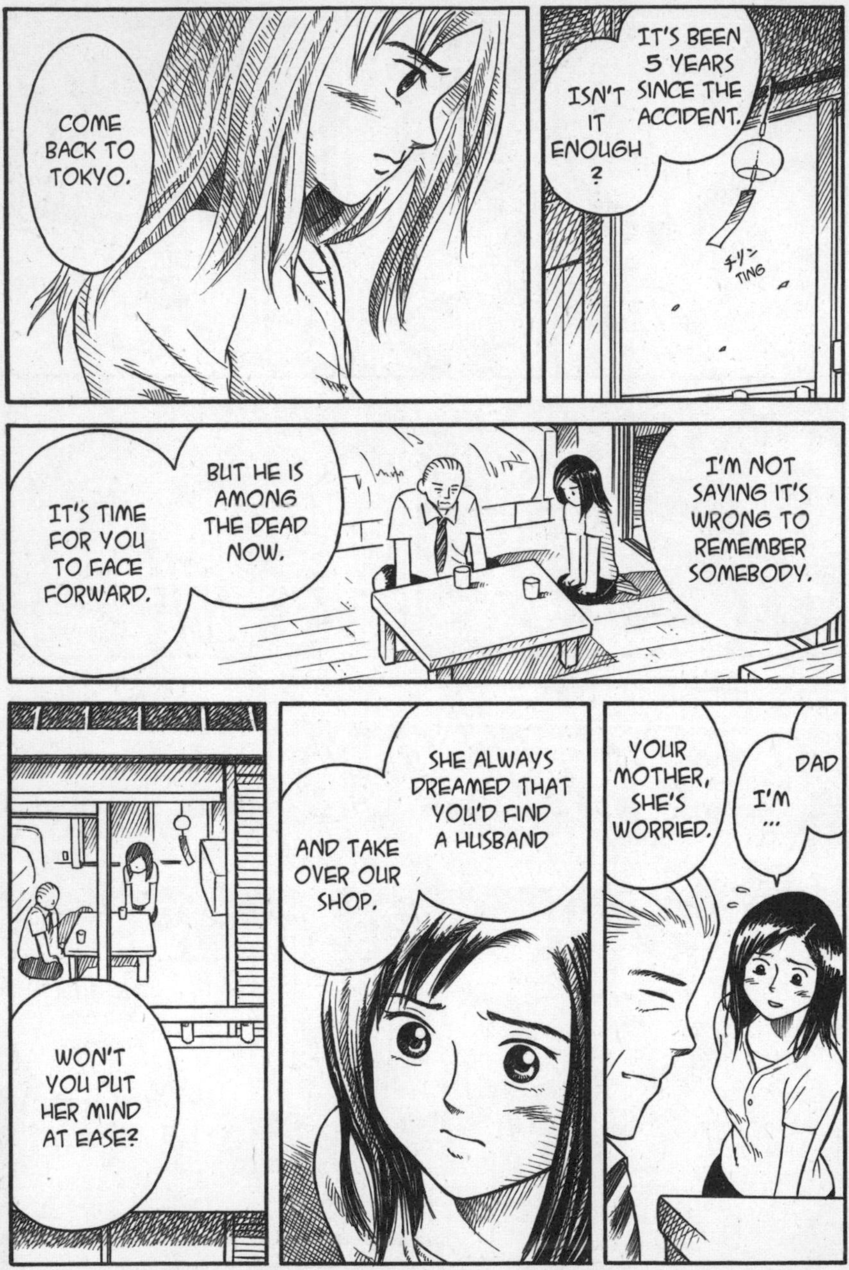
IT'S BEEN 5 YEARS SINCE THE ACCIDENT.
ISN'T IT ENOUGH?
チリン
TING
COME BACK TO TOKYO.
I'M NOT SAYING IT'S WRONG TO REMEMBER SOMEBODY.
BUT HE IS AMONG THE DEAD NOW.
IT'S TIME FOR YOU TO FACE FORWARD.
DAD
I'M ...
YOUR MOTHER, SHE'S WORRIED.
SHE ALWAYS DREAMED THAT YOU'D FIND A HUSBAND
AND TAKE OVER OUR SHOP.
WON'T YOU PUT HER MIND AT EASE?

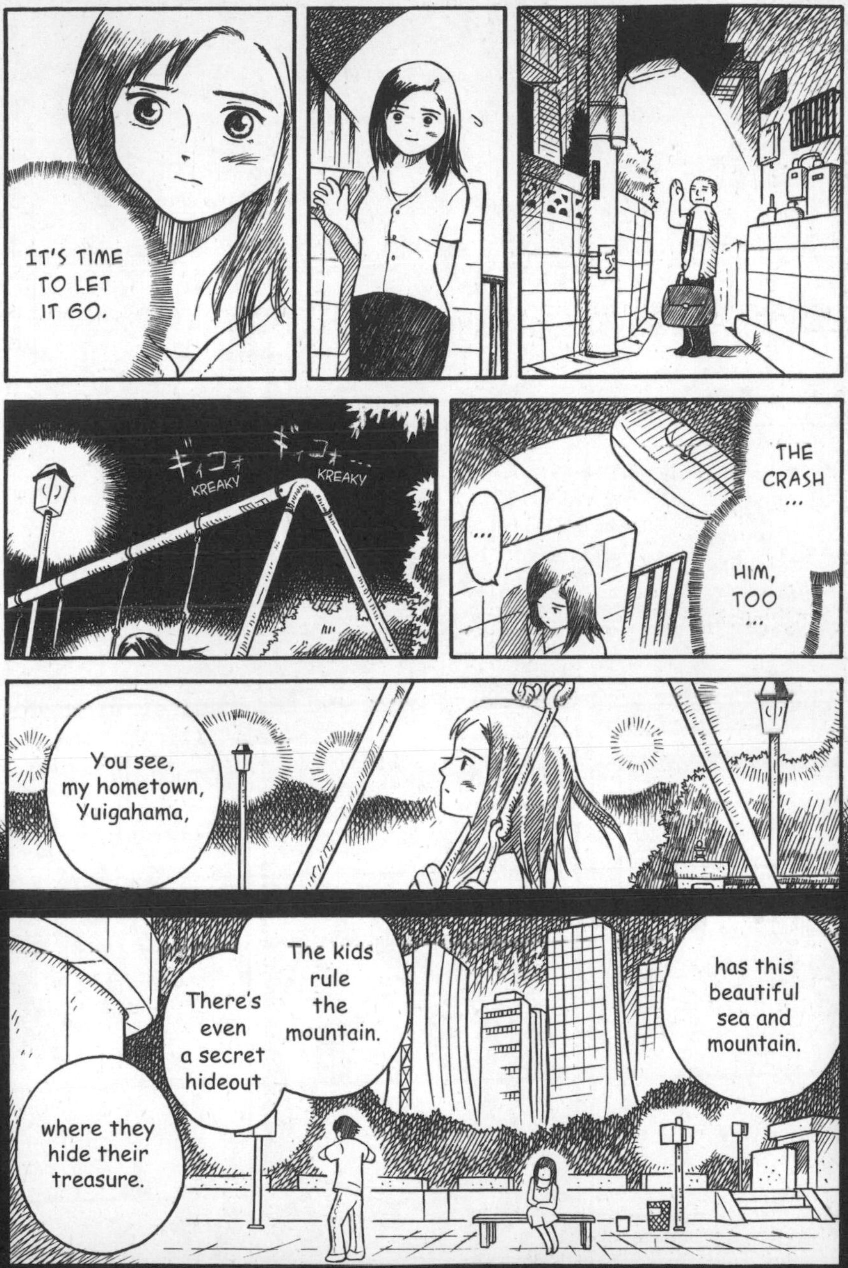
IT'S TIME TO LET IT GO.
THE CRASH ...
HIM, TOO ...
...
ギィコォ… KREAKY
ギィコォ KREAKY
You see, my hometown, Yuigahama,
has this beautiful sea and mountain.
The kids rule the mountain.
There's even a secret hideout
where they hide their treasure.

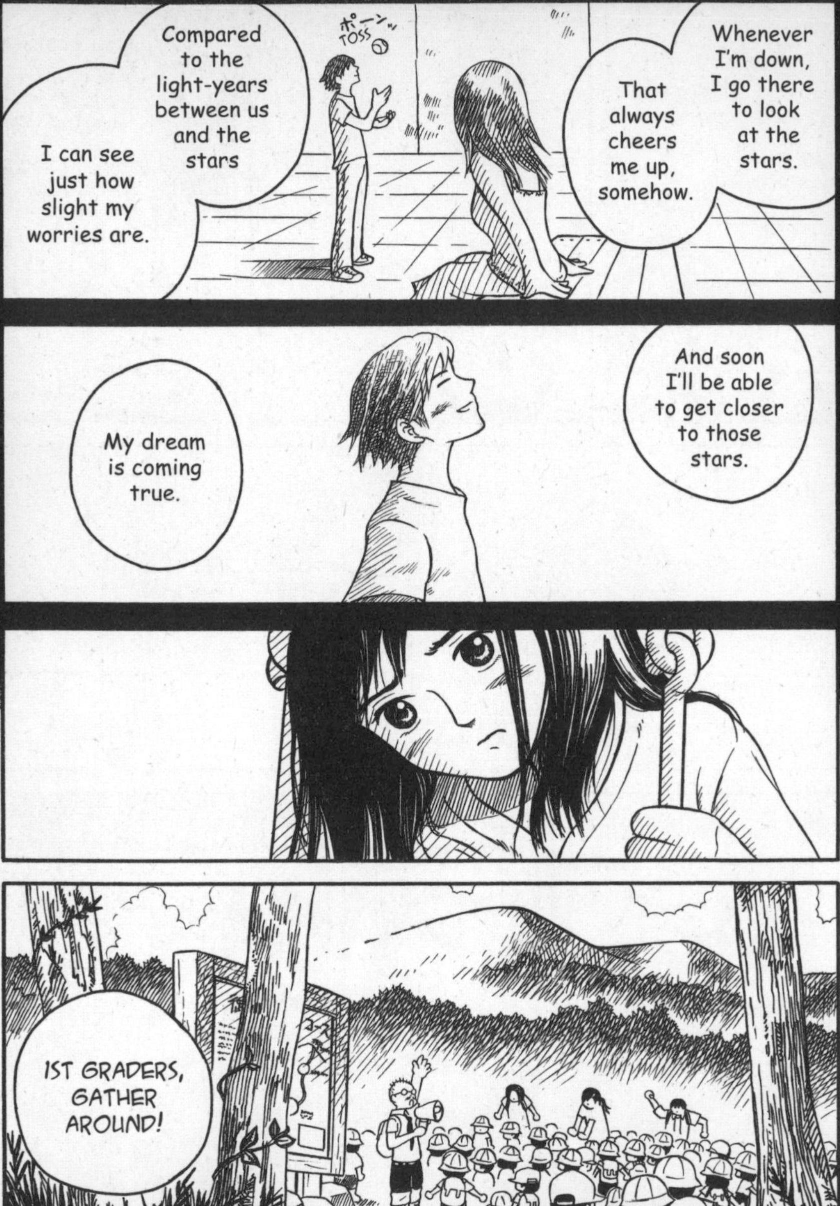
Whenever I'm down, I go there to look at the stars.
That always cheers me up, somehow.
ポーン TOSS
Compared to the light-years between us and the stars
I can see just how slight my worries are.
And soon I'll be able to get closer to those stars.
My dream is coming true.
1ST GRADERS, GATHER AROUND!

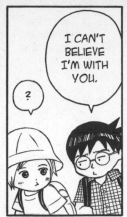

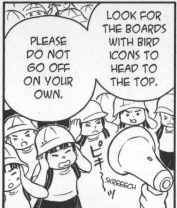

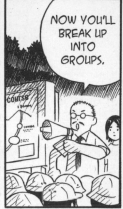

NOW YOU'LL BREAK UP INTO GROUPS.
LOOK FOR THE BOARDS WITH BIRD ICONS TO HEAD TO THE TOP.
PLEASE DO NOT GO OFF ON YOUR OWN.
ピキ
SKREEECH
ッ
I CAN'T BELIEVE I'M WITH YOU.
?
THERE !!
- 3 -
SUN
WHERE ?
THERE !
THAT'S THE 3RD ONE.

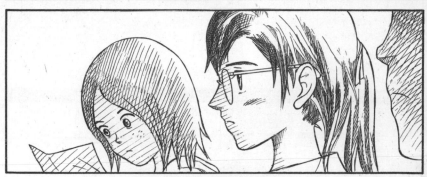

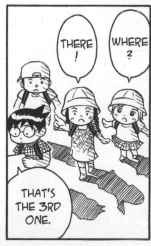

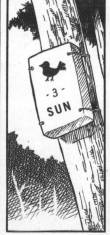

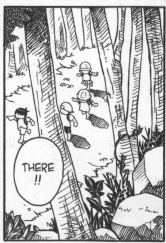

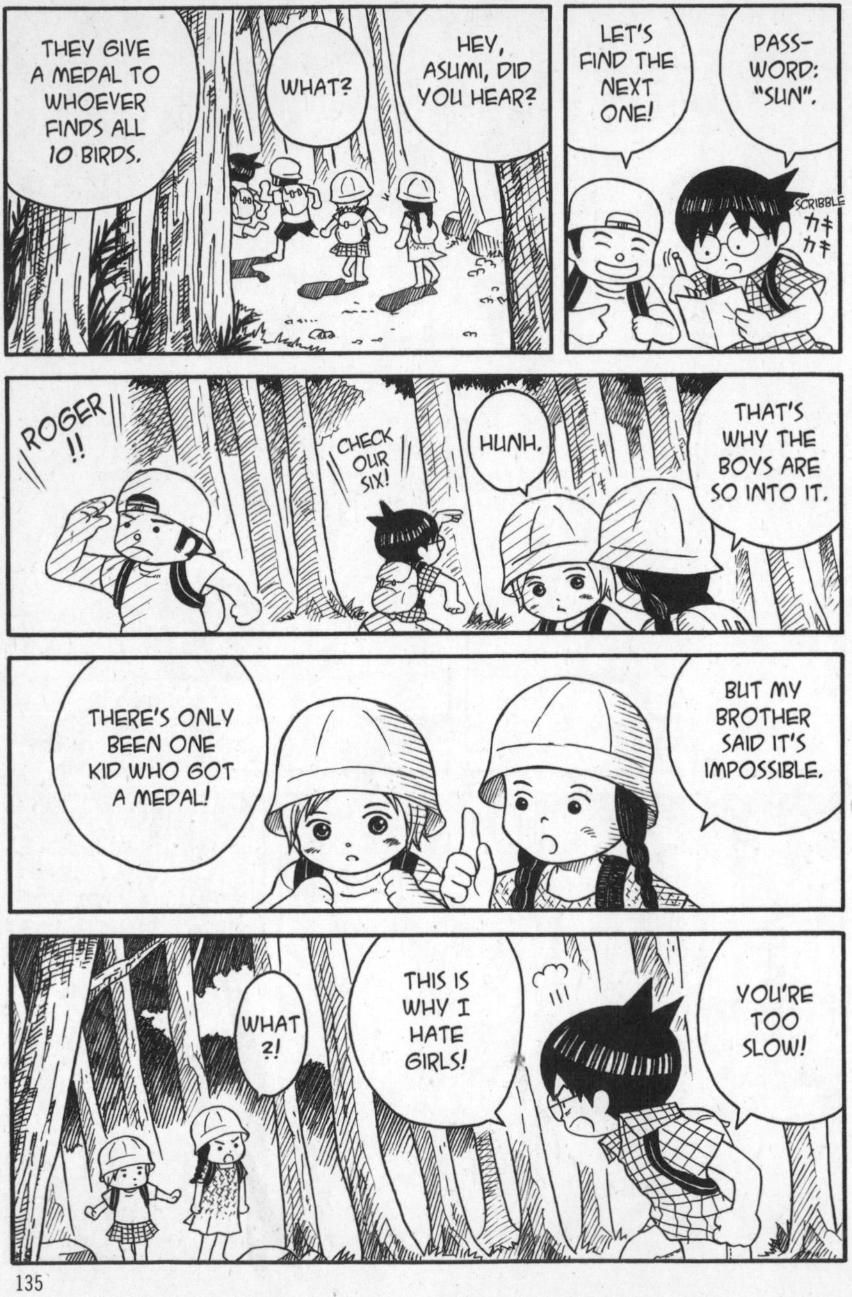
PASS-WORD: "SUN".
LET'S FIND THE NEXT ONE!
SCRIBBLE
カキカキ
HEY, ASUMI, DID YOU HEAR?
WHAT?
THEY GIVE A MEDAL TO WHOEVER FINDS ALL 10 BIRDS.
THAT'S WHY THE BOYS ARE SO INTO IT.
HUNH.
CHECK OUR SIX!
ROGER!!
BUT MY BROTHER SAID IT'S IMPOSSIBLE.
THERE'S ONLY BEEN ONE KID WHO GOT A MEDAL!
YOU'RE TOO SLOW!
THIS IS WHY I HATE GIRLS!
WHAT?!

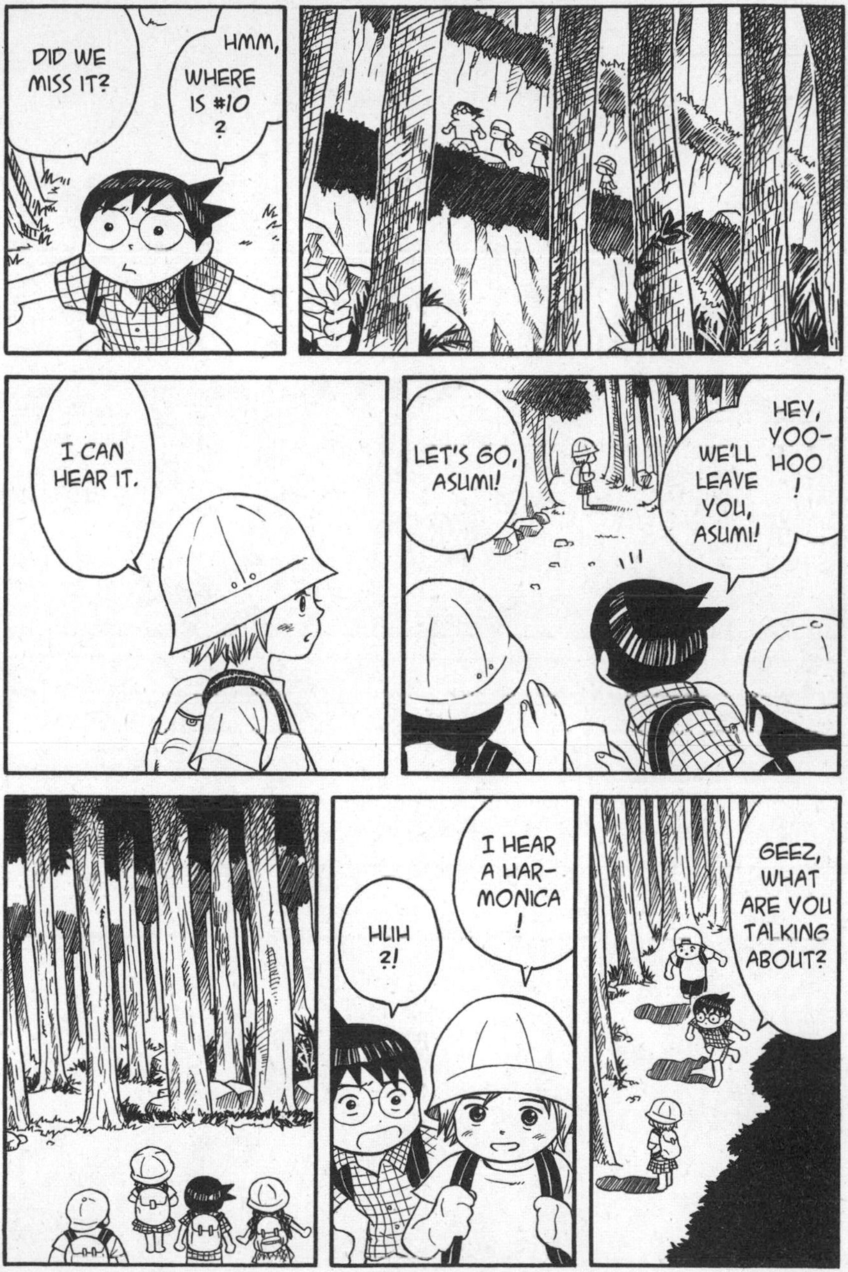
HMM, WHERE IS #10 ?
DID WE MISS IT?
HEY, YOO-HOO !
WE'LL LEAVE YOU, ASUMI!
LET'S GO, ASUMI!
I CAN HEAR IT.
GEEZ, WHAT ARE YOU TALKING ABOUT?
I HEAR A HAR- MONICA !
HUH ?!

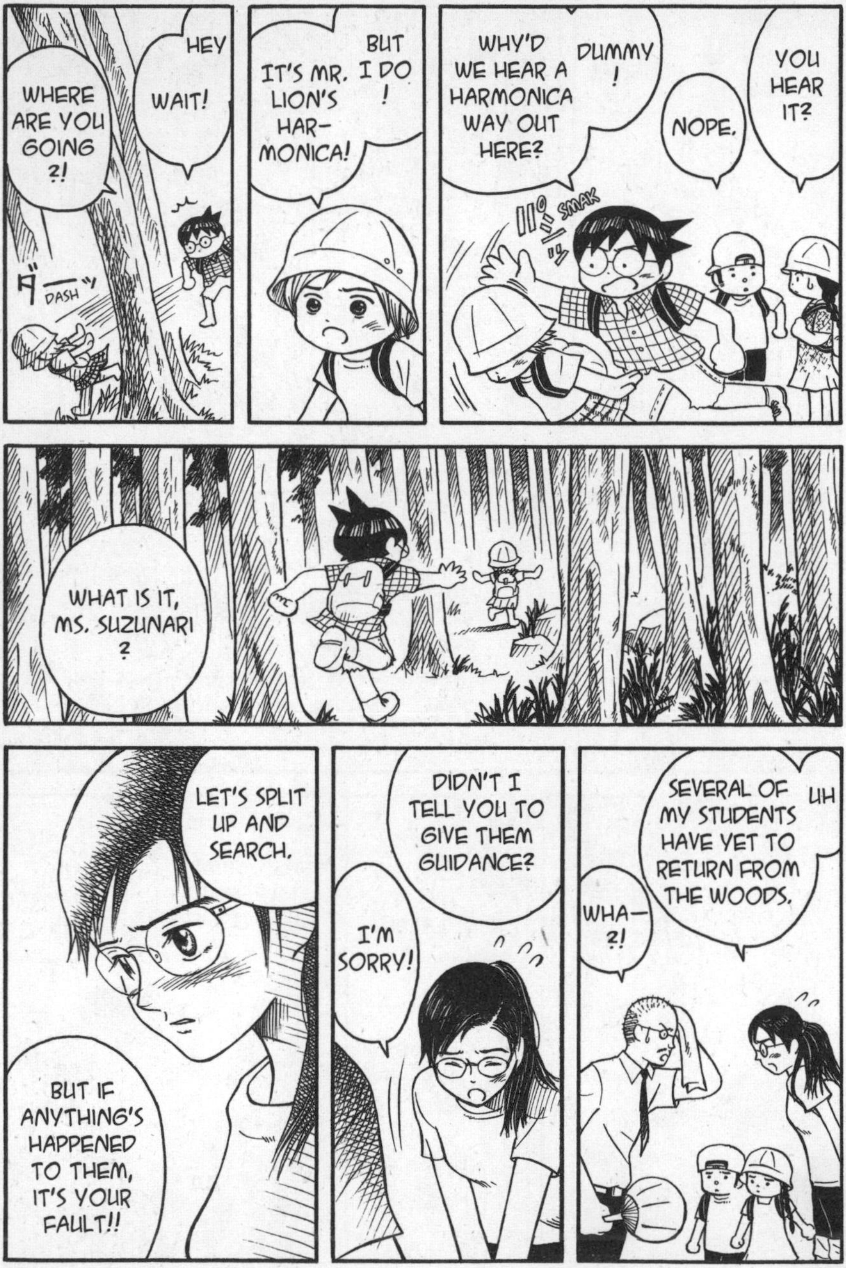
YOU HEAR IT?
NOPE.
WHY'D WE HEAR A HARMONICA WAY OUT HERE?
DUMMY!
SMAK
BUT I DO!
IT'S MR. LION'S HAR-MONICA!
HEY
WAIT!
WHERE ARE YOU GOING?!
DASH
WHAT IS IT, MS. SUZUNARI?
UH
SEVERAL OF MY STUDENTS HAVE YET TO RETURN FROM THE WOODS.
WHA—?!
DIDN'T I TELL YOU TO GIVE THEM GUIDANCE?
I'M SORRY!
LET'S SPLIT UP AND SEARCH.
BUT IF ANYTHING'S HAPPENED TO THEM, IT'S YOUR FAULT!!

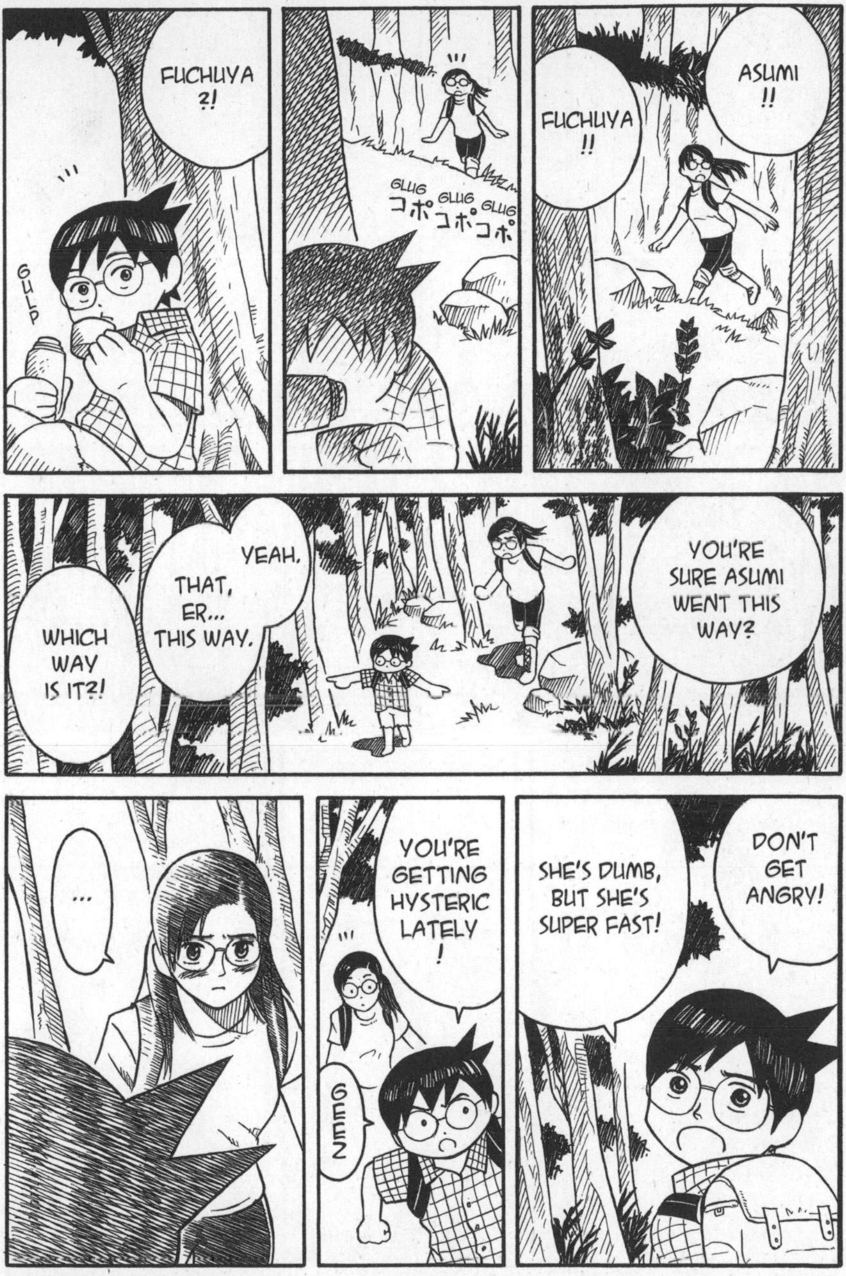
ASUMI !!
FUCHUYA !!
GLUG GLUG GLUG
コポコポコポ
FUCHUYA ?!
GULP
YOU'RE SURE ASUMI WENT THIS WAY?
YEAH.
THAT, ER... THIS WAY.
WHICH WAY IS IT?!
DON'T GET ANGRY!
SHE'S DUMB, BUT SHE'S SUPER FAST!
YOU'RE GETTING HYSTERIC LATELY !
GEEZ
...

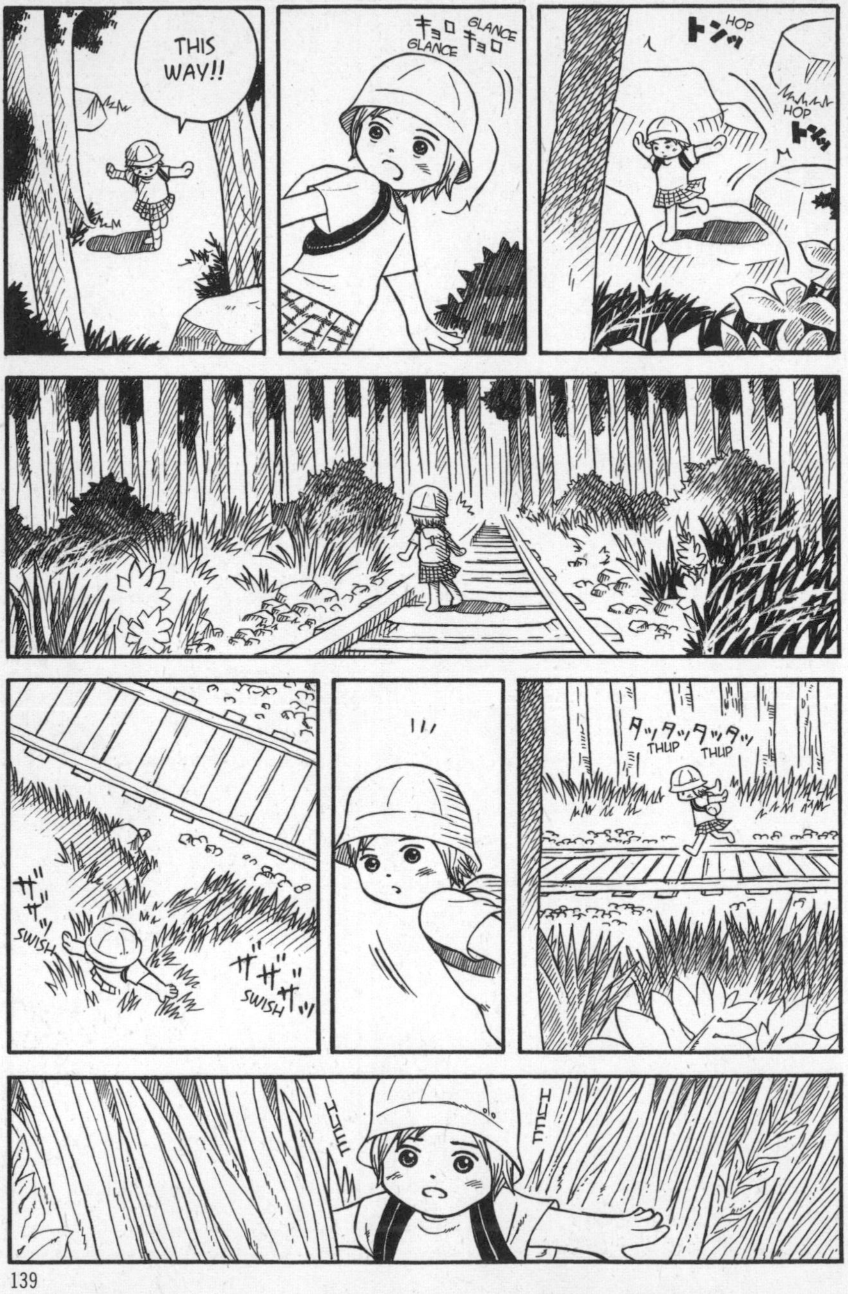
HOP
トンッ
HOP
トンッ
キョロ
GLANCE
GLANCE
キョロ
THIS WAY!!
タッタッタッタッ
THUP THUP
!!!
ザザッ
SWISH
ザザザッ
SWISH
HUFF
HUFF

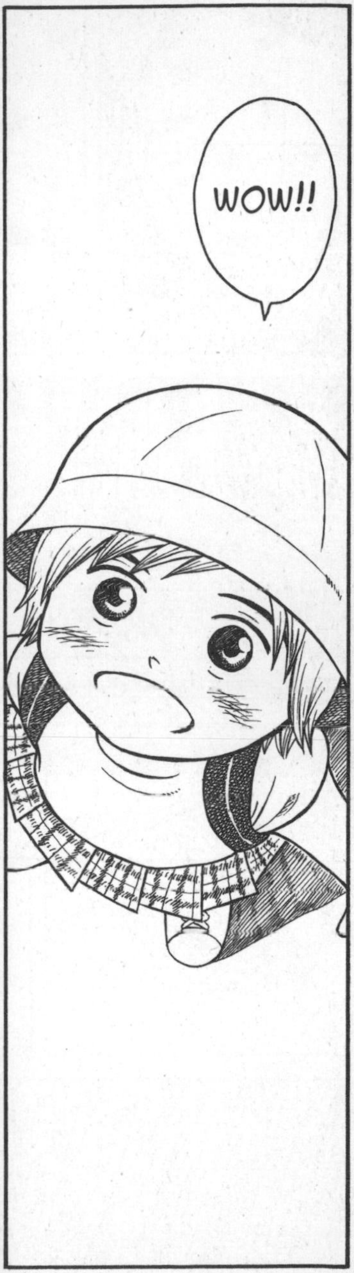
WOW!!

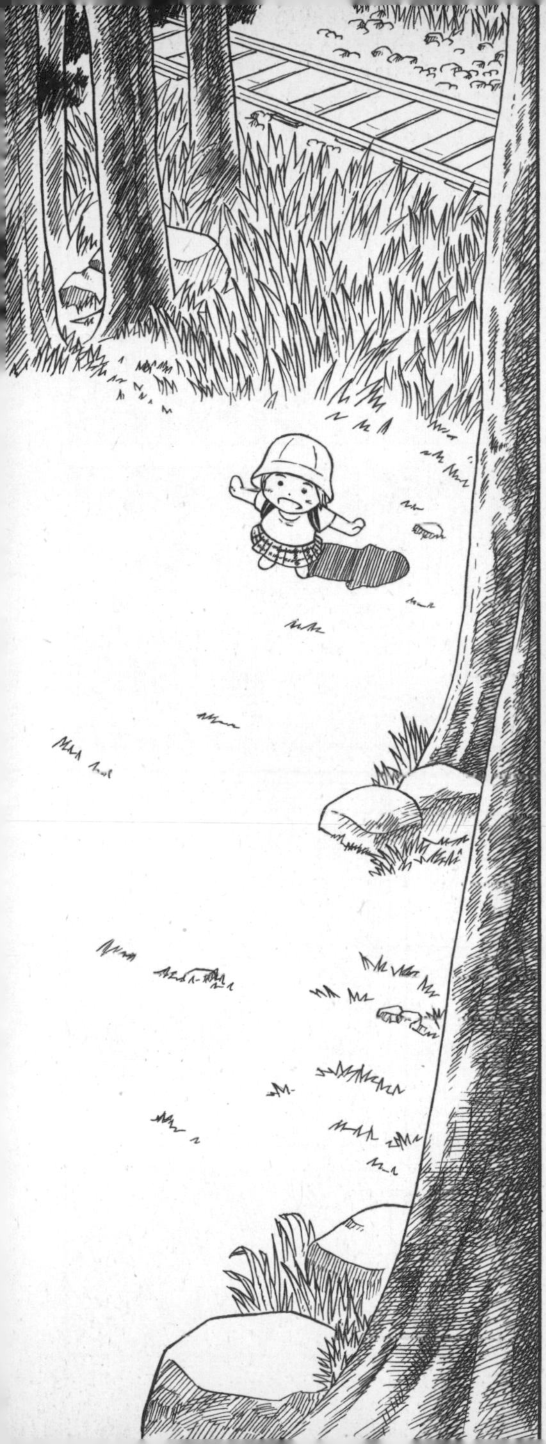

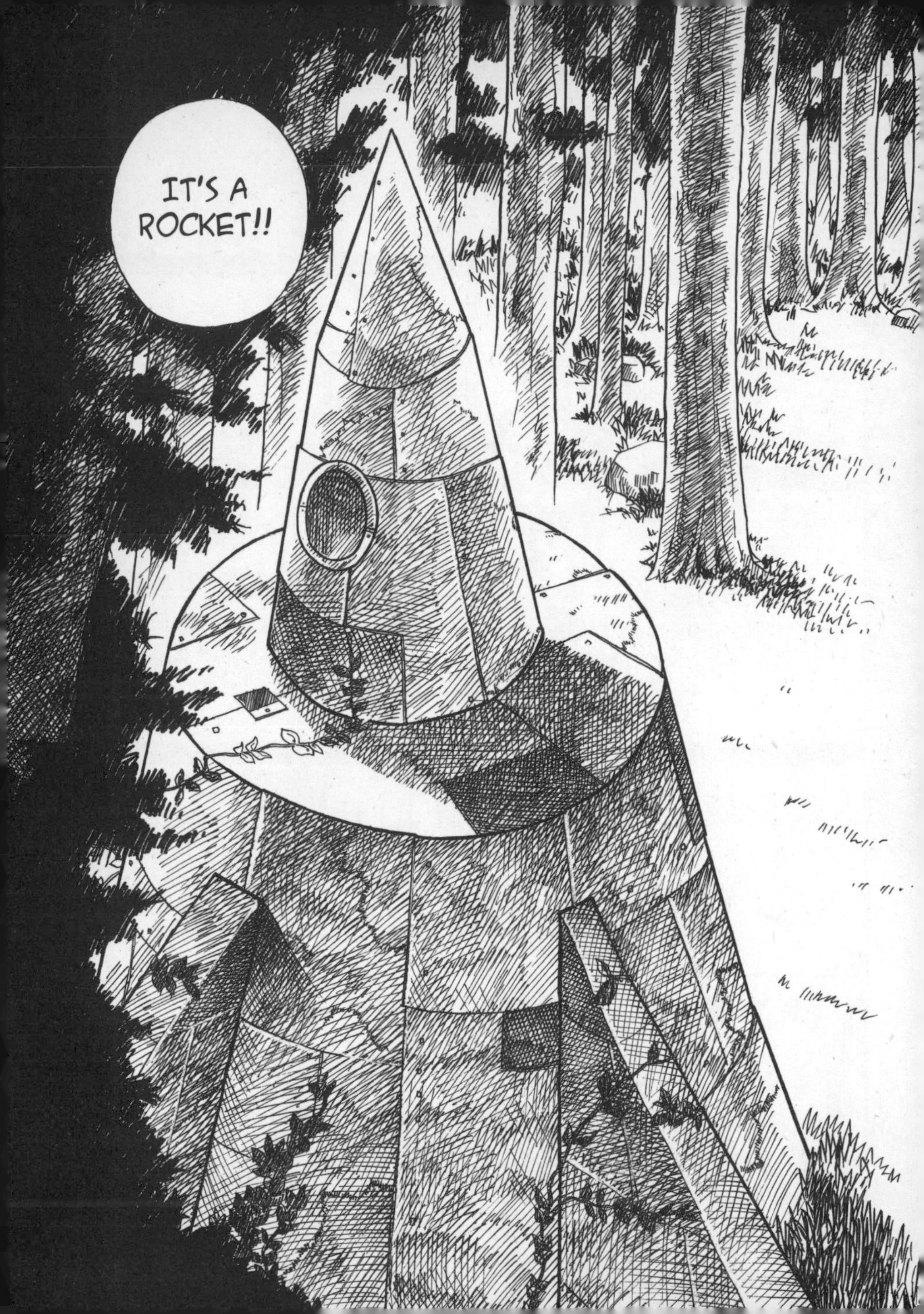
IT'S A ROCKET!!

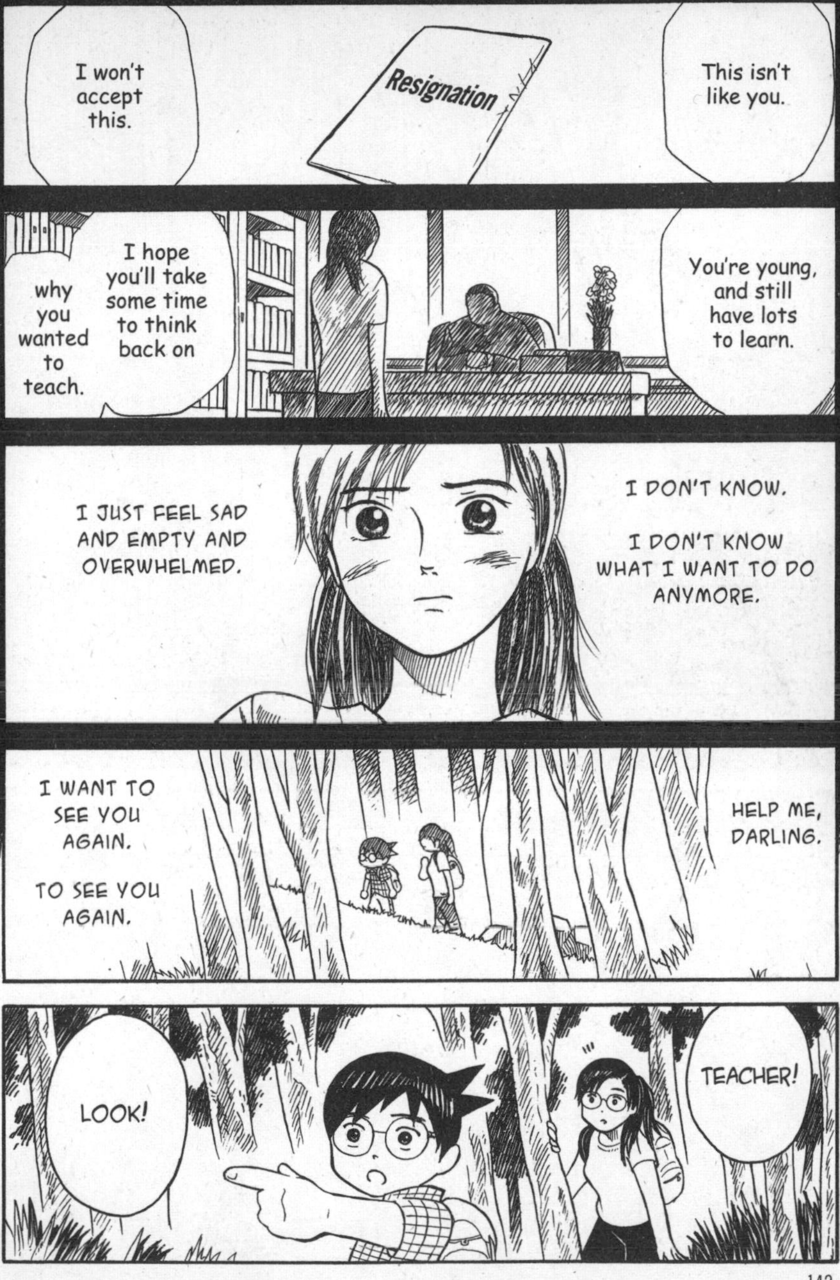
This isn't like you.
Resignation
I won't accept this.
You're young, and still have lots to learn.
I hope you'll take some time to think back on
why you wanted to teach.
I DON'T KNOW.
I DON'T KNOW WHAT I WANT TO DO ANYMORE.
I JUST FEEL SAD AND EMPTY AND OVERWHELMED.
HELP ME, DARLING.
I WANT TO SEE YOU AGAIN.
TO SEE YOU AGAIN.
TEACHER!
LOOK!

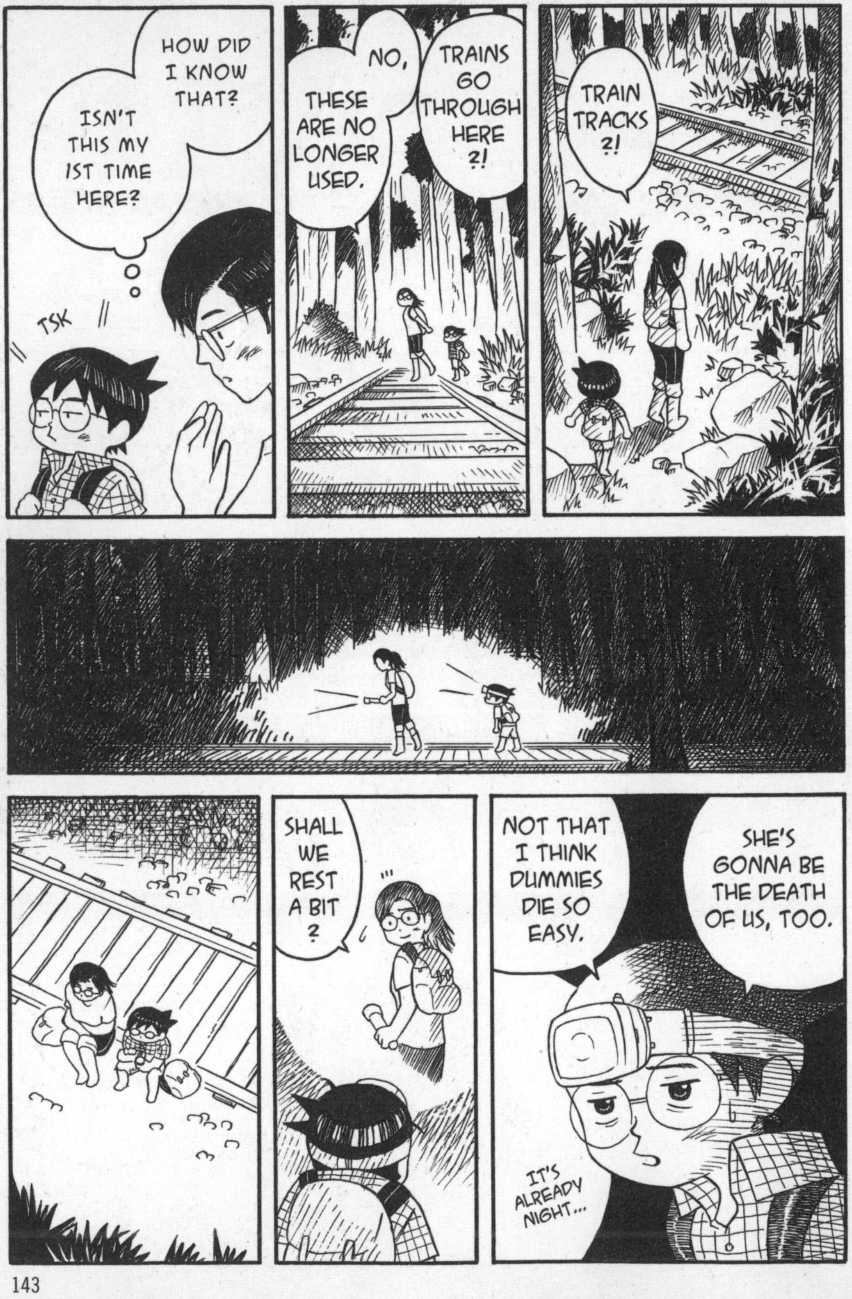
TRAIN TRACKS ?!
TRAINS GO THROUGH HERE ?!
NO, THESE ARE NO LONGER USED.
HOW DID I KNOW THAT?
ISN'T THIS MY 1ST TIME HERE?
TSK
SHE'S GONNA BE THE DEATH OF US, TOO.
NOT THAT I THINK DUMMIES DIE SO EASY.
IT'S ALREADY NIGHT...
SHALL WE REST A BIT ?

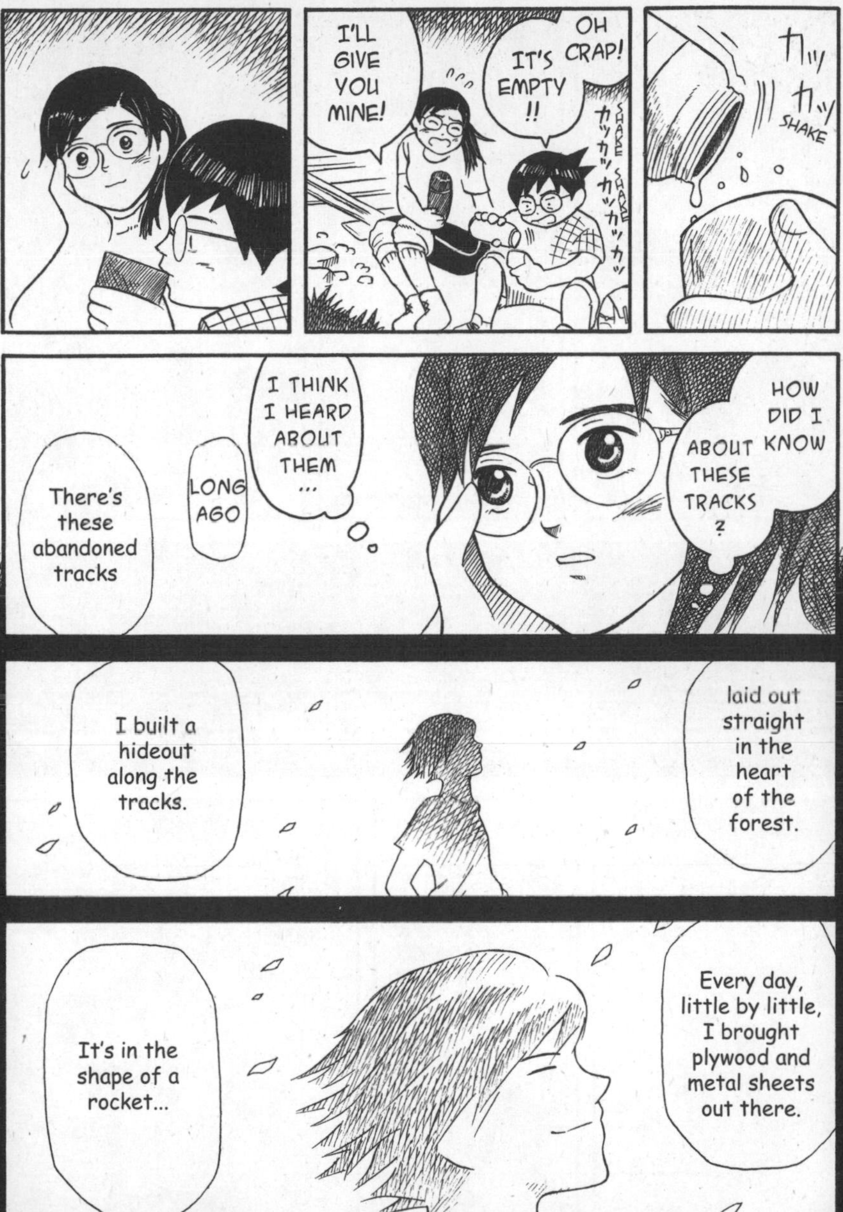
カッ
カッ
SHAKE
OH CRAP!
IT'S EMPTY!!
カッカッ
SHAKE
SHAKE
カッカッカッ
I'LL GIVE YOU MINE!
HOW DID I KNOW ABOUT THESE TRACKS?
I THINK I HEARD ABOUT THEM ...
LONG AGO
There's these abandoned tracks
laid out straight in the heart of the forest.
I built a hideout along the tracks.
Every day, little by little, I brought plywood and metal sheets out there.
It's in the shape of a rocket...

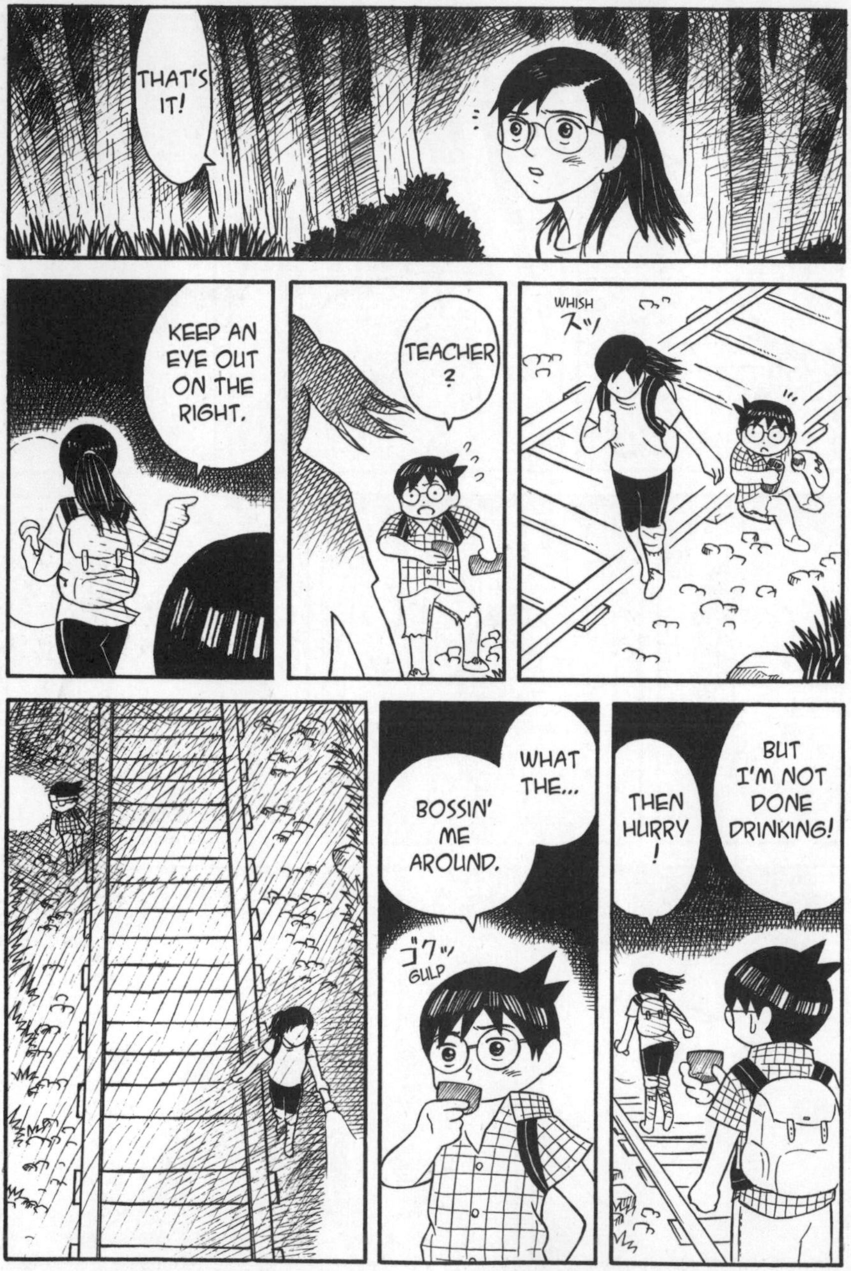
THAT'S IT!
WHISH
スッ
TEACHER?
KEEP AN EYE OUT ON THE RIGHT.
BUT I'M NOT DONE DRINKING!
THEN HURRY!
WHAT THE...
BOSSIN' ME AROUND.
ゴクッ
GULP

!!
THERE IT IS !!
TEACHER ?!
SWISH
ザザザッ
W- WHAT'S THAT ?!
ポロ DRIP ポロ DROP
ポロ DRIP ポロ DROP
POOR THING ...
WHEW

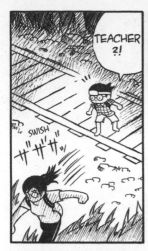

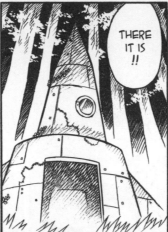

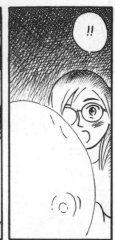

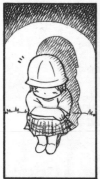

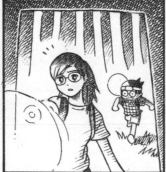

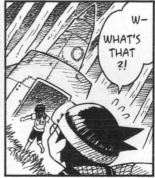

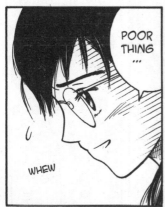

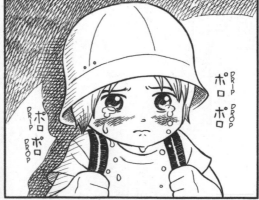

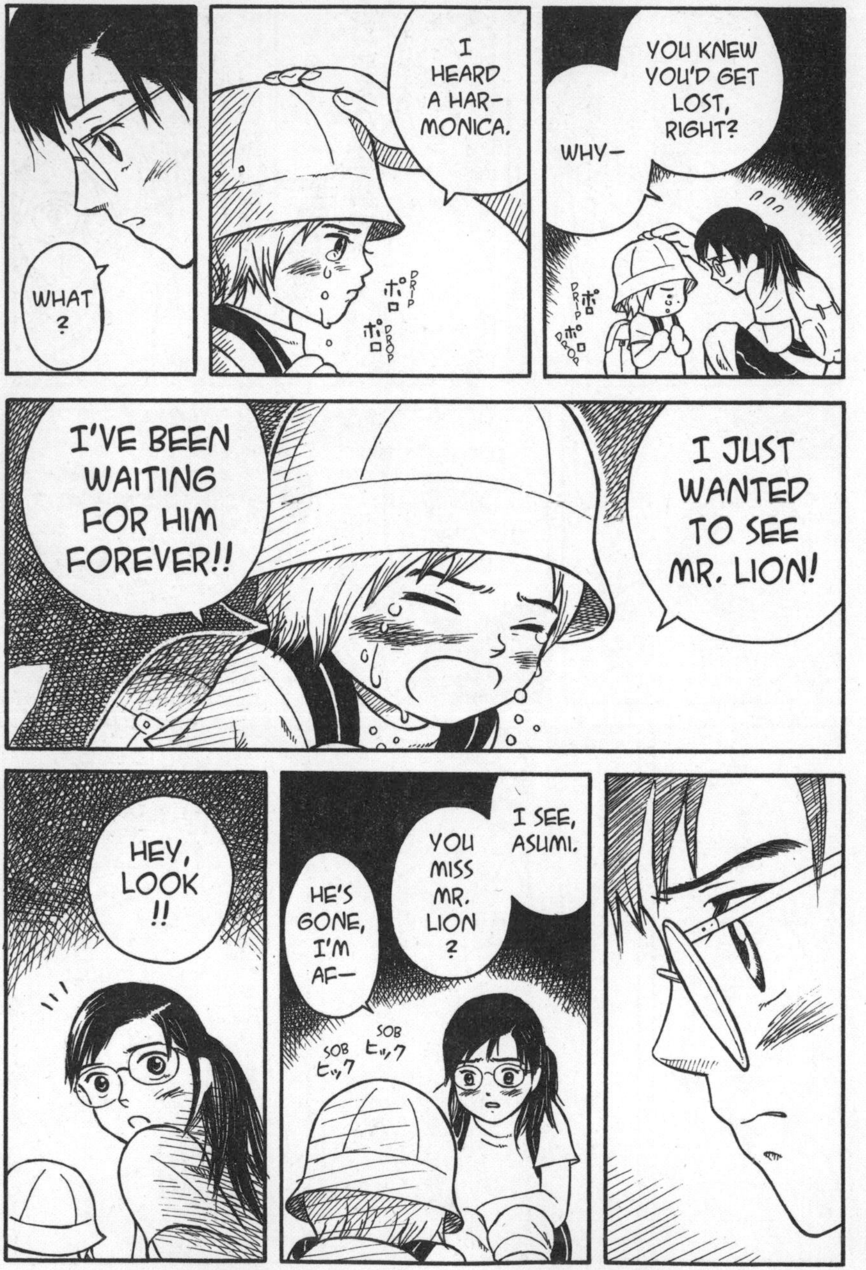
YOU KNEW YOU'D GET LOST, RIGHT?
WHY—
ポロ DRIP
ポロ DROP
I HEARD A HAR-MONICA.
ポロ DRIP
ポロ DROP
WHAT?
I JUST WANTED TO SEE MR. LION!
I'VE BEEN WAITING FOR HIM FOREVER!!
I SEE, ASUMI.
YOU MISS MR. LION?
HE'S GONE, I'M AF—
SOB ヒック
SOB ヒック
HEY, LOOK!!

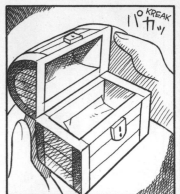

IT'S A HIKING MEDAL!
WHAT'S THIS DOING HERE?
IT WAS IN THE TREASURE CHEST.
CHEST?
HIC
KREAK
パカッ
WHAT'S THIS PHOTO?
DUDE'S WEARING A REALLY OLD SPACE SUIT.
CCCP
THERE'S SOMETHING WRITTEN ON THE BACK.
LESSEE...
WHEN I...
HM?
!!
WHEN I G-GROW UP...
AH
I HEAR IT!
TURN
くるっ

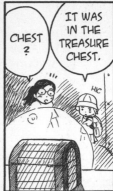

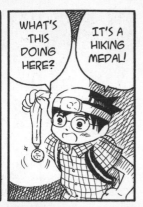

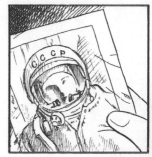

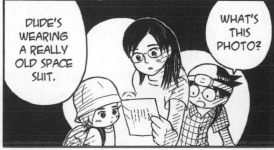

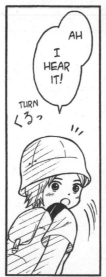

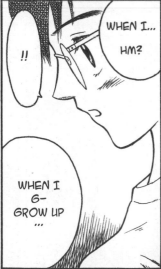

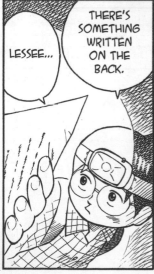

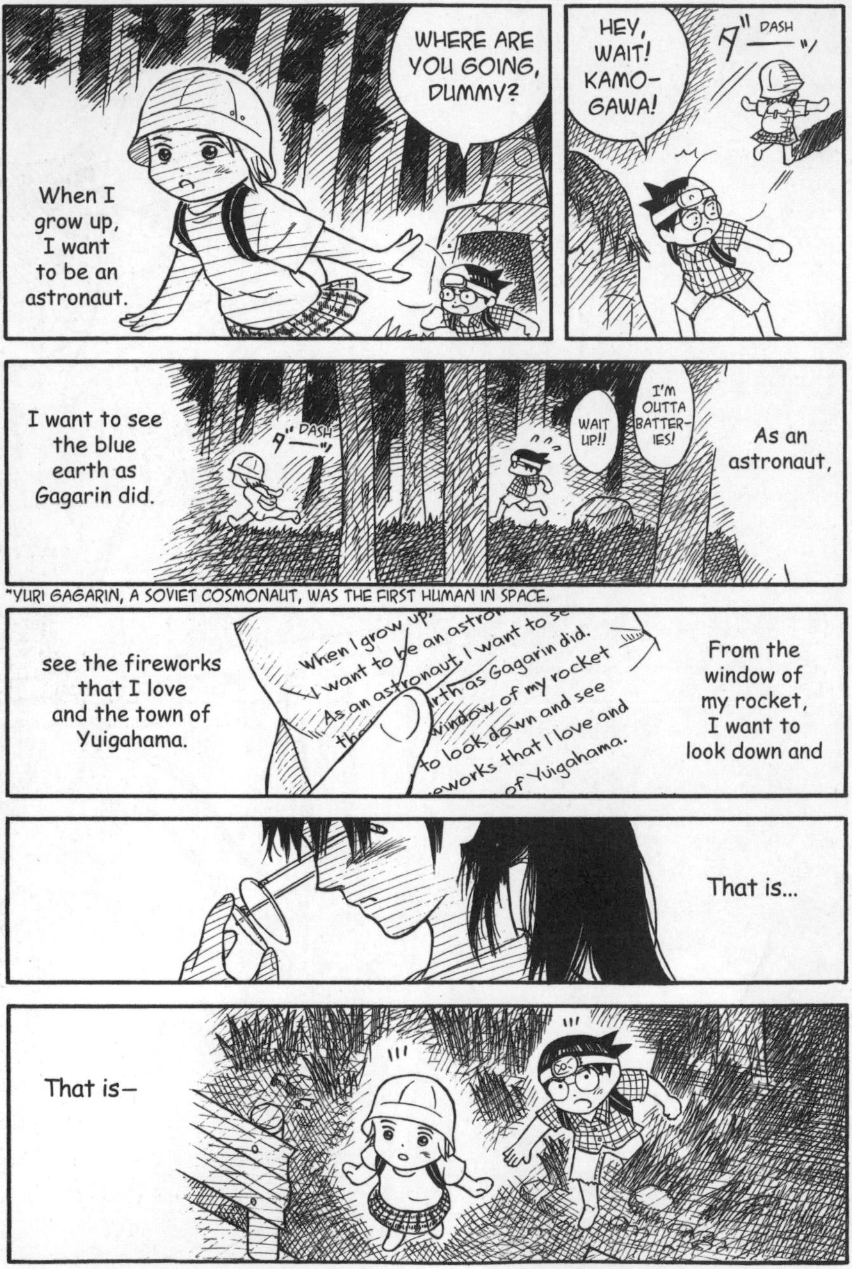
HEY, WAIT! KAMO-GAWA!
DASH
WHERE ARE YOU GOING, DUMMY?
When I grow up, I want to be an astronaut.
As an astronaut,
I'M OUTTA BATTER-IES!
WAIT UP!!
DASH
I want to see the blue earth as Gagarin did.
*YURI GAGARIN, A SOVIET COSMONAUT, WAS THE FIRST HUMAN IN SPACE.
From the window of my rocket, I want to look down and
When I grow up,
I want to be an astron
I want to se
As an astronaut,
rth as Gagarin did.
window of my rocket
to look down and see
eworks that I love and
of Yuigahama.
see the fireworks that I love and the town of Yuigahama.
That is...
That is—

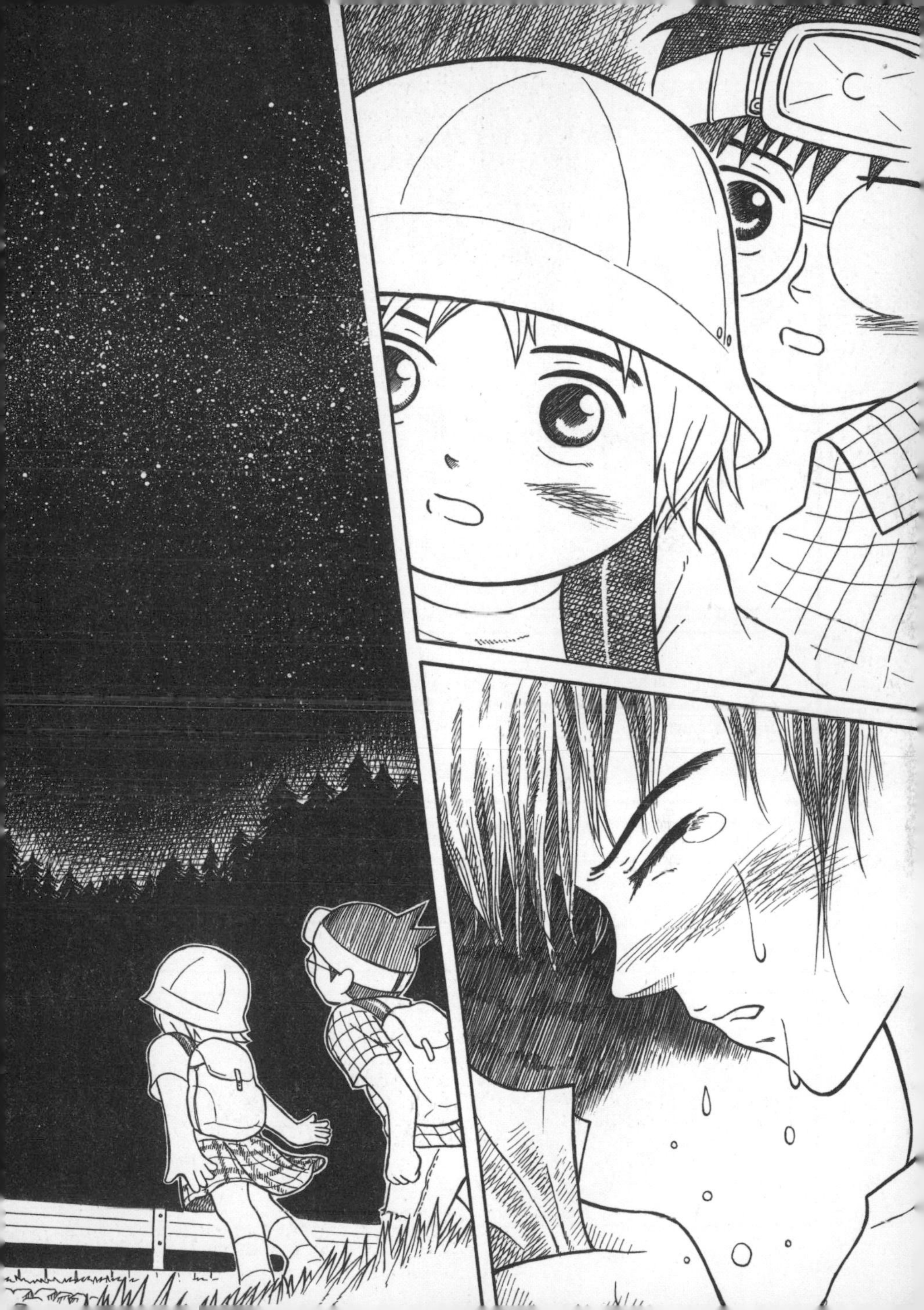

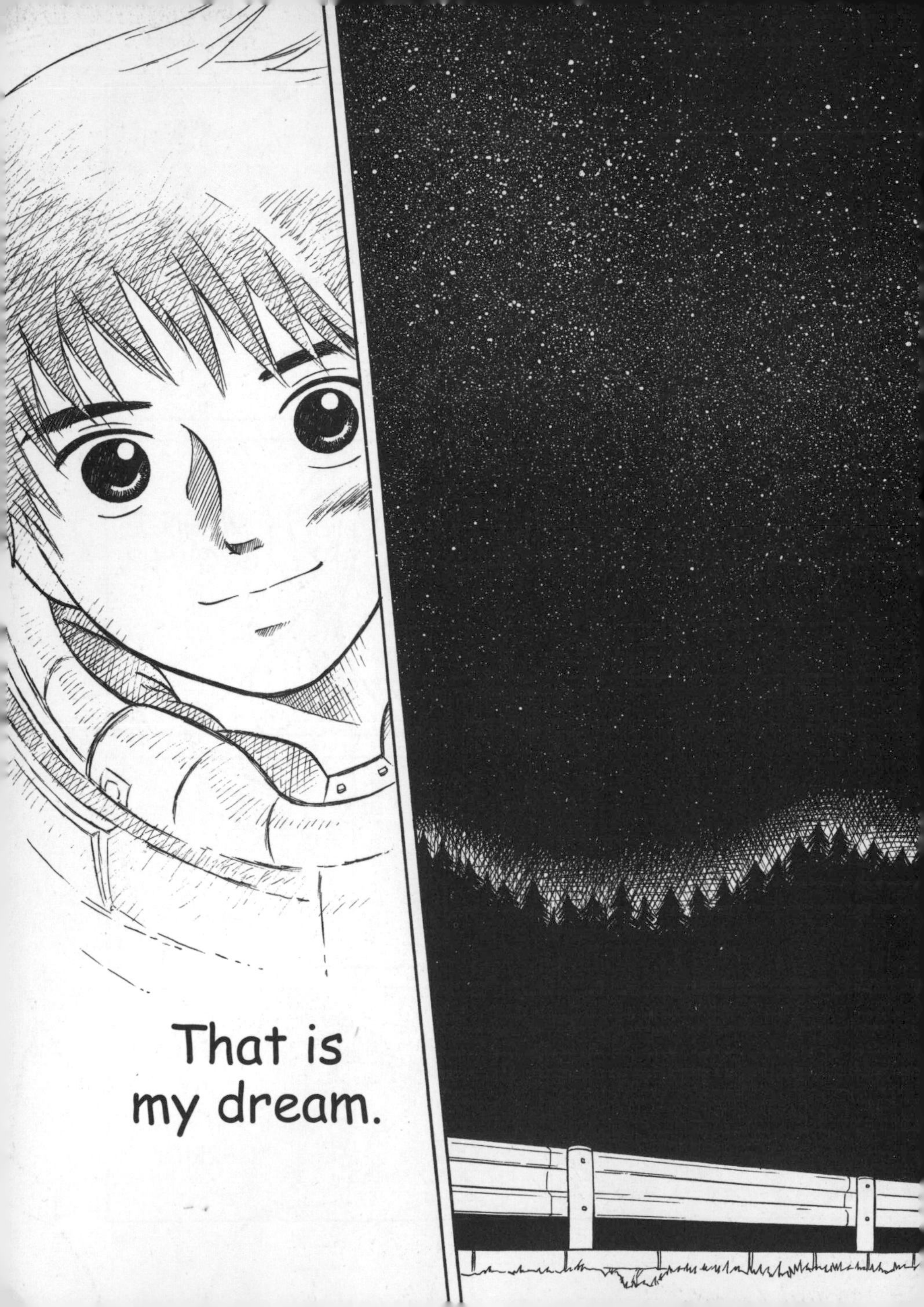
That is
my dream.

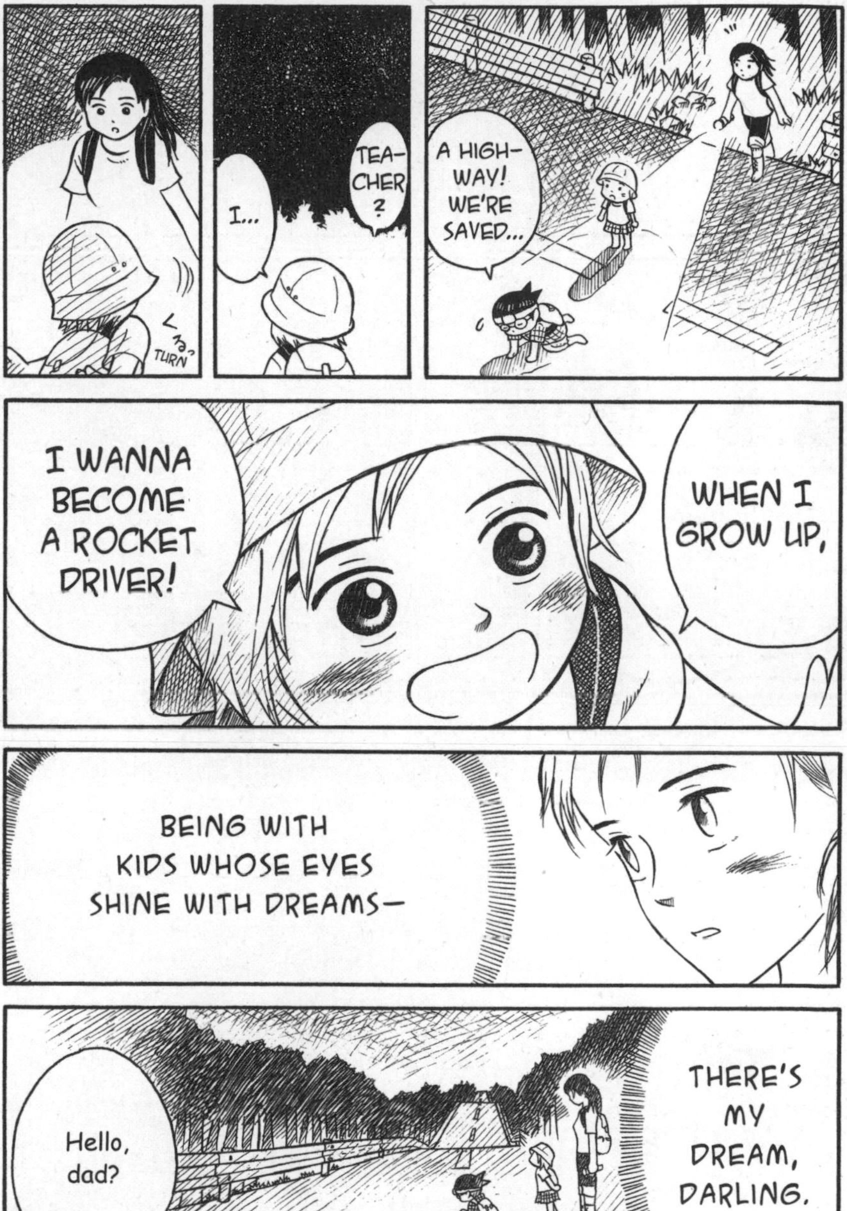
A HIGH-WAY! WE'RE SAVED...
TEA-CHER?
I...
TURN
WHEN I GROW UP,
I WANNA BECOME A ROCKET DRIVER!
BEING WITH KIDS WHOSE EYES SHINE WITH DREAMS—
THERE'S MY DREAM, DARLING.
Hello, dad?

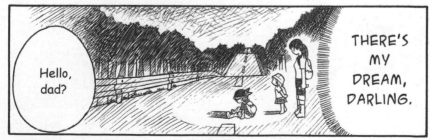

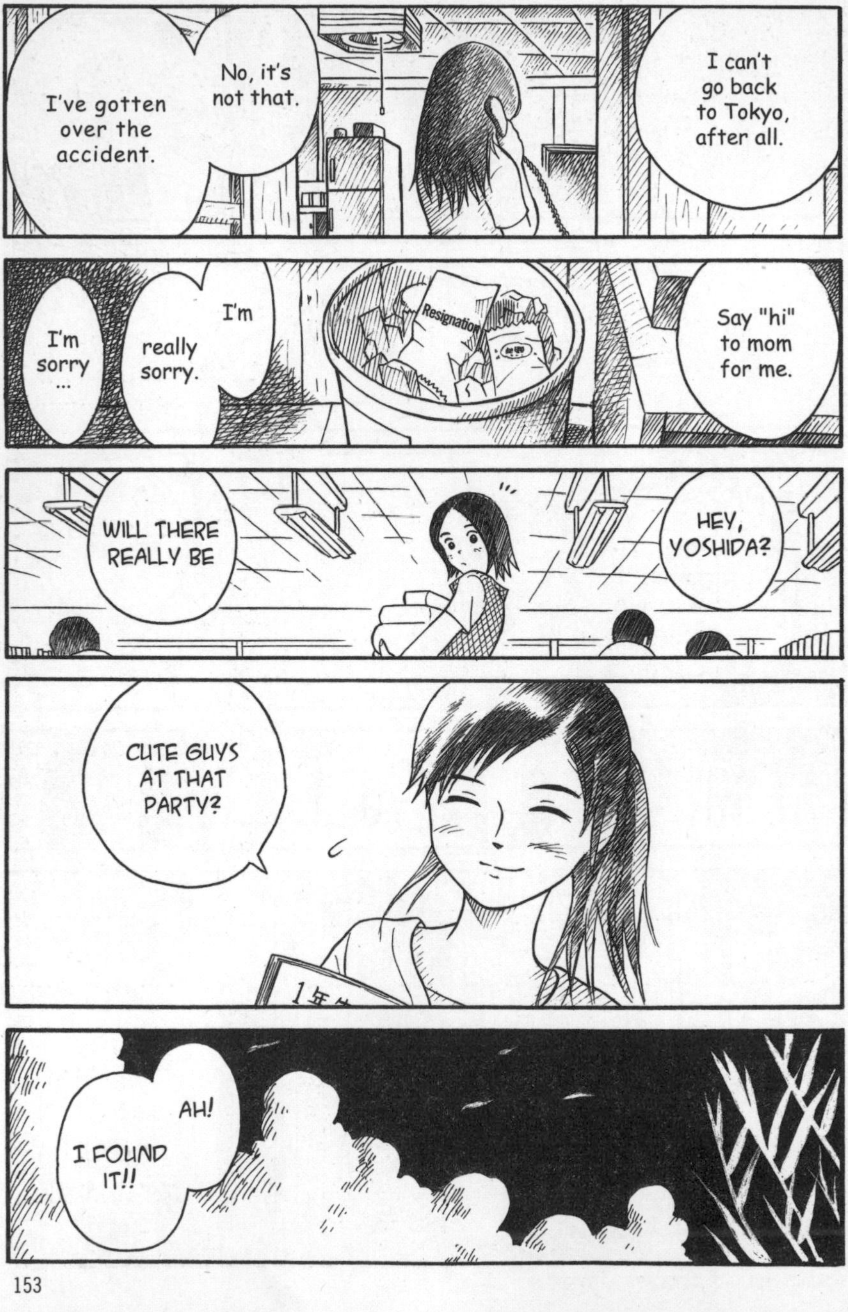

I can't go back to Tokyo, after all.
No, it's not that.
I've gotten over the accident.
Say "hi" to mom for me.
Resignation
I'm really sorry.
I'm sorry ...
HEY, YOSHIDA?
WILL THERE REALLY BE
CUTE GUYS AT THAT PARTY?
AH! I FOUND IT!!

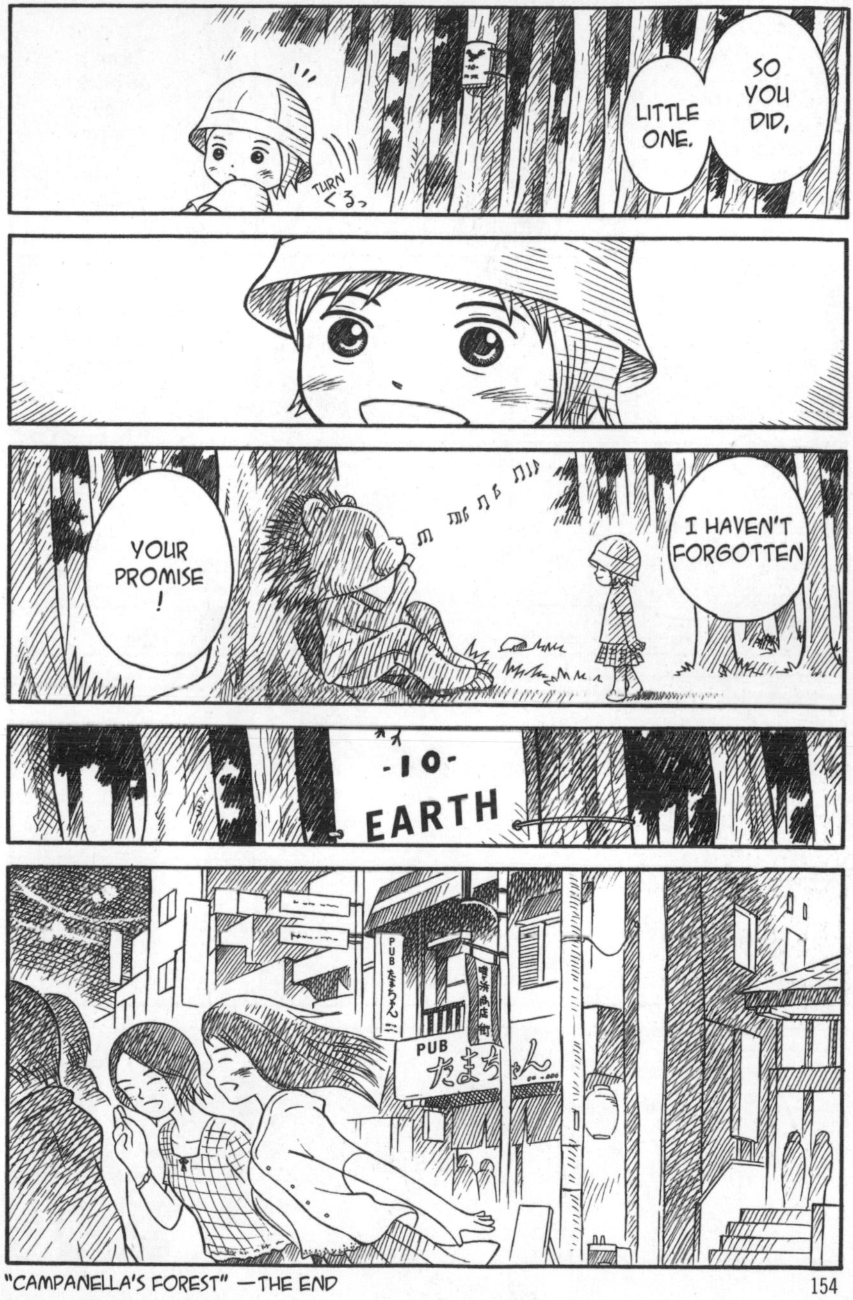
SO YOU DID,
LITTLE ONE.
TURN
くるっ
I HAVEN'T FORGOTTEN
YOUR PROMISE !
-10-
EARTH
PUB
たまちゃん

"CAMPANELLA'S FOREST" —THE END

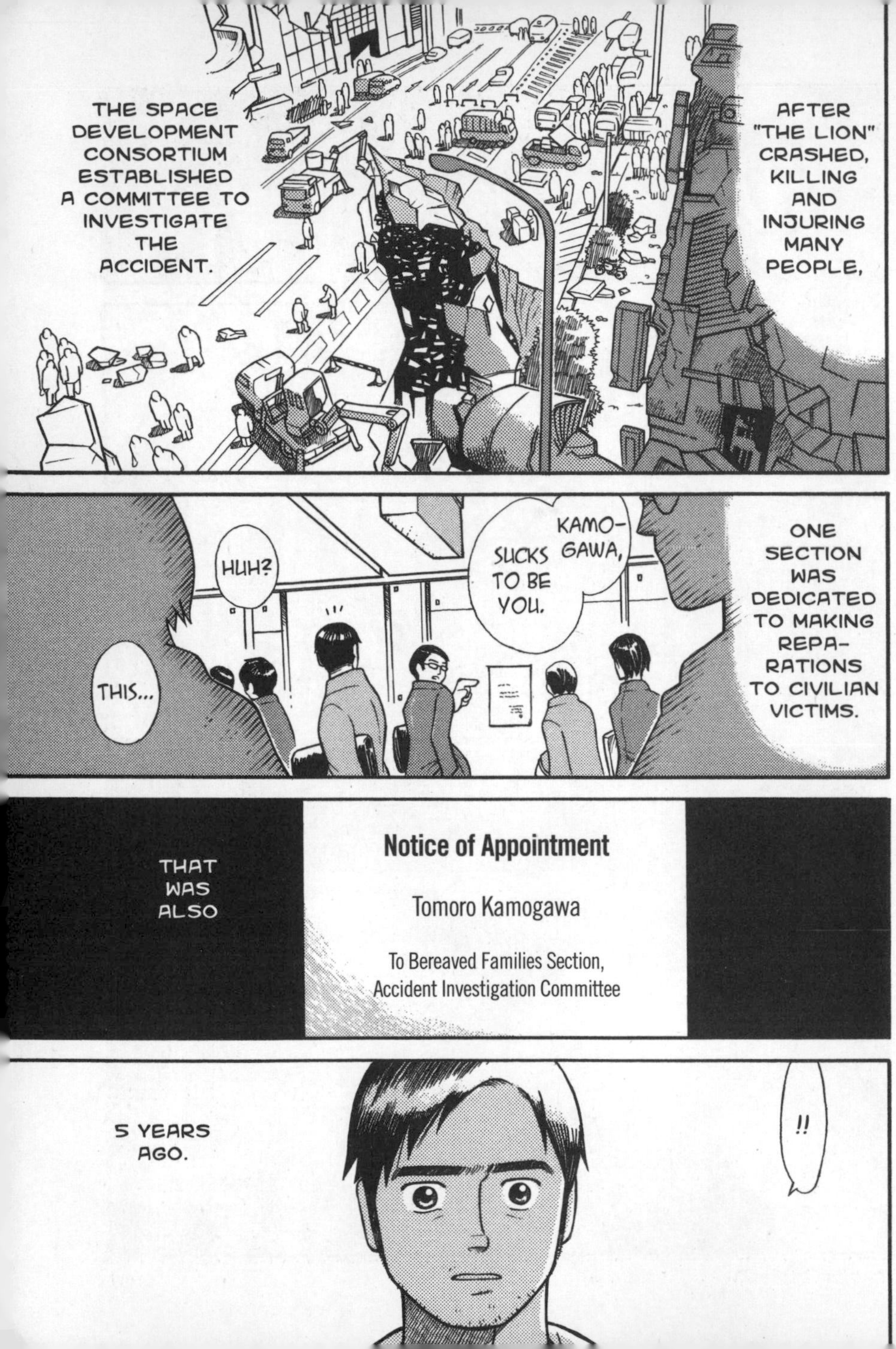
AFTER "THE LION" CRASHED, KILLING AND INJURING MANY PEOPLE,
THE SPACE DEVELOPMENT CONSORTIUM ESTABLISHED A COMMITTEE TO INVESTIGATE THE ACCIDENT.
ONE SECTION WAS DEDICATED TO MAKING REPA-RATIONS TO CIVILIAN VICTIMS.
KAMOGAWA, SUCKS TO BE YOU.
HUH?
THIS...
Notice of Appointment
Tomoro Kamogawa
To Bereaved Families Section, Accident Investigation Committee
THAT WAS ALSO
!!
5 YEARS AGO.

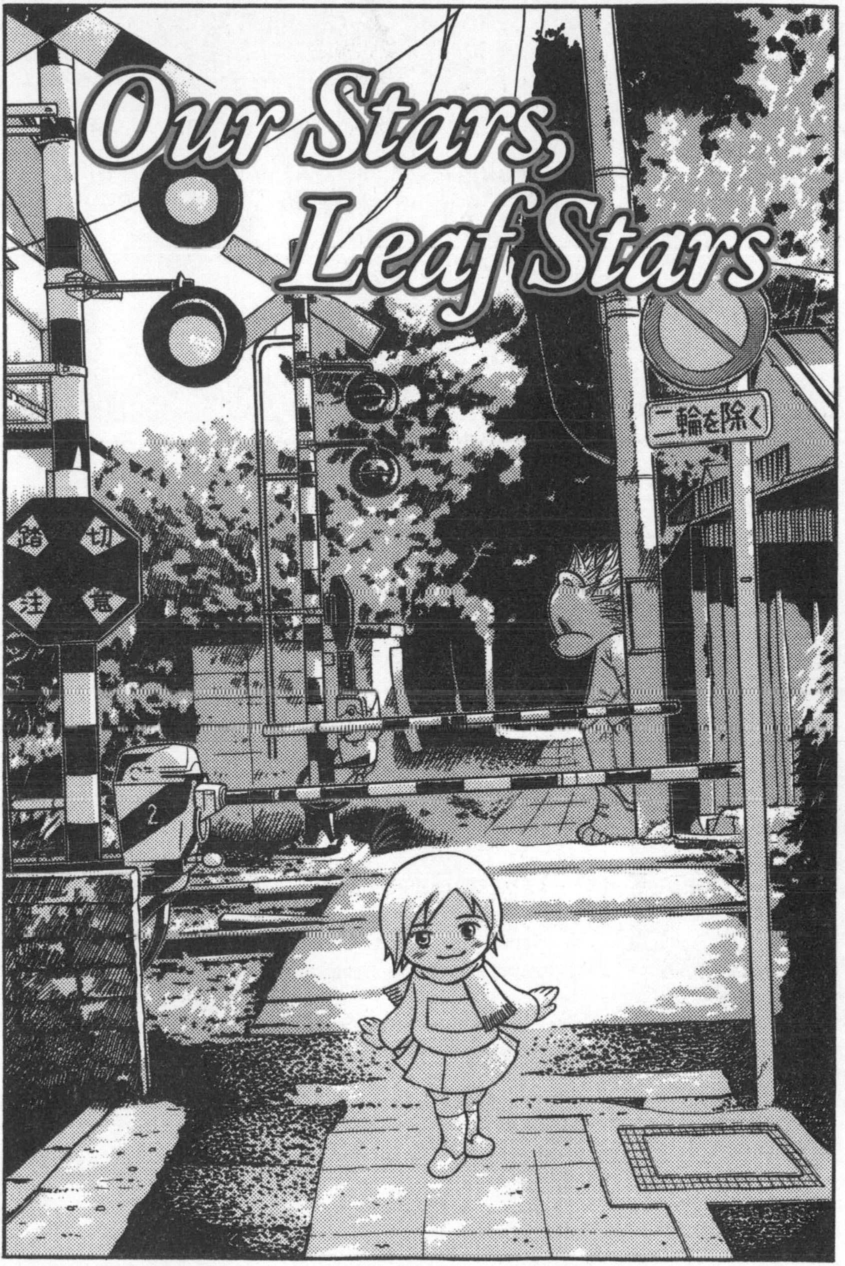
Our Stars,
Leaf Stars
二輪を除く
踏切
注意
2

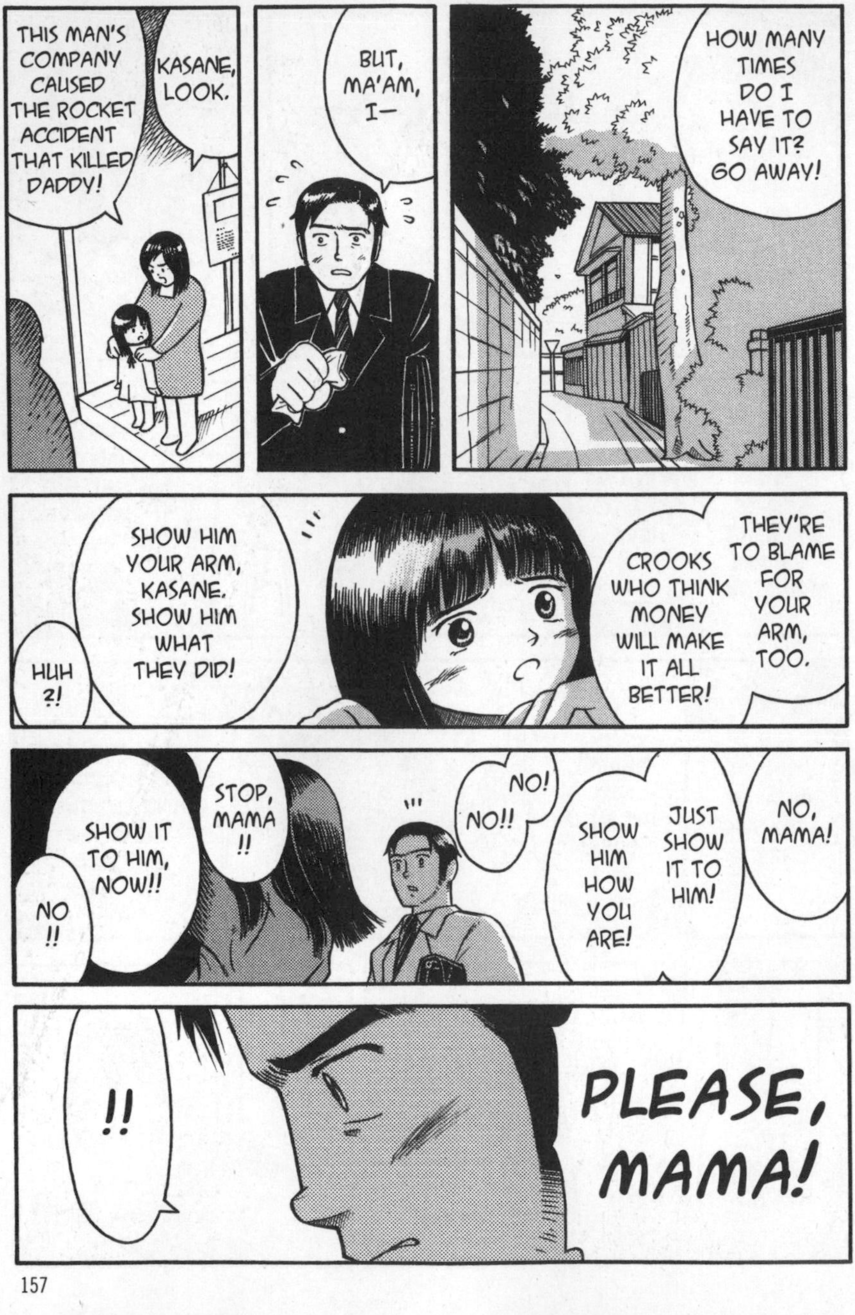
HOW MANY TIMES DO I HAVE TO SAY IT? GO AWAY!
BUT, MA'AM, I—
KASANE, LOOK.
THIS MAN'S COMPANY CAUSED THE ROCKET ACCIDENT THAT KILLED DADDY!
THEY'RE TO BLAME FOR YOUR ARM, TOO.
CROOKS WHO THINK MONEY WILL MAKE IT ALL BETTER!
SHOW HIM YOUR ARM, KASANE. SHOW HIM WHAT THEY DID!
HUH?!
NO, MAMA!
JUST SHOW IT TO HIM!
SHOW HIM HOW YOU ARE!
NO!
NO!!
STOP, MAMA!!
SHOW IT TO HIM, NOW!!
NO!!
PLEASE, MAMA!
!!

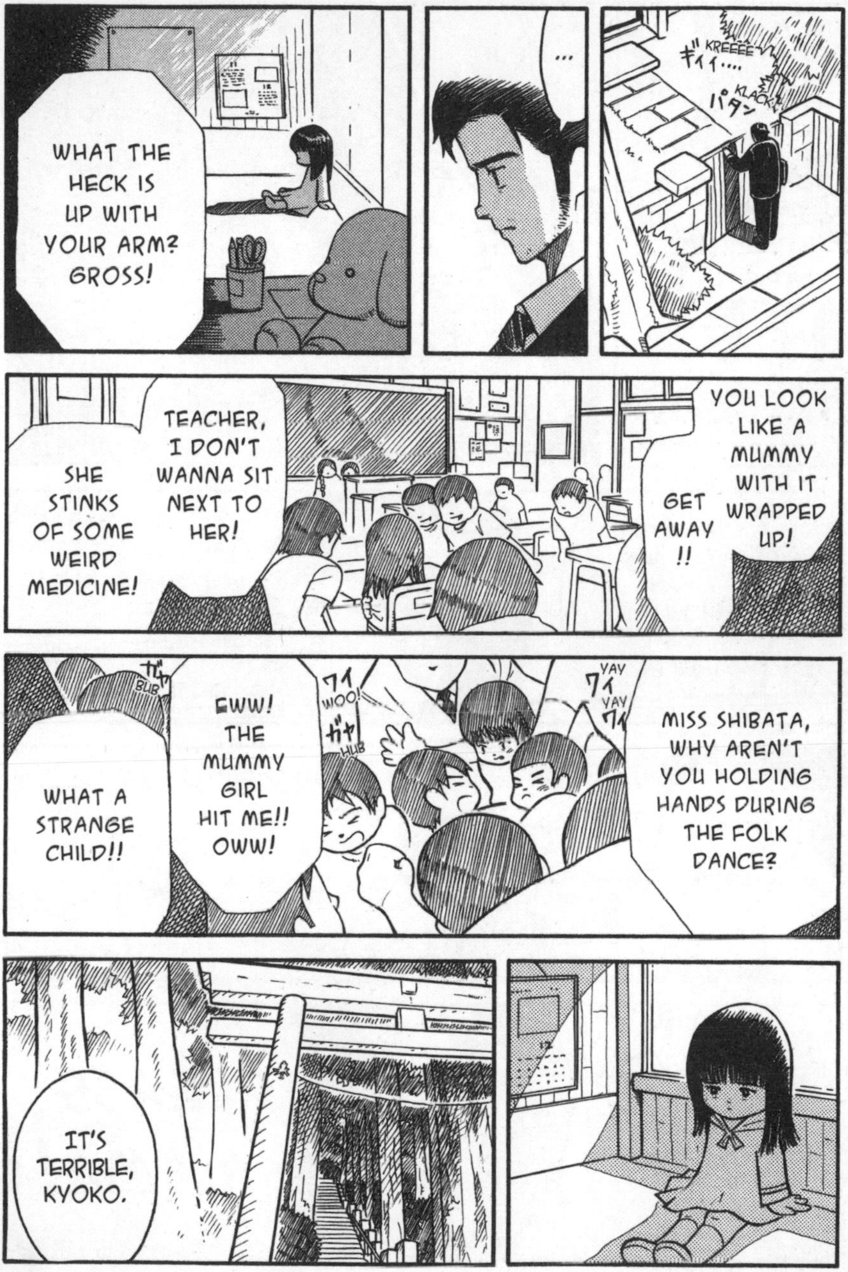
KREEEEE
ギィィ….
KLACK
パタン
…
WHAT THE HECK IS UP WITH YOUR ARM? GROSS!
YOU LOOK LIKE A MUMMY WITH IT WRAPPED UP!
GET AWAY!!
TEACHER, I DON'T WANNA SIT NEXT TO HER!
SHE STINKS OF SOME WEIRD MEDICINE!
MISS SHIBATA, WHY AREN'T YOU HOLDING HANDS DURING THE FOLK DANCE?
YAY
ワイ
YAY
ワイ
ワイ
WOO!
ガヤ
HUB
EWW! THE MUMMY GIRL HIT ME!! OWW!
ガヤ
BUB
WHAT A STRANGE CHILD!!
IT'S TERRIBLE, KYOKO.

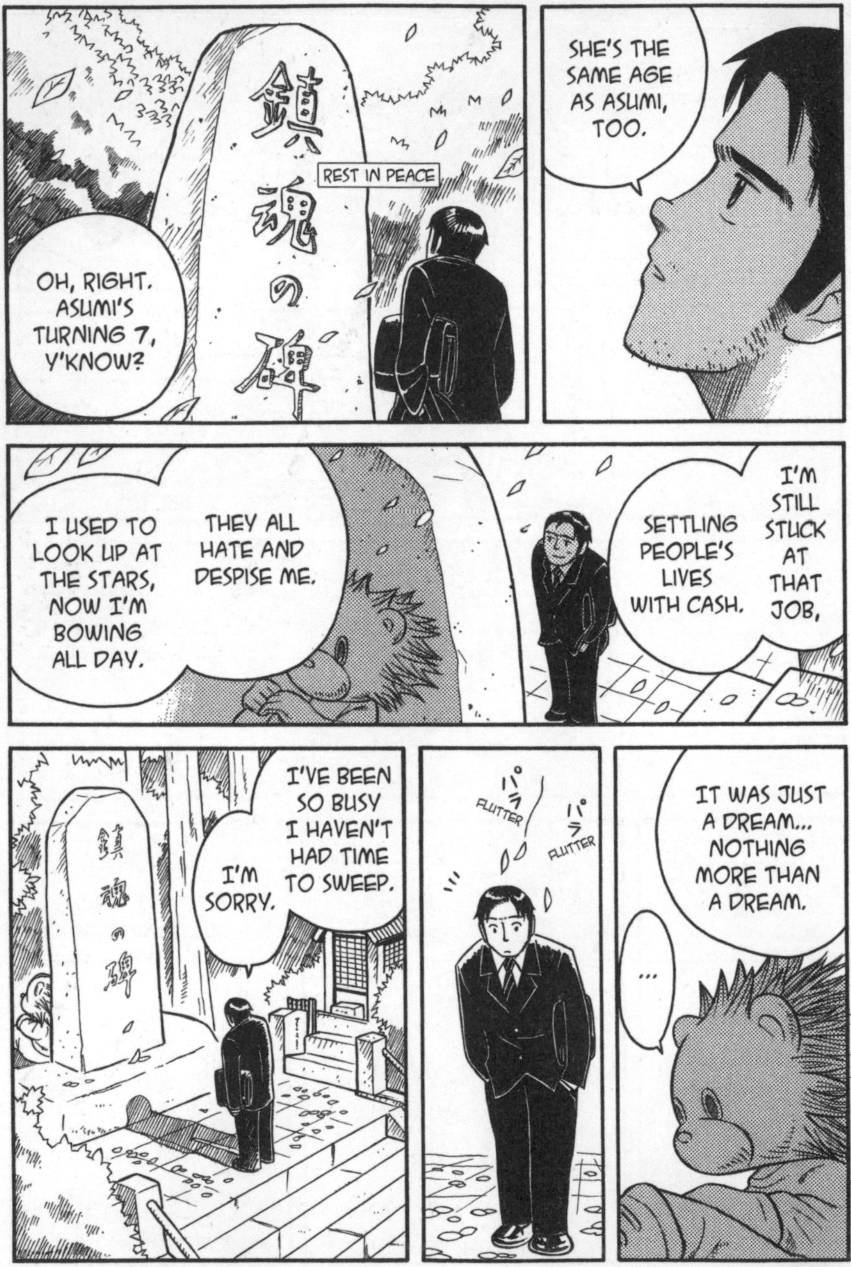
SHE'S THE SAME AGE AS ASUMI, TOO.
鎮魂の碑
REST IN PEACE
OH, RIGHT. ASUMI'S TURNING 7, Y'KNOW?
I'M STILL STUCK AT THAT JOB,
SETTLING PEOPLE'S LIVES WITH CASH.
THEY ALL HATE AND DESPISE ME.
I USED TO LOOK UP AT THE STARS, NOW I'M BOWING ALL DAY.
IT WAS JUST A DREAM... NOTHING MORE THAN A DREAM.
...
パラ
FLUTTER
パラ
FLUTTER
I'VE BEEN SO BUSY I HAVEN'T HAD TIME TO SWEEP.
I'M SORRY.
鎮魂の碑

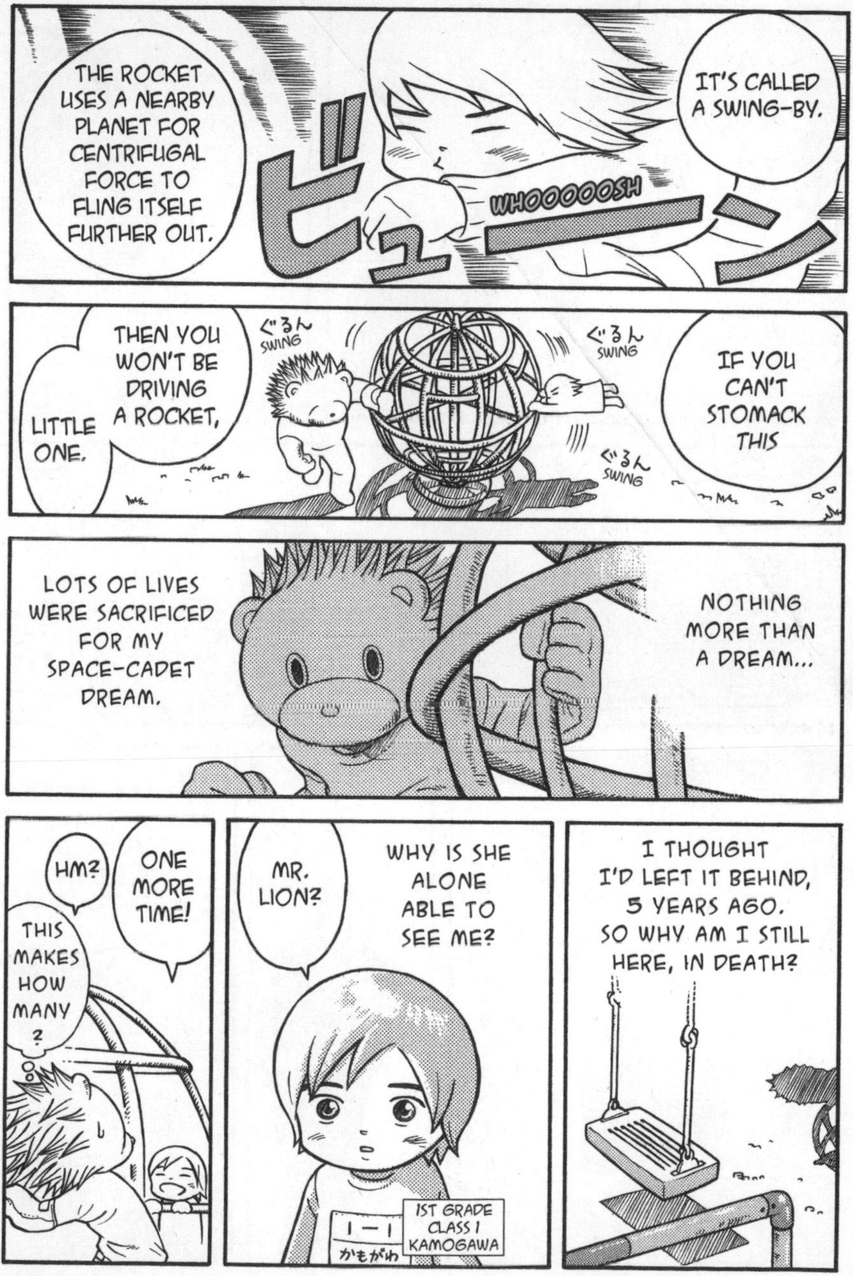
IT'S CALLED A SWING-BY.
THE ROCKET USES A NEARBY PLANET FOR CENTRIFUGAL FORCE TO FLING ITSELF FURTHER OUT.
ビューーン
WHOOOOOSH
IF YOU CAN'T STOMACK THIS
ぐるん
SWING
ぐるん
SWING
ぐるん
SWING
THEN YOU WON'T BE DRIVING A ROCKET,
LITTLE ONE.
NOTHING MORE THAN A DREAM...
LOTS OF LIVES WERE SACRIFICED FOR MY SPACE-CADET DREAM.
I THOUGHT I'D LEFT IT BEHIND, 5 YEARS AGO. SO WHY AM I STILL HERE, IN DEATH?
WHY IS SHE ALONE ABLE TO SEE ME?
MR. LION?
1ST GRADE CLASS 1 KAMOGAWA
1-1
かもがわ
ONE MORE TIME!
HM?
THIS MAKES HOW MANY?

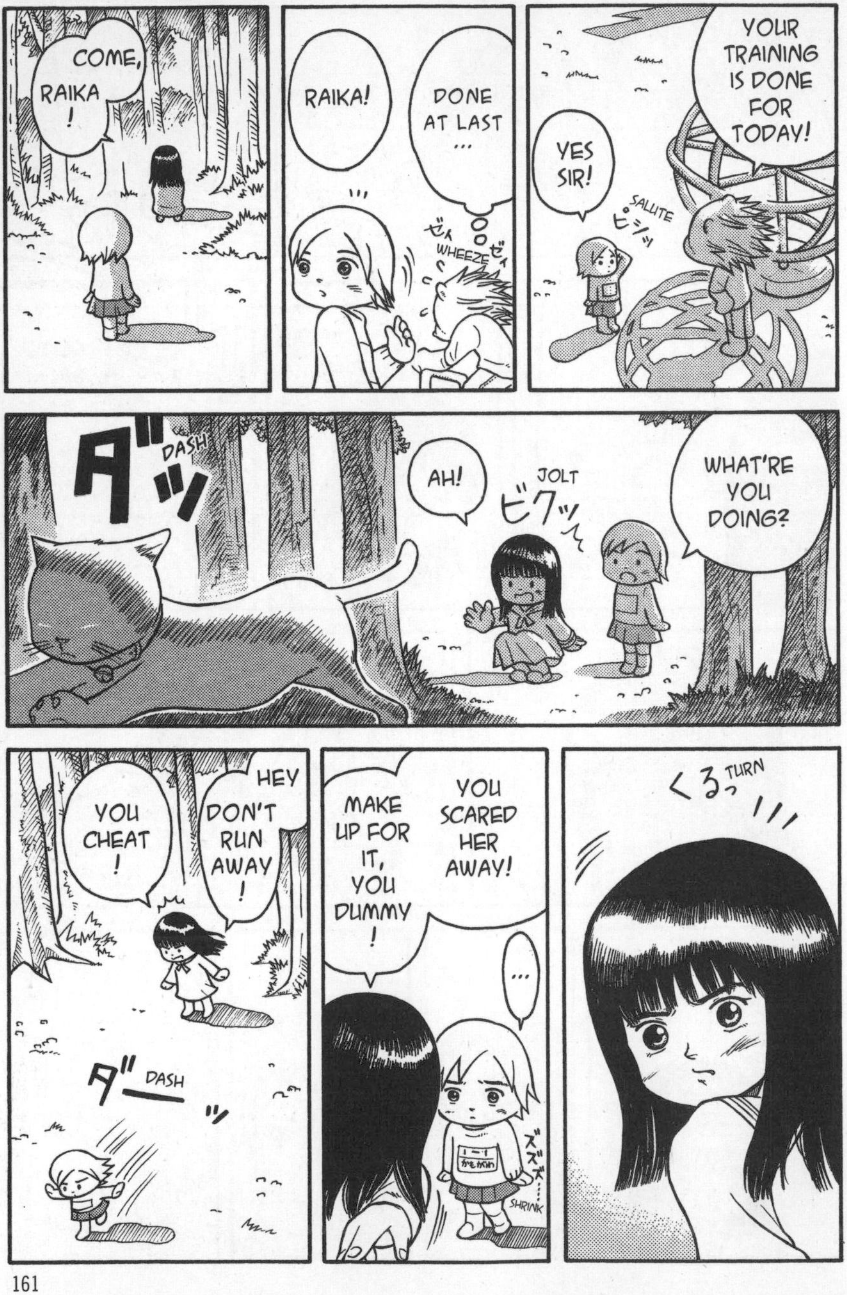
YOUR TRAINING IS DONE FOR TODAY!
YES SIR!
ピシッ SALUTE
RAIKA!
DONE AT LAST ...
ぜぃ ぜぃ WHEEZE
COME, RAIKA!
WHAT'RE YOU DOING?
ビクッ JOLT
AH!
ダッ DASH
くるっ TURN
YOU SCARED HER AWAY!
MAKE UP FOR IT, YOU DUMMY!
...
ズズズ... SHRINK
HEY DON'T RUN AWAY!
YOU CHEAT!
ダー DASH

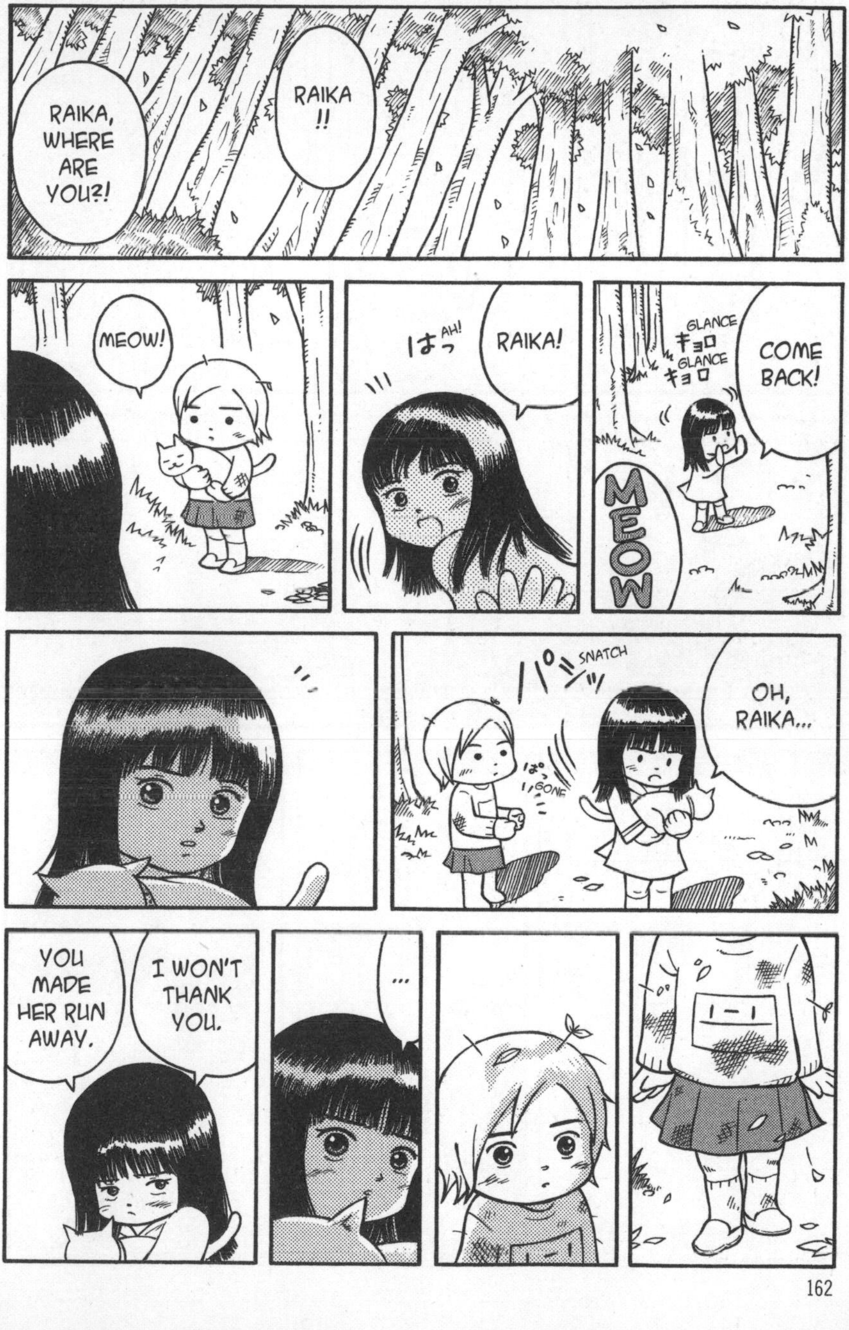

RAIKA !!
RAIKA, WHERE ARE YOU?!
GLANCE キョロ GLANCE キョロ
COME BACK!
MEOW
はっ AH!
RAIKA!
MEOW!
パシッ SNATCH
OH, RAIKA...
ぱっ GONE
...
I WON'T THANK YOU.
YOU MADE HER RUN AWAY.

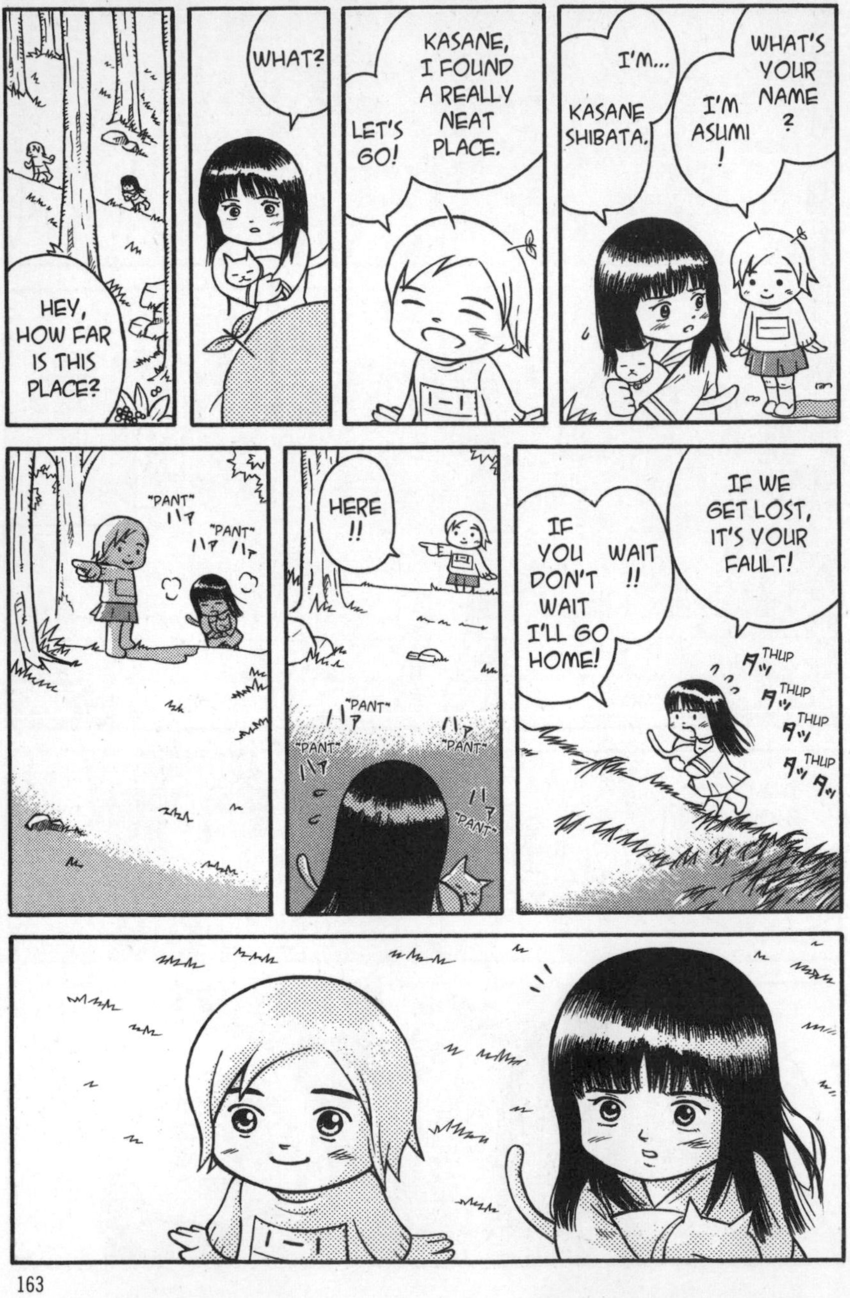
WHAT'S YOUR NAME?
I'M ASUMI!
I'M...
KASANE SHIBATA.
KASANE, I FOUND A REALLY NEAT PLACE.
LET'S GO!
WHAT?
HEY, HOW FAR IS THIS PLACE?
IF WE GET LOST, IT'S YOUR FAULT!
WAIT!!
IF YOU DON'T WAIT I'LL GO HOME!
THUP タッ
THUP タッ
THUP タッ
THUP タッ タッ
HERE!!
"PANT" ハァ
"PANT" ハァ
"PANT" ハァ
"PANT" ハァ
"PANT" ハァ
"PANT" ハァ ハァ

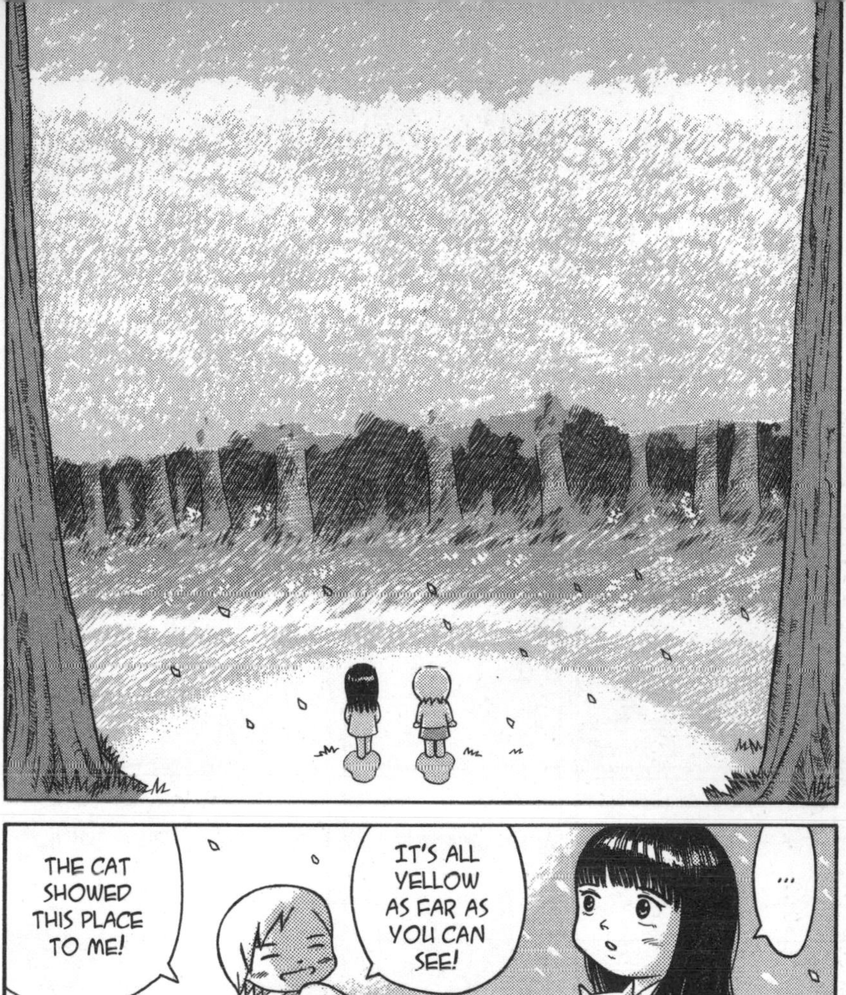

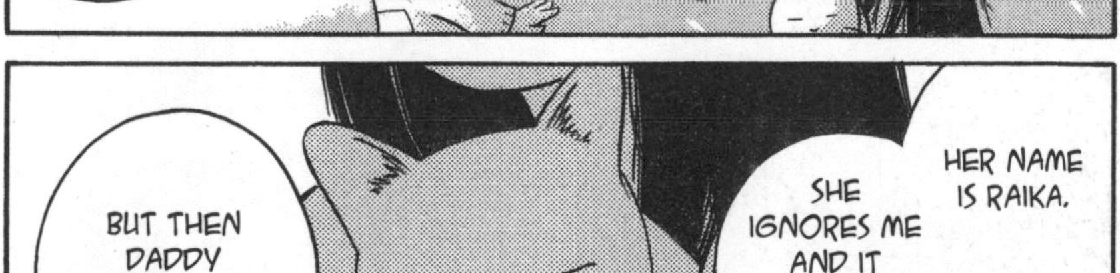
...
IT'S ALL YELLOW AS FAR AS YOU CAN SEE!
THE CAT SHOWED THIS PLACE TO ME!

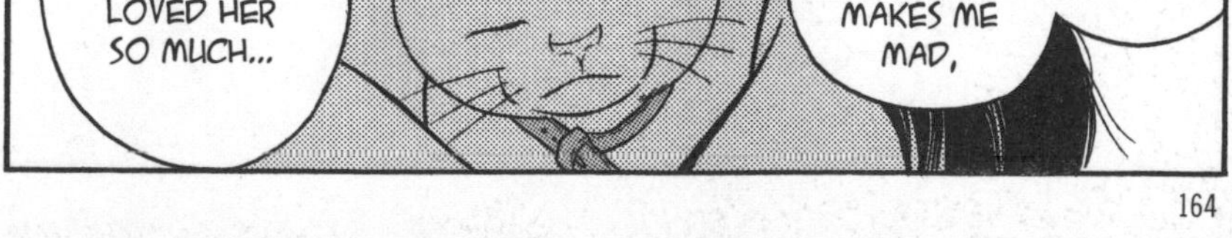
HER NAME IS RAIKA.
SHE IGNORES ME AND IT MAKES ME MAD,
BUT THEN DADDY LOVED HER SO MUCH...

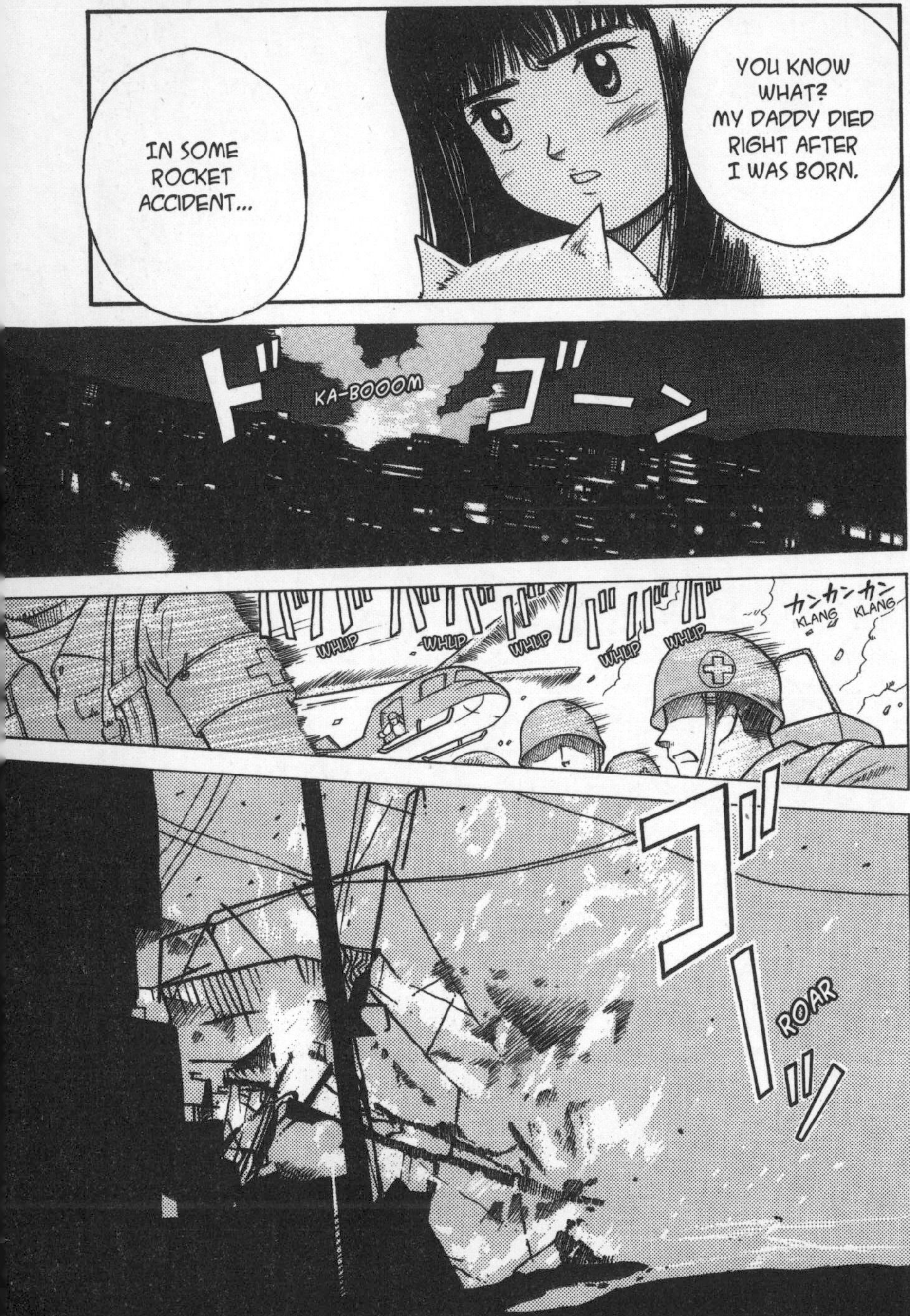
YOU KNOW WHAT? MY DADDY DIED RIGHT AFTER I WAS BORN.
IN SOME ROCKET ACCIDENT...
ドゴーン
KA-BOOOM
カンカンカン
KLANG KLANG
WHUP
WHUP
WHUP
WHUP
WHUP
ゴーッ
ROAR

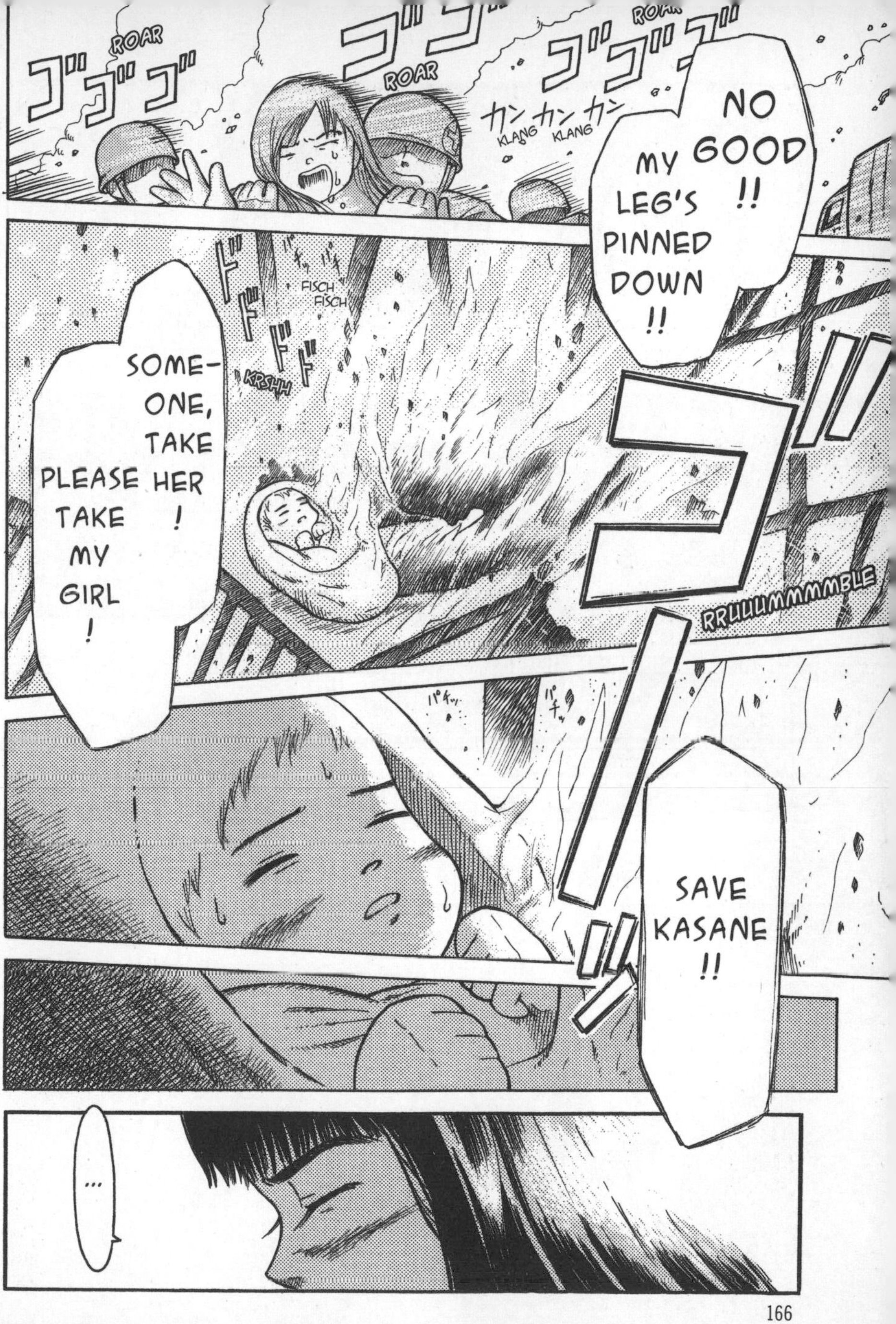
ROAR
ROAR
ROAR
ゴゴゴ
カンカンカン
KLANG KLANG
NO GOOD!! MY LEG'S PINNED DOWN!!
FISCH FISCH
KRSHH
RRUUUMMMMBLE
SOME-ONE, TAKE HER! PLEASE TAKE MY GIRL!
SAVE KASANE!!
...

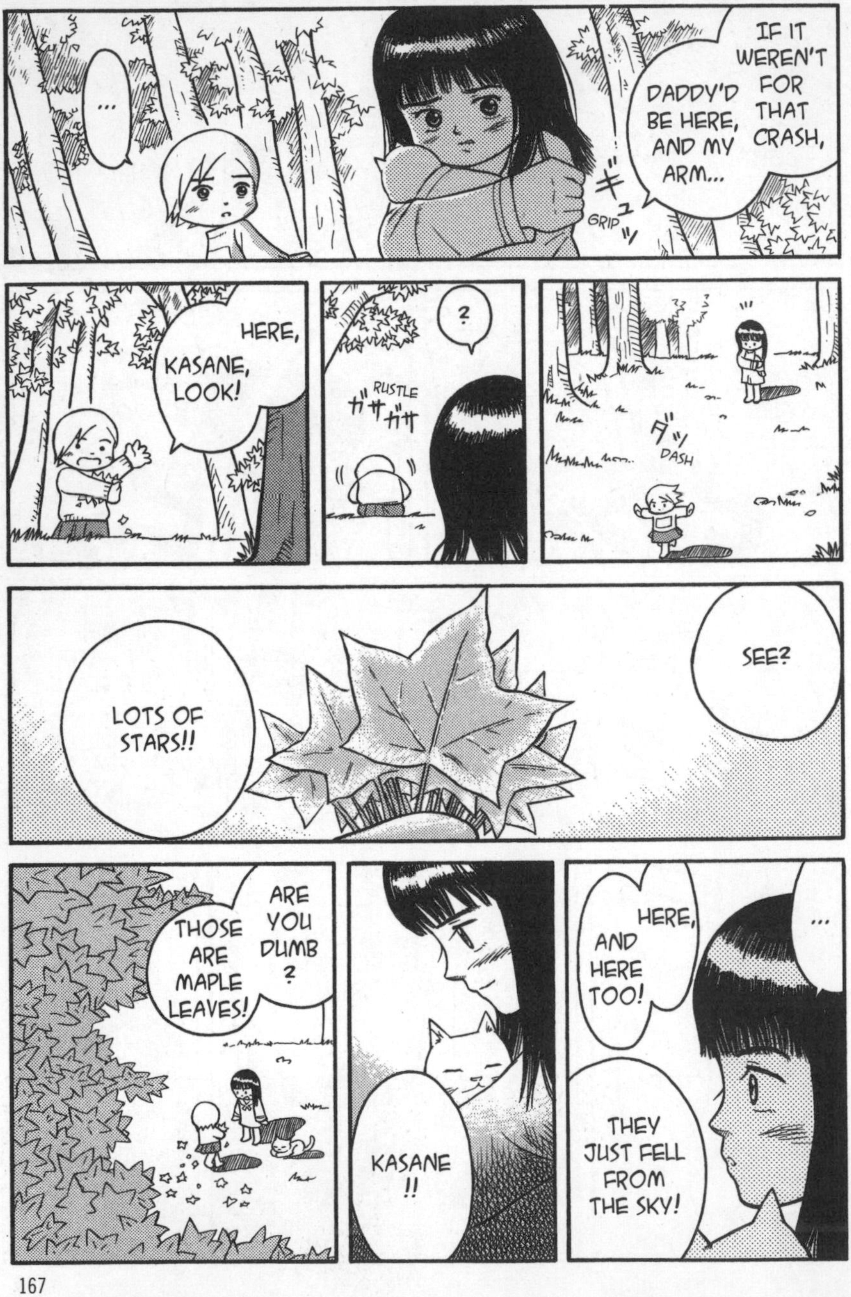
IF IT WEREN'T FOR THAT CRASH, DADDY'D BE HERE, AND MY ARM...
ギュッ
GRIP
...
ダッ
DASH
?
RUSTLE
ガサガサ
HERE, KASANE, LOOK!
SEE?
LOTS OF STARS!!
...
HERE, AND HERE TOO!
THEY JUST FELL FROM THE SKY!
KASANE!!
ARE YOU DUMB?
THOSE ARE MAPLE LEAVES!

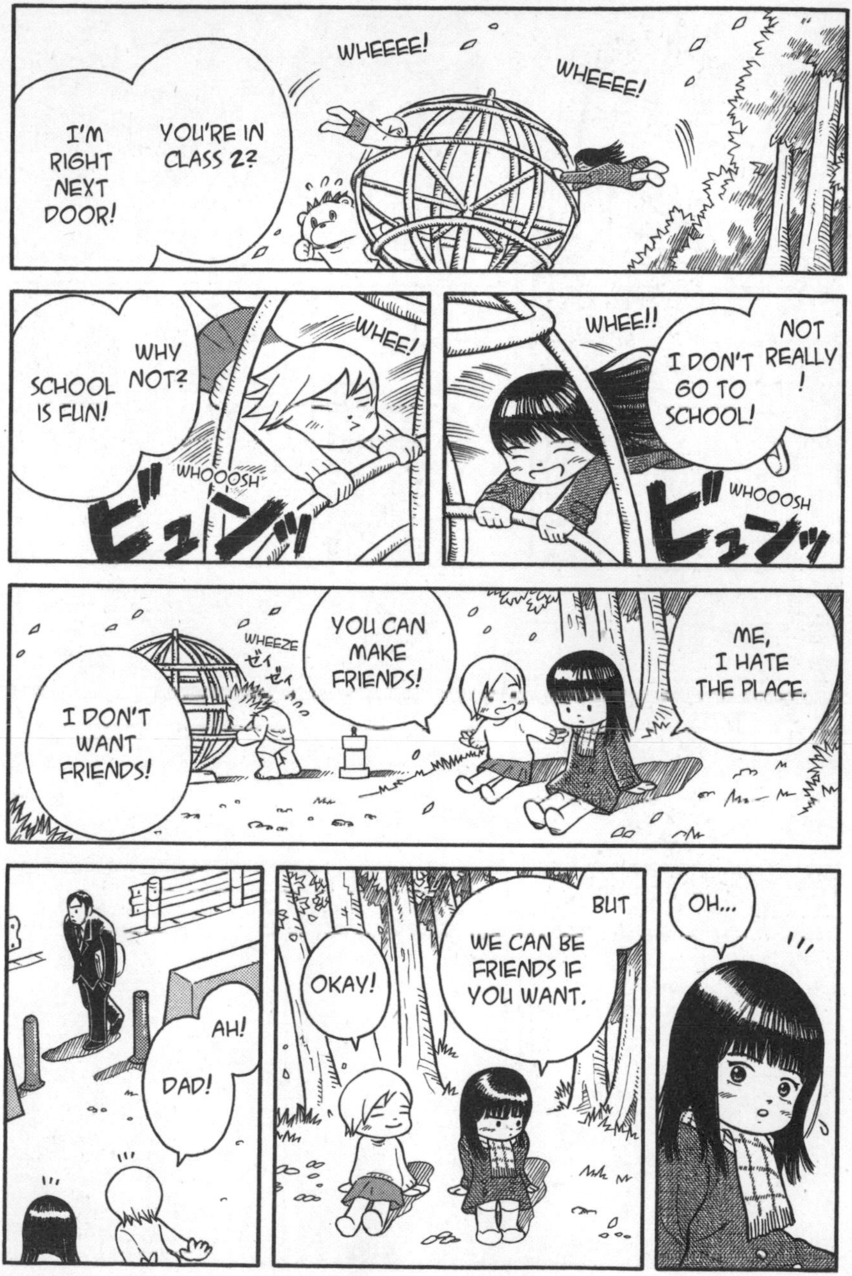
WHEEEE!
WHEEEE!
YOU'RE IN CLASS 2?
I'M RIGHT NEXT DOOR!
NOT REALLY!
I DON'T GO TO SCHOOL!
WHEE!!
WHOOOSH
ビュンッ
WHEE!
WHY NOT?
SCHOOL IS FUN!
WHOOOSH
ビュンッ
ME, I HATE THE PLACE.
YOU CAN MAKE FRIENDS!
WHEEZE
ゼィ ゼィ
I DON'T WANT FRIENDS!
OH...
BUT
WE CAN BE FRIENDS IF YOU WANT.
OKAY!
AH!
DAD!

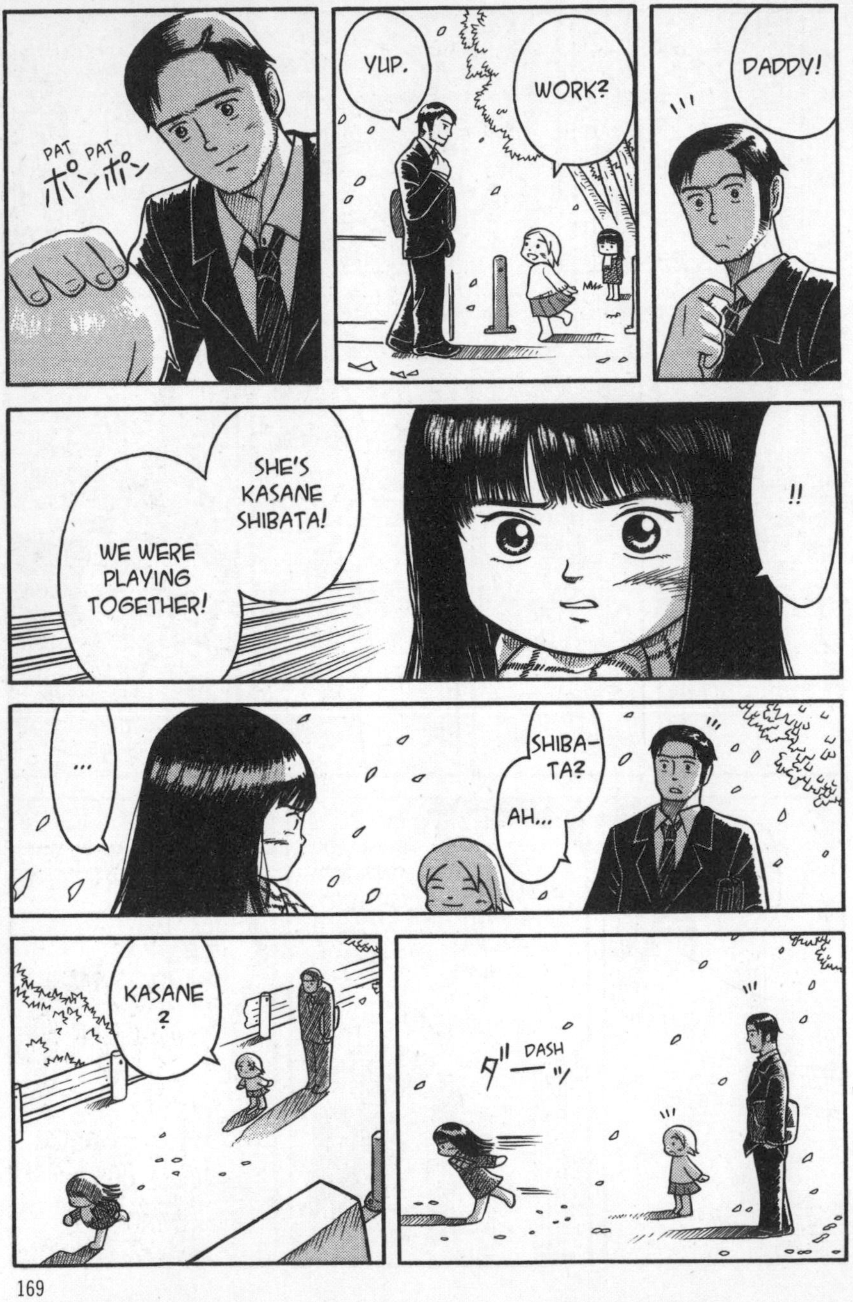
DADDY!
WORK?
YUP.
PAT PAT
ポンポン
!!
SHE'S KASANE SHIBATA!
WE WERE PLAYING TOGETHER!
SHIBA-TA?
AH...
...
ダーッ
DASH
KASANE?

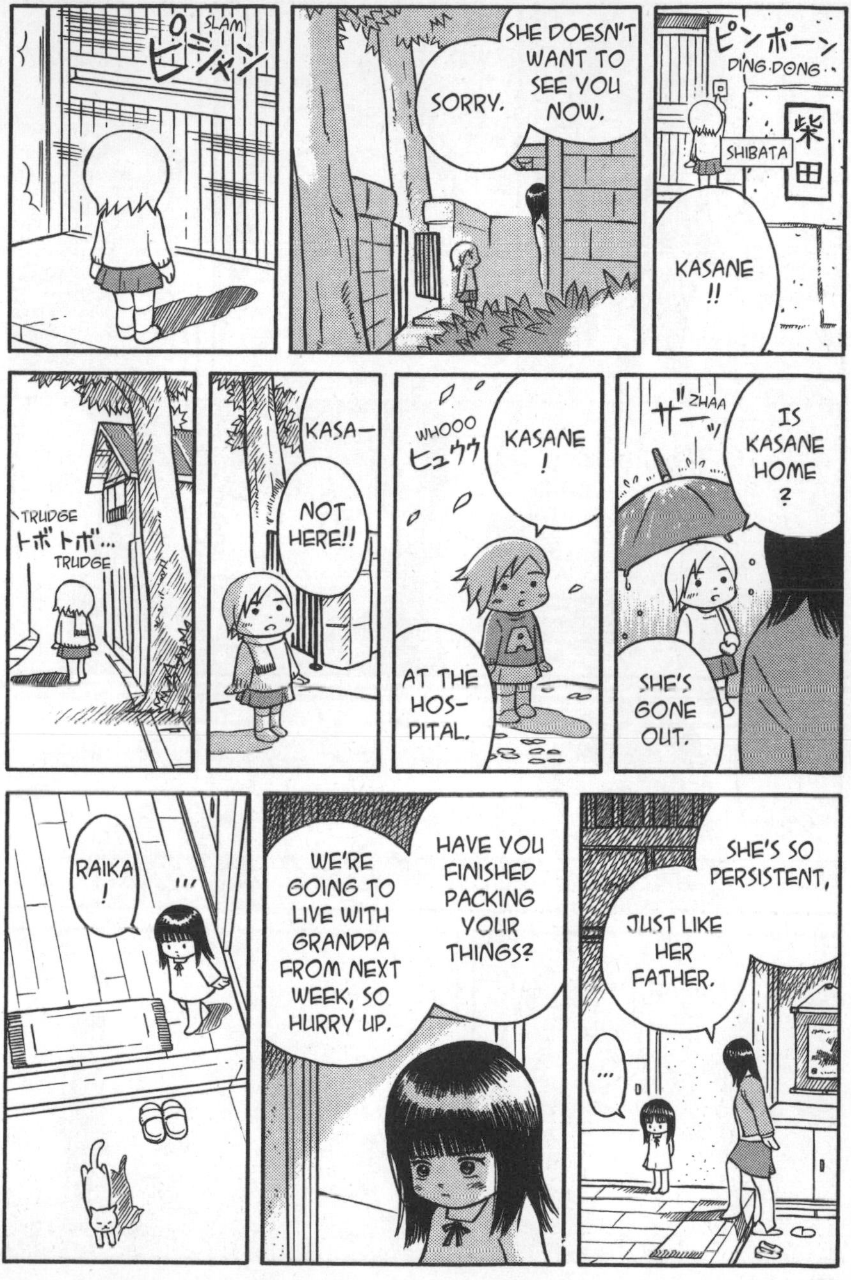
ピンポーン
DING DONG
柴田
SHIBATA
KASANE !!
SHE DOESN'T WANT TO SEE YOU NOW.
SORRY.
SLAM
ピシャン
ザーッ
ZHAA
IS KASANE HOME?
SHE'S GONE OUT.
WHOOO
ヒュウウ
KASANE !
AT THE HOS-PITAL.
KASA—
NOT HERE!!
TRUDGE
トボトボ...
TRUDGE
SHE'S SO PERSISTENT,
JUST LIKE HER FATHER.
...
HAVE YOU FINISHED PACKING YOUR THINGS?
WE'RE GOING TO LIVE WITH GRANDPA FROM NEXT WEEK, SO HURRY UP.
RAIKA !

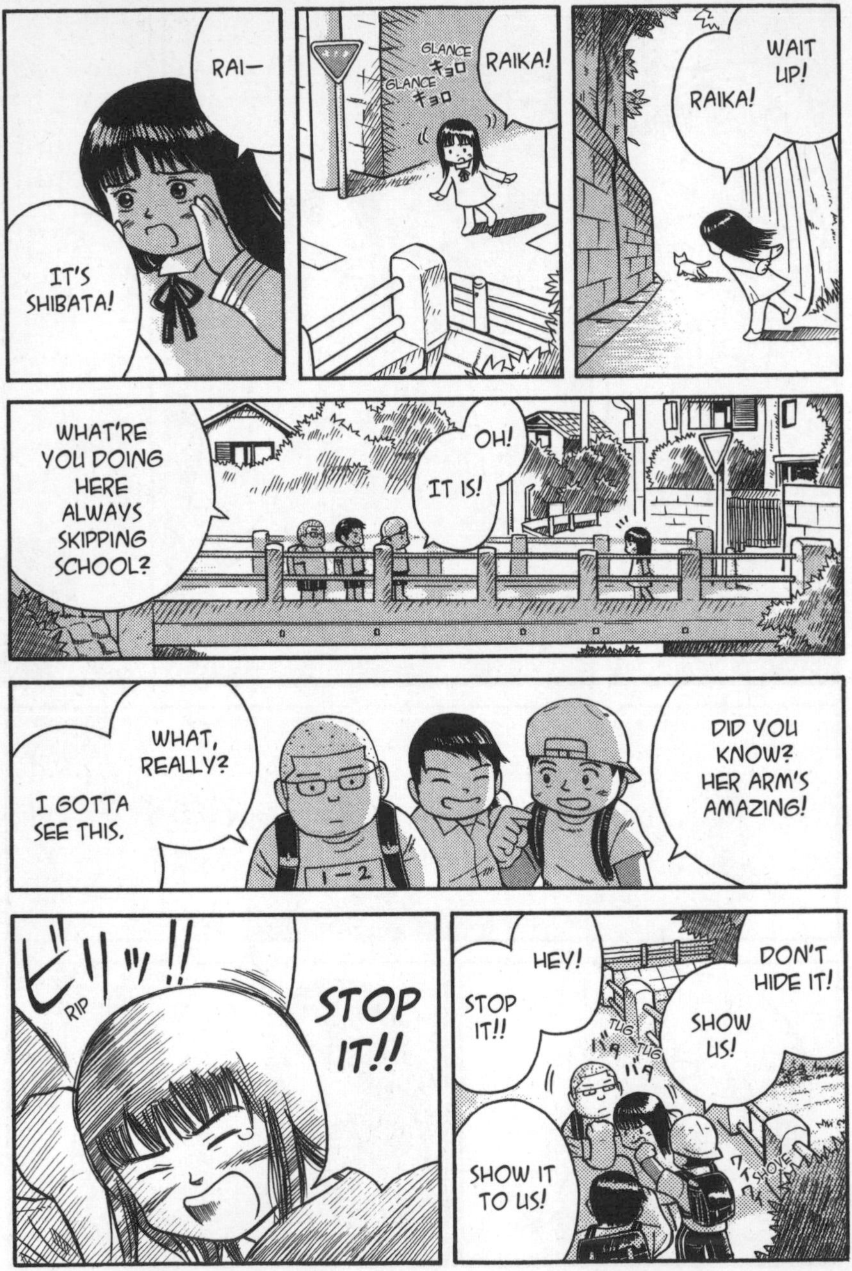
WAIT UP!
RAIKA!
GLANCE キョロ
GLANCE キョロ
RAIKA!
RAI—
IT'S SHIBATA!
OH!
IT IS!
WHAT'RE YOU DOING HERE ALWAYS SKIPPING SCHOOL?
DID YOU KNOW? HER ARM'S AMAZING!
WHAT, REALLY?
I GOTTA SEE THIS.
1-2
DON'T HIDE IT!
SHOW US!
HEY!
STOP IT!!
TUG バタ
TUG バタ
SHOVE ワイワイ
SHOW IT TO US!
ビリッ!!
RIP
STOP IT!!

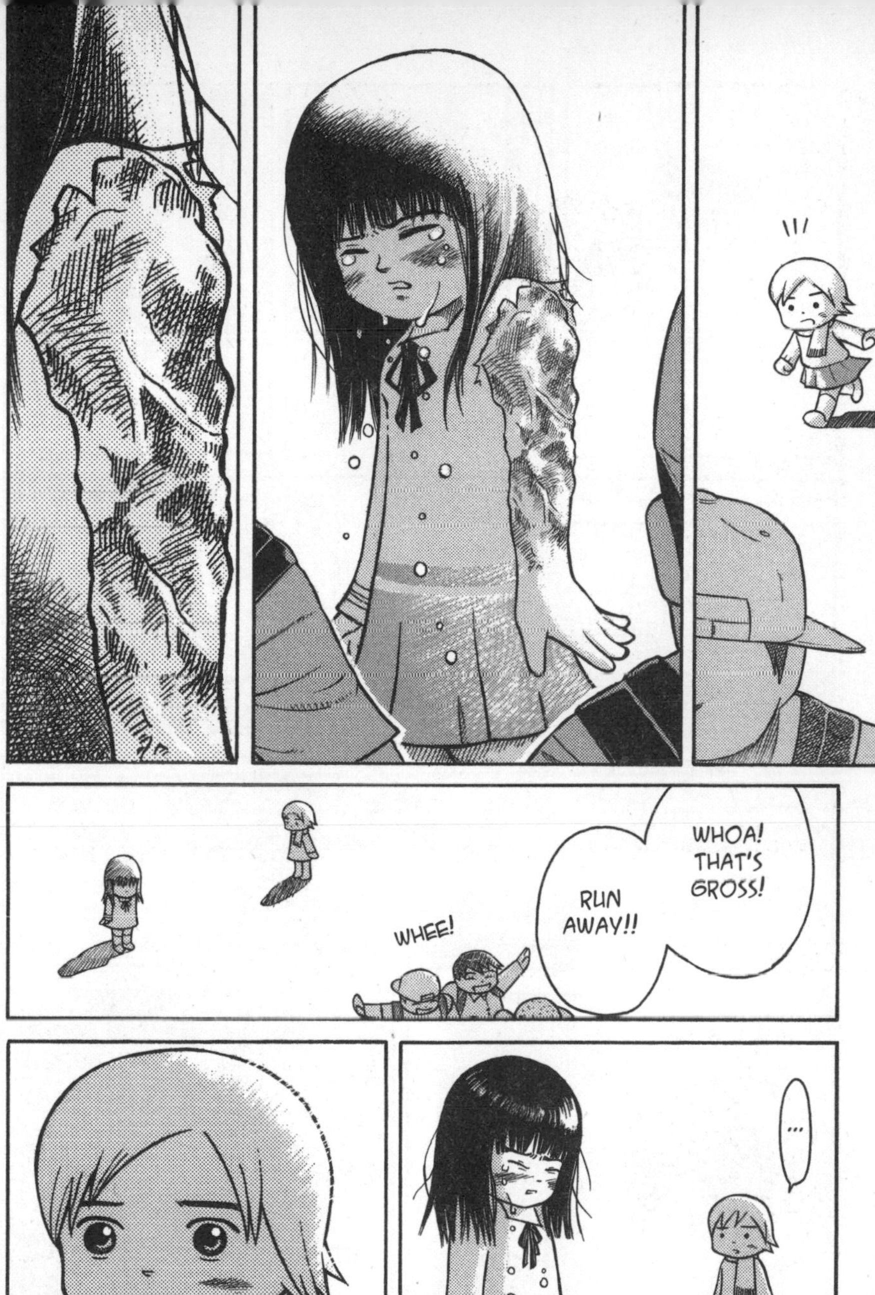
WHOA! THAT'S GROSS!
RUN AWAY!!
WHEE!
...

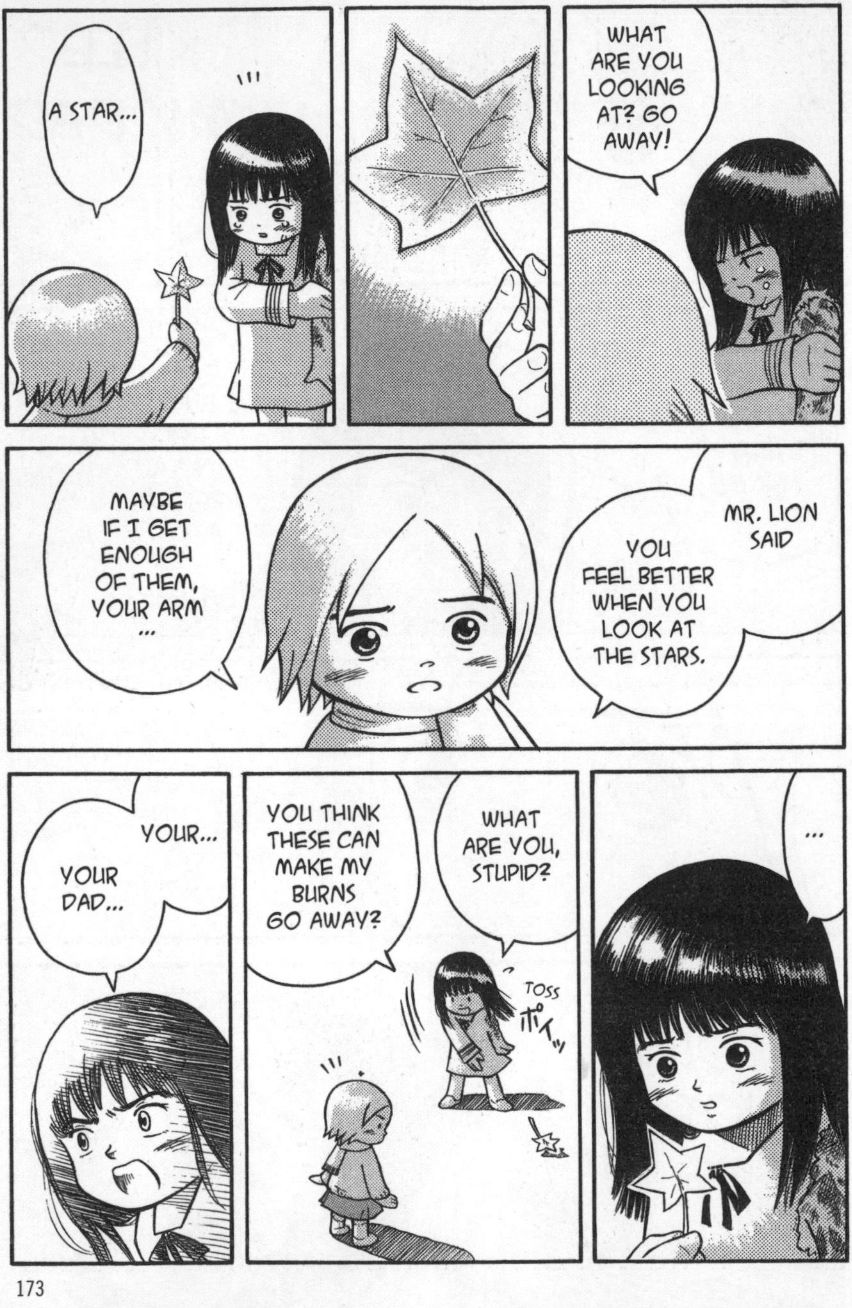
WHAT ARE YOU LOOKING AT? GO AWAY!
A STAR...
MR. LION SAID
YOU FEEL BETTER WHEN YOU LOOK AT THE STARS.
MAYBE IF I GET ENOUGH OF THEM, YOUR ARM ...
...
WHAT ARE YOU, STUPID?
YOU THINK THESE CAN MAKE MY BURNS GO AWAY?
TOSS
ポイッ
YOUR...
YOUR DAD...

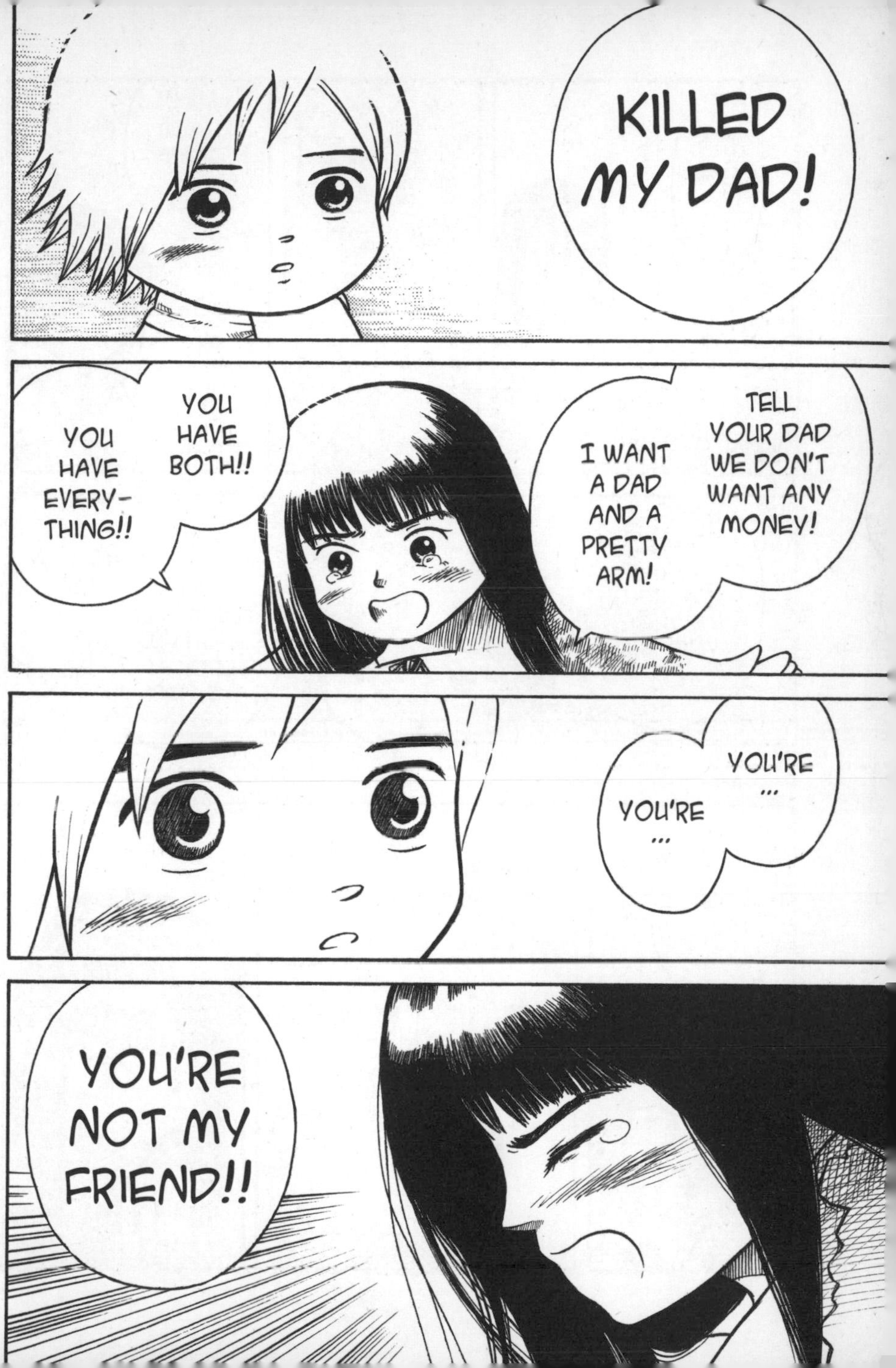
KILLED MY DAD!
TELL YOUR DAD WE DON'T WANT ANY MONEY!
I WANT A DAD AND A PRETTY ARM!
YOU HAVE BOTH!!
YOU HAVE EVERY-THING!!
YOU'RE ...
YOU'RE ...
YOU'RE NOT MY FRIEND!!

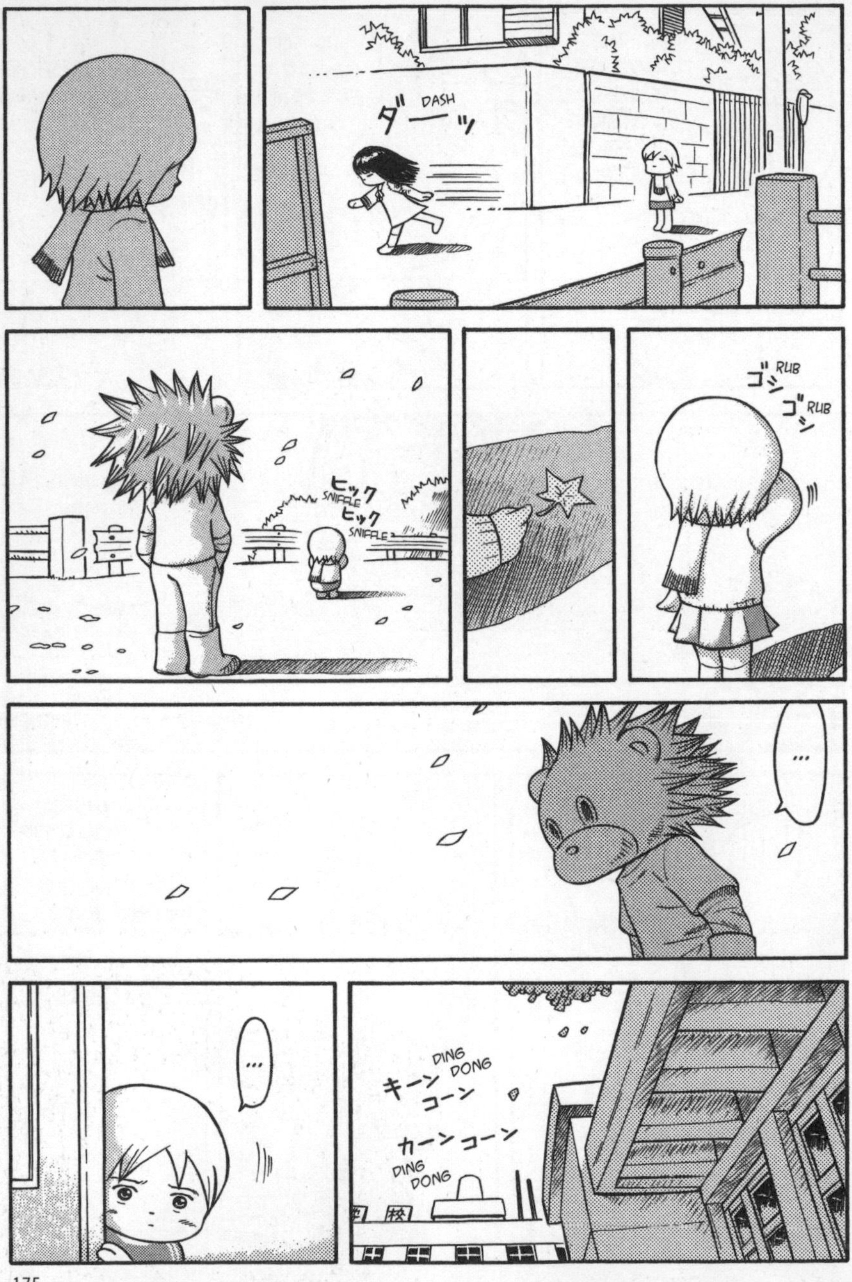
ダーッ
DASH
ゴシ RUB
ゴシ RUB
ヒック SNIFFLE
ヒック SNIFFLE
...
キーン DING
コーン DONG
カーン コーン
DING DONG
...

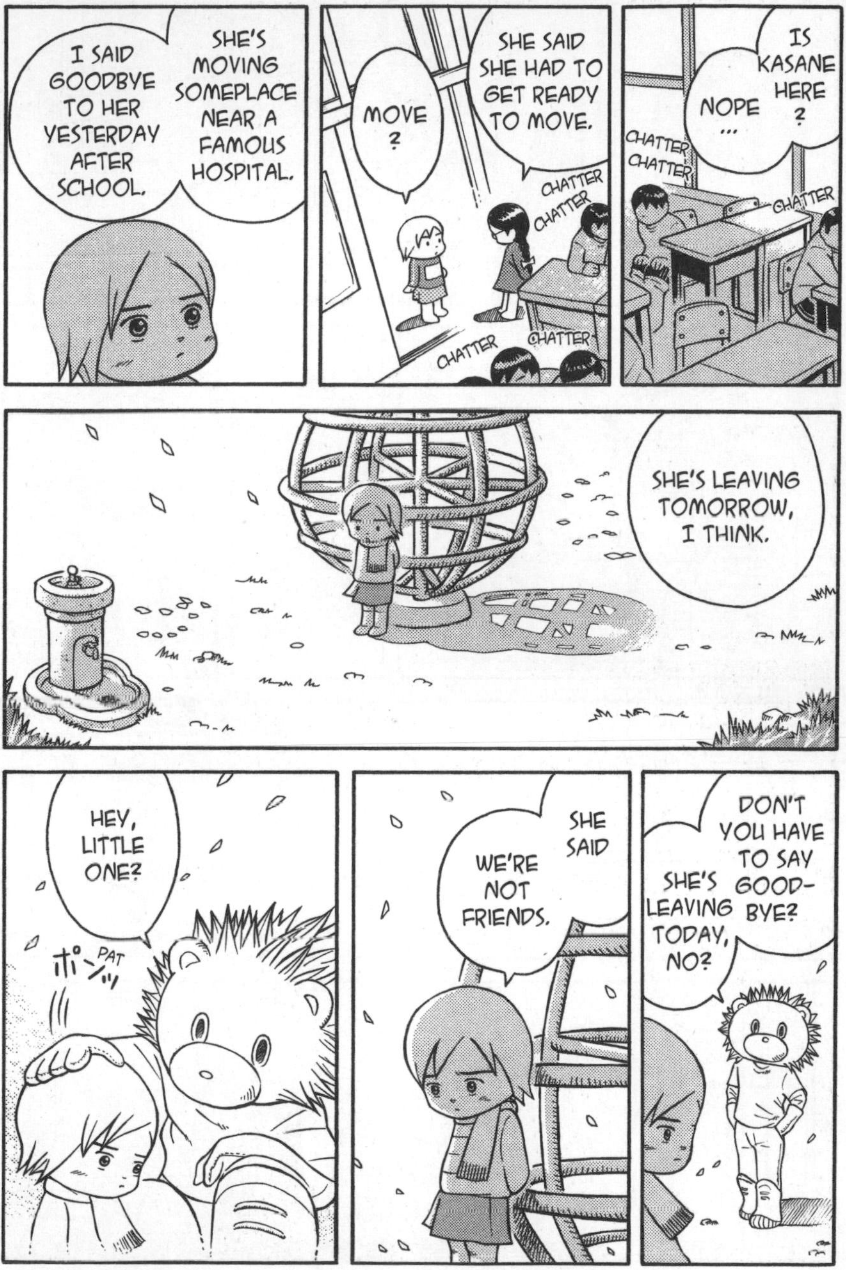
IS KASANE HERE?
NOPE ...
CHATTER
CHATTER
CHATTER
SHE SAID SHE HAD TO GET READY TO MOVE.
MOVE?
CHATTER
CHATTER
CHATTER
CHATTER
SHE'S MOVING SOMEPLACE NEAR A FAMOUS HOSPITAL.
I SAID GOODBYE TO HER YESTERDAY AFTER SCHOOL.
SHE'S LEAVING TOMORROW, I THINK.
DON'T YOU HAVE TO SAY GOOD-BYE?
SHE'S LEAVING TODAY, NO?
SHE SAID
WE'RE NOT FRIENDS.
HEY, LITTLE ONE?
ポンッ
PAT

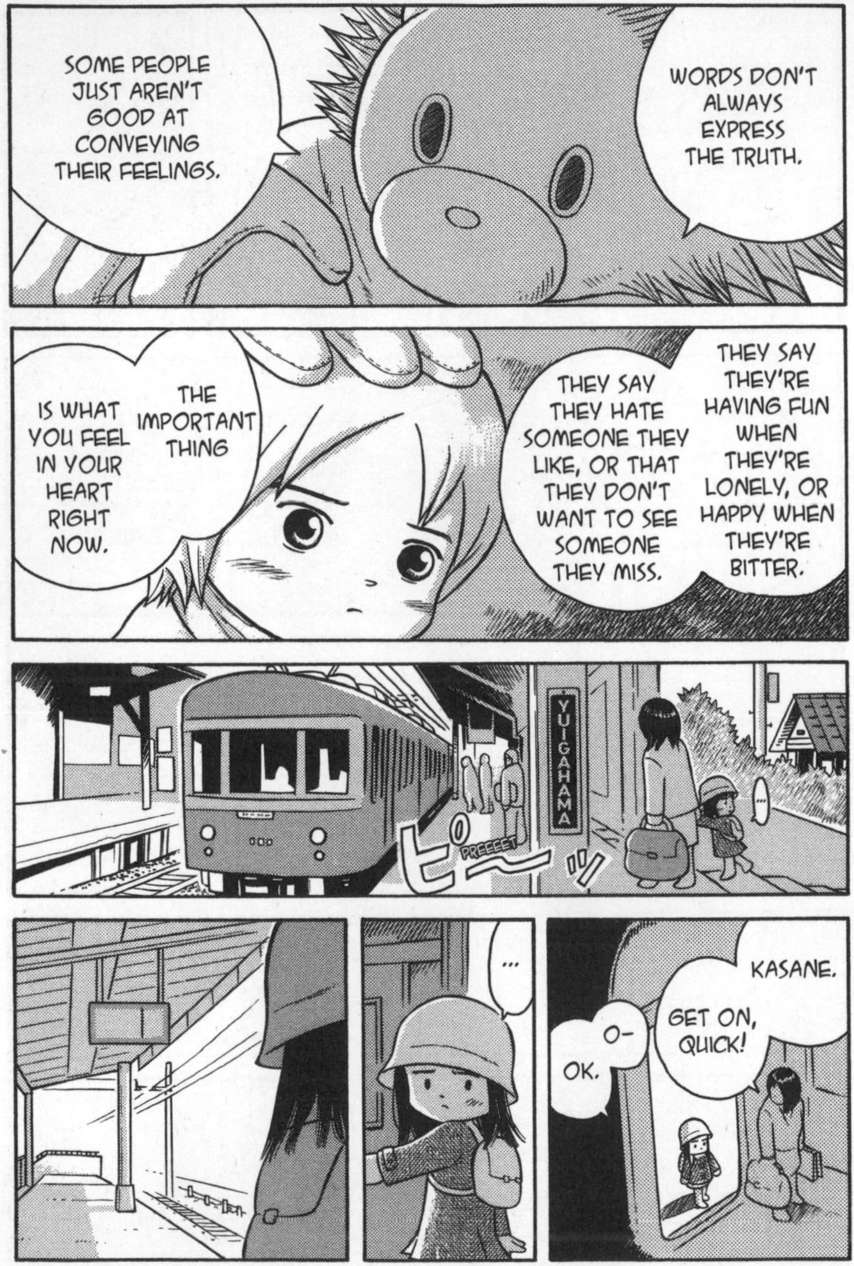
WORDS DON'T ALWAYS EXPRESS THE TRUTH.
SOME PEOPLE JUST AREN'T GOOD AT CONVEYING THEIR FEELINGS.
THEY SAY THEY'RE HAVING FUN WHEN THEY'RE LONELY, OR HAPPY WHEN THEY'RE BITTER.
THEY SAY THEY HATE SOMEONE THEY LIKE, OR THAT THEY DON'T WANT TO SEE SOMEONE THEY MISS.
THE IMPORTANT THING
IS WHAT YOU FEEL IN YOUR HEART RIGHT NOW.
...
YUIGAHAMA
PREEEET
KASANE.
GET ON, QUICK!
O- OK.
...

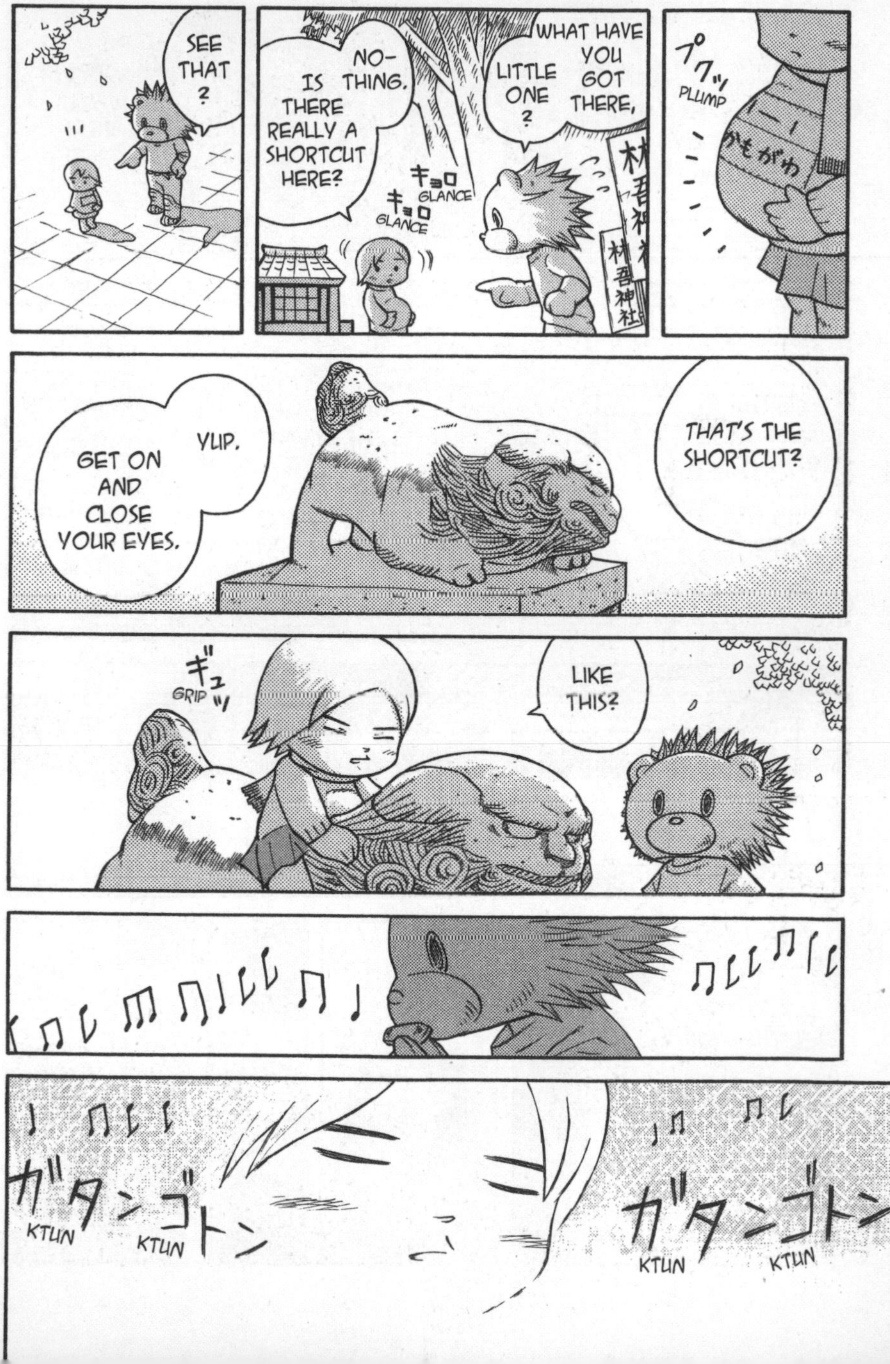
プクッ
PLUMP
かもがわ
WHAT HAVE YOU GOT THERE, LITTLE ONE?
林吾神社
キョロ
GLANCE
キョロ
GLANCE
NO-THING. IS THERE REALLY A SHORTCUT HERE?
SEE THAT?
THAT'S THE SHORTCUT?
YUP. GET ON AND CLOSE YOUR EYES.
LIKE THIS?
ギュッ
GRIP
ガタンゴトン
KTUN KTUN
ガタンゴトン
KTUN KTUN

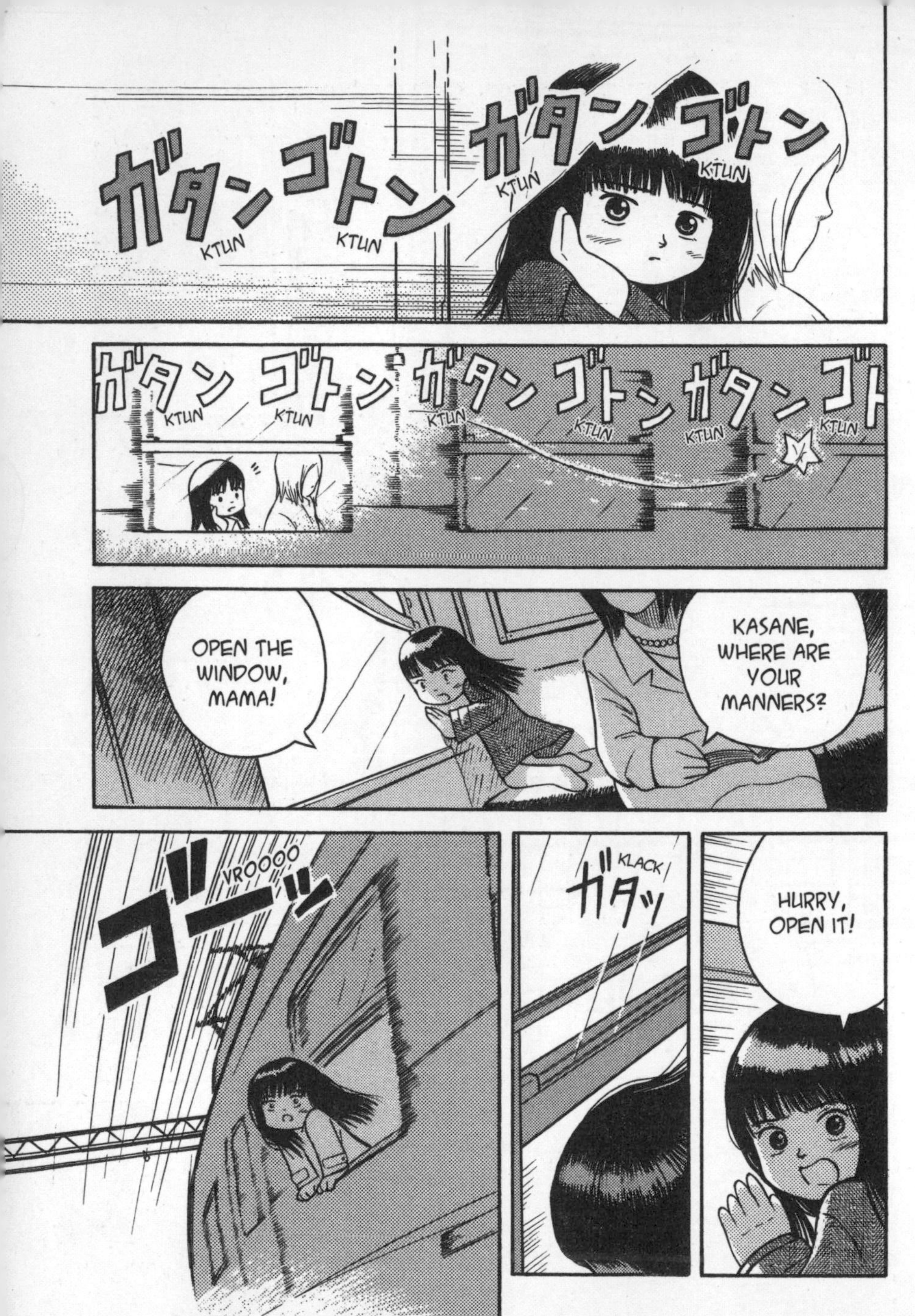
ガタンゴトン
KTUN
KTUN
ガタンゴトン
KTUN
KTUN
ガタン ゴトン ガタン ゴトン ガタン ゴト
KTUN
KTUN
KTUN
KTUN
KTUN
KTUN
KASANE, WHERE ARE YOUR MANNERS?
OPEN THE WINDOW, MAMA!
HURRY, OPEN IT!
ガタッ
KLACK
ゴーッ
VROOOO

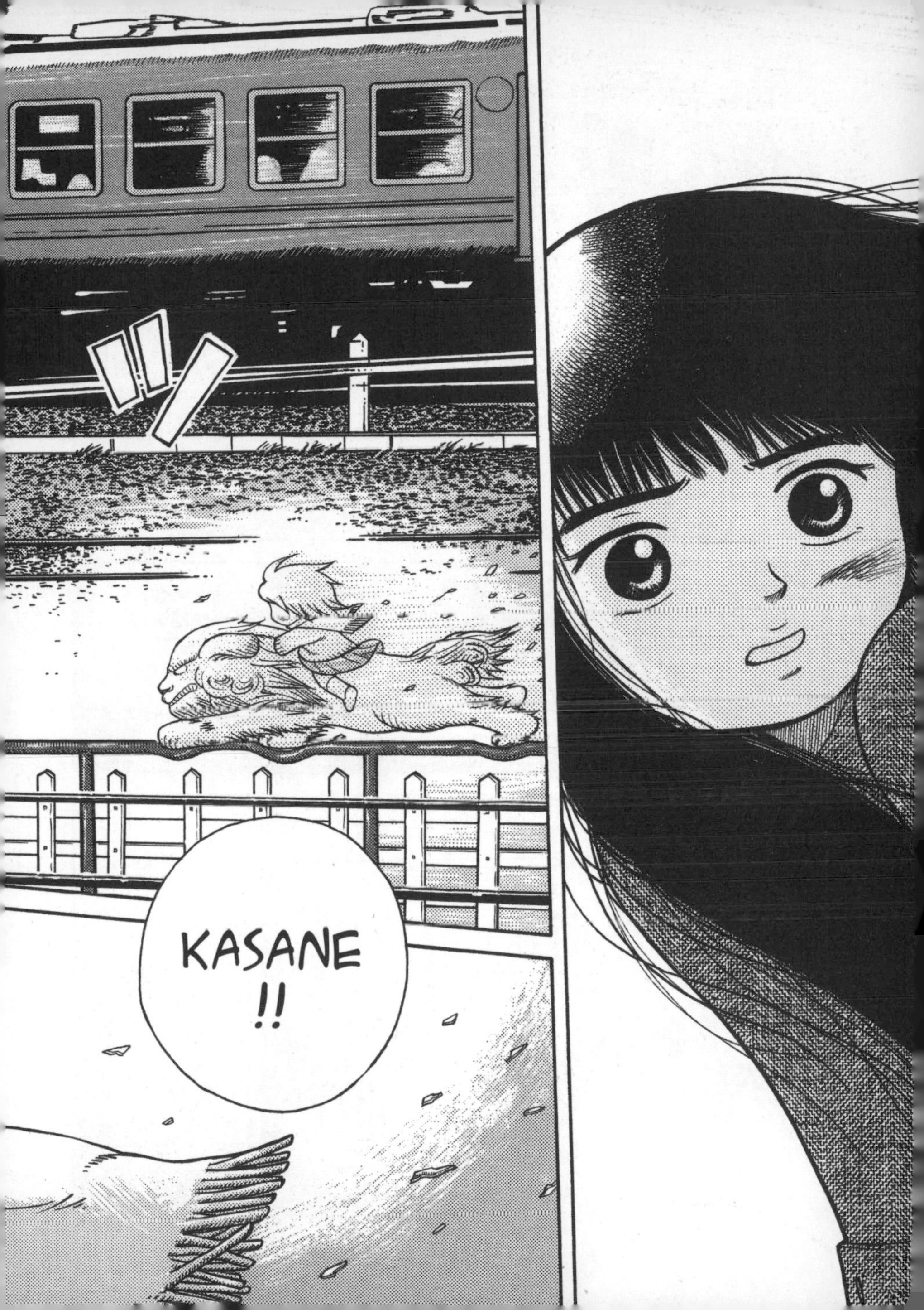
KASANE !!

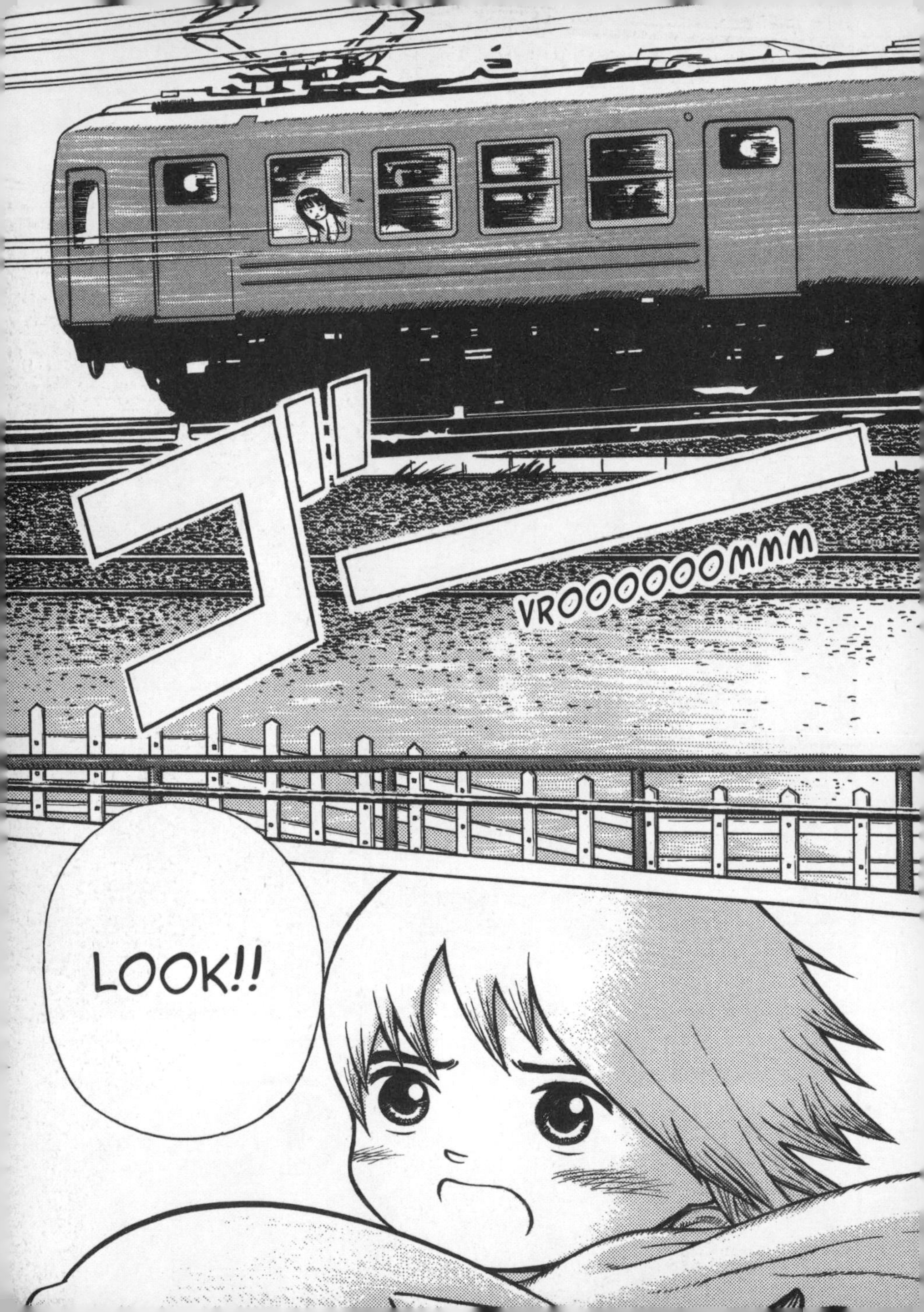
ゴー
VROOOOOOOMMM
LOOK!!

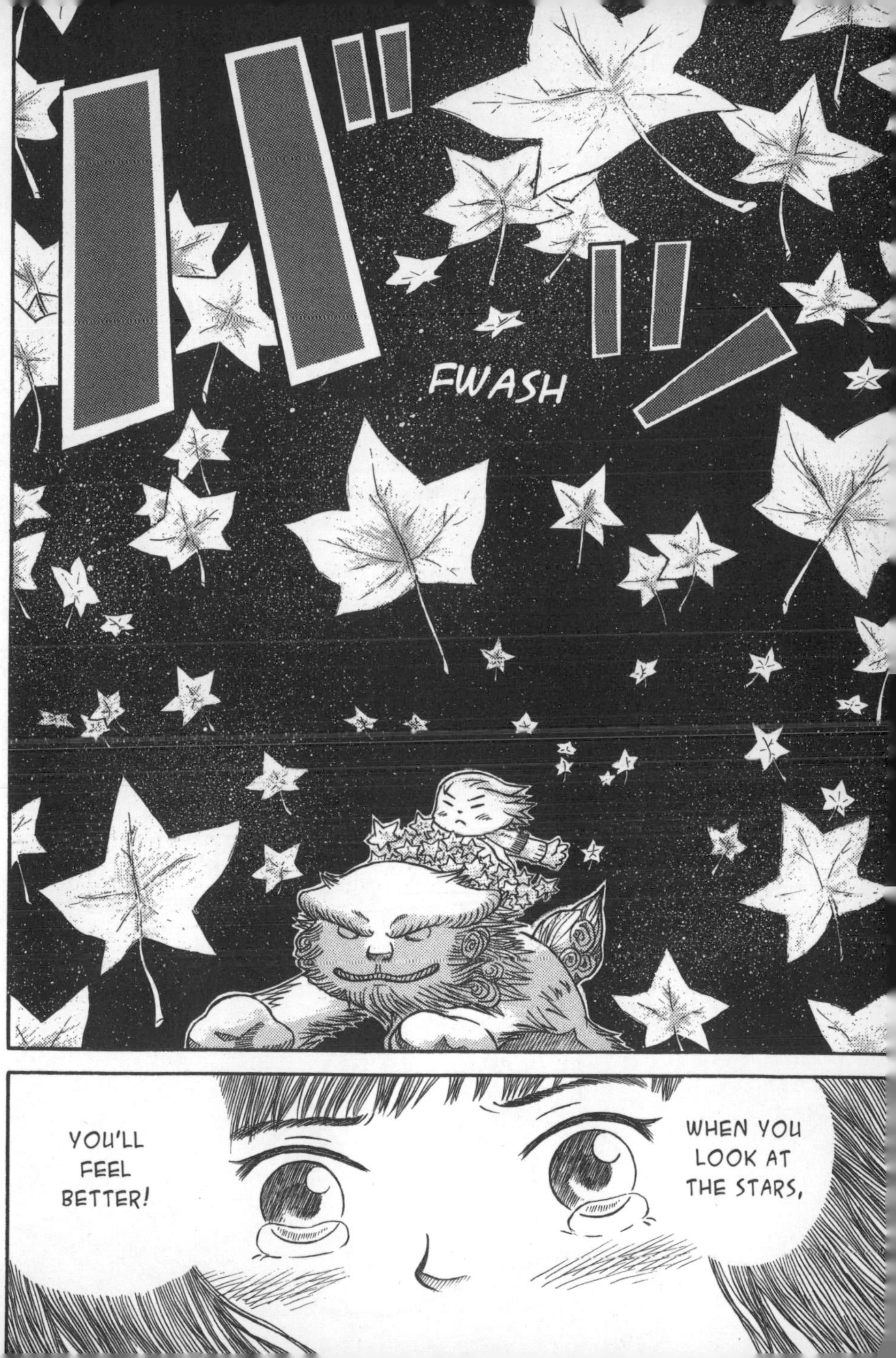
FWASH
WHEN YOU LOOK AT THE STARS,
YOU'LL FEEL BETTER!

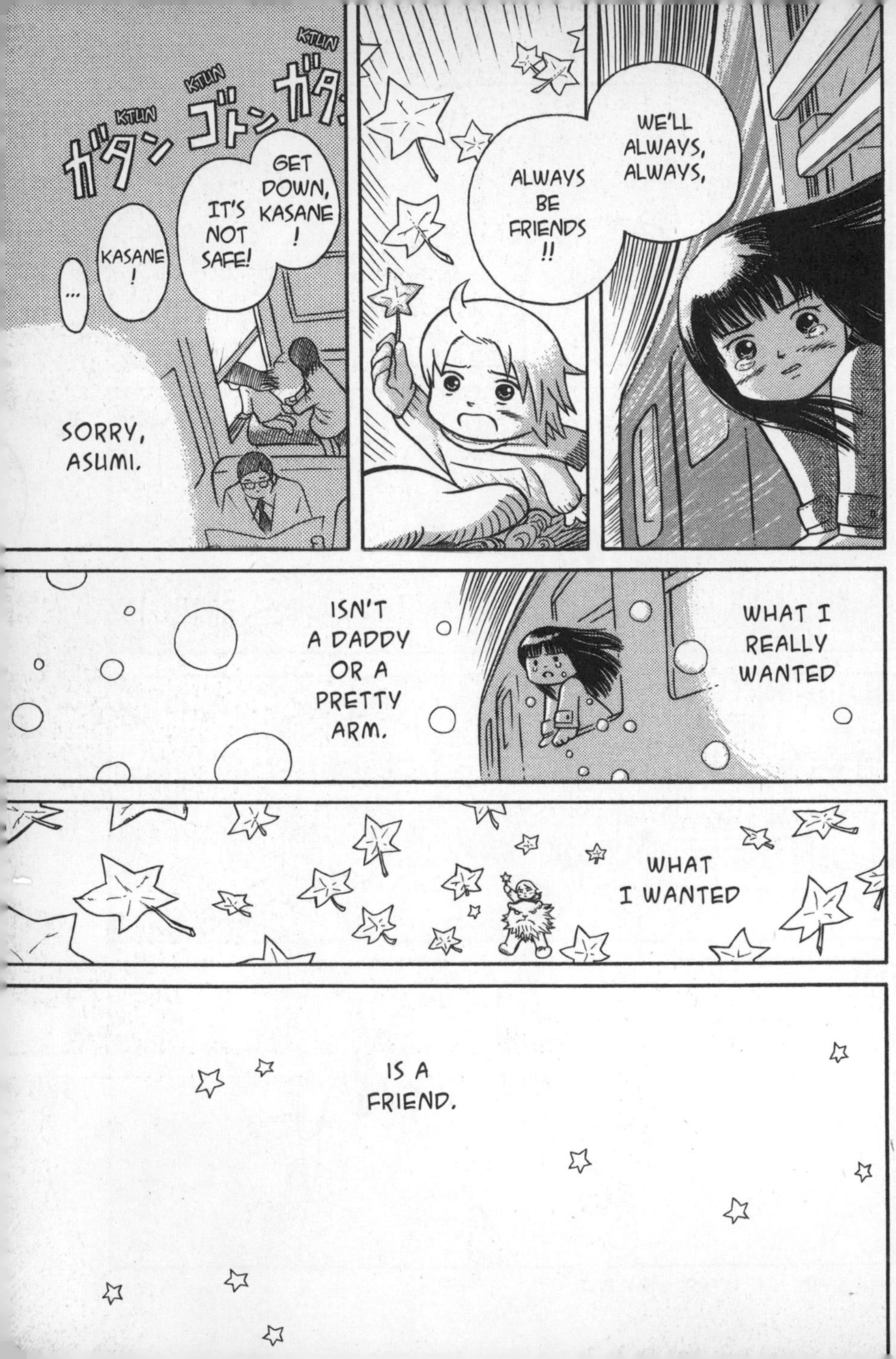
WE'LL ALWAYS, ALWAYS,
ALWAYS BE FRIENDS !!
KTUN
ガタ
KTUN
ゴトン
KTUN
ガタン
GET DOWN, KASANE!
IT'S NOT SAFE!
KASANE!
...
SORRY, ASUMI.
WHAT I REALLY WANTED
ISN'T A DADDY OR A PRETTY ARM.
WHAT I WANTED
IS A FRIEND.

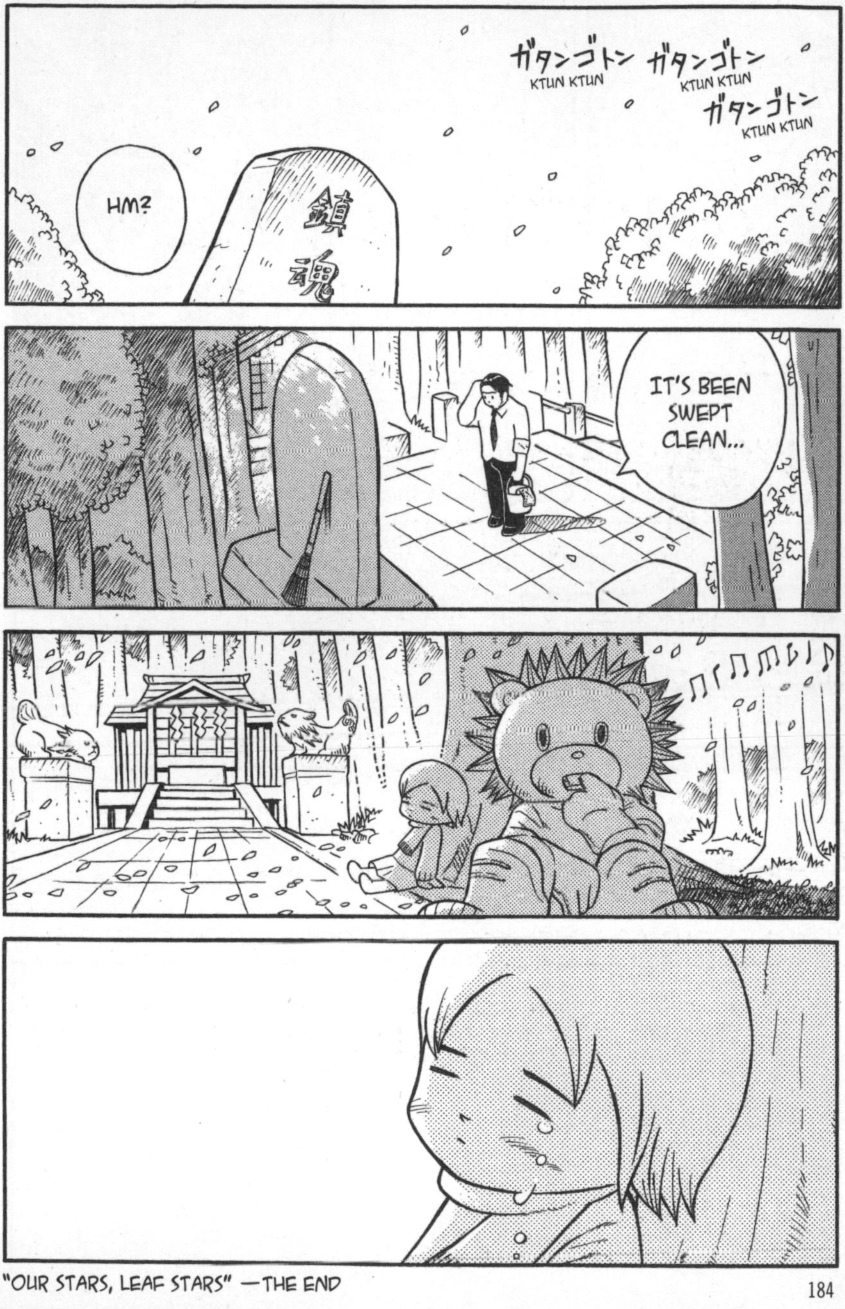
ガタンゴトン
KTUN KTUN
ガタンゴトン
KTUN KTUN
ガタンゴトン
KTUN KTUN
鎮魂
HM?
IT'S BEEN SWEPT CLEAN...

"OUR STARS, LEAF STARS" —THE END

ANOTHER SPICA

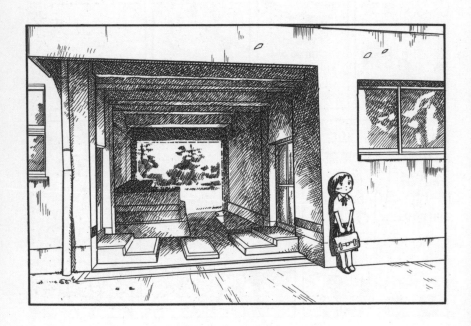

KOU YAGINUMA

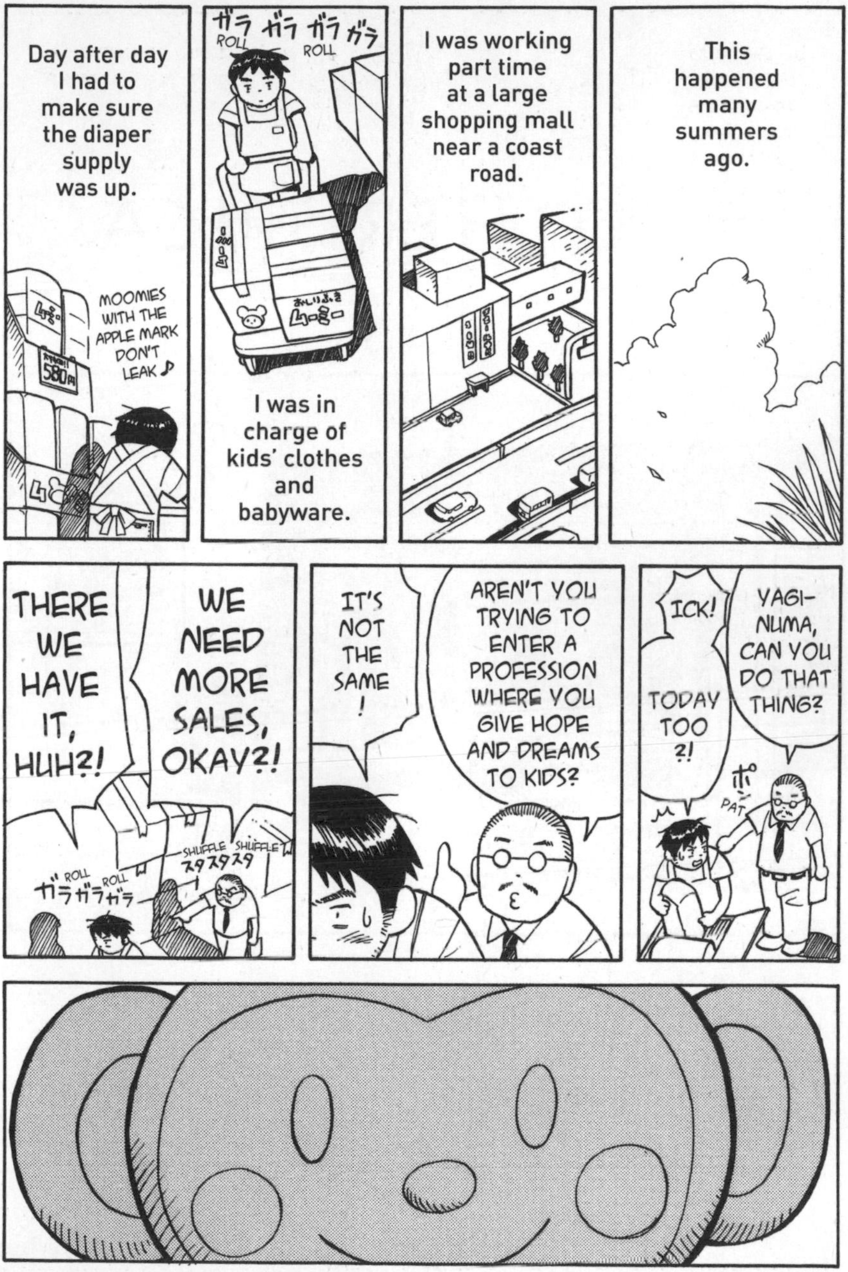
This happened many summers ago.
I was working part time at a large shopping mall near a coast road.
ガラ ガラ ガラ ガラ
ROLL ROLL
I was in charge of kids' clothes and babyware.
Day after day I had to make sure the diaper supply was up.
MOOMIES WITH THE APPLE MARK DON'T LEAK ♪
580円
YAGI-NUMA, CAN YOU DO THAT THING?
ICK!
TODAY TOO?!
ポン
PAT
AREN'T YOU TRYING TO ENTER A PROFESSION WHERE YOU GIVE HOPE AND DREAMS TO KIDS?
IT'S NOT THE SAME!
WE NEED MORE SALES, OKAY?!
THERE WE HAVE IT, HUH?!
SHUFFLE SHUFFLE
スタスタスタ
ROLL ROLL
ガラガラガラ

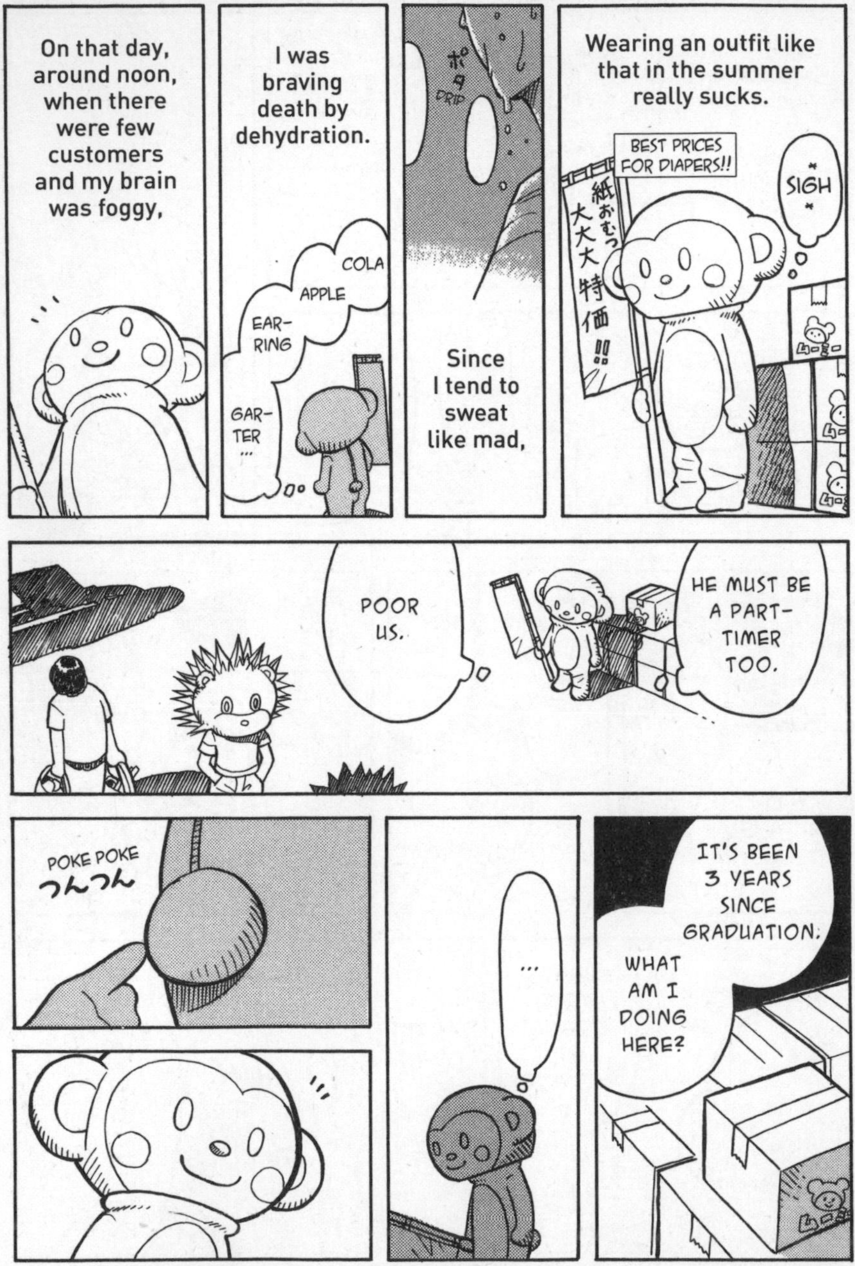
On that day, around noon, when there were few customers and my brain was foggy,
I was braving death by dehydration.
GAR-TER...
EAR-RING
APPLE
COLA
ポタ
DRIP
Since I tend to sweat like mad,
Wearing an outfit like that in the summer really sucks.
BEST PRICES FOR DIAPERS!!
紙おむつ大大大特価!!
SIGH
POOR US.
HE MUST BE A PART-TIMER TOO.
POKE POKE
つんつん
...
IT'S BEEN 3 YEARS SINCE GRADUATION.
WHAT AM I DOING HERE?

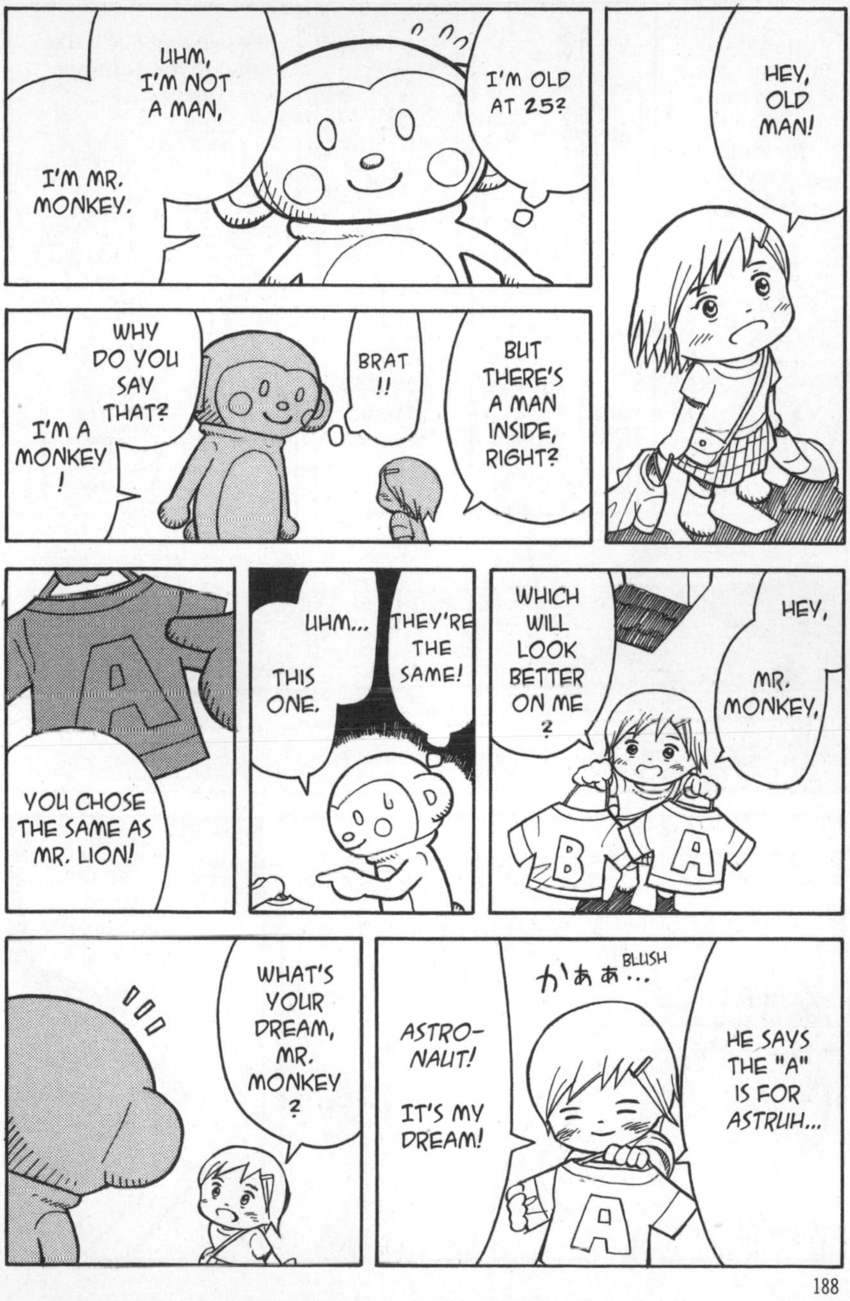
HEY, OLD MAN!
I'M OLD AT 25?
UHM, I'M NOT A MAN,
I'M MR. MONKEY.
BUT THERE'S A MAN INSIDE, RIGHT?
BRAT!!
WHY DO YOU SAY THAT?
I'M A MONKEY!
HEY, MR. MONKEY,
WHICH WILL LOOK BETTER ON ME?
THEY'RE THE SAME!
UHM... THIS ONE.
YOU CHOSE THE SAME AS MR. LION!
かあぁ…
BLUSH
HE SAYS THE "A" IS FOR ASTRUH...
ASTRO-NAUT!
IT'S MY DREAM!
WHAT'S YOUR DREAM, MR. MONKEY?

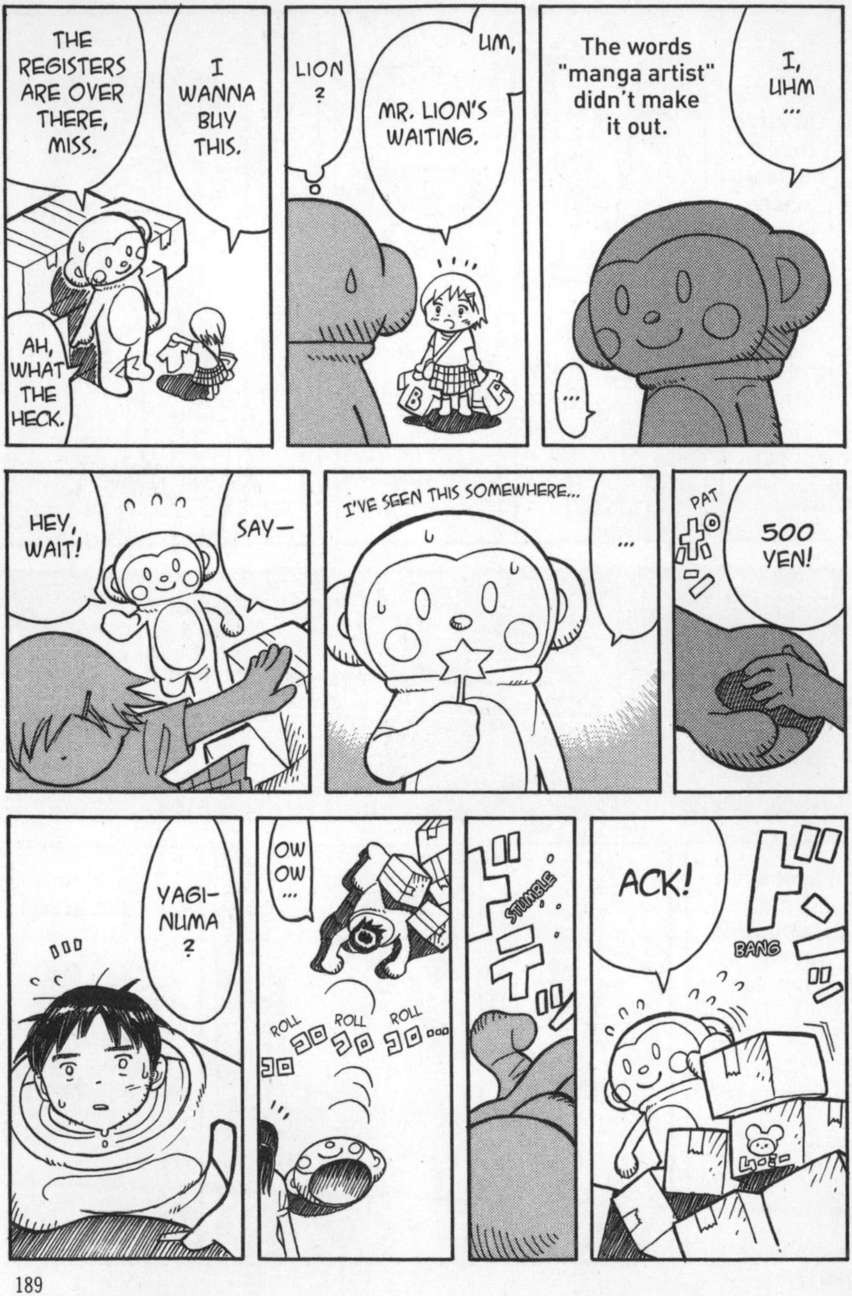
I, UHM ...
The words "manga artist" didn't make it out.
...
UM, MR. LION'S WAITING.
LION?
I WANNA BUY THIS.
THE REGISTERS ARE OVER THERE, MISS.
AH, WHAT THE HECK.
500 YEN!
PAT
...
I'VE SEEN THIS SOMEWHERE...
SAY—
HEY, WAIT!
ACK!
BANG
STUMBLE
OW OW ...
ROLL ROLL ROLL
YAGI-NUMA?

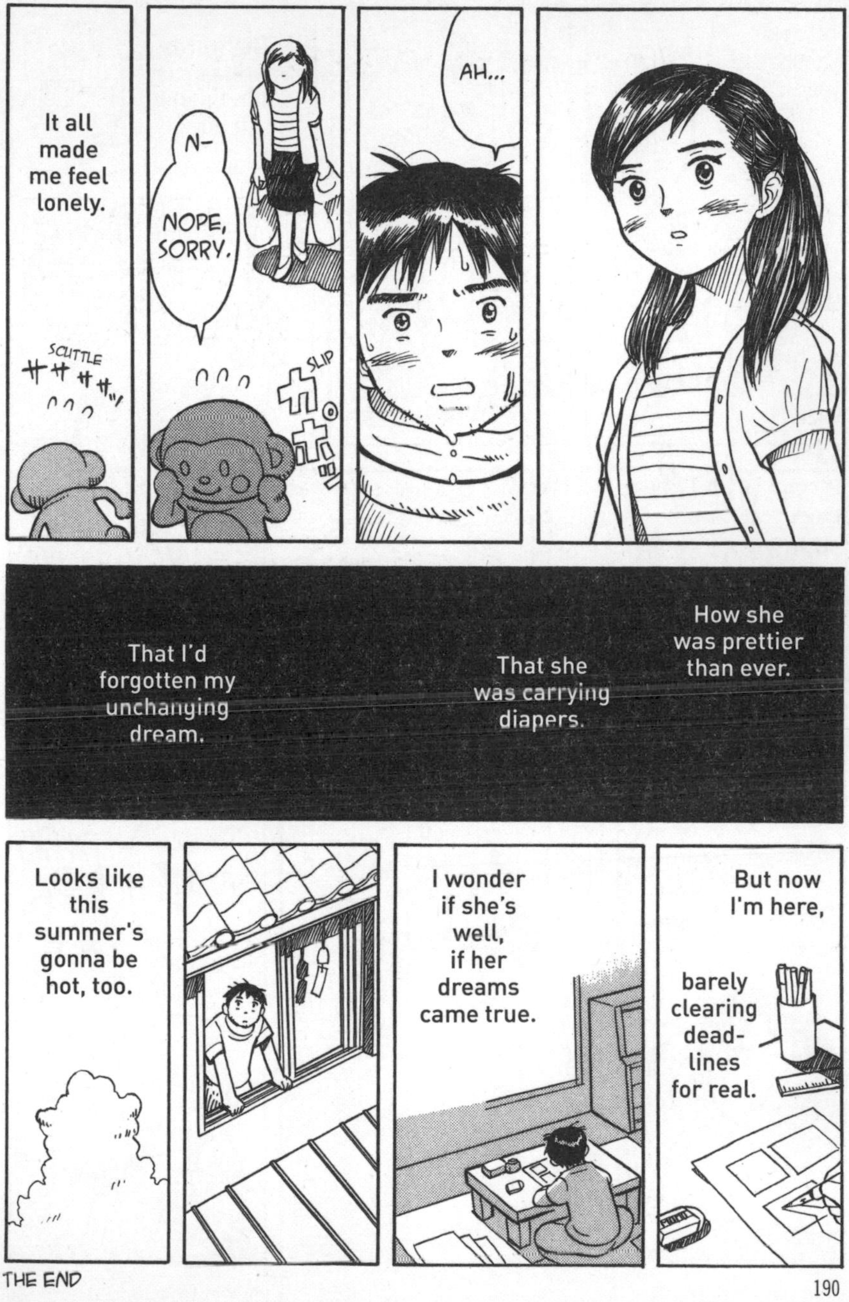
AH...
N-
NOPE, SORRY.
SLIP
カポッ
It all made me feel lonely.
SCUTTLE
ササササッ
How she was prettier than ever.
That she was carrying diapers.
That I'd forgotten my unchanging dream.
But now I'm here,
barely clearing dead-lines for real.
I wonder if she's well, if her dreams came true.
Looks like this summer's gonna be hot, too.

THE END

Notes on the Translation

P. 59

In Japanese folklore, a *zashiki warashi* is a beneficial child spirit that lurks mostly unseen in prosperous houses.

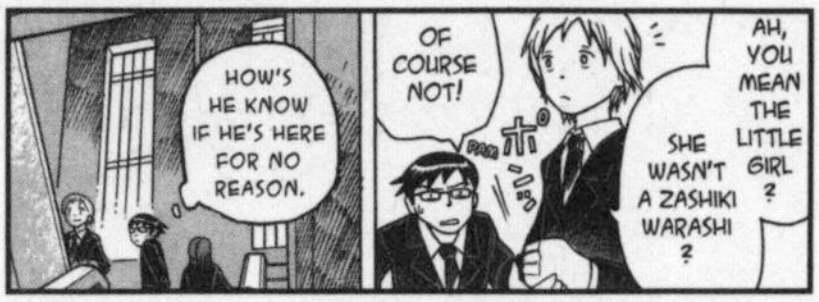

AH, YOU MEAN THE LITTLE GIRL?
SHE WASN'T A ZASHIKI WARASHI?
OF COURSE NOT!
HOW'S HE KNOW IF HE'S HERE FOR NO REASON.

P. 126

Campanella is the name of the protagonist's friend and companion in Kenji Miyazawa's fantasy novel *Night on the Galactic Railroad.*

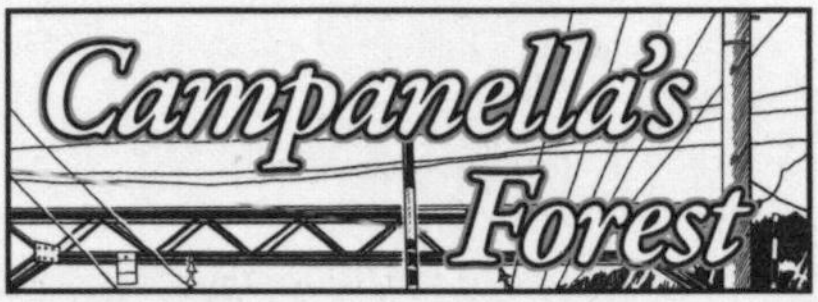

Campanella's Forest

Translation - Maya Rosewood
Production - Hiroko Mizuno
Rina Nakayama

Published by Vertical, Inc., New York

Originally published in Japanese as *Futatsu no Supika*
by MEDIA FACTORY, Inc., Tokyo 2002
Futatsu no Supika first serialized in Gekkan Comic Flapper,
MEDIA FACTORY, Inc., 2001-2009
"Kamupanerura no Mori" first published in Gekkan Comic Flapper,
MEDIA FACTORY, Inc., 2000
"Futari no Hoshi Happa-boshi" first published in Gekkan Comic Flapper,
MEDIA FACTORY, Inc., 2001

This is a work of fiction.

ISBN: 978-1-934287-86-6

Manufactured in Canada

First Edition

Vertical, Inc.
1185 Avenue of the Americas, 32nd Floor
New York, NY 10036
www.vertical-inc.com